THE
UNVEILING

THE
UNVEILING

Freeing Prophetic Reality from
Academic Kabbalistic Metaphors

R. Ariel B. Tzadok

The Unveiling

Freeing Prophetic Reality from Academic Kabbalistic Metaphors

The KosherTorah School
for Biblical, Judaic & Spiritual Studies
www.koshertorah.com
arieltzadok@gmail.com

Hardcover ISBN: 979-8-393-10399-6
Softcover ISBN: 979-8-393-10381-1
Layout, graphic and cover design by: Dovid S. Brandes

About the Cover Art: *The image represents Man's internal struggle between his intuitive side and his academic side (right brain vs. left brain). When the Primordial Kings shattered and fell, they caused elements of good to become encased in evil. This is represented here as the Nahash (serpent) whispering into Man's left (academic) ear, inciting him not to listen to his higher (intuitive) Self, which is naturally connected to the Living Torah, portrayed by the text of the Ketoret (Incense Offering), which is known to have deep mystical properties.*

PROUDLY PRINTED IN THE USA

Also by R. Ariel B. Tzadok:

WALKING IN THE FIRE

Classical Torah/Kabbalistic Meditations, Practices & Prayers.

PROTECTION FROM EVIL

Exposing & Neutralizing Harmful Spiritual Forces.

ALIENS, ANGELS, & DEMONS

Extraterrestrial Life in Judaism/Kabbalah & its Vital Relevance for Modern Times.

VISIONS OF THE END OF DAYS

A Kabbalistic View of the Book of Daniel with a Guide to Dream Interpretations

THE EVOLUTION OF GOD

Experiencing the Fractal Sefirot of the Kabbalah

SECRETS OF THE CYCLE OF TIME

A Prophetic Kabbalah Journey through the Jewish Year

LET THERE BE… KNOWING!

Using the Prophetic Kabbalah & Ma'aseh Merkavah to Expand the Powers of the Mind/Soul

USING THE HOLY NAMES OF GOD

Developing Psychic Abilities Using the Secret Codes within the Torah

THE GREATEST STORY NEVER TOLD

Torah: Not for Jews Only! The Bedrock of Universal Spirituality

THE KABBALAH OF RELATIONSHIPS

Between Men & Women You & Your Soul You & Your Body

THE SIMPLE PATH

Uncommon Common Sense from Psalm 119

FOR I HEARD FROM

BEHIND THE VEIL

Insights & Messages Regarding Current Events in Light of the Teachings of the Prophetic Kabbalah

Available on Amazon.com

Check out our courses in all areas of study

Available at **www.koshertorah.com**

YouTube: **KosherTorah School of Rabbi Ariel Bar Tzadok**

TABLE OF CONTENTS

SECTION TWO
THE UNVEILING OF THE VEILED

SECTION THREE
ECHOES FROM THE VOICE

<u>The Unveiling, What You Need to Know...</u>

The Difference Between the Academic Kabbalah of Today & the True "Prophetic" Kabbalah of R. Hayim Vital
We Are Not Being Taught the "Real Deal"

<u>Kabbalah Today</u>

So you study Kabbalah, do you? How would you respond if you were shown that the Kabbalah that you study and learn from the books is not the true Kabbalah at all?

I call this book, The Unveiling, because I have something very important for you to see with your own eyes, and to experience with your own mind!

Read this introduction, and you will have the beginnings of understanding. Let me begin by explaining what I just said above.

I hate the way that Kabbalah is being taught these days. I hate it, and so should you!

Almost all Kabbalah study for the past many decades is taught like any other academic topic. Such an academic path is not true to Kabbalistic experience.

Real Kabbalah, the authentic version, the one that came forth from the teachings and experiences of the Biblical prophets, was never learned from books!

Real Kabbalah, the authentic version, the one that came forth from the teachings and experiences of the Biblical prophets was not an academic exercise. It was not philosophical. Heck! It wasn't even metaphysical.

The real authentic Biblical Kabbalah was an interactive experience where the conscious mind of the aspiring prophet (male and female) made actual contact with entities and realities beyond the scope and limitation of what we think our world to be.

Real, authentic Kabbalah was not something that you learned. It was something that you experienced. Real authentic Kabbalah did not come out of one's head, but rather it came out of one's heart.

This is what is missing from all modern Kabbalah. The modern Kabbalah is no different from all the other academic courses of study within Judaism. Today, Kabbalah is a subject of academic pursuit, not too dissimilar from the pursuit of Talmud and Halakha. And this is where Kabbalah has gone off course! But this is not a recent problem. This problem of academia replacing experience goes back centuries. Let me digress to discuss a little bit of history, so as to put our problem into a proper context.

There is something very important to understand about the most popular school of modern Kabbalah, which of course is the Kabbalah of the Ari'zal, as brought to us by his faithful student R. Hayim Vital.

The Real R. Hayim Vital

R. Hayim authored all the numerous books that make up for us the body of Lurianic Kabbalah. So much of this comes from R. Hayim Vital himself, that to be more accurate, we should not refer to these teachings are the Torah of the Ari'zal, we should instead call it by its rightful name, the Torah of Marhu (Moreynu, Rabbeynu Hayim Vital – our teacher, our Rabbi Hayim Vital).

For some, such a statement on my part is entirely academic, of interest only to scholars or those who seek rigid historical accuracy. In other words, what difference does it make if we call the system after the man who brought it to us, or after the man whom he claims he learned it from. But there is a difference. Let me explain it.

Historically speaking, R. Hayim only studied under his master, R. Yitzhak Luria (the Ari'zal) for a period of less than two years. The Ari'zal succumbed to an untimely early death at age 38 in 1572. For the last 48 years of his life, R. Hayim was left without a teacher. But then again, no, he was not. For after the passing of the Ari'zal, over the many years that followed, R. Hayim wrote down his teachings. As he did this, R. Hayim claimed that the Ari'zal would speak to him in dreams and visions, to continue their studies together. Apparently, R. Hayim Vital was in touch with the Neshama soul of the Ari'zal in Heaven, who continued as his master and guide long after his mortal body returned to the Earth.

Whether or not R. Hayim was actually in touch with the Neshama soul of the Ari'zal is irrelevant, for it is clear from the nature of his writings that R. Hayim did receive revelations directly from an off-world higher dimensional source. R. Hayim claimed it was the Neshama of the Ari'zal who taught him, while others said it was the immortal prophet Eliyahu HaNavi. It doesn't matter which one came to him to instruct him. The point is that there was an active higher dimensional Presence involved, and R. Hayim knew how to be in touch with it.

R. Hayim was shown many different things. He did not make up stuff out of his own head. Granted, R. Hayim was also a worthy Rabbinic scholar, but his Kabbalistic revelations did not come to him from his books, nor from his scholarly learning. Unlike the many modern Kabbalists who devote all their days to the study of the works of R. Hayim Vital, R. Hayim himself was very different. R. Hayim delved into the true Kabbalah and sought to practice and to experience the worlds of which he wrote so much about.

Only those who have ever directly read R. Hayim Vital's works in the original Hebrew will appreciate what I am about to reveal here.

When R. Hayim sat down to write about the order of the Supernal Worlds, of Adam Kadmon, of the Akudim, Nikudim and the Berudim, of the Lights of the AHaF and rest of the Seder HaHish'tal'sh'lut (which is the subject of my book, The Evolution of God), how do you think he received all this information? It certainly wasn't from any book, because he himself is the author of all such books. No such books like his existed before him. R. Hayim could not read about these things, like everyone does today. No, on the contrary, R. Hayim entered into deep meditative trances, and within them, he saw the order of the worlds visually appear before him in his mind's eye (the proverbial "third eye").

What R. Hayim Vital brings down to us as the Lurianic Kabbalah did not come from books, it came directly from spirit, from psychic, telepathic communion with higher-dimensional forces that communed directly with R. Hayim's mind and showed him the things that he saw. Only afterwards did he write it all down. And thus we have the prolific writings of our teacher, R. Hayim Vital.

Now, one who reads R. Hayim's books can also close one's eyes and imagine seeing the things written about. But there is a big difference between imagining seeing these things, and actually seeing them with psychic, intuitive inner-vision. Those today who read the books do not know what they are looking at, whereas R. Hayim did!

R. Hayim saw the entirety of the worlds, from Adam Kadmon to the Malkhut of Asiyah and he understood their subjective nature (Olam HaPenimi, HaPrati). R. Hayim never claims that his visions, and his Torah speak about objective nature (Olam HaHitzoni, HaKlali). This is a vital point when it comes to understanding what R. Hayim saw, and what he taught. (This also is also related to R. Hayim's belief that the pre-Adamic civilizations could not have physically existed, a subject briefly discussed in my commentary to Masekhet Atzilut, section one of this book).

The point that I am trying to make here should be clear. All the academic Kabbalists who follow in the footsteps of R. Hayim Vital are not following in his footsteps at all! Granted, R. Hayim was a true Rabbinic scholar, but his Kabbalah was not meant to be of the exclusively academic kind. R. Hayim both knew and practiced the older school of meditative, prophetic Kabbalah. R. Hayim knew the importance of experiential Kabbalah, and this is what he practiced.

What is sad is that a good portion of R. Hayim's works outlining meditative practice and the techniques used to acquire telepathic abilities, and possibly even prophecy, were censored and silenced soon after his death in 1620. His little book, Sha'arei Kedusha (Gates of Holiness), which was written to be a guide and a path towards prophecy, originally had four parts to it. But Part 4 that dealt with the practical methods of meditation and Prophetic Ascent was, for 370 years, censored and never published.

Thank God that times have finally changed, and Heaven has had mercy on us. Not too long ago, Sha'arei Kedusha, Part 4 along with all its meditative wisdom, guidance, and instructions was finally published for the first time. Also soon after this, the entire library of the writings of Abraham Abulafia were also published for the first time, some 750 years after they were "cancelled." We do not need to explore why this happened. We just need to run with it, and so I have. I have been publicly teaching the meditative ascent lessons from Sha'arei Kedusha, Part 4, and other similar sources for many years now. These teachings permeate all my books, and I even have a thirteen hour audio course on the subject.

Today most Kabbalists say that they follow in the footsteps of R. Hayim Vital, but for the most part they most certainly do not. R. Hayim was a practitioner of the meditative ascent school, and humbly, so am I. And it is the teachings of this school that I am here to teach in this book, as well as in my many others.

As far as I am concerned while the other systems of academic Kabbalah study are all fine, well, and good, still none of them should rightly be called Kabbalah after the original, and authentic Biblical model, because none of them teach their students authentic ascent (Ma'aseh Merkava) meditation and how one can and does travel out of body and into direct experience with the other dimensions, and those who dwell there.

When one reads the words of R. Hayim, one enters a world built entirely upon symbolism, metaphors, and archetypes. R. Hayim makes it ever so clear that what he discusses is nothing literal, and that he only uses the framework and terminology that he does in order to offer some sense of rational understanding. But this becomes a problem.

Almost everyone reads the metaphors, and symbols without ever understanding the underlying reality beneath R. Hayim's entire system. As such they understand the symbolic to be literal and in doing so completely miss what it is that Kabbalah is supposed to be teaching.

Kabbalah and the Human Psyche

I must state, what should be the obvious. Kabbalah does not speak about, nor address matters in the physical universe. What is going on beyond our planet in other realms and dimensions is only of interest with regards to how these other realities interact with our own, and how they have direct influence upon us. And the only way that we human beings become aware of such interactions is through our senses of psychic intuition and perception.

When Kabbalah discusses the Four Worlds of Atzilut, Beriah, Yetzirah and Asiyah, these are not physical locations to which one can travel. Rather these are psychic, psychological realms accessed by various grades of expanded human consciousness through which one travels.

When R. Hayim gazed and saw the pattern of the universe(s), what he saw was the fullness of Greater Man, (that which he knew so well as Zeir Anpin, the "Small Face" of God). All the worlds that he saw, from the Ayn Sof down to the Malkhut of Asiyah, all of them were seen through the gazing third eye of man below (R. Hayim, himself).

R. Hayim saw the Man Above. And this Man Above is the Supernal Pattern of all human consciousness and all human experience. This Supernal Pattern, that R. Hayim saw so clearly, is Zeir Anpin, the Image of Supernal Man. It was not the Image of all reality (the Image of Arikh Anpin). For this is an Image that no human mind is presently capable of receiving. This is the underlying message that God told Moses that no man can see the Face of God and live (ref. Exodus 33:20). We human beings can see everything in the universe from within the context of our humanity. But outside of that context is presently beyond the scope of our reality.

Needless to say, for most, one's level of awareness and perception is very dull. Most do not have a clue as to what is going on around them. This is true with regards to everyday affairs in one's life, and all the more so with regards to higher, more lofty realities which one does not even know exist.

The study of Kabbalah is designed to awaken the sleeping mind to become more aware and more perceptive. In order for Kabbalah to achieve this lofty goal, it must be understood within its proper context. To put it bluntly, Kabbalah needs to be understood as a guide to human psychology, as well as the path for the development of expanded consciousness through the cultivation and usage of what we today call psychic abilities.

Kabbalah is psychology, through and through. It is not metaphysics, it is the internal pattern and operation of the collective human mind and consciousness itself.

Ma'aseh Merkava is thus the psychoanalysis of the human mind and soul. In order for one to gain from the benefits of Kabbalah study, one must be internally transformed by the power of its teachings. All the symbolisms of Kabbalah, while well and good on their own, still must be stripped down, and understood for what they really mean. And very few Kabbalists have succeeded in doing just this.

Kabbalah speaks about Ten Sefirot, Four Worlds and Twelve Partzufim. Yet, just what is a Partzuf, a World or a Sefirah is only understood by what books say about them. No one has any direct experience with any of them. And without any direct experience, all speculation, no matter how deep, is only a bunch of ideas in a person's head. Without direct experience with these realities, they remain theoretical concepts in the mind of the many students of Kabbalah, devoid of any clarity and true knowing.

All the Sefirot, Worlds and Partzufim are constructs of definition whose reality exists within the human mind, and soul.

These constructs, and everything that R. Hayim saw, is the pattern of Man, both Supernal above, and us below. All the lessons included in the books, Etz Hayim, Otzrot Hayim and the like are events happening within the ever fluctuating consciousness of human beings.

The Akudim, Nikudim, and Berudim are lessons in the development of human psychic and psychological identity. Just as the evolution of these worlds led to the manifestation of the rectified world of Atzilut, and the establishment of a grounded and balanced Zeir Anpin (ZA), so too is this the psychological role model for each of us. The Seder HaHish'tal'sh'lut is our personal story. And this is why we study it. We study it to learn more about ourselves! R. Hayim saw all this in his meditative gaze.

Today, because the students of R. Hayim lack psychic intuitive insight that comes from practicing the Prophetic Kabbalah, all their speculations come from the World of Beriah, the realm of intellectual, academic understanding. Without psychic intuitive insight, one has not touched, nor received anything from Atzilut.

Pathway to Psychic Development – Ruah HaKodesh

The way to experience authentic Biblical Kabbalah comes from the meditative techniques that originated out of the schools of the Biblical prophets. One of the important lessons of this school is that all instruction is meant to be one-on-one, from master to student, as we learn from the Biblical example of Elijah and Elisha.

So fundamental is this personal teaching relationship that it was even codified into law with the writing of the Mishna in the second-century (Tractate Hagigah 2). This one-on-one teaching method was not established with the intent to keep down the number of practitioners. Rather, this school, Ma'aseh Merkava, is like modern in-depth psychotherapy. Just like with psychotherapy, Ma'aseh Merkava can only be taught one-on-one because no two persons are alike. Each one learns in one's own way.

In my past books, Let There Be... Knowing, and Using the Holy Names of God, I took upon myself to reveal many different techniques and practices. When used correctly, they will enable the individual to become aware of the greater reality, to cultivate the necessary intuitive psychic insight, and tap in to the reality of Atzilut, as it is able to be manifest here on Earth in human consciousness.

In my previous book, Behind The Veil, I discussed the serious nature of our present global predicament. I had to speak very cautiously and only reveal certain things in a certain way. This book, The Unveiling, should be considered a continuation of Behind The Veil. In that book, I suggested what there is to be seen. Now, I am being even more blunt, getting down to business to discuss realities that each of us desperately needs to see with each our own eyes!

I have included within this book, both academic and psychic material. The outline of The Unveiling is as follows:

Section 1

Masekhet Atzilut is a wonderful short text that I have often taught to my KosherTorah School students. The commentary that I included will not follow in the footsteps of the academic Kabbalists who see only through the philosophical eye of Beriatic rationalism. As you read what I wrote, you will see the difference between the Prophetic Way and theirs.

Section 2

The next short section deals with the subject of Psychic Warfare. Some do not like this term, and feel that it has no place in Torah literature. Little do such objectors know how very wrong they are! Psychic warfare is very much an active battleground in which we are all unwilling participants. Psychic attacks come to us (knowingly or unknowingly) from other human beings, as well as from other entities who exist in dimensions unseen by the physical human eye. It is imperative that we recognize what is happening to us, and what we must do to deal with it.

Section 3

The major part of this book, and the actual reason for its publication, is to disseminate the teachings of my Sihot, my weekly writings that I share with my KosherTorah School student body. In these, I break down the teachings of the Ma'aseh Merkava and the Kabbalah and present them in real down-to-Earth words, free from the multiple layers of Kabbalistic metaphor that has become the norm. In order for the wisdom and knowledge of the Biblical prophets to be properly disseminated, they need to be properly understood. I know that some readers prefer all the Kabbalistic metaphors and symbolic language. But again, the problem is that most who study the Pshat (surface level) of Kabbalah never achieve revelation of the Sod (deeper level). Too many people pay too much attention to the metaphors, and not enough attention on the actual meaning and intent. The Sihot are here to address this problem, and with the Grace of God, to provide at least a minor correction.

Section 4

The forth section of the book is a collection of related essays on topics of very relevant immediate importance to everyone. I again address the topic of actual Dark Side (demonic) activity in society today. I divulge the difference between Earthbound human souls, Shed/Jinn entities, and the descendants of the Fallen Angels spoken of in Torah literature. I also reprinted my original translations from R. Yehuda Fatiyah's Minhat Yehuda, on the topic of (demonic) possessions. Due to the proclivity of the Occult and New Age movements these days, creating more awareness about the spiritual problems that they create is of vital importance.

Section 5

I can't conclude the material of this book without including at least one meditative technique that will assist the practitioner to expand one's psychic awareness and natural consciousness. I have already published two books on the greater details of this vital subject matter, these being the two volumes of my Yehi Deah, which are Let There Be... Knowing and Using the Holy Names of

God. These two works explain the meditative system in the proper depth that it deserves. For here in this book, I have included an updated, revised version of the Kavanot of the Merkava that I published in 2007 in my book Walking in the Fire. The version included in this book, I am calling "YHWH (Hawaya) Meditations. The Practice of the YHWH Merkava Using the Name YHWH as a Tool for Psychic Diagnosis, and Spiritual Healing. A Ritual Practice of the Lurianic Kabbalah as Practiced in the School of the Prophetic Kabbalah." Rather than be yet another academic exercise, I offer the reader something more tangible.

So here you have The Unveiling. Read on. I am sure that you will not be disappointed.

My blessings to you all. Shalom.

R. Ariel Tzadok
27 April 2023
6 Iyar 5783

Section One

Masekhet Atzilut

An Ancient Kabbalistic Text
with original translation & commentary

Masekhet Atzilut

Introduction

There are many treasures of Kabbalistic literature mostly unknown to the general public.

Masekhet Atzilut is one of these treasures.

Subject Matter

This short text contains within it profound revelations that are rarely discussed in other Kabbalistic texts.

I have divided the text into seventeen segments for easy elaboration and individual commentary.

These subjects are:

1. The Way of Ma'aseh Merkava
2. The Importance of Concealment
3. The Dark Light and the Light Darkness
4. Secrets of the Pre-Adamic Civilization
5. Secrets of Atzilut
6. Secrets of Beriah
7. Secrets of Yetzirah
8. Secrets of Asiyah
9. Secrets of the Du Partzufim
10. Secret of the Shekhina
11. Secrets of Metatron and Sandalphon
12. The Hokhma-Binah Union, the Tzadik & Tal.
13. Wisdom and the Fear of God

בעזהי"ת

מסכת אצילות

היא ברייתא בחכמת הקבלה לחכמים קדמונים מזמן דוד המלך ע"ה בעניין עשר ספירות ונתחברה על ידי יערישיה וזכריה אליה בני ירוחם הנזכרים בדברי הימים א' ח'

ונוסף על זה פירוש גנזי מרומים להגאון המקובל ר' יצחק אייזיק חבר ז"ל בעל פתחי שערים, וכל ענינו להראות כיצד רמוזים הקדמות האריז"ל במסכת זו. וכן מובאים בו התומר דבורה להרמ"ק על עשר ספירות בדרך הנהגה ומוסר, ופירוש האילן לר' שלמה לוריא המהרש"ל, ובסופו מסילות החכמה והם ל"ב כללים בחכמה על פי הקדמות האריז"ל ממהר"ם פפיראש. ועל פירוש גנזי מרומים ציונים ועיונים ומפתח הקדמות וערכים

14. Origins of the Sefirot
15. The First Triad of Sefirot
16. HaGaT NaHiY, the Middle and Lower Sefirotic Triads
17. Malkhut

What is interesting to note is that Masekhet Atzilut apparently predates Zoharic Kabbalah by a good period of time. And yet, the text speaks about the four Kabbalistic worlds of Atzilut, Beriah, Yetzirah and Asiyah, knowledge of which was mostly unknown (or concealed?) at that time. Some scholars have suggested that Masekhet Atzilut may be the first of the Kabbalistic texts to discuss the four worlds in their present format.

The Encyclopedia Judaica says this about Masekhet Atzilut:

"The Treatise on Emanation.

The earliest literary product of the speculative Cabala is the work "Masseket Aẓilut," [sic] which contains the doctrine of the four graduated worlds as well as that of the concentration of the Divine Being. The form in which the rudiments of the Cabala are presented here, as well as the emphasis laid on keeping the doctrine secret and on the compulsory piety of the learners, is evidence of the early date of the work. At the time when "Masseket Aẓilut" was written the Cabala had not yet become a subject of general study, but was still confined to a few of the elect. The treatment is on the whole the same as that found in the mystical writings of the time of the Geonim, with which the work has much in common; hence, there is no reason for not regarding it as a product of that time. The doctrines of Metatron, and of angelology especially, are identical with those of the Geonim, and the idea of the Sefirot is presented so simply and unphilosophically that one is hardly justified in assuming that it was influenced directly by any philosophical system."

https://www.jewishencyclopedia.com/articles/3878-cabala#anchor29

The text is an excellent example of what I call the "older" Kabbalah that predates the Zohar and Zoharic influence. Masekhet Atzilut therefore discusses certain secrets of the Torah which, for the most part, were either concealed or forgotten by the later generations of the philosophical Kabbalists.

When the Zohar first was publicized (as the Midrash of R. Shimon Bar Yohai) it spread throughout Judaism like a wildfire. For the most part, the Zohar was widely received to be the authentic work of the 2nd century Tana (teacher) Rebbe Shimon. As such, what the Zohar taught quickly became the new face of Kabbalah. Indeed, the very term Kabbalah that we use today is for the most part associated with the Zohar and the vast number of mystical schools that emanated out of it, only one of which is the great school of the Ari'zal in 16th century Tzfat.

The Older, & Original, Biblical Kabbalah

The Zoharic Kabbalah did not invent Kabbalah; but it did radically reinterpret and replace the older schools of Kabbalah that has been in existence since Biblical times. Since Biblical times, authentic Biblical Kabbalah was built upon the teachings and experiences of the Biblical prophets. This Kabbalah was not a body of academic information learned from books. The original Kabbalah of the Prophets was an experiential learning system. It could not be taught in a classroom setting, nor could its teachings ever be captured by words on the page of a book.

The system of Biblical, prophetic Kabbalah was given a specific name by the Rabbinic Sages of the Second Temple period. They called the prophetic Kabbalah by the name of Ma'aseh Merkava (the work of the Chariot). This reference to a chariot comes from Ezekiel's famous vision, recorded in Chapter One of his Biblical book. Hidden within the metaphors and symbols of that chapter are recoded various and numerous secrets about how the Biblical prophets would rise up and out of normal waking consciousness, ascend into a state of greater psychic awareness, and in that state interact with whatever forces and form that the prophet would there encounter. The Biblical episode of the prophet Elijah recorded in 2 Kings also contains many of these secrets and hidden lessons. I have already written a detailed commentary on this section of 2 Kings, titled Secrets of the Prophet Elijah, published in my book, Behind The Veil.

The Zoharic system and everything that was born from it is today referred to as the Theoretical (or Academic) Kabbalah. The reason for this is that the system is, in reality, nothing more than a unique expression of Jewish metaphysical philosophy. The system contains no functional meditative system that enables a practitioner to escape the limits of waking consciousness, so as to explore the higher dimensions. As such the Zoharic system and the Ari'zal system based upon it are both academic systems. The students of these system spend all their time learning what the books say. Only the rare few who study the books ever discover what they really mean.

It is also very relevant to say that the many authors who follow the Zoharic/Ari'zal systems firmly believe that their path is the authentic and original way of understanding the Older Kabbalah. Since Zoharic times (from about the 14th century) almost all commentaries written on pre-Zoharic mystical texts have been written by Zoharic/Ari'zal influenced authors who reinterpret everything old in light of everything new. For some, this is understood to be a good thing. Whereas for others such modern commentaries that interpret pre-Zoharic material in light of Zoharic philosophy is a scholarly inaccuracy.

The original authors of pre-Zoharic material did not know the Zohar and the system that it presents. As such their written works contain nothing related to a Zoharic understanding of things. Therefore to reinterpret non-Zoharic material in the light of the Zohar, in my opinion, is fundamentally unhistorical, and mostly not in accordance to the intentions of the original authors! One does not come to a proper understanding of a text all the while that one is interpreting it in a way and fashion that is clearly foreign to the text writers themselves!

The one commentary to Masekhet Atzilut, published in Yalkut HaRo'im, and independently, is titled, Ginzei Meromim, (the Genizah Above), authored by the Kabbalist, R. Itzhak Isaac Haver, (author of the Kabbalistic text, Pit'hei She'arim). The Rabbi was a student of the Gaon of Vilna, and based his understanding of Kabbalah, and his writings on the system of the Ari'zal as seen through the eyes of the Gaon. Ginzei Meromim takes the pre-Zoharic, pre-Ari'zal teachings of Masekhet Atzilut and interprets them all in light of the Ari'zal. Like I said, almost all authors of the

Ari'zal school will applaud R. Haver and insist that he did the right thing. In their eyes, the teaching of Kabbalah before the Ari'zal, and certainly before the Zohar were either illegitimate or incomplete. These authors feel totally justified to reinterpret all older material in light of their present more-modern understandings. While this is all well and good, and indeed R. Haver's works are scholarly brilliant, still, nevertheless, they are not the original teachings and do not express the original intentions of the authors, with Masekhet Atzilut being here the example of this.

There are numerous writings from the pre-Zoharic schools. These include the Sefer Yetzirah, and most importantly the writings of the Hasidei Ashkenaz, which includes Rabbi Yehuda the Hasid, and Rabbi Eliezer of Worms. The prolific works of these two great Torah Sages include the Sefer Hasidim, and the Book of the Angel Raziel. This entire genre of Torah mysticism is based upon the older Biblically based Ma'aseh Merkava school. It predates the Zohar, and is thus absent of it influence. And this is why the system of the Hasidei Ashkenaz still contains elements within it that are valuable aspects of Merkava psychic ascents. While our present text, Masekhet Atzilut does not seem to emanate out of the schools of the Hasidei Ashkenaz, nevertheless, it is clearly evident that there is a common denominator between the two.

Masekhet Atzilut speaks about the Ten Sefirot and the Four Worlds in similar fashion to the later Zoharic Kabbalah. Such types of discussion are completely absent in the earlier Kabbalah schools. Even when the Sefer Yetzirah introduces to us the concept of Sefirot, as discussed in its first chapter, it is very clear right there in that first chapter that the Sefirot discussed therein are described very differently than later interpretations.

What Masekhet Atzilut discusses with regards to the Sefirot reveals a very early layer of teachings that became embodied in the later Zoharic Kabbalah, and at the same time, it contains elements from the older schools. This is what makes our text so unique and important. It is a blend of both worlds, the older Kabbalah and the newer. As such, it serves as a bridge between the two.

<u>Authorship</u>

The text is clearly ancient. Just how ancient seems to be anybody's guess. Historically, the text is an anomaly. No one knows for sure when the text was written, and by whom.

According to the Introduction Page to the version of Masekhet Atzilut, published in the book, Yalkut HaRo'im (published by Nezer Shraga, Jerusalem, 2016 edition), the text is called a Baraita, (an external Mishna), and is given an awesome pseudepigraphal authorship.

The Introduction Page says,

"Masekhet Atzilut... is a baraita of the wisdom of the Kabbalah of the ancient Sages from the days of King David (upon him be peace), discussing the subject of the Ten Sefirot. It was written by Y'ari'shiya, Zekharia, and Eliyah the sons of Yeruham, mentioned in 1 Chronicles 8."

Regardless of any claims to the opposite, there was definitely no discussion of knowledge about Sefirot in the days of King David. The idea of Sefirot did not dawn in the Jewish mind until many (many) centuries later. To ascribe an otherwise unknown text a pseudepigraphal authorship is a very common Jewish practice. For example, most scholars will readily agree that the Book of Enoch most certainly had no real connection to the Biblical character whose exploits are discussed therein. The Sefer Yetzirah is said to have its connection to Avraham Avinu (the Biblical Patriarch). This list goes on, and even includes the opinion of those who believe that the Zohar, is only ascribed to Rebbe Shimon Bar Yohai, and not really actually written by him.

Once a legend is born, it is sometimes hard to weed out what parts of it may have been historical from what parts of it are embellishments. The true authorships of texts is a concern for scholars, mostly of the secular kind. For the faithful, knowledge of the identity of the actual historical author is mostly irrelevant. What is important are the teachings of the texts themselves. The truths of the texts cry out and proclaim their wisdom, regardless of who actually wrote them. Therefore, the identities of actual authors is of second interest, at best.

Conclusion

Masekhet Atzilut contains within it secrets of the Ma'aseh Merkava school seldom discussed outside the confines of this school. The two topics of the pre-Adamic civilizations and the revelations about angels are two cases in point.

The secrets of the pre-Adamic civilization is a subject matter that was condemned by R. Hayim Vital. Being that the existence of the pre-Adamic world contradicted his own understanding of pre-Adamic times, he had no room for this knowledge in his Kabbalistic system. Yet just because it was rejected by R. Hayim Vital did not make this system disappear. I have written about the pre-Adamic world in many of my other writings, most specifically in my books Aliens, Angels, and Demons, and Behind the Veil. Many great Kabbalists before and after R. Vital embraced the knowledge of the pre-Adamic civilizations, including some of R. Vital's students. No true student of Torah and Kabbalah should thus turn a blind eye to this most important of topics.

The lesson about the pre-Adamic times is only one of the many great lessons brought to us in this sacred, short text. In order to provide the reader with the best exposure to the text, I have decided to present the first version of it here without commentary. In this way the reader can follow the flow of the text undisturbed and receive a direct experience of the material as it was originally written. After one has received this, only then do I introduce to you, my commentary. I have tried to stay as true to the original meaning of the text as I possibly could. I did not deviate into later kabbalistic systems to reinterpret the old in light of the new. I will allow my readers to decide for themselves how much or little value they find my commentary to be.

One way or another, I believe that Masekhet Atzilut has valuable lessons to offer the reding public. For this reason I have translated it here. I have always included Masekhet Atzilut as a topic of study in my KosherTorah School. I even have a 16 hour audio course on the text available online through our website www.koshertorah.com. Needless to say, in audio format I cover more material than the written word allows me.

The following is my lesson-by-lesson syllabus of the audio course on Masekhet Atzilut.

Lesson 1, Yirat Shamayim & Sitrei Torah

An opening introduction into the nature and purpose of pseudepigraphal writings. What is the meaning and purpose of Yirat Shamayim. It is the proper psychological alignment of one's inner self. Once this alignment is achieved between one's emotional state and one's mental state, one become sensitive to higher, more subtle levels of awareness. These then are the secrets of the Torah. The process of this alignment is Ma'aseh Merkava. All Kabbalah is essentially psychology. Any study of it that does not pursue this course is superficial, and misdirected. When one achieves this psychological/spiritual accomplishment it is said that one has achieved the level of Yirat Shamayim, in other cultures, called enlightenment.

Lesson 2, Light & Darkness: Understanding vs. Ignorance.

Truth can be found in many places, even within fiction. Truth should be embraced, regardless of its source. Truth needs to be understood for what it really is, and for what it really is not. Light is the metaphor for intellectual, rational understanding. One who has "the light" is considered mature. Lack of light defines immaturity. This lesson discusses the pursuit of truth and understanding, and describes the arduous psychological journey of how the path to light often takes us along roads of darkness (and why this is so). Example of Elisha Aher, why he became an apostate, what this means, and what we need to learn about communal responsibility, and the need to safeguard secrets.

Lesson 3. The Fall of the Prehistoric Worlds.

How what a text says, might not be what some interpret it to be. The worlds before Adam, and what happened to them. This subject is discussed from two points of view, the classical, which speaks of physical pre-Adamic human civilizations, and the Lurianic, which speaks about the evolution of the spiritual realms (even though the text does not fit the model). The costs of selfishness. An elaboration of modern political, and social problems that could lead to societal collapse. Has this happened all before? A discussion about prehistoric America, life before Adam, the existence of Atlantis. What happened in the past? Were their ancient societies that collapsed? What lesson does this hold for us today.

Lesson 4. The Four Worlds, Part 1.

An extended discussion about the nature of alternate realities, and the experience of their physical counterparts. Other worlds includes within its definitions, other physical inhabited planets, and other equally inhabited parallel dimensions, some physical like our own, and others radically different. How travel and communication between worlds occur. Examples of Ezekiel's and Elijah's chariot. Vortexes, wormholes, astral travel, and star-gates are all discussed within the context of extraterrestrial and inter-dimensional travel. Numerous examples are given from modern media. Atzilut, the first world, the domain of revealed energy, which we call YHWH, God. What and why this level exists, where it is, and the meaning of Divine Presence (Shekhina) as the foundation of intelligence in all atomic Intelligent Design.

Lesson 5. The Four Worlds, Part 2.

The Realm called Beriah, what exactly is it. The domain of collective souls, the beginning of differentiation between the Creator, and the creation. Why this is called, "something from nothing." Energetic life forms, orbs, how they appear to us at a distance, and how we communicate with them, and thus see them within the mind's eye in composite forms compatible to one's present level of consciousness. Akatriel Yah YHWH Tzvaot, is this God, an angel, or both? What is the Livnat Sapir, sapphire stone, and its relationship to Nefesh/Qi/Orgone. The Heavenly palaces, actual domains, the experience thereof is a matter of perception.

Lesson 6. The Four Worlds, Part 3.

All about angels. In-depth discussion into the actual reality, purpose and function of the other-worldly beings that we call "angels." The sons of God in Genesis 6, their relationship to the Watchers in Daniel, and the Heavenly Sanhedrin. The Teli dragons, who rule in the universe. The ten classes of angels, understanding their forms of projection, and how we perceive them, as opposed to how they are in reality, the different views of RaMBaM, and RaMBaN. Selected readings from the book, Shoreshei Shemot about how certain angels are invoked, and for what purpose. The continuing practices of angelic invocations, interactions, and communions. Metatron and Sandalphon. The nature of collective prayer, being a global energetic telepathic broadcast, and what happens when the signal is weakened by one siphoning off energy from it. The reality and meaning of avodah zara, idolatry.

Lesson 7. Heaven & Earth, Dual Dimensions of a Shared Reality.

All of live in parallel dimensions simultaneously. In Lurianic Kabbalah, they are called Asiyah (Earth) and Yetzirah (Heaven). These "worlds" are not really one higher than the other, but more-like one alongside the other. Passage between them is by expansion of consciousness. This is the underlying purpose of meditation and spiritual growth. But passage is no easy thing. Human emotions play a strong role here. Emotions must be balanced before "successful ascent" can be achieved. Balanced emotions only come about through a balanced mind (intellect/Binah, and wisdom/Hokhma). This lesson expands on the practical reality of what the classical Kabbalah calls the "Du Partzufim," and explains them using the oriental metaphor of the Yin/Yang symbol. Significant references to Metatron, Sandalphon, Samael, and the Watchers

Lesson 8. Consciousness in Nature, the Metatron/Sandalphon Relationship.

Metatron, Sandalphon and their relationship to levels of human consciousness. What exactly is Ruah HaKodesh, and who can receive it. What exactly is Israel, and how this title applies to all enlightened souls, regardless of origins. The actual doorways/vortexes of how consciousness travels from one dimension to the next in kind-of-like a quantum entanglement state. Warnings about the path. The secret of destiny, and how one fulfills one's own, but never that of another. Leviathan, what is it, a Godzilla, Teli, or something else, a lesson about understanding midrash. The true identity of Samael and Lillith, and how they challenge to us is also their service to God, and what this all means. The actual reality of Hekhalot ascent.

Lesson 9. Wisdom, Understanding, the Honor Due Heaven, & the Secret of the TAL.

More midrashic metaphors to describe the correct state of mind and being necessary for the proper alignment of the physical and spiritual dimensions. Mind development is the entire purpose, and destiny of every human soul. Healing the inner turmoil (tikkun), bring order into the inner chaos, this is symbolized in the in-depth metaphors of the Lurianic system, and in his lesson completely unmasked and explained in depth. The natural order of the development of psychic powers of the mind. The influence of the individual on to the collective human consciousness, regardless of time, place, and form. The falsehood of superficiality in life, specifically in religion, and how it is a waste of time and a terrible distraction for the soul, keeping it away from its appointed pre-ordained tikkun. A full explanation of the metaphor of Dew (Tal), as being the teleological director that guides individuation.

Lesson 10. The Natural Fall of Evil, the Sefirot in Nature.

According to the Sefer Yetzirah, morality is a natural force. Evil will naturally collapse. The essence and purpose of universal Torah, and nationalistic Judaism, how they are different, and yet complement one another. The meaning of Shabat, a level of consciousness, a vessel/tool through which to manifest the state of natural alignment. The Sefirot are also natural tools created by the Unknowable, and Unknown Sentience of Existence, the Cosmic Mind (God) through which the Unknown can become known. This class explores the multi-dimensional reality in which we live, and includes discussion about the actual function, and parameters of astrological influences, and the quantum entanglement that unites all of existence.

Lesson 11. The Sefirah Keter, & the Psychic Powers of the Mind.

A discussion of the older Kabbalah, prior to its philosophical forms. The Golem, what it really is, and how one is really made. Reading the commentary of R. Shlomo Luria (the Maharshal), and reference to his student, R. Eliyahu Ba'al Shem, the original creator of the Golem. The older Kabbalah of the Ashkenazim. The power of mind, the formation of the abstract into the concrete. The actual form of a Tulpa. Why and how Chakras are different from Sefirot. The Keter in the older Kabbalah is different from the later Kabbalah, and is more akin to the Collective Unconscious, a described in later psychological literature. This class delves into the psychic parameters of the mind to instruct students in actual, and practical matters, applicable to everyone.

Lesson 12. The Sefirot of the Mind in the Maharshal.

More about the Pre-Lurianic concepts of the Keter, and its relationship with the other powers of the mind, Hokhma and Binah. Reference to the book Sha'arei Orah of R. Yosef Ibn Giktalia. Different cultural expressions used to describe similar concepts (do not mistake the finger for the moon). The Keter's role of Giver, the conduit between individual and collective consciousness. How originality, "divine" inspiration, and prophecy all come from the same psychic source. Telepathic Torah on Sinai, the forces of Mind, Voice and Speech. The need for Voice and Speech in psychic healing and prayer. The sefirot as symbols within the human body (when in reality they are psychological, and not physical). The role of Mazal, and astral (astrological and astronomical) cosmic forces. The Torah in the Hekhal, why Torah law must be defined by human needs, and not by higher needs, or standards. Due to a technical failure with a recording device, the class ends abruptly, but no material was lost.

Lesson 13. Hokhma & Binah in the Mind & its Materialization into Reality.

Practical direction how to focus the power of the imaginative mind (Hokhma) into construct form (Binah), and then how to charge it with passion (Heshek/heart) to motivate, and thus create the reality which one seeks. Numerous examples from cultures around the world how this inner power is tapped into, concentrated, and projected. The power of Faith. The strength of Passion. This lesson details how all spiritual systems (including magical ones) work to manifest inner power into the outer world. It is a vital lesson for personal transformation, and the accomplishment of individual desires, and destiny. This lesson sums up and knits together the previous two, making these a complete three that discuss the powers of mind over matter. Also more sefirotic references from the Sha'arei Orah found in the Maharshal commentary.

Lesson 14. The Seven Attributes. How Emotions Translate Thought into Action.

The transformation of unconscious compulsions into emotional passions and how these drive the manifestation of congealed thought-forms. Hesed, the first of the sub-conscious emotions. The metaphorical descriptions of Hesed along with their psychological significance. An overall discussion of the 72 Triad Name(s) of God (and mention of the 42), and how and why they are used in meditative context in association with their specific attributes. The relationship to the archetypes of the Patriarchs, iconic representation of personality types. The secret of the Merkava and a system of psychological transformation, and how this understanding is what underlies the law as mentioned in Tractate Hagigah. Masekhet Atzilut – Classical Kabbalah

Lesson 15. Gevurah, the Attribute of Discipline & Severity.

Human psychology is always fluctuating between the opposite poles of "too much," and "too little." This class explains the vital psychological nature of the attribute of Gevurah, and how one must embrace it in one's life. Even anger has its rightful place.

There is no duality in Torah, therefore, both right side and left side are equal in value, and have their context, and place. Practical examples are given from modern fiction, with references to modern social issues, and the place of enlightened western civilization (the symbolic head of Esau buried in the lap of Jacob). The psychic/psychological differences between Jacob and Israel. This class addresses the topic of the sefirotic triad within the context of human psychological reality.

Lesson 16. Tiferet, the Inner Man & Malkhut, Unleashing the Inner Man in Outer Man.

Final class in this course. The final five sefirot are understood as a concentric whole explaining the relationship of what we call the Inner/Higher Self, and one's conscious physical being. How does the inner ideal of the Higher Self (Torah) become manifest in fruition in real life. This comes about through the motivational emotional aspects of wanting to impose (Netzah) order in the world for its own sake (Hod) and betterment. This only comes about when one is properly motivated (Yesod), the do the right things (Malkhut). Also discussed are the metaphors used to describe this psychological process, and an in-depth analysis of what Kabbalah calls Sefirotic Faces (Partzufim).

Masekhet Atzilut

Full Original Text, Translated

Masekhet Atzilut 1 – The Way of Ma'aseh Merkava

"Eliyahu Ben Yosef opened, it is written, (Psalm 25:14), "the secret of God is for those who fear Him and His covenant is for those who acknowledge it." From this we learn that the Holy One blessed be He does not reveal His secrets other than to those who fear Him.

Even if a man of Israel were to study Bible, Mishna, Talmud, Aggadah and Tosafot, but he has no fear [of God], then in vain does he swim in the mighty waters. All his efforts are for naught.

And the one who [truly] fears Heaven [he] pursues the concealed and [the] Ma'aseh Merkava which is the essence of wisdom and knowledge, as it is written, (Psalm 111:10), "the beginning of wisdom is the fear of God."

The fear [of God] is a brass shield and an iron sword and [the] one [who possesses it] will not be afraid of anything, as it is written, (Isaiah 33:14), "the sinners in Zion were in fear." They were in fear of sinning, but they were not afraid. [This is] because the Shekhina was adorned before them and protects them and reveals to them sublime secrets.

This is "the secret of God is for those who fear Him." And it is written, (Job 28:28) "the fear of God is wisdom and turning from evil is understanding."

Masekhet Atzilut 2 – The Importance of Concealment

"Y'arishiah ben Yosef opened, (Proverbs 25:20), "It is Kavod (glory/respect) to God is to conceal a thing." This teaches [us] that the words of Ma'aseh Merkava should be concealed, for this is the Kavod (glory/respect) to God. Another thing [with regards to] the Kavod (glory/respect) of God; when is it when one extends (glory/respect) to God? At the time one works with the hidden [things]. Don't read "a thing" (davar), but rather read [the last word in the verse above as] "a word" (dibur).

Masekhet Atzilut 3 – The Dark Light & the Light Darkness

It is written (Job 38:19), "Upon which path will Light dwell, and darkness, what is its place?" And it is written, (Daniel 2:22), "He knows what is in darkness, and Light dwells with Him." This teaches us that the Holy One, blessed be He created a place for Light, and a place for darkness.

The Light [is for] the pleasure of the righteous who do His Will, and the darkness [is] to punish the wicked who go against His Will. Even though Light is with Him, we learn that the Holy One, blessed be He constricts his Light.

He knows what is in the dark, meaning that He knows what to do with the darkness. For darkness [is how] the Holy One, blessed be He pays back [those] who violate His Will. For it says of them, darkness, and it is said, like Light, like darkness.

Just as darkness is payback to the wicked, for they darken their deeds, so too was Light created to give good reward to the righteous, for their deeds enlighten the world. This is what Solomon said (Kohelet 7:14)," this corresponding to that God has made."

Isaiah 45:6-7 states, "So that they may know, from East to West, that there is none but Me. I am YHWH and there is no one else, I form light and create darkness, I make peace and create evil. I YHWH do all these things."

Masekhet Atzilut 4 – Secrets of the Pre-Adamic Civilization

"Opening. We are taught (Proverbs 20:21), "An estate acquired in haste in the end will not be blessed."

We learn that the Holy One, blessed be He originally created [other] worlds and then destroyed them. [He planted] trees and [then] uprooted them, [all because] they were terrified.

They were jealous of one another. [By way of] example, [let's take] ten trees that are planted in the field all in a single straight line. There is not any space between each of the trees. Each tree [thus] wishes to dominate the others, and to absorb all the moisture in the ground. [In the end] they all end up dry. Thus it was with the [primordial] worlds. Their end was not blessed, for the Holy One, blessed be He withdrew His Light from them.

They remained [in the] dark so as to punish the wicked. Thus the verse says, "in the end [they] will not be blessed."

Masekhet Atzilut 5 – Secrets of Atzilut

"It is written [in] Isaiah 43:7, "All that is called by My Name and by My Honor, I created it, I formed it, I even made it."

We learn [from this] that the Holy One, blessed be He created four worlds corresponding to His blessed Name that contains four letters. And these are their names: (1) Atzilut.

This [name] teaches us that the Holy One blessed be He emanated from His Light (as if to say) and made it like a dress and like a garment. He "wrapped [Himself] with Light like a garment" (Psalm 104:2). He placed [there] His Name and the Name of His Glory (Kavod). And there is no [mention of] His Glory (Kavod) other [than in reference to the] Shekhina, as it is written, "And they saw the Glory (Kavod) of YHWH" (Numbers 17:7).

From which Light was this world created? From the Light created at first that was originally terrifying. The Holy One, blessed be He added Light upon their Light and created from them His world, and planted within them His Light, thus "YHWH is one, and His Name is One" (Zecharia 14:9), and it says, "I will not give my Glory (Kavod) to another" (Isaiah 42:8)."

Masekhet Atzilut 6 – Secrets of Beriah

"I created it. [This is] the world of (2) Beriah. Herein are the Neshama (souls) of the righteous. Also, [herein] are the storehouses of blessing and life.

Here [also] is the Throne of Glory (Kavod) for the Holy One, blessed be He, and Akatriel Yah Tzvaot who sits upon the Throne.

Herein are the (1) Palaces of Pleasures (oneg), (2) the Palace of Desire (ratzon), (3) the Palace of Love (ahavah), (4) the Palace of Merit (zekhut), (5) the Palace of Glowing Light (nogah), and (6) the Palace of the Essence of Heaven (etzem hashamayim).

And beneath them [all] is (7) the Sapphire Brick, as it is written (Exodus 24:10), "and under His Feet was like a brick of sapphire."

It is also the Foundation of the World (Yesod HaOlam), as it is written, "the Righteous is the foundation of the world" (Proverbs 10:25). And El Shadai dwells within them all."

Masekhet Atzilut 7 – Secrets of Yetzirah

"I have formed," (3) the World of Yetzirah. Therein are the holy Hayot that were seen by Ezekiel son of Buzi the Kohen priest.

Therein are His servants who perform the Will of the Holy One, blessed be He. Also here are the Palaces of pleasure (oneg) and desire (ratzon), because these corresponding to those.

For the lower raises the fear of God… [missing text]. And there are a number of faces [facing] towards faces.

And therein are the ten types of His angels each in accordance to their stature. And these are them:

1. *Serafim; Shamunga'el rules over them; and there are those who say that Yahuel rules over them.*

2. *Ofanim; Rifael, and the Light of Peniel rules over them.*

3. *Kiruvim; Kiruviel rules over them.*

4. *Shinanim; Tzadkiel and Gavriel rules over them.*

5. *Tarshishim; Tarshish and Shalu'yael rules over them.*

43

6. *Ishim; Tzfaniah rules over them.*

7. *Hashmalim; Hashul rules over them.*

8. *Malakhim; Uziel rules over them.*

9. *Benei Elohim; Hhafniel rules over them.*

10. *Erelim; Mikhael rules over them.*

And these are the ten [types] of angels who perform His Will.

[These are the ones who] were created first and who rule over the [other] mentioned camps. And Metatron who was changed from flesh and blood to devouring fire rules over them [all].

Therein are the spirits (Ruhot) of human beings, and the stones of war, and soldiers, and chariots (merkavot), and princes of the chariots, as it is written (Psalm 68:18), "the chariots of Elohim are myriad, thousands upon thousands." And Elohim shines upon them and rules over them all."

Masekhet Atzilut 8 – Secrets of Asiyah

"I even made it" (Isaiah 43:7). [This is world #4], the world of Asiyah.

Herein are Ofanim, those who receive prayers and supplications, and those who are in charge of the desires of men.

Herein are the Nefesh souls of men, and the masters of fists (martial artists?), the Princes of the army, arrows, stones, and catapult stones.

Many above are directors of the ship, arrangers of the [supernal] system corresponding to the evil Samael, and his associates, to prevent them from entering the openings of prayer, those who pass by the way and fear not the power of God.

Therein are the guardians who witness the deeds of men. And Sandalphon [who] ties [the] crowns rules over them. And Adonai God radiates them and rules over all, as it says, "And His Kingdom is in all places" (Psalms 103:19)."

Masekhet Atzilut 9 – Secrets of the Du Partzufim

Zechariah ben Yosef opened, "With wisdom YHWH founded the Earth, [He] established the Heavens with intelligence" (Proverbs 3:19). This teaches us that with wisdom was the Earth founded (established). And there is never any mention of "the Earth" other than to signify the Shekhina (Divine Presence), as it is written, "The whole Earth is full of His glory" (Isaiah 6:3).

However, the Earth was attuned with intelligence, as it is written, "with wisdom is a house built, and with intelligence it is attuned" (Proverbs 24:2). And there is never any mention of "house" other than to signify the Shekhina (Divine Presence), as it is written, "And the Glory of YHWH filled the house" (2 Chron. 7:1).

This teaches us that with wisdom (Hokhma) was the house built. And it is written, "like the beauty (Tiferet) of man, to dwell in [a] house." (Isaiah 44:13). And with intelligence he is attuned.

This teaches that with intelligence he is attuned, and being that this is so, what then is judgment (Din), of which it says, "attuned Heaven with intelligence."

Rather interpret it [like this], with wisdom and with understanding was the Earth and the Heavens created. And there is never any mention of "the Heavens" other than to signify the Holy One, blessed be He, as it is written, "the Heavens are the Heaven of YHWH" (Psalm 115:16).

Which one was created first? We have been taught (M.R. Ber. 1:15), R. Shimon B. Yohai said that the Heavens and the Earth were created together, like a cooking pot with its cover.

R. Eliezer, his son said that the two are equal, for at times Heaven is mentioned before the Earth, [and at other times] the Earth is mentioned before the Heavens. This teaches us the that the two are equal."

Masekhet Atzilut 10 – Secret of the Shekhina

"It is written, "One to one they touch, and not even a breath comes between them" (Job 41:8). This teaches us that to every place that the Shekhina goes, the King, the Holy One, blessed be He is with

Her. [This is so] so that the spirit of the nations, God forbid, will not come, and finish off Keneset Yisrael.

[Here is] a parable about a King that sent his esteemed woman to go on a mission to a place far away to redeem her children from imprisonment. But the King feared to send her concerned that she may encounter highwaymen. So, he decided to join her. Thus we have, one to one they touch. It is also written, "In all of their suffering, He suffers" (Isaiah 63:9)."

Masekhet Atzilut 11 – Secrets of Metatron & Sandalphon

"It is written regarding them, "Each clings to one other; they are interlocked so that they cannot be parted" (Job 41:9). This teaches us that the Princes, Metatron and Sandalphon, each clings to one other, even if they are interlocked with the sins of Israel, they do not break apart nor separate.

Metatron's "sneezing flashes forth light, and his eyes are like the rays of dawn" (Job 41:10). "From his mouth go firebrands" (Job 41:11). "His breath kindles coals" (Job 41:13). This teaches us that he was transformed from flesh and blood to fire. "The coals ignite, in his neck resides strength" (Job 41:13-14). All of these sayings are speaking about Metatron.

"No arrow can put him to flight" (Job 41:20). This is Samael who [acts] as accuser, and who shoots arrows at Israel. "And (s)he plays at the noise of the harpoon" (Job 41:21). This is the evil Lilith.

"Behind him he shines a path" (Job 41:24). This teaches us that Samael and his seventy Princes do not take pleasure from the Light above other than from the backside of Metatron.

"On the dust there is none that rules over him" (Job 41:25). "He looks at all high things" (Job 41:26), meaning that he receives strength and support from Akatriel, who is higher than him, He is king over all the children of arrogance who are Samael and his Princes; for they are arrogant and full of pride."

Masekhet Atzilut 12 – The Hokhma-Binah Union, the Tzadik & Tal.

Yeruham ben Yosef opened, "Happy is the man who finds wisdom (Hokhma), and a man who gives forth intelligence (Tevunah)" (Proverbs 3:13).

Come and see, in the place where wisdom (Hokhma) is mentioned, right next to it stands understanding (Binah) and intelligence (Tevunah). This is to teach us that wisdom (Hokhma) and understanding (Binah) are both equal. One never, ever separates from the other.

It is written, "With His knowledge the depths were split, and the heavens dripped dew" (Proverbs 3:20). In the mind of the Holy One, blessed be He the depths of the 50 gates of understanding (Binah) were split, meaning as it says, "From whose womb did the (awesome) ice emerge" (Job 38:29).

"And the heavens dripped dew" (Proverbs 3:20). How [to whom] are the heavens dripping dew? To he who is a Tzadik, who is the Foundation of the world. For it is impossible for the world not to have dew.

And the dew does not stop, meaning, as the Holy One, blessed be He spoke to Israel, fear not for my head is full of dew" (Song 5:2). And it is written, "I will be like dew to Israel" (Hoshea 14:6)."

Masekhet Atzilut 13 – Wisdom & the Fear of God

"Better a little [knowledge of Torah] with the fear of YHWH, than a great treasury that comes with turmoil" (Proverbs 15:16).

Better a little [bit of] Torah and there be with it the fear of God, for one who has [the] fear [of God], goes in straight ways, as it is written, "He who fears YHWH goes in his uprightness" (Proverbs 14:2).

Then he has revealed to him the mysteries of wisdom, as it is written, "but His counsel is with the upright" (Proverbs 3:32). For we have learned, one can do much or one can do little, just as long as he focuses his heart to Heaven.

From great treasure comes turmoil. One who is full of the treasure of Torah and who suffers turmoil therein is because he has no fear [of God]. For then all the days rumble against him.

Woe to him for what he studied, woe to him for what learned, and woe to him that he serviced the Sages. Let this rule be established in your hand, one who has no fear [of God], has no wisdom.

And we learned (Avot 3:17), "if there is no fear [of God, then there is no wisdom. Woe to such a one because of [the] judgment [to come], as it is written, "Behold, the fear of YHWH is wisdom and shunning evil is understanding"(Job 28:28). Thus, even a little [Torah knowledge] is good [as long as it has] the fear of God."

It is written (2 Sam. 23:6-7), "But the wicked are all as thorns thrust away, for they cannot be taken in hand. But if a man touch them, he should be armed with iron and the staff of a spear; and with fire they shall be utterly burned in their place."

These verses speak about Samael and his associates and how they will be burned up, toppled, and destroyed, [they will be] burned in their place (ba'shavet). Do not read [the word] as ba'shavet, but rather as b'Shabat (the Shabat of creation).

There are those who say that on Erev Shabat, his host will be torn [up] in Judgement, "When the wicked flourish like grass, and all workers of violence blossom, only to be destroyed to eternity." (Psalm 92:8).

But we are saved with a single verse, "But, as for me, let my prayer to You, YHWH, be in an Et Ratzon (an auspicious time). With Your abundant kindness, Elohim, answer me with the truth of Your salvation." For then (on Erev Shabat) it is an Et Ratzon (an auspicious time), and the accusers are nullified and concealed in their place. This is what makes it be an Et Ratzon (an auspicious time).

Fear [of God] is so great [a thing] that our teacher Moses (upon him be peace), commanded [us] with regards to it, "And now Israel, what does YHWH your God, ask of you? Only to fear YHWH your God, to walk in all His ways, and to love Him, and to worship YHWH your God, with all your heart and with all your soul." (Deut. 10:12).

All who wish to enter into the [inner] sanctums of wisdom and who have no fear [of God] will lose all that one has gained, as it is written, "The beginning of wisdom is the fear of YHWH, and the knowledge of the holy ones is understanding." (Proverbs 9:10).

Masekhet Atzilut 14 – Origins of the Sefirot

"It is written, "To You YHWH is the greatness, the might, the glory, the victory, and the majesty. For all that is in the Heavens and on the Earth [is Yours]. Yours is the kingdom, and it is You who is the exalted Head over everything." (1 Chron. 29:11).

We have been taught in the Sefer Yetzirah (1:2) of Avraham Avinu (upon him be peace) that there are Ten Sefirot Blimah. What is Blimah? It is as it is written (Job 26:7), "He suspends the Earth on Blimah (nothing), for therein is no image, nor similarity." Blimah, they are the work of the fingers of God. They are the artisan tools of the Holy One, blessed be He.

For example, an artisan metal-worker has a crucible for [melting] silver, and a kiln for [melting] gold. Even though the crucible and the kiln are both made from clay their names are different. So it is with the attributes and praises of the Holy One, blessed be He.

Why are their names called Sefirot? Because it is written (Ex. 28:18), "sapphire (sapir) and diamond." And it is written (Job 38:37), "who will speak of (yi'saper) the Heavens with wisdom."

And by His artisan's tools the Holy One blessed be He strikes down the boastful, and raises up the humble, one is impoverished, one is made wealthy, this one falls, and this one arises. And if the righteous act righteously and straightforward in the world, and labor in Torah, which is called "a fortress," then the Shekhina says, "If they would grasp My fortress, they would make peace for Me" (Isaiah 27:5).

And if the wicked and sinners proliferate throughout the land, then the world collapses. The Shekhina then cries out, my head is destroyed, my arm is destroyed.

For life and peace only grow throughout the world when there are the righteous therein. For the world of the righteous is for life, and the fruits of evil are for sin."

Masekhet Atzilut 15 – The First Triad of Sefirot

"These are them. The first is called Keter. It is divided into 620 paths and beams of light. Regarding this it is written, "and the Ancient of Days sat; His raiment was as white as snow, and the hair of His head was like clean wool." (Daniel 7:9). Therein are the thirteen gates of wisdom and compassion that were referenced in the Torah by Moses our teacher, peace be upon him. Regarding this, they said, that which is too wondrous for you do not seek to elaborate upon it, for you have no business with hidden things.

The second. The Spirit of the Living God, Hokhma. It is divided into thirty-two paths of light. Therein are the depths of hidden wisdom, and perceived wisdom. "For with wisdom did God form the Earth" (Proverbs 3:19).

The third. "For, if you call for Binah (understanding)." (Proverbs 2:3). Therein are the pleasures of the World to Come, and the rest for souls. It is divided into three gates, Hokhma, Binah and Da'at. They are never parted. Regarding them it says, "Has the rain a father, or who begot the waves of dew?" (Job 38:28). Thus, "For YHWH gives wisdom; from His mouth [come forth] Da'at (knowledge) and Tevunah (discernment)." (Proverbs 2:6)."

Masekhet Atzilut 16 – HaGaT NaHiY, the Middle & Lower Sefirotic Triads

The Fourth. Mercy (Hesed) to Avraham (Micah 7:20). This is the attribute of our father Avraham. Water of rest and joy. [It is] called the Right [side or hand] of the Holy One, blessed be He, as it is written (Isaiah 62:8), "YHWH swore by His right hand."

The Fifth. The Fear (Pahad) of Isaac, father of Jacob. This is the attribute of our father Isaac who was bound [upon the altar] by [his father] Abraham. Therein is scorching fire, for YHWH is a devouring fire (Deut. 4:24). [It is] called the Left [side or hand] of the Holy One, blessed be He, as it is written, (Isaiah 62:8), "the arm of His strength."

The Sixth. Glory/Beauty (Tiferet). "And it is his glory to pass over a transgression" (Proverbs 19:11). This is the attribute of our father Jacob. From here was the Torah of Moses our teacher given. It is called the Heart of Heaven, regarding this it is written (Isaiah 44:13), "like the beauty of man to sit [in] the house."

The Seventh. [The] Victory (Netzah) of Israel will not lie. This is the attribute of Moses our teacher, upon him be peace. In his merit did the manna descend from Heaven, that grinds the manna for the righteous.

The Eight. [The] Splendor (Hod) and Majesty of the Holy One, blessed be He. This is the attribute of Aaron, upon him be peace. In his merit there were six clouds covering over Israel in the wilderness. Regarding them is it written, (Song of Songs 5:15), "His legs are [as] pillars of marble."

The Ninth. [The] Righteous [is the] foundation (Yesod) of the world. This is the attribute of Yosef the Righteous (Tzadik), upon him be peace. From herein comes all the influences of the mercy, grace, and severity of the Holy One, blessed be He. [From here comes] sustenance and support to Collective Israel (Knesset Yisrael). Regarding this it is written (Judges 6:24), "and he called it, "YHWH peace (Shalom)."And it is [also] says (Genesis 28:12), "and its top reached to Heaven."

Masekhet Atzilut 17 – Malkhut

"The tenth. His Kingdom (Malkhut) is the Kingdom over all worlds. For all of them give radiance and blessing to Her through the attribute of peace that makes peace between Knesset Yisrael and the Holy One, blessed be He.

Therein enter the voices of prayer and supplication. Therein is the reward and punishment of the righteous and justice. It says, "Righteousness and justice are the base of Your throne." (Psalm 89:15).

Therein is the attribute of King David, upon him be peace. Regarding him, it says, "in this I am confident." (Psalm 27:3). "This is from God." (Psalm 118:23)."

Masekhet Atzilut 1

The Way of Ma'aseh Merkava

"Eliyahu Ben Yosef opened, it is written, (Psalm 25:14), "the secret of God is for those who fear Him and His covenant is for those who acknowledge it." From this we learn that the Holy One blessed be He does not reveal His secrets other than to those who fear Him.

Even if a man of Israel were to study Bible, Mishna, Talmud, Aggadah and Tosafot, but he has no fear [of God], then in vain does he swim in the mighty waters. All his efforts are for naught.

And the one who [truly] fears Heaven [he] pursues the concealed and [the] Ma'aseh Merkava which is the essence of wisdom and knowledge, as it is written, (Psalm 111:10), "the beginning of wisdom is the fear of God."

The fear [of God] is a brass shield and an iron sword and [the] one [who possesses it] will not be afraid of anything, as it is written, (Isaiah 33:14), "the sinners in Zion were in fear." They were in fear of sinning, but they were not afraid. [This is] because the Shekhina was adorned before them and protects them and reveals to them sublime secrets.

This is "the secret of God is for those who fear Him." And it is written, (Job 28:28) "the fear of God is wisdom and turning from evil is understanding."

These wise words speak for themselves. Unfortunately, although people read the words, they often overlook their message. The text here clearly states that without one possessing the honest and sincere personality trait of Yirat Shamayim (fear of Heaven) any and all study of Torah, the greatest mitzvah of them all, is consider null and void. Without the fear of Heaven all religious observances are hypocritical (Sefer Ba'al Shem Tov, Shemot 1).

Our text here does not simply state nebulously that one has to be Yirat Shamayim; it actually spells out for us what the expected Yirat Shamayim needs to be. One who is truly Yirat Shamayim will by nature have a personality that first seeks out the secrets of Torah as an academic pursuit and then continues in the meditative practices of transcending physical space/time through the expansion of consciousness here called Ma'aseh Merkava.

Read the words above; they are quite clear. Without these two pursuits of the study of the secrets of Torah and the practices of Ma'aseh Merkava, one is not considered to be Yirat Shamayim; and without being Yirat Shamayim, one is considered to be a hypocrite, whose entire efforts in Torah study are a complete waste of time. These are strong and harsh words, but disagree as one may wish, these are the words written by the ancients who proclaim them to be true!

Learning the secrets of Torah can never be accomplished through academic pursuits alone. One can read and learn all the books about Kabbalah ever written and still walk away completely ignorant of what it means to bond with God and to practice Ma'aseh Merkava. Like with all other mitzvot of the Torah, it is not the learning that counts but the doing (*Lo HaMidrash HaIkar Eleh HaMa'aseh*).

When it comes to embracing the secrets of Torah one cannot do this from the pages of a book, one needs practice. The practices of Ma'aseh Merkava are meditative exercises used to expand human consciousness. Only in this higher enlightened state can one gaze into the Torah and intuitively perceive the secrets therein. Mere human academic accomplishments do not expand human consciousness to the point of granting one this psychic insight.

Fear is instinctual. Love is acquired. Fear is innate and natural; one does not need to learn it. Either one has it or one does not. Look to the natural world for example. Animals have instinctual fear of that which can cause them harm. Because we human beings have lost our connection to the natural, we have lost our natural instinct of fear. This is much to our own harm. As we can see with society's ills, all our societal and individual harm comes about because we have forgotten our instinct to stay away from that which harms us. We use our intellect to justify all type of unjustifiable behaviors. Such lack of vision always leads to death.

When one learns the secrets of Torah one is not learning a topic but rather a new way to think and see. One learns to see the depths in everything, even the depths of that which is on the surface. The depths of a thing in Torah language are called the heart of the matter. And we are taught to love God with all our hearts and to place His words upon our hearts (Deut. 6:5-6). Love is something acquired. We do not naturally love; we learn to love. Yet, we are equally commanded to fear God. Indeed, our Sages teach that the fear of God comes before the love of God.

The beginning of wisdom, like the verse says above, is the fear of God, not the love of Him. Fear is instinctual. When we regain our instincts, we are using our physic intuitive knowing. When we reacquire that, we achieve wisdom. Wisdom is the Sefirah Hokhma. Hokhma is intuition and therefore also instinct. Thus when we regain the instinctual, we have regained wisdom/Hokhma. The Sefirat Hokhma corresponds in Kabbalah to the Olam (dimension) of Atzilut, the domain of the Divine. Therefore to regain instinct is to touch the Divine. This is the beginning of wisdom/Hokhma/Atzilut. This and only this is the true Torah, like the section above clearly states.

Yirat Shamayim serves as both a shield of defense and a sword to attack. How is this so? The answer again is instinct. Every martial artist and warrior knows that in spite of however much training they receive in theory, their ability to be victorious is based upon their experience. Like I said above, *Lo HaMidrash HaIkar Eleh HaMa'aseh*. Every fighter fights on instinct. He/she knows in advance when to block and when to strike. One can in essence sense the next move of one's opponent faster than one's eyes or brain can process it. One acts with a speed faster than intellectual processing and is already blocking or striking, without having to think about it. The mind actually slows down the warrior. His/her body acts instinctually, faster than what the senses can process. Every successful warrior knows this to be true.

As it is with a warrior of the flesh, so is this true with warriors of spirit. They fight with instinct. They know in advance what is and what is not proper. They can instinctually recognize the good and with equal instinct recognize the bad. They have awareness that transcends words and still can be justified with simplicity without the need to be overly-philosophical and having to convince or "brainwash."

True Yirat Shamayim is not superficial superstitions and fears. Such is the way of the fool, never the way of the wise. Only those who know living Torah know wisdom. Only that which is alive can keep one alive. Thus living Torah keeps one alive. Without this wisdom/Yirat Shamayim, one's Torah is dead, and like the text says above, all one's efforts in learning such "dead" Torah is worthless. This is the difference between what we call the "dead" Torah of Mashiah Ben Yosef and the living Torah of Mashiah Ben David. Those with wisdom will understand here the secret of redemption.

Instinctual wisdom keeps one away from harm; whereas evil is understood and recognized intellectually. Evil is harmful; this should not only be instinctual; it should also be logical. Therefore when we approach something that we may or may not feel to be dangerous, we use our senses coupled with our intuitive internal wisdom and explore, analyze, and discover the truth of the matter. Once we have discovered the truth of a thing it is easy to explain its danger (or lack of it). Proper understanding brings with it simplicity and clarity. Simplicity is here the key.

When something is clearly understood one can explain it simply and easily. Without such an understanding we must question what one really knows. Too much talk covers up ignorance. Simple, straight, logical talk shows understanding. Yet, if someone says something simple, but stupid, we recognize the lack of understanding and also the lack of wisdom in such words and ideas. These must be dismissed.

The instinctual mind of wisdom "smells" in superficiality the weakness and falsehoods in such positions. This is how we use our intellects to ascertain truth. We distinguish between fears of foolishness and the fear of Heaven.

Embracing living Torah means using both our Binah brain and our Hokhma brain. Only when the two are merged together do we then use our full minds. Without a full mind, no one can have full Torah. Without full Torah, there is a great shortage in the soul and thus in the world.

In Pirkei Avot it is said that a Voice cries out from Sinai everyday saying, *"woe to the world for the disgrace shown to Torah."* Who today has the inner ear to hear the inner Voice? Only those with combined understanding (Binah) and wisdom (Hokhma) have the inner ear to hear (Ta Shema) and the inner eye to see (Ta Hazeh). The proof of this is not in words, but in actions; actions of simplicity, actions of instinct, actions of wisdom (not superstitious foolishness) and actions of truth. This is the living Torah, the mighty shield and sword in our hands.

Masekhet Atzilut 2

The Importance of Concealment

"Y'arishiah ben Yosef opened, (Proverbs 25:20), "It is Kavod (glory/respect) to God is to conceal a thing." This teaches [us] that the words of Ma'aseh Merkava should be concealed, for this is the Kavod (glory/respect) to God. Another thing [with regards to] the Kavod (glory/respect) of God; when is it when one extends (glory/respect) to God? At the time one works with the hidden [things]. Don't read "a thing" (davar), but rather read [the last word in the verse above as] "a word" (dibur).

Why must anything be kept a secret? Secrets are concealed for their protection, to prevent them from being exposed to elements that may be harmful to them. We learn the way of this from nature itself. There are many pathogens in nature that attach to living organisms and cause them great harm, if not death. The way nature protects these organisms is to provide for them some form of husk or shell to keep out harm.

We human beings are part of nature, and so too is human knowledge and experience. As we learned from the Garden of Eden, Knowledge can be either good or evil. Some knowledge can bring life, and some knowledge can bring death.

Knowledge, like other elements in nature needs to be protected from any external contaminates that can compromise its integrity. This is why certain aspects of knowledge are protected under a veil of secrecy. This is to protect the knowledge from falling into the hands (minds) of those not able to properly receive it and work with it in the way originally intended by nature.

The untrained and the unprepared human mind often acts like a pathogen. One's thoughts and attention attach on to something, and then uses that something in a way that is harmful to that thing. One very relevant example of this is the knowledge of the Kabbalah.

Kabbalah is a very intricate system compromising many different levels of knowledge and expanding awareness. These levels must be approached each in its proper way and time. If and when the natural order of things is not follow, the resulting conclusions are dreadfully harmful.

Thus, because certain Kabbalistic teachings have fallen into the wrong hands, of those not able to receive it properly and to understand it correctly, what has happened is that Kabbalah has been transformed into something very profane, instead of being something very sacred.

One merely needs to look at the wide variety of non-kosher Kabbalah books so readily available to the general public, for example. These books pervert the Kabbalah and thus pervert the public's perception and expectations of the Kabbalah. Needless to say it would be best that such books had never been written.

It is an ancient law that states the secrets of Ma'aseh Merkava were only taught one-on-one, from master to student, and even then, the student had to already have expressed some semblance of psychic ability to understand matters without having to have them explained in detail.

The reason for this exclusivity underscores the real essence of what the Ma'aseh Merkava really is. For the real Ma'aseh Merkava was not a study of external forces, regardless of how angelic or extraterrestrial these forces may be. Real Ma'aseh Merkava was the art and science of developing psychic consciousness that enabled an aspiring prophet to reach out and commune with actual and real other-worldly, holy entities.

The nature of this work was intensely psychological. It requires of the aspiring prophet to delve deep into oneself and to discover therein that unique way which works only for the specific individual. Thus those practicing Ma'aseh Merkava were said to descend to the Merkava, not ascend to it.

And being that the work was almost totally psychological, it was intensely personal. Therefore, the discoveries that one student discovered were different from those of another. Each experienced what they did within the context of each individual personality. Thus no two individuals could experience the same thing, in the same way, at the same time. This is why Ma'aseh Merkava had to be taught only one-on-one, and in no other way.

Now, what happens if this rule gets violated? This is how blurred teachings are born, this is how mistakes are made; this is how knowledge becomes perverted. Thus the secrets of Ma'aseh Merkava are kept safely concealed, and out of the hands of those who are at present incapable of in-depth self-discovery.

Thus we say that it is glory/respect to God for the aspiring prophet to lead the right things, in the right way and at the right time. For by doing so, this enables the aspiring prophet to enter into communion with higher powers not of this Earth. And this restoration of the soul's connection with the dimension from which it came, is a major accomplishment, and it is one of the reasons why our souls incarnate here on Earth, in the first place.

Prophetic meditation always involves chanting. Chanting is verbal, and often melodic. It always uses one's voice, and this one's words as well. This is the reason why the text of Masekhet Atzilut references the word Dibur (a word) instead of Dvar (a thing). For it is known that by the power of sound, specifically the right and correct combination of sounds, the word chanted can have a tremendous effect upon the world around us.

Masekhet Atzilut 3

The Dark Light & the Light Darkness

It is written (Job 38:19), "Upon which path will Light dwell, and darkness, what is its place?" And it is written, (Daniel 2:22), "He knows what is in darkness, and Light dwells with Him." This teaches us that the Holy One, blessed be He created a place for Light, and a place for darkness.

The Light [is for] the pleasure of the righteous who do His Will, and the darkness [is] to punish the wicked who go against His Will. Even though Light is with Him, we learn that the Holy One, blessed be He constricts his Light.

He knows what is in the dark, meaning that He knows what to do with the darkness. For darkness [is how] the Holy One, blessed be He pays back [those] who violate His Will. For it says of them, darkness, and it is said, like Light, like darkness.

Just as darkness is payback to the wicked, for they darken their deeds, so too was Light created to give good reward to the righteous, for their deeds enlighten the world. This is what Solomon said (Kohelet 7:14)," this corresponding to that God has made."

Isaiah 45:6-7 states, "So that they may know, from East to West, that there is none but Me. I am YHWH and there is no one else, I form light and create darkness, I make peace and create evil. I YHWH do all these things."

Although it is clearly written in Scripture, the fact that it is God alone who is the Author of both good and evil, and of both Light and darkness remains a profound truth unknown to most.

Although many modern religions want to portray good and evil as opposites sides in a cosmic battle, where God and Satan are fighting over the control of human souls, such a duality is unheard of in Torah.

Unlike other religions, who have built their beliefs upon this dualism, Torah proclaims a simple unity. God and God alone is in charge of all things. God, and God alone, creates both Light and darkness, both good and evil. Both Forces are designed to serve their Creator.

Anything and everything that ever happens is because it was the Divine Will for such things to happen. This apparent determinism, and the fact that evil and darkness both exist simply in order to serve the Divine Will may come as a shock to many. Not for naught are the secrets of the Kabbalah kept hidden and concealed. Not everyone is able to handle the truth of things.

It is well known that the Sefirotic Tree of Life has to it both a right column expressing Divine mercy, and a left column expressing Divine severity. One column is a opposite reflection of the other. Between the tension of the two opposites is balance and harmony established. Without the tension between the two, there could be more movement, and no change. There would be no balance simply because imbalance could not exist. And what would be the meaning and experience of balance if there did not exist awareness and knowledge of the lack of it?

Reflections also follow the rules of their existence. Just like a reflection can reflect in one direction, it can also reflect in the opposite direction. So, while the right column of the Sefirot can reflect towards its left, and thus contribute to the building of the center column of the Sefirot, the right column can also reflect further to the right, completely outside of the Sefirotic pattern. When this occurs there is created a perverted right column, which overextends itself, without any possible center for balance.

This perverted right column is called the Klipah, the husk or shell of the right. This is the genesis of the proverbial "Other Side" (Sitra Ahra). And just like this occurs on the right column, so too does it happen on the left. Thus we have the existence of the Sitra Ahra, the true Dark Side of the Force. And all this was also created by God. Like King Solomon said (Kohelet 7:14)," *this corresponding to that God has made."*

God has made this to be. God created the Force and forces of evil that in our eyes stand up to oppose the Divine Way. Why would God create His own opposition? God creates Life and growth; why would He equally create Death and decay?

I can say that God created the opposites so that between them balance would be created and established. This, at least, makes sense to me. But, alas, I cannot think with the Divine Mind. I cannot fathom the wisdom and purpose of our Divine Creator. As a mortal human being all that I can do is to observe, become aware of what is, and then to learn how to interact with what is in a way that works towards my betterment.

As for why God does what God does, no mortal human can say. Yes, we can offer all types of wise insights, but without Divine insight, who among us can understand the secret workings of the Divine Way?

When we speak about the creation of darkness, we are not speaking about the left column of the Sefirot. Rather, we are speaking about the Klipah, those overextended reflections of both the right and left columns of the Sefirot that extend outwards outside the true primordial Divine pattern. These create perverted forms of both right and left. The perverted form of the right is too much leniency. The perverted form of the left is too much strictness. We see both of these Klipot forces very much active in society today.

Just as souls emanate from the true Sefirot, so too do souls emanate from their perverted forms. These perverted souls each reflect the nature of their origins. They are the forces of the Klipot, who seek to influence others to either overly indulge on the right, or opposite it to be overly restrictive on the left. Again, we see these extreme polarities throughout society today.

All this was created by God to further advance the purpose of creation. Yes, I can express human, mortal ideas as to why this is so, but who other than God can proclaim the ultimate Truth of the matter? These things are very deep and profound. Not every human mind can entertain these thoughts. For many, the idea that God is behind the creation of evil, and its continued maintenance and upkeep is too much to handle. Best that this knowledge remains hidden and kept secret. God is the only Author, and the only Creator of all things. This we know, and this is the message that we must proclaim, "YHWH our God, YHWH is one"!

This is only one of the many secrets treasured within the teachings of the Ma'aseh Merkava. Learn it, and then be silent about it. This is how one gives Kavod (respect) to God.

Masekhet Atzilut 4

Secrets of the Pre-Adamic Civilization

"Opening. We are taught (Proverbs 20:21), "An estate acquired in haste in the end will not be blessed."

We learn that the Holy One, blessed be He originally created [other] worlds and then destroyed them. [He planted] trees and [then] uprooted them, [all because] they were terrified.

They were jealous of one another. [By way of] example, [let's take] ten trees that are planted in the field all in a single straight line. There is not any space between each of the trees. Each tree [thus] wishes to dominate the others, and to absorb all the moisture in the ground. [In the end] they all end up dry. Thus it was with the [primordial] worlds. Their end was not blessed, for the Holy One, blessed be He withdrew His Light from them.

They remained [in the] dark so as to punish the wicked. Thus the verse says, "in the end [they] will not be blessed.

The primordial worlds referenced herein are not those from before the Big Bang, but rather this is a reference to the pre-Adamic civilizations that existed here on Earth.

It is a well-known and documented teaching of the Kabbalists that prior to Adam in Eden there were other great and advanced human (or proto-human) civilizations here on Earth. The earliest literature said that this is hinted to in the Torah within the verse (Gen. 36:31), *"these are the Kings who reigned in the Land of Edom prior to there being a King in Israel."*

The reality of pre-Adamic human civilizations is accepted as fact by almost all Kabbalists, with the one exception being R. Hayim Vital and those who embrace his outlook. R. Hayim Vital, the famous redactor of the Torah of the Ari'zal contradicted dozens of earlier Kabbalists authorities, including the Zohar (T.K. 36), by clinging to his version of spiritual evolution (*Seder HaHishtalshlut*), and claiming that it is historical (in the context of time) instead of figurative (in the context of mind).

R. Hayim's understanding of the Order of the Worlds, specifically the worlds of the Akudim, Nikudim and Berudim, for him outline the whole of time, and therefore there could not have been another time for other pre-Adamic civilizations. With the exception of most of those who call themselves the students of R. Hayim, all the later Kabbalists continued to embrace the reality of the pre-Adamic civilizations, regardless of R. Hayim's objections. Indeed, even one of the most authoritative commentators to R. Hayim's works (R. Shalom Cohen in his book, Sha'at Ratzon) penned an involved commentary to the Tikunei Zohar 36 to attempt to show how R. Hayim's version of the past and the pre-Adamic civilizations do not need to be contradictory.

One must recognize that in the world of Kabbalah there does not need to be a consensus of ideas. Halakha requires consensus because with regards to rituals each community does indeed need to practice in the same way (for this is what identifies a community). However, with ideas and beliefs this is not the case.

There does not need to be consensus on all ideas and beliefs, especially Kabbalistic ones. Therefore, one may indeed hold the majority opinion of embracing the reality of the pre-Adamic civilizations, or one may hold the minority opinion of R. Hayim and those who follow in his stead. Indeed, one may even embrace both positions as did R. Cohen in his commentary to T.K. 36. As we say *Elu v'Elu Divrei Elohim Hayim*.

Now, let us turn to the actual teachings of our text.

The reference to the ten trees is clearly a reference to the Ten Sefirot. However, the nature of their primordial struggle, as being ten in a tight row, each fighting for space and nourishment, is not exactly how R. Hayim Vital describes the primordial worlds, some centuries later. This is significant in that our text provides for us insights into primordial times that is not Zoharic or Lurianic in nature.

We should not view our text as merely an alternative view, but rather as a primary one. After all, Masekhet Atzilut, from most scholarly opinions, is from the early 1300's or earlier, possibly even pre-dating the revelations of the Zohar in the 1270's. As such it represents an independent view of things that is worthy of our consideration.

Awareness of the primordial worlds being created and destroyed is recorded in the Midrash (G. R. 3:7). Who knows for how long this teaching existed in oral form before it was redacted into writing? It is ancient knowledge. Yet, as for the details of what these earlier worlds were like, very little has been committed into writing. In many of my other works I have discussed this topic and have provided many translations and details. We have no need to repeat them here.

What we have here, in the metaphor of the trees is a unique approach to the underlying reason as to why there was a collapse of the primordial worlds. This indicates that these worlds fell due to direct fault of their own, as opposed to just a whimsical desire on part of the Creator.

Remember, the Midrash, and our text based upon it, echoes the teaching that God destroyed the primordial worlds. Our parable of the trees here indicates that God did not destroy them (at least directly), but rather that they destroyed themselves. And this is of great significance.

Centuries later R. Hayim Vital elaborates how his primordial worlds of the Akudim, Nikudim and Berudim were in a sense evolutionary. These worlds evolved one from the other is proceeding grades of greater refinement and perfection. The previous world was not perfect enough, and so the next world came to replace it and to improve upon it. Our text here in Masekhet Atzilut does not teach this exact same thing. However, while the details differ, the end result is the same. But we all know that details reveal to us very important matters, so let us turn to the details of the ten trees to extract its very important message.

Ten trees all in a row, each with limited space, each one fighting with the others for finite resources in order to survive. Sound familiar? This metaphor describes human civilizations perfectly. The cause of most wars, past and present, is for the control of resources. From the sound of this parable, wise King Solomon was right, there is nothing new under the sun. The pre-Adamic civilizations suffered from the same finiteness as do we modern humans.

Were ancient, pre-Adamic humans (proto-humans, or non-humans) fighting with one another in the same way as we do today? If we look back at the myths and legends of every culture from around the world, there are always stories about the wars of the ancient "gods." And aside from stories and legends, there does seem to be a good amount of archeological evidence to suggest that our ancient ancestors did indeed possess levels of science that we do not believe possible. Even many of our Midrashim acknowledge this. These ancient ancestors of ours may indeed have been involved in devastating wars using weapons devised with a technology equal to, if not surpassing our own. Maybe this is what happened to "the ten trees."

I am certain that what really did happen in the past is well known in certain circles, while this closely guarded knowledge is almost unknown to the masses. Even in Kabbalah, the secrets of the past are meant to remain hidden and mysterious. But our Sages have revealed to us the little that we are entitled to know. What more is known we can only speculate. We have a good amount of titillating tips revealed to us in books like Sefer Temunah and in Yalkut Reuveni. As I mentioned above, I have already addressed these works in my other writings, and I choose not to repeat that work here.

This section of our text concludes by saying, "*the Holy One, blessed be He withdrew His Light from them. They remained [in the] dark so as to punish the wicked.*"

If God withdrew His Divine Light from them (whomever "they" really are), then obviously it was an intentional act, and a deserving one. What did the ancients do that caused them to be plunged into darkness so as to punish the wicked? Like I said, legends from around the world speak about the ancient "wars amongst the gods." In each of the legends, the "gods" are never described in any benevolent way.

I believe that we can safely conclude that the ancient "gods" were no gods at all. Rather, they were the advanced humans (?) of their day, fighting and destroying one another. The folly that blinds the eyes of political leaders, and that compels them to fight suicidal wars can most rightly be called a withdrawal of the Divine light.

Just ask Pharaoh and the Kings of Canaan, who as Scripture records had their hearts hardened by God so as to bring about their doom. It makes one wonder in fear and trepidation when we look upon our modern-world political leaders and see them acting with the same hardness of heart, and blindness of eyes.

The ancient pre-Adamic global world order was destroyed. Atlantis was swallowed up by the sea, literally or figuratively. All that was, was no more. All that was left was the devastated bands of survivors, who without any source for technologies or advanced knowledge soon reverted to primitive lifestyles. Maybe this is the origins of those whom we today call, cavemen? What better way to describe the loss of Divine Light, and remaining in the dark than this? What greater way to punish the wicked? Can you imagine if something like this were to happen today?

Can you imagine if we today were to have a global war that would wipe out modern civilization, how would the survivors be living in one or two generations after such a holocaust? Most of them, without access to modern schooling and amenities would revert back to a primitive life style, without even remembering the advanced technologies that we embrace as normal today. Our descendants would revert to uneducated and ignorant individuals. What a terrible judgment! Yet, what better way is there to describe the loss of Divine Light?

We are told that before our first-recorded historical civilizations popped up (some seemingly very fast, and from out of nowhere) that people lived like the proverbial cavemen for many centuries. If this is indeed the case, then those intervening centuries were surely enough for all the ways of the past pre-Adamic worlds to have been forgotten.

Strange, but this scenario also seems to be echoed in a teaching of our Sages. The Talmud (B. Sanhedrin 97a) states that our world will only survive for 6,000 years, and afterwards for a thousand years, our world will lay devasted. There are those who say that just as this will happen to our world, that so too did this already happen to the world (the global civilization) that preceded ours.

The Kabbalists who discuss the pre-Adamic world refer to it by the Biblical term of Shemitah. Just as the land is worked for six years and then given a year of rest (its Sabbatical, or Shemitah), so too is it with human civilization (as referenced in the Talmud).

The Kabbalists say that the Shemitot are seven in number, corresponding to the seven-year cycle referred to in the Torah. These seven also correspond to the seven lower Sefirot HaGaT, NaHiY'M (Hesed, Gevurah, Tiferet, Netzah, Hod, Yesod, Malkhut).

The first Shemitah was the one before us. It is said to correspond to the Sefirah Hesed. Hesed as we know is expansive and blessed. This may be why the legends of old speak about the days of the ancient "gods" as being both wondrous and wonderful. With the coming of the second Shemitah of the Sefirah Gevurah, judgment, and darkness entered the world. This seems to fit the description of our text above, and its description of the struggle of the ten trees.

Today, we are in the Shemitah of Gevurah. It is dominated by the forces of severity and judgement which is the Force that rules (and defines) Gevurah. The Kabbalists say that this is why our present society, since our ancient times (as in Cain and Abel) has been full of bloodshed, violence and evil. Yet, this too must come to an end with the dawning of the Age (Shemitah) of Tiferet. Tiferet promises to be a much better time for humanity and our planet than our present time in the Shemitah of Gevurah.

And so, our text here in Masekhet Atzilut offers us a simple parable, yet within its simple words there is the entire history of humanity, both in ancient pre-Adamic past, and its prophesied near future. Time will tell what our future holds, but our Torah does teach us to look to the past for lessons about our future. Indeed, maybe we have just done this exact thing!

Masekhet Atzilut 5

Secrets of Atzilut

"It is written [in] Isaiah 43:7, "All that is called by My Name and by My Honor, I created it, I formed it, I even made it."

We learn [from this] that the Holy One, blessed be He created four worlds corresponding to His blessed Name that contains four letters. And these are their names: (1) Atzilut.

This [name] teaches us that the Holy One blessed be He emanated from His Light (as if to say) and made it like a dress and like a garment. He "wrapped [Himself] with Light like a garment" (Psalm 104:2). He placed [there] His Name and the Name of His Glory (Kavod). And there is no [mention of] His Glory (Kavod) other [than in reference to the] Shekhina, as it is written, "And they saw the Glory (Kavod) of YHWH" (Numbers 17:7).

From which Light was this world created? From the Light created at first that was originally terrifying. The Holy One, blessed be He added Light upon their Light and created from them His world, and planted within them His Light, thus "YHWH is one, and His Name is One" (Zecharia 14:9), and it says, "I will not give my Glory (Kavod) to another" (Isaiah 42:8)."

The dating of the text's writing becomes significant with this selection. Our text introduces us to the four worlds of A'Be'Y'A (Atzilut, Beriah, Yetzirah, Asiyah). These names and their descriptions are well known in all the later Kabbalah, especially through the Kitvei HaAri'zal. What is significant is the antiquity of this text. According to most scholars Masekhet Atzilut predates the Zohar and the rise of modern Kabbalah in 13th century Spain and France. If this is indeed so, then our text here is the first Kabbalistic text to reference the four worlds in this format which would later be adopted as the Kabbalistic norm.

This selection quotes Isaiah 43:7 which is the source of the names Beriah (created), Yetzirah (formed) and Asiyah (made). There is no overt reference to the name Atzilut, but its presence is inferred through the reference to the Glory (Kavod) of God. As is made clear, the Kavod is a reference to the Shekhina. The Shekhina is the Sefirah Malkhut, and is thus an expression of God, and an emanation of the Divine Presence. The Shekhina is the emanation, thus She exists in Her own world, the world of Emanation (Atzilut). The text then proceeds to elaborate for us what is this world of Atzilut.

Atzilut is the first of the four created worlds. Today, in light of centuries of Lurianic Kabbalah, this statement is nothing other than obvious. However, in its day, this was a significant revelation. Four worlds, one each to correspond to the four letters of the Holy Name, Yod Hey Wav Hey. Again, this is well known to us today, but it was a revelation in the pre-Zoharic past.

Remember this, prior to the revelation of the Zohar and the theoretical Kabbalah, all the Sitrei Torah (secrets of the Torah) addressed the upper worlds (higher realities) within the context of psychic (astral – prophetic) ascent. Those who descended before the Merkava actually went to some "place" that was out of body.

The Talmud (B. Hagigah) and other sources enumerate the names of the seven Heavens. And, while the later Kabbalah merged the identity of these seven Heavens with the Sefirot and the concepts expressed in the theoretic school, nevertheless, in the original experiential literature, the seven Heavens were clearly actual, tangible domains (destinations), and not just symbolic references to states of altered higher consciousness.

Thus to those who ascended there was no Asiyah, Yetzirah, Beriah or Atzilut to go to. These four were not travel destinations. No ascender ever said, "today, I will ascend the Yetzirah or Beriah."

The categorization of these four worlds introduced to ascenders and to the speculators a vocabulary of contextual differences. Thus when the ascender ascended, he could say that while "traveling" off Earth that he had either a Yetziratic or Beriatic experience, based on the type of encounter that he experienced.

One famous example of this is found in the Talmud (B. Berakhot), where it is recorded that R. Yishmael envisioned himself in the Holy of Holies of the Sacred Temple, wherein which he encountered Akatriel Yah YHWH Tzvaot. In the Talmud no mention is made whether or not this was a Yetziratic or Beriatic experience. However in light of the later Kabbalah (which came about over 1000 years after R. Yishmael's experience), we can categorize his encounter as being Beriatic, and not Yetziratic. More so, the categories enable a student to understand why such an identification is important, and what it means to modern-day ascenders.

Historically, R. Yishmael would never have said that he ascended to the world of Beriah. Neither would Ben Azai, Ben Zoma, R. Elisha, and R. Akiva have said that their trip to the Pardes (B. Hagigah) took them into the world of Yetzirah. These terms, these descriptions and these concepts did not exist in the minds of the ascenders of those days.

In ancient times, ascenders ascended into the Seven Heavens. Sometimes they would ascend into the Seven Palaces (Hekhalot). However, it is important to remember that the Seven Palaces described in ancient Hekhalot literature are not the same Palaces as those described in the Zohar and the later Kabbalah.

The earlier ascenders ascended to specific places. The four worlds as discussed here in Masekhet Atzilut are not places of location. They are not destinations in any sense of travel. Rather the four world are layers and levels of experiencing all worlds, all places, and all destinations. This is why we say that the four worlds of A'Be'Y'A describe a dimensional ascent wherein which levels of ascent are applicable to every place. So, even right here on physical, mundane Earth, one can expand consciousness to experience a higher Yetziratic, Beriatic and even an Atzilutic level of Earth, with each level (dimension) becoming more and more refined, and more and more in tuned with, and more like the primary world of Atzilut.

This section marks the shift from Merkava ascent being an astral projection and into a more subtle way of understanding the psychological origins of what ascents actually are.

Atzilut is the first of the worlds from above to below. According to the later Kabbalah there is even one world higher than Atzilut; this being the world of Adam Kadmon. When correlating the worlds to the Sefirot, Adam Kadmon corresponds to Keter, and Atzilut corresponds to Hokhma. The Sefirah Hokhma and thus Atzilut are clearly #2. Being that this is so, why is Atzilut called world #1 of the 4 worlds?

The answer to this reveals how the four worlds are indeed levels of consciousness as opposed to merely being destinations of psychic travel as previously discussed. The four worlds correspond to levels of human consciousness. Being that Adam Kadmon is Keter, and the Keter sits on top of the head and not in it, Adam Kadmon and Keter is by definition above human consciousness. In the language of psychology we would say that Adam Kadmon/Keter is the collective unconscious, which connects the individual to a whole new world greater than oneself. Hokhma/Atzilut is the beginning of the individual human identity. As such this level is the highest any human being can achieve.

From our human point of view this is the level of the Divine; what we would call the archetypes of the collective unconscious. For Keter is never directly revealed other than through Hokhma, so too the collective unconscious is only made manifest through the archetypes of the collective unconscious.

The archetypes are the forms of the higher domain that cannot be experienced other than through a symbolic form. Here, our text refers to this exact same process when it states that *the Holy One blessed be He emanated from His Light (as if to say) and made it like a dress and like a garment.* This is a reference to the primordial Light above (the Sefirah Keter), emanating out of itself to manifest the world of its emanation. And thus Atzilut was born.

No angels are mentioned herein, nor Palaces. The only thing that resides here in Atzilut is the Glory of God, and this is the Divine Presence, the Shekhina. Thus the world of Atzilut is the Divine World, the world of the Prime Sefirot. While Adam Kadmon, technically is the Ultimate Pattern of all existence, still, Adam Kadmon is above our experiential grasp. Therefore our perception of the Supernal Pattern is the world of Atzilut, our subjective world #1.

Also, when we address Adam Kadmon in Keter, due to its high and sublime nature, we often do not distinguish it from the Ayn Sof, the Source of all. So, Ayn Sof is the Primordial Nothing. It manifests itself in Keter. This is the revealed Essence of God (the Ayn Sof being the concealed Essence). Anything below this are the garments of God, here referred to as God's Name. Thus YHWH is one and His Name is one. All Names of God, including YHWH is but a garment through which the Divine Essence is manifest and made perceptible to creation.

Masekhet Atzilut 6

Secrets of Beriah

"I created it. [This is] the world of (2) Beriah. Herein are the Neshama (souls) of the righteous. Also, [herein] are the storehouses of blessing and life.

Here [also] is the Throne of Glory (Kavod) for the Holy One, blessed be He, and Akatriel Yah Tzvaot who sits upon the Throne.

Herein are the (1) Palaces of Pleasures (oneg), (2) the Palace of Desire (ratzon), (3) the Palace of Love (ahavah), (4) the Palace of Merit (zekhut), (5) the Palace of Glowing Light (nogah), and (6) the Palace of the Essence of Heaven (etzem hashamayim).

And beneath them [all] is (7) the Sapphire Brick, as it is written (Exodus 24:10), "and under His Feet was like a brick of sapphire."

It is also the Foundation of the World (Yesod HaOlam), as it is written, "the Righteous is the foundation of the world" (Proverbs 10:25). And El Shadai dwells within them all."

Beriah is the domain of the Neshamot souls. It is also the Upper Garden of Eden. Beriah is indeed the domain of the Divine Thone, but not the Divine Essence.

This selection opens with a reference to the Neshama souls. These are the higher Selves of the collective whom we call Israel, and whom the text calls, the righteous. As we know, when we use the term "Israel" we cannot limit it just to the mention of the members of a single tribe, the Jews. Israel consists of twelve tribes, and if Israel and the righteous are synonymous terms then there must be many righteous souls in this world who are of Israel, but who do not know their true identities as such.

Beriah is the dimensional plane wherein which resides the Divine Throne, the Kiseh HaKavod, the Throne of Glory. And upon the throne sits Akatriel Yah YHWH Tzvaot. So, who and what is this Akatriel, and why is It sitting on God's Throne. If we attempt to interpret any of this as having any physical foundation in reality, then those who make such interpretations are one step away from the spiritual crime of idolatry! From a physical standpoint there is no Divine Throne, or anything else physical. What is a Throne, and what is the Shekhina (Divine Presence)? Without understanding these no one will be able to grasp the true meaning of Kabbalistic metaphors.

Being that Atzilut is the domain of the Divine, this world alone is the one that we call the "garments of the Creator." For as I said above, Ayn Sof, Adam Kadmon and Atzilut serve as the Supernal Pattern for what would become the triad soul NaRaN. This would also serve as the Supernal Pattern for its reflection, the lower three worlds of Be'Y'A (Beriah, Yetzirah and Asiyah). Thus, Ayn Sof, Adam Kadmon and Atzilut serve, as if, like the Neshama, Ruah, and Nefesh of the Creator. Mind you, this is symbolism. We speak in this way only to make matters understandable to us and relatable to our human experience. God is one, in the ultimate of unity. We must never mistake metaphors and symbolisms as being actual in any manner.

Being that Atzilut serves, as if, like the Nefesh of the Creator, our text refers to it as the "garments." Again following our usage of metaphors, the Creator created His worlds, Beriah, Yetzirah and Asiyah in order to dwell within them. Thus we have the NaRaN of the Creator, and opposite it we have the NaRaN of creation!

Beriah is the highest realm of creation. It is the realm of the Neshama soul of human beings. The Neshama soul is the collective of all human souls. It is thus called Supernal Man (not to be confused with Zeir Anpin, who is also called Supernal Man, but within another context).

The Throne is not a literal seat. God does not have an anatomy that needs to sit down. The Throne is a profound metaphor. For just as an actual physical chair/throne enables the one sitting on it to lower one's body and to securely rest it in a lowered position, so does the world of Beriah serve such a function for the Divine Presence. As Atzilut serves as the "Nefesh" for the Creator, Beriah serves as the dwelling of the "Nefesh" of the Creator, where Creator meets creation. As such, Beriah is the beginning of creation.

What resides in Beriah? We just said it; the collective Neshama soul, the source soul of all humanity, the higher (united) Self. In other literature, this would be called the "head" of Metatron (for his "body" is of Yetzirah). So, God the Creator takes up residence within His dwelling. And what is the Supernal Dwelling for the Divine Presence? This is the Supernal Neshama Soul! God dwells within the Collective Soul, a spark within the greater Neshama. Thus the Shekhina is called Knesset Yisrael.

Even the Neshama soul itself is a triad. Within the Neshama soul resides the Hayah and Yehida levels of soul. This indwelling Presence of God dwells within the Yehida. As such, the Presence of God lowers itself below its Atzilutic essence to settle into and to be secured into the lower domain of the Yehida of the Neshama. This bond between Creator and Creation is the secret of the Kiseh HaKavod, the Divine Throne.

And this is the secret of Akatriel Yah YHWH Tzvaot that was experienced by R. Yishmael. How is it that an angel such as Akatriel has attached to its name the sacred Names of Yah and YHWH? We do see this with certain other angels, but certainly this is rare! We do not see the names Yah or YHWH being attached to Michael, Gavriel, Uriel or Rifael. This is because there are angels of Yetzirah, and then there are other entities whom we call angels but are really of a higher order (of Beriah).

Certain entities, whom we call angels are actually part of the higher collective which we call the Supernal Neshama Soul. In other literature, we refer to them as being the Race of the Metatron (whose head is in Beriah). These entities have many different names, even as Metatron has 70 names as does his Master (Shadai YHWH).

Whenever we see an entity (an angel) who has the name Yah or YHWH attached to It we recognize such an entity as being a representative of the Beriah collective. Such an entity acts as the conduit for YHWH here in the lower dimensions of Be'Y'A.

This is who (what) R. Yishmael saw in his vision. He saw an image of the collective Supernal Neshama. He saw the Crown (Keter) of Beriah, serving as the Kiseh HaKavod. Thus the name of the entity is Akatriel, which translates as the Keter of El, or as the Crown of God. What I have revealed to you now is considered one of the deepest secrets of the Ma'aseh Merkava. It gets even deeper than this; it is related to the image of the man upon the throne that was witnessed by Ezekiel in his vision. No more about this is allowed to be said.

The seven Palaces mentioned herein are not those that are referenced in the older Hekhalot literature. The Palaces in Hekhalot literature usually correspond to the Seven Heavens as mentioned in the Talmud (B. Hagigah 2). The Palaces mentioned here, in our text, are well known and spoken about in the Zohar (Parshat Pekudei) and the later Kitvei HaAri'zal. But these seven Palaces are correlated to the seven Sefirot in Yetzirah. They do not belong in Beriah as our text enumerates.

While there are seven Palaces in Beriah, they are usually considered to be the inner sanctums of the seven Palaces of Yetzirah. Remember, Beriah and Yetzirah are not places, they are depths of dimensional experience. As such Beriah is a deeper level within Yetzirah. Thus the Palaces, from our point of view are experienced Yetziratically, in the domain of the angels, and not from the perspective of their inner sanctum in Beriah.

This section of the text concludes with a reference to the Tzadik Yesod Olam and the holy Name Shadai. Again, these are both references to the Metatron(s). Metatron in gematria is the same as Shadai (314). Tzadik Yesod Olam corresponds to the Sefirah Yesod. True, the forms of all these things are in Yetzirah, but their source is in Beriah, and this is what our text is saying. It is all too easy for

Beriatic and Yetziratic realities to be confused with one another. Essentially, the two are one, in the same way as the Neshama and the Ruah are one. Yes, they are two different things, but in reality, the two are only dual perceptions of a singular reality.

Masekhet Atzilut 7

Secrets of Yetzirah

"I have formed," (3) the World of Yetzirah. Therein are the holy Hayot that were seen by Ezekiel son of Buzi the Kohen priest.

Therein are His servants who perform the Will of the Holy One, blessed be He. Also here are the Palaces of pleasure (oneg) and desire (ratzon), because these corresponding to those.

For the lower raises the fear of God... [missing text]. *And there are a number of faces [facing] towards faces.*

And therein are the ten types of His angels each in accordance to their stature. And these are them:

1. *Serafim; Shamunga'el rules over them; and there are those who say that Yahuel rules over them.*
2. *Ofanim; Rifael, and the Light of Peniel rules over them.*
3. *Kiruvim; Kiruviel rules over them.*
4. *Shinanim; Tzadkiel and Gavriel rules over them.*
5. *Tarshishim; Tarshish and Shalu'yael rules over them.*
6. *Ishim; Tzfaniah rules over them.*
7. *Hashmalim; Hashul rules over them.*
8. *Malakhim; Uziel rules over them.*
9. *Benei Elohim; Hhafniel rules over them.*
10. *Erelim; Mikhael rules over them.*

And these are the ten [types] of angels who perform His Will.

[These are the ones who] were created first and who rule over the [other] mentioned camps. And Metatron who was changed from flesh and blood to devouring fire rules over them [all].

Therein are the spirits (Ruhot) of human beings, and the stones of war, and soldiers, and chariots (merkavot), and princes of the chariots, as it is written (Psalm 68:18), "the chariots of Elohim are myriad, thousands upon thousands." And Elohim shines upon them and rules over them all."

Consider this metaphor. God, in Atzilut, is like the CEO, the Chief Executive Officer of a company, which in this case is the universe. The Neshamot soul in Beriah are like the management team that runs the company for the CEO. The angels in Yetzirah are like the support staff that executes the orders and directives of the CEO and his staff of managers. This pretty much sums up how our universe operates. The multiple races of angels in Yetzirah are the civil service and the mechanical workers that maintain the machine of creation.

Now that we can ascribe meaning to the function of the beings of Yetzirah, we can now address the very confusing issue of their identities. For our text here enumerates ten types (species?) of Yetziratic beings. And corresponding to our text we have other books that also enumerate ten species of Yetziratic beings, but of all these different books, none of them have the same list, in the same order. So, in spite of the fact that we have lists, we, nevertheless, do not have an agreed-on order.

Yetziratic beings serve a function; their job is to perform a service on behalf of their Lord in Atzilut (as delivered to them through their Managerial Entities of Beriah). Essentially, Yetziratic beings are messengers. And this is where the name Malakh comes from.

Malakh comes from the Hebrew root verb HaLaKh, which means "to go." Thus, someone who goes for you, representing you, is your MaLaKh, "one who goes," as is one who goes on a mission of representation. So, a Yetziratic being is a messenger entrusted with fulfilling a task on behalf of his Atzilut Lord. Thus the Yetziratic beings are called MaLaKh'im (angels). The English word "angel" does not even hint to the actual function or purpose of Yetziratic beings. We still use the word out of linguistic convenience, but we must be aware of how meaningless it is with regards to a discussion of the actual nature and mission of these beings.

There are ten types or species of Yetziratic beings enumerated. The Kabbalists lose no time in pointing out how the number ten (10) is the number of the Sefirot, and therefore the angelic types must, in some way, correspond to the order of the Ten Sefirot. There is no shortage of lists of such associations along with many similar other details attached to the primary concept.

Are any of these enumerations and associations real? This depends upon whom you ask! For the believer in one system, his system is the one and only. For the believer in another system, he too is just as convinced of the absolute correctness of his way. And the third person learns all the different opinions, and either does, or just as often does not, come up with yet a third opinion. In the end, with regards to our discussion about angels, we are left with far more questions than with answers that we can all accept.

Our selection opens with a mention of the Hayot angels witnessed by the prophet Ezekiel. And it is interesting to note that when enumerating the ten types (classes or species) of angels, our author does not mention the Hayot among them. To include them would make a list of eleven (11) types. This would imbalance the list in corresponding with the Sefirot.

Here are some more questions. The four Hayot of the Merkava are in many sources identified as being the angels Michael, Gabriel, Uriel and Rifael. This would imply that these four are Hayot. And yet here in our text, Michael is identified as being of the Erelim; Gabriel is identified as being of the Shinanim; Uriel is not mentioned at all, but Rifael is identified as being of the Ofanim. So, how can Michael, Gabriel, Uriel and Rifael all be Hayot, when Michael is also an Erel, Gabirel is also a Shinan, and Uriel an Ofan? Are the Erelim, Shinanim, and Ofanim, all synonymous with the Hayot? If so, then why bother to enumerate different types (classes, species) if they are all one and the same? And if they are not all one and the same, but they are completely different from one another, then how can we have conflicting identities for specific angels?

Many might want to peruse the available literature to research these questions, but in the end, all that one will have is yet another opinion to add to the batch of already recorded multiple opinions. Ultimately, an academic approach to angelology might sound fascinating to some, but the entire field is merely conjecture and theory, with no real solid Yetziratic ground to stand upon!

With regards to the types of angels, there is even disagreement with their names and types. One such disagreement is worth nothing here because it is recorded by Rabbi Yitzhak Isaac Haber in his commentary to Masekhet Atzilut, titled Ginzei Meromim.

With regards to the class of angels enumerated here in our text as (5) the Tarshishim, the Rabbi has written: *"Here the Tarshishim are thought to be in the number of the ten types. However, our great Rabbi, the Gra, (Rabbi Eliyahu, the Gaon of Vilna), in his commentary to Tractate Berahot, chapter HaRoeh, has written that this is a mistake of the copier (of the text) in every instant that it is recorded such. For the Tarshishim are not a separate class, for it is written in Ezekiel in the Merkava [vision], that [he saw] what looked like tarshish (a glow), meaning that is was a hue [or color] as seen by the eye. He included in their place the Erelim and the Benei Elohim."*

Rather than clear up any confusion, Rabbi Haber's comments in the name of the Gaon of Vilna only add more questions. While we can remove the name of the Tarshishim as being a separate class of Yetziratic beings, we do need to replace them with some other order. But how can they be replaced with the Erelim and the Benei Elohim when both of these orders are already enumerated on the list?

There are a number of sources that provide a list of the angelic beings. Maimonides provides one list in his Hilkhot Yesodei Torah. The Zohar provides a similar list. There are others in a number of Kabbalistic texts.

What is important for us to acknowledge about angels is not what we do know, but rather just how much that we do not know.

Like many other authors before me, I can digress to analyze the lists and examine all their similarities and differences. But once this is done, what is it that we expect to learn? Even after all such endeavors, all we will have is more questions, more speculations, and more theories. Therefore, I chose not to digress to elaborate on lists.

It is wiser to learn about what angels do, rather than to speculate on their true identities. All we can say about angels is that they are not humans and they are not of this Earth. By every criteria of judgment this makes angels to be the very definition of extraterrestrial. And this association should not take us down the road of science fiction, but rather we really must start merging our knowledge of religion and our knowledge of science. Angels are real, they are not religious myths. Angels are extraterrestrials, but they don't travel in flying saucers, and shoot ray guns. Our text grants us some insight into angelic activity. Let us turn to this for further insights.

Like I mentioned at the beginning of this present discussion, angels serve as the mechanics and operators of the great machine which we call our (Asiyatic) universe. Angels operate behind the scenes in higher dimensional realities (the Yetziratic dimension). They serve and function within the multiple contexts of that which we call the Seven Palaces. Essentially, these Palaces, as revealed by their names, are actually forces of cosmic energy that are in need of alignment and balance. Angels working in each Palace therefore, must operate within their parameters and work to make sure that the processes of creation operate in accordance to the Supernal Pattern of Atzilut.

Angels seem to operate in a very rigid hierarchical order. There is always a specific angel in charge of a group of other angels. How and what is the nature of angelic authority and government, we can only speculate. There are a good number of ancient Kabbalistic texts that enumerate the names of many angels and identify what forces each angel works with. Knowledge of these angels and their charges is highly classified Kabbalistic intel. Interaction with these entities and revelations about their activities is the very definition of the Ma'aseh Merkava. We have no better proof of this than the vision experienced by Ezekiel.

But Ezekiel's vision as great and sublime as it was, does not even compare to the close encounter that was experienced by the ancient Enoch. It is well documented in Midrashic and Kabbalistic literature that the Biblical Enoch was taken up into Heaven (wherever this place really is). Here Enoch was genetically transformed. Enoch stopped being human, as he was genetically transformed into a powerful extraterrestrial form. Enoch became Metatron. But as we know, the story of this transformation is not as simple as some are led to believe.

So Enoch became Metatron. Now, this creates an interesting contradiction. According to the Talmud (B. Yevamot 16b) Metatron was present with God at the time of the creation of the universe. But how can this be? If Metatron is Enoch, and Enoch is the seventh generation descendant of Adam, how could he have been in the beginning with God, long before he (and Adam) were ever created? This curiosity has been noticed in the past and has been addressed by the authors of the Tosafot commentary to the Talmudic section in Yevamot. Their answer is straightforward. They say that Metatron did indeed pre-existed the universe. And later, Enoch was absorbed into an already present Metatron. So Enoch became a part of an already existing Metatron. This lesson in Yevamot is one of the sources that reveal to us that Metatron is not actually an individual, but rather a race of beings.

And Metatron rules over them all. It is said of Metatron that his head is in Beriah, his body is in Yetzirah and his feet are in Asiyah. And Metatron is a race of beings and not an individual. So any reference to head, body and feet needless to say must be understood as metaphor. Head, body and feet are metaphors for specific functions, as well as specific levels of being (evolution? appearance?).

The Metatron race that rules over all clearly has its forms of manifestation that are different from one another in the different dimensions as parts of the human anatomy are different from one another and perform different tasks. Thus Metatron in Beriah is head, in Yetzirah is body and in Asiyah is feet. Each of these descriptions symbolically describe the functions and activities of the Metatron each in its own place, each n its own way. And yet of all these different parts, Metatron is still one. The big secret of course is who is Metatron really, and why is he selected to wield such tremendous heavenly power.

According to the book Emek HaMelekh (Sha'ar HaYetzirah), Metatron is the collective of Adamic souls who prior to the fall, split off from Adam and remained above in Heaven unblemished. Since then the Metatrons (our higher Neshama selves) have served as guides to the lower Adamic souls that have fallen and become stuck here on Earth. So, essentially the Metatron is Collective Israel, the Knesset Yisrael. This would explain his intimate connection with God's Divine Presence, the Shekhina. This also sheds light on the Zoharic teaching (3, 73a) how God, Torah and Israel are one and the same in concept. As we see, there is much more to the Metatrons than meets the eye.

The Metatrons are Supernal Israel. This is why they are so intimately bound to terrestrial Israel. This also helps us to understand how Ya'aqob Avinu (the Patriarch Jacob) became Israel, in similar fashion as to how Enoch became Metatron. Both were absorbed into a Pre-existing Collective, which is the same collective for them both. Enoch became what we call a Metatron, and Ya'aqob became a Yisrael. The two are one and the same.

The final part of this selection of our text addresses the Rual level of human consciousness that is indigenous to the Yetziratic dimension. Ruah is the source of human emotions. It corresponds to the Haluka d'Rabbanan, that which many today call the Astral Body. The Yetziratic dimension is governed by the Six-Sefirot that form the Sefirotic Face of Zeir Anpin, which is centered in the heart. As such Yetzirah is the dimensional plane of the emotions. The Libido of the Yesod is here present in the form of intense sexual passion. This passion in the supernal sense motivates and creates the Supernal Union, which is the unity of the Holy One, blessed be He (in Tiferet) and His Shekhina (in Malkhut).

However, when there is no unity, then there is strife and conflict. And thus Yetzirah is in a constant state of movement in the attempt to maintain and balance the dimensional planes above it and below it. In times of peace, there is harmony, in times of war, however, there is chaos, strife, division, and conflict. Thus our text speaks about war and soldiers. These are the forces within Yetzirah that manifest conflict both within their own dimensional plane and in ours.

Masekhet Atzilut 8

Secrets of Asiyah

"I even made it" (Isaiah 43:7). [This is world #4], the world of Asiyah.

Herein are Ofanim, those who receive prayers and supplications, and those who are in charge of the desires of men.

Herein are the Nefesh souls of men, and the masters of fists (martial artists?), the Princes of the army, arrows, stones, and catapult stones.

Many above are directors of the ship, arrangers of the [supernal] system corresponding to the evil Samael, and his associates, to prevent them from entering the openings of prayer, those who pass by the way and fear not the power of God.

Therein are the guardians who witness the deeds of men. And Sandalphon [who] ties [the] crowns rules over them. And Adonai God radiates them and rules over all, as it says, "And His Kingdom is in all places" (Psalms 103:19)."

Asiyah is the realm of the physical. Yet there is much more to Asiyah than just our physical dimension. R. Hayim Vital properly elaborates in his Sha'arei Kedusha (Section 3), and in his Etz Hayim (Gate 50) that like the other dimensional planes, the dimension of Asiyah comprises its own unique Ten Sefirot. What this simply means is that Asiyah, the domain of the physical, is itself, multi-dimensional. Not only is Asiyah the domain of space and time, but it is also the domain of many different variations of space and time.

R. Hayim enumerates that our physical dimension is just the Malkhut plane of Asiyah, and that above it are other dimensional planes emanating from the Yesod of Asiyah up to the Keter of Asiyah. All these planes are Asiyatic; they are not Yetziratic. But from our limited human point of view from the Malkhut of Asiyah, we, for the most part, cannot distinguish the difference between something (or someone) from the Yesod of Asiyah and/or the Malkhut of Yetzirah.

Intervening between the dimensional plane of Yetzirah and Asiyah resides those forces whom we call the Klipot. These forces and the entities which manifest them are half-physical, and half-ethereal. And even this description is not completely accurate! Herein reside many other races of beings who bridge the Yetzirah-Asiyah divide. The most well-known of these races is one that resides here on Earth alongside human beings. These are the Shedim, the Jinn.

It is said of the Shedim that in three ways they are like the Malakhim of Yetzirah and in three ways they are like the human beings of Asiyah. Like angels, Shedim can fly, be invisible, and foresee the future up to thirty days out. Like human beings, Shedim eat and drink, sexually procreate, and they die. So, they are not Yetziratic beings, they are Asiyatic, but in a dimensional level of Asiyah above our own.

I suspect that many of the real extraterrestrial beings who travel to and from our Earth are also higher-dimensional Asiyatic beings, whose reality is one of the other sefirotic manifestations of Asiyah.

We need to understand that these different dimensional planes exist! Although we cannot realistically recognize the differences between Yetziratic beings and higher Asiyatic beings, we still need to know that they are not one and the same.

Throughout recorded human history, all too often human beings have had close encounters with Shedim of Asiyah and misunderstood the encounters to be with Malakhim of Yetzirah. These mistakes have been the cause of many harmful human affairs.

These mistakes continue to this day, especially in the realms of extraterrestrial contacts. Many civilian and government encounters are with Shedim who are masquerading as Yetziratic beings. None of those involved are any the wiser as to the true identity of those with whom they are in contact.

Needless to say, Shedim have an agenda of their own, and clueless human being succumb to their manipulative influences. Most alien abductions scenarios are perpetrated by Shedim, and not off-world extraterrestrials. Yet, not all E.T.s are Shedim, and not all E.T.s are from the Malkhut of Asiyah as we are.

So, how is one to know the difference between one group of beings and the next? The Kabbalists and other ancient orders of Servants of Heaven know how to distinguish between the sacred and the profane. As for all others not so adequately trained, it is best not to solicit interaction with other-dimensional Asiyatic beings.

With these understandings firmly before us, we can now address the other Asiyatic beings mentioned in our text. We will begin with the Ofanim.

We first learn about Ofanim from their mention in Ezekiel's Merkava vision (Ezekiel 1:15-21). The original Hebrew text is not the easiest to translate in a literal fashion. Here is my translation alongside the tradition translation from the Jewish Publication Society Bible (1985 edition).

Original Translation, R. Ariel B. Tzadok 2022

And I saw the Hayot and behold there was one Ofan by each of the four faces of the Hayot.

The appearance of the Ofanim and their behavior looked like tarshish (beryl?), there was one image for all four, and their appearance and their behavior were as if there was an Ofan within an Ofan.

Upon the four fourths on their goings, they did not turn as they moved.

Their structure and their height was visible as they moved. Their structure was full of eyes around all four of them.

As the Hayot went, the Ofanim went next to them, and when the Hayot lifted off the ground they lifted the Ofanim.

And as the wind (spirit) was to go, the spirit (wind) went, and the Ofanim moved alongside them, for the wind (spirit) of the Hayah was in the Ofanim.

And when these went, those went and when these stood, those stood, and when they were lifted off of the ground, the Ofanim lifted alongside them, for the wind (spirit) of the Hayah was in the Ofanim.

Jewish Publication Society (JPS) 1985 edition

As I gazed on the creatures, I saw one wheel on the ground next to each of the four-faced creatures.

As for the appearance and structure of the wheels, they gleamed like beryl. All four had the same form; the appearance and structure of each was as of two wheels cutting through each other.

And when they moved, each could move in the direction of any of its four quarters; they did not veer when they moved.

Their rims were tall and frightening, for the rims of all four were covered all over with eyes.

And when the creatures moved forward, the wheels moved at their sides; and when the creatures were borne above the earth, the wheels were borne too.

Wherever the spirit impelled them to go, they went—wherever the spirit impelled them—and the wheels were borne alongside them; for the spirit of the creatures was in the wheels.

When those moved, these moved; and when those stood still, these stood still; and when those were borne above the earth, the wheels were borne alongside them—for the spirit of the creatures was in the wheels.

Whether one reads my literal translation, the JPS version or another, one thing seems to be clear from the text: the description of the Hayot and the Ofanim does not sound like the description of living, thinking beings. This peculiarity in the text has led secular Gentile authors, such as Josef Blumrich, and Erich von Daniken, to speculate that what the prophet Ezekiel actually saw was some sort of a mechanical spaceship. Of course, anyone with knowledge of Hebrew, and especially those trained to receive and interpret such psychic events as Merkava visions know the fanciful fallacies of these uninitiated authors. But nevertheless, one cannot blame an outsider from making certain grave errors based upon a casual surface perusal of the text.

Ofanim are living, thinking entities with minds of their own. But with that being said, one must understand the nature of the relationship between groups of entities. Sometimes entities with different group names are not as separate from one another as we might think based upon our understanding of relationships here in the space time realm of physical matter. Without elaborating too much, understand that the Hayot and the Ofanim have an intimate relationship with one another, which may very well be metaphorically described as sexual.

Ofanim are Asiyatic beings. Hayot are Yetziratic beings. These two share a bond of association in the same way as do their two heads, Metatron and Sandalphon. Remember how we said that Metatron has his head in Beriah, his body in Yetzirah and his feet in Asiyah. This is the relationship being hinted to here.

The Hayot and Ofanim relate to one another as do soul and body. This is the relationship that is hinted to in Ezekiel's description. The Ofanim, like the Metatron are a collective sharing a hive mind. They are the mechanics that operate the great machine of the physical universe. While it is God YHWH that ordains natural law, it is God's many servants who execute the Divine plan and keep God's creation "well-oiled" and fully functional.

Not only do the Ofanim deal with the proper maintenance of physical space time, but they also are in charge of the proper channel and flow of universal life force energy. They are the ones who handle the flow and distribution of the universal life-force energy that is called by many different names. While in Torah this energy is called Nefesh, it other cultures it is called: Hiyuli, Qi, Prana, Vril or Orgone. Whatever the name the energy is one and the same.

The Life-force energy has its source in the highest of the Supernal Realms. In Kabbalah, the energy is called Ohr (Light) and Shefa (Radiance). It is the source of all life and blessing. The Shefa emanates from the highest levels in the Unknown, descends below to the lowest levels, and from there it needs to ascend in reverse in order to complete the cyclical flow of Light and Life-force energy.

In Kabbalah we call this flow Ohr Yashar (descending Light) and Ohr Hozer (ascending Light). The job of the Ofanim is to serve as collectors of Ohr Hozer and to process the Light for its ascent back up through the higher dimensional planes.

Referencing this, our text states, "*Herein are Ofanim, those who receive prayers and supplications, and those who are in charge of the desires of men.*"

Human thought and human emotion generate a real and tangible Life-force energy of their own. Each thought and each emotion emanates from our bodies, maybe from our organic brains in the form of brain waves and similar forms. Each of these has its own unique frequency and vibration. When our individual frequencies and vibrations calibrate properly with the universe around us then our vibrations are called good, and manifest as righteousness. These promote natural harmony, balance, and growth inside ourselves and in the world around us. When, however, our vibrations are out of sync with the universe around us, this is bad, and manifests as evil.

The original Primal Force (Shefa, Ohr Yashar) that comes down to our dimensional plane travels a long journey through multiple dimensional realities. This Force (Ohr Yashar) is subject to the various grades, and frequencies of the vibrations through which it passes.

There are entities at each location along the way; Beriatic entities, Yetziratic entities and Asiyatic entities in dimensions higher than our own. Each of these entities is nourished and sustained by the Primordial Life-Force that emanates from Atzilut (the Creator). However, the further the Primal Force flows from the Source, the narrower (weaker) it becomes.

As this occurs, the entities receiving the lower grades of the Primal Force more and more begin to gravitate away from the natural order and become out-of-sync with the greater Supernal Pattern. Thus, the further away from the Source, the greater the existence of evil. For whatever reasons known in the Divine Wisdom, this system was established as is, on purpose.

The Creator then reached down to the very bottom and placed a representative of Himself, a very reflection of YHWH itself, to serve and act as an anchor of balance at the very bottom, so as to coordinate the proper reception of the Primal Force (Ohr Yashar) below, and to then property redirect its flow above (Ohr Hozer).

It is the human race, (Adam) created in the Divine Image (of the Ten Sefirot) whose job it is to serve as the Divine reflection, and to elevate the Ohr Hozer, in a form that the Kabbalah of the Ari'zal calls MahN, Mayim Nokbin.

MahN (in Malkhut) is desire (ratzon). It is the same Force (along the Sefirotic Center Column) as is the Sefirah Keter, the Supernal Will (Ra'avah Ila'ah). Keter descends down as Shefa, Ohr Yashar, and Malkhut, (specifically human beings here in the dimension of the Malkhut of Asiyah) then catches the Ohr Yashar, and elevates it back up as Ohr Hozer, thus completing the universal energetic circuit, and thus maintaining the balance and harmony of all creation.

So, we human beings capture the Ohr Yashar here in the Malkhut of Asiyah, and through our thoughts, emotions, and deeds, reverse its flow, allowing its natural and necessary return ascent (Ohr Hozer). All of the energy emanating from our thoughts, feeling and deeds are collected by the Ofanim, in the dimensions of the Yesod through the Keter of Asiyah, and they are the ones charged to refine it, and prepare it for its ascent into the Yetziratic dimensions.

In this Malkhut of Asiyah we find our present state of human consciousness. We call this our Nefesh level of soul. Nefesh is the raw Life-force energy that permeates this physical dimensional plane. Our identity of self as it relates to this energy is what we call Nefesh consciousness. We reflect the Image of YHWH here in this place. And here in this place the Image of YHWH is cloaked within the natural Life-force energy of this dimension. The cloak is called Tzelem Elohim, the Image of God (Elohim, in gematria, is equal to HaTeva, Nature). Thus human beings are meant to represent and manifest the natural Way of the universe.

Of course, there are other species that are not human and do not share this inner, innate ability to reflect YHWH or Elohim. One such race of beings we have already mentioned: Shedim, but there are also others.

In this dimensional plane where awareness of the Higher Worlds is very limited, there is constant struggle and even outright warfare in order to control the flow of Life-Force energy. These other entities are not interested in returning the Life-Force (Ohr Yashar) to Above. They want to keep all that they can get for themselves. Such selfishness is the manifestation of their lower levels of universal consciousness. They see themselves as entities separate from the greater universe and thus seek to nourish themselves even at the expense of others, whom they hold to be of lesser value.

Thus in Asiyah, there is always a struggle, a war, for humans to do their divinely appointed jobs. Many entities with whom human beings need to psychically fight are symbolically referred to as "masters of fists, Princes of the army, arrows, stones, and catapult stones. All of these metaphors reflect the reality of the aggressive nature of these entities who seek to steal Life-Force energy at whatever cost. Yet, they do not go about performing this task haphazardly; they do have a plan, and a method of operations. We call this system the Sitra Ahra, the real Dark Side of the (Life) Force.

The system of the Sitra Ahra operates with rigid discipline and order. It is often compared to a ship at sea, and its operators as soldiers, or sailors. Thus our text says, *Many above are directors of the ship, arrangers of the [supernal] system corresponding to the evil Samael, and his associates.*

It is the job of the Ofanim angels to raise the Life-Force energy of Ohr Hozer back up to Yetzirah, and to prevent the Sitra Ahra from subverting their endeavors. Thus our text says that it is the job of the Ofanim *"to prevent them* (the forces of the Sitra Ahra) *from entering the openings of prayer, those who pass by the way and fear not the power of God."* This is the battle that we human being face every day. It is a battle to control the thoughts, emotions, and deeds of human beings, in order to control the flow of Life-Force energy that comes forth from them.

Samael and his associates, they are the ones who are stealing the Ohr Hozer Life-Force energy. But to what end do they do this? Sam is Yetziratic in origins. His dominions are in both Yetzirah and Asiyah. Surely, they recognize the need for the smooth operations of the machinery of the universe. Surely, they do not and cannot thwart the operations of the universal machine. Why would God tolerate the presence of that which would thwart the Divine work? Why would God create such a force that is devoted to thwart and destroy everything that God Himself has made and has put into operation?

Such things cannot be! Such things are not what we think them to be! Yes, opposition to the working of the universal machine does exist! Yes, God created this opposition. And we are taught that Samael is actually one of God's most trusted servants. Samael is the Dark Side of Metatron. Samael is Metatron's dark twin. Why would God create such a force, such an entity. Why does this being exist?

Sam and his minions exist because God created them and gave them a harsh task, one which they take very seriously and fulfill with due diligence. Sam and his minions are the force of polar opposition. Sam and his minions create the circumstances of opposition. Sam and his minions create the opposition force that when reacted against, causes the force of energy that shoots the Ohr Hozer back along its ordained route.

The old saying is that when the going gets tough, then the tough get going. It's Sam's job to get the tough to become tougher, and by doing so, pushing them to remarkable accomplishments that would not be possible without his subtle and persistent intervention. This is what the Talmud (B. Berakhot 34b) is hinting to when it teaches in the name of R. Abahu that *"in the place where the Ba'al Teshuva (the penitent) stands, the fully righteous cannot stand."*

God uses both light and darkness, good and evil to accomplish the Divine Will. This is one of those mysteries not understood by mortal human beings today. But God did tell us about this when he revealed through the prophet Isaiah (55:7-11) the following words:

"The wicked shall give up his way, and the man of iniquity his thoughts, and he shall return to YHWH, Who shall have mercy upon him, and to our God, for He will freely pardon. For My thoughts are not your thoughts, neither are your ways My ways," says YHWH. As the Heavens are higher than the Earth, so are My ways higher than your ways and My thoughts [higher] than your thoughts. For, just as the rain and the snow fall from the Heavens, and it does not return there, unless it has satiated the Earth and fructified it and furthered its growth and has given seed to the sower and bread to the eater, so shall be My word that emanates from My mouth; it shall not return to Me empty, unless it has done what I desire and has made prosperous the one to whom I sent it."

Let the one with wisdom contemplate the secrets that I have revealed to you here. In this will one understand the secret of Yihud (unity) and the profundity of the revelation that *Ayn Ohd M'lavdo*! There is none other than He!

Masekhet Atzilut 9

Secrets of the Du Partzufim

Zechariah ben Yosef opened, "With wisdom YHWH founded the Earth, [He] established the Heavens with intelligence" (Proverbs 3:19). This teaches us that with wisdom was the Earth founded (established). And there is never any mention of "the Earth" other than to signify the Shekhina (Divine Presence), as it is written, "The whole Earth is full of His glory" (Isaiah 6:3).

However, the Earth was attuned with intelligence, as it is written, "with wisdom is a house built, and with intelligence it is attuned" (Proverbs 24:2). And there is never any mention of "house" other than to signify the Shekhina (Divine Presence), as it is written, "And the Glory of YHWH filled the house" (2 Chron. 7:1).

This teaches us that with wisdom (Hokhma) was the house built. And it is written, "like the beauty (Tiferet) of man, to dwell in [a] house." (Isaiah 44:13). And with intelligence he is attuned.

This teaches that with intelligence he is attuned, and being that this is so, what then is judgment (Din), of which it says, "attuned Heaven with intelligence."

Rather interpret it [like this], with wisdom and with understanding was the Earth and the Heavens created. And there is never any mention of "the Heavens" other than to signify the Holy One, blessed be He, as it is written, "the Heavens are the Heaven of YHWH" (Psalm 115:16).

Which one was created first? We have been taught (M.R. Ber. 1:15), R. Shimon B. Yohai said that the Heavens and the Earth were created together, like a cooking pot with its cover.

R. Eliezer, his son said that the two are equal, for at times Heaven is mentioned before the Earth, [and at other times] the Earth is mentioned before the Heavens. This teaches us the that the two are equal."

This section introduces us to the ancient Kabbalistic concept of the "Du Partzufim." This is the underlying structure of the dual-reality in which we live, of what we call the spiritual and the physical domains. The Torah refers to these two sides of reality as the Heavens and the Earth. But as we can see from our text, Heaven and Earth have far greater depths of meaning that what a surface perusal of the Torah text infers.

I must be very clear here to state that my usage of the term "Partzufim" is very different from how the word is used in the later Torah of the Ari'zal. The word "Du" here actually means two, with Du being similar in meaning to our word, dual. The Two Faces, the Du Partzufim are the two "faces of reality," which we call the spiritual and the physical. In the earliest stages of Kabbalistic literature everything about the worlds was packaged into this easy and simple formula. There was "here" in our world, and then, there was "there" in the worlds (many worlds) above.

The two worlds are again neatly summed up as being the Heavens and the Earth, But at the same time, these two are understood to be metaphors for the Holy One, blessed be He (Heaven) and His Shekhina (Earth). This correlation is what our text is describing using Midrashic metaphors to associate verses of Scripture with their greater underlying concepts.

In the pre-Ari'zal Kabbalah, the Du Partzufim are readily discussed. Usually the discussion revolves around the question asked in the text itself; which was created first, the Heavens or the Earth. Here is a selection from a pre-Ari'zal text, Sefer Ohel Moed, that in short words elaborates this point.

(Written in 1559 by Rabbi Yosef Menahem of Egypt, Sefer Ohel Moed was published together with two other books under the general title, Sifrei HaMekubalim HaKadmonim, Sha'ar HaKabbalah v'Sidra. Published in Jerusalem in 2002 by R. Yosef Eliezer Elimelech Parush. The selection quoted here is from page 64 in the Ohel Moed section, specifically Section 20, The Tenth Light, Malkhut, and Section 21, Secret of the Du Partzufim).

"And this was the disagreement between the Sages (Hagigah 12a). This one said that the Heavens were created first, and the other said that the Earth was created first. And along comes a third verse that decides between them. The secret is (Isaiah 48:13), "I call upon them and they stand together." This means that potentially [only] one, meaning that Du Partzufim (two faces) were created. This is the example of male and female (B. Berakhot 61a), meaning a giver and a receiver.

And their example below is that the first Man (Adam) was created male and female, Du Partzufim....

For at first one was created, which in the end became two..."

Since the Torah of the Ari'zal, the older expositions upon the nature of the worlds, both the spiritual (now called Atzilut, Beriah and Yetzirah) and the physical (now called Asiyah), have become a bit antiquated and outdated. The older understandings have been replaced, with the more complex and explanatory Torah of the Ari'zal becoming dominant.

Now, let us explain our text before us within its original, pre-Ari'zal context.

Our text is addressing the relationship between what we call the spiritual-physical divide. In the language of the later Kabbalah, this would technically be a discussion on the relationship between the worlds of Yetzirah (the angelic) and Asiyah (the physical). But our text begins with a discussion of Hokhma (wisdom) and Tevunah (intelligence).

The Hokhma mentioned herein is clearly a reference to the Sefirah Hokhma (and the later world of Atzilut). Tevunah, in the context of our text, refers to what today we call the Sefirah Binah (and the later world of Beriah). It seems to be that the reference to the verses is also the source of the Ari'zal's teaching that Tevunah is the name of the lower Partzuf within the Sefirat Binah

Although our text may indeed be the first text to introduce the Four Worlds by their names A'Be'Y'A, at this point in the text, it is not using these names to describe the Du Partzufim. Nevertheless, with or without these names being used, describing the genesis of the Du Partzufim is exactly what this section of our text is doing.

Our text opens with the discussion about how our Earth (and thus all physicality, the general world of Asiyah) was founded upon Hokhma (wisdom), whereas the Heavens (the Yetziratic realms of the angels) is established with Tevunah (intelligence-Binah). This correlation of Atzilut (wisdom) with Asiyah (Earth) is a very ancient Kabbalistic teachings. It is usually referred to by the statement, Abba Bara Batra, (Abba/Father created His daughter).

Putting aside all the speculative Kabbalah and its many attempts to expound upon this teaching (which includes many different schools, some based upon the Ari'zal, and others that are not), its meaning is really rather simple. Abba is a reference to Heaven (although in the speculative Kabbalah such a correlation needs much further elaboration), and Batra (daughter) is simply a reference to the Shekhina (the Divine Presence, Malkhut). Like I said above, the Torah of the Ari'zal has for centuries now added much needed depth and insight into these teachings. What we have before us is a pre-Ari'zal, and most likely pre-Zoharic text which (for its day) was radically revelatory.

While the Earth is made with Hokhma, it is fine-tuned with Tevunah. In other words, the genesis of creation begins with Hokhma, and the continuation of it proceeds with Tevunah (Binah). This coincides with all the later Kabbalah teachings about the Seder HaHishtalshlut, the Order of Spiritual Evolution, but like I said, in much simpler words. Let me put the message of our text into the language of the Ari'zal. Atzilut is the Source world, the Creator of all the lower worlds of Beriah, Yetzirah, and Asiyah. Atzilut (Partzuf Abba) refines creation through Beriah (Partzuf Imma). Together these give rise to Yetzirah (the Heavens) and Asiyah (the Earth).

Our text here is addressing the general relationship between the spiritual and the physical dimensions. Its purpose is not to expand into a discussion of the Four Worlds. So while many of the Four World terms are being used (such as Hokhma and Tevunah), they are not being used as in the context of the later Kabbalah.

This is what is important about our text. Aside from providing us with profound Kabbalistic knowledge, it is also giving us a history lesson about how these concepts were communicated in earlier times, prior to the adoption of modern terminologies. It is important that we recognize both the older and the newer forms of wordage so as to never confuse the two. This is what scholarship is all about!

So, in brief, the Heavens (referred to here) regardless of its association with Hokhma (here in the text) is actually a reference to (what we today call) Yetzirah (the spiritual world). The Earth (as referred to here) is a reference to (what we call today) Asiyah (the physical world). Both are created by Higher Forces (Atzilut/Abba and Beriah/Imma), and both contain many concealed secrets.

Our text proceeds to ask an age-old question discussed in many older sources. Which came first, which was created first, the Heavens or the Earth?

The source of this discussion is the Gemara (B. Hagigah 12, Koren – Steinsaltz translation).

"Beit Shammai and Beit Hillel dispute the order of Creation, as the Sages taught: Beit Shammai say: The Heavens were created first and afterward the Earth was created, as it is stated: "In the beginning God created the Heavens and the Earth" (Genesis 1:1), which indicates that Heaven came first. And Beit Hillel say: The Earth was created first, and Heaven after it, as it is stated: "On the day that the Lord God made Earth and Heaven" (Genesis 2:4).

But the Rabbis say: Both this and that were created as one, for it is stated: "Indeed, My hand has laid the foundation of the Earth, and My right hand has spread out the Heavens; when I call to them, they stand up together" (Isaiah 48:13), implying that they were created as one."

Our text then turns to the Midrash Rabbah, (Genesis 1:15), and paraphrases its lesson, although no reference is made to identify this source.

"Rabbi Shimon son of Yochai said, "I am amazed at how the fathers of the world, Beit Shammai and Beit Hillel, were divided on the creation of the Heavens and the Earth, I would say to both of them that they were not created [separately], but [rather] they are like a stew pot and its lid, as it is said "I call unto them, they stood up together" (Isaiah 48:13).

Said Rabbi Eliezer the son of Rabbi Shimon "if it is according to the opinion of my father, why in one place does the Earth precede the Heavens and in the other place the Heavens precede the Earth? This teaches that they both have weight on either side (are equal)."

In conclusion, our text establishes that the Heavens and the Earth were made together, and thus both should be considered equal in stature. This is how the older schools of Kabbalah understood the relationship between the physical and spiritual worlds. The Heavens and the Earth, while being considered to be in a male-female, giver-receiver relationship with one another still did not accord superiority to the Heavens and inferiority to the Earth. The point of our text is clear that both of these dimensions are equal in importance with the suggestion that they are also equal in stature.

In the language of the later Kabbalah, this would mean that Yetzirah and Asiyah are equal in stature. In light of the Torah of the Ari'zal, this might be a controversial conclusion. Nowhere in the writings of the Ari'zal does it say that Yetzirah and Asiyah are equal in any sense. On the contrary, the opposite is taught. The Olam HaYetzirah is clearly on a higher level than Olam HaAsiyah.

Is there here a disagreement between the older school of Kabbalah and the newer school? Yes, we can debate about the relationship between Yetzirah and Asiyah, but all such debate would be nothing more than mere metaphysical speculations. And speculations, while intellectually entertaining, they do not necessarily provide for us any real insights into the reality of the higher dimensions. Such insights can only come through the experience of actual practitioners, such as the four Sages who entered the Pardes, and the countless others who have followed in their footsteps.

This is why we must remember what text it is that we are dealing with, and what is that text's message. How the later Kabbalah wants to view the worlds is one thing. How our text is viewing the worlds is faithful to the teachings of the Kabbalah of its day.

Our text is simply stating that we live in a dual-dimensional reality, Du Partzufim. Each dimension, the spiritual and the physical are equally important, and each plays a vital role in the order of creation. Our text is able to draw this conclusion based upon Midrashic insights of the verses quoted, and upon an unreferenced quote from the Midrash Rabbah. The rest is left up to us to explore.

Masekhet Atzilut 10

Secrets of the Shekhina

"It is written, "One to one they touch, and not even a breath comes between them" (Job 41:8). This teaches us that to every place that the Shekhina goes, the King, the Holy One, blessed be He is with Her. [This is so] so that the spirit of the nations, God forbid, will not come, and finish off Keneset Yisrael.

[Here is] a parable about a King that sent his esteemed woman to go on a mission to a place far away to redeem her children from imprisonment. But the King feared to send her concerned that she may encounter highwaymen. So, he decided to join her. Thus we have, one to one they touch. It is also written, "In all of their suffering, He suffers" (Isaiah 63:9)."

We will now discuss the secret of the Shekhina, the Divine Presence. As we will see, knowledge and awareness about the true and actual Divine Presence has devolved over the years. What was understood in the past is not what is popularly understood in the present. Thing have changed over the centuries, but many of the secrets of the Torah, in spite of the proliferation of Kabbalah, still remain safely guarded secrets.

In Biblical times, the Shekhina, the Divine Presence is clearly portrayed as a tangible, sentient, and conscious energetic field. This energy field the Torah calls the Kavod, the Glory of YHWH. We see a very clear example of this in Lev. 9:23-10:2, when Nadav and Avihu, the two sons of Aharon, approached the Tabernacle to offer incense once the Kavod of YHWH had descended upon the Ark of the Covenant.

The narrative makes it clear how a fire of sorts came forth from YHWH, killing them both on the spot. The commentaries describe the method in which they died, and it sounds very much like a modern-day electrocution. We learn from this and other Biblical examples that the Kavod of YHWH, the original portrayal of the Shekhina, is something significantly tangible, and not just another concept contemplated with metaphysical speculations about the Sefirat Malkhut.

It is clear from the written Scriptures that the Kavod (Glory) of YHWH, His Divine Presence, His Shekhina, is something tangible in this world. This leads to many questions of contemplation that have occupied the Sages for many centuries. The question is even asked as to what exactly is this Divine Presence? Is it an actual expression of the Divine Himself, or is it something less than this?

Some might thing that this line of questioning is not significant today in light of the absence of the Divine Presence. But without a clear understanding of just what is the Shekhina, how can we conclude for sure whether or not there is (or is not) such an absence.

It is easy to refer to the Divine Presence, the Shekhina, in some metaphysical sense, or even in a psychological way. It is easy to refer to the Shekhina as the Sefirat Malkhut, and disregard, or reinterpret any tangible manifestations. But such mystical speculations leave us bereft of understanding the lesser-than-metaphysical teachings.

R. Moshe Cordovero in his Pardes Rimonim (Gate 23, Chapter 13, 27A) expresses his opinion that the archangel Metatron is the garment of the Shekhina. What kind of metaphysical speculation is this? Does the Kavod of YHWH actually cloak itself in a garment. What kind of garment could the Divine Presence possibly wear? How literal, or how metaphorical is such a teaching!

When describing his Merkava vision, Ezekiel (1:28) refers to what he saw as the *"vision of the image of the Kavod of YHWH."* So, the image upon the Merkava, and the fire that came forth from the Tabernacle are somehow both related to Metatron, who is the garment of the Shekhina, the Kavod of YHWH. These correlations do seem to fit together, but what is the picture that is coming forth from them?

Avraham Abulafia takes these correlations even further. In his Sitrei Torah, (#6, Angel and Mind), Abulafia, based upon Maimonides' Guide to the Perplexed, reveals some of the deepest secrets of the Ma'aseh Merkava. The ramifications of these secrets is still best left unelaborated. Here is the text from Abulafia (Sitrei Torah #6, Barzano/Gross ed. page 53):

"I need to make known to you that the thing that is able to manifest our minds from potential to actual is mind that is separated from all form.

This is called in our language by many names.

This is the Prince of the World, he is Metatron, the Prince of the Presence, who is called Prince of Armies in the movement of the Sphere.

His Name is Shadai like the Name of His Master.

His alias is Metatron, and his numerical value is Angel of the Moon, and to him there is ancient knowledge.

But he bears witness to himself, and says I am created.

And he is the Sage who speaks. He is the General Spirit.

And the Sages of investigation (philosophers) call him the Active Intelligence, he who sees, but is not seen.

They also called him Ishim, Ruah HaKodesh, the Shekhina, the Faithful Spirit, the Kingdom of Heaven.

Like them, and those similar to them, they called him with many names.

However the intent of all who call his name is a single intent upon which all agree.

Thus the mind, in our language, is called an angel or a keruv (cherub).

Also in places he is called Elohim, like we have said on the subject that his name is the same as his Master's.

Our Sages called him Enoch and said that Enoch is Metatron.

And R. Eliezer of Germiza said that he has seventy names as our Sages have discussed in Pirkei d'R. Eliezer."

Abulafia's revelations herein are quite profound. By "putting two and two together" Abulafia is able to connect the pieces of the puzzle and is able to show the connections between the Shekhina and Metatron. One can extrapolate from here to draw other conclusions.

When going back to our text here in Masekhet Atzilut which makes reference to the King traveling with his Queen, we can understand this symbolism in light of Abulafia's revelation about the relationship between Metatron and the Shekhina. This helps us also understand what is underlying the statement quoted by R. Cordovero.

There are some secrets that, to this day, are best left unexplained. While it is usually my personal intent to reveal what can be revealed of hidden secrets, sometimes even I cannot proceed freely in this direction. I have hinted to and spoken about these secrets in my other writings. Interested readers and my students should explore those writings for further insights into what I have written here.

What we learn from all this is a very important lesson. Our text states that *"One to one they touch, and not even a breath comes between them" (Job 41:8). This teaches us that to every place that the Shekhina goes, the King, the Holy One, blessed be He is with Her."* The two, the Holy One, blessed be He and His Shekhina touch one another. Nothing comes between them, but nevertheless, it is clear from the parable of the King and Queen that the two are not one and the same!

The Holy One, blessed be He and His Shekhina are not synonymous with one another. Nor is the Angel of the Lord (mentioned in Exodus 23:20-21), the same as the Lord, (YHWH) Himself. The Name of YHWH is in the Angel, but not YHWH Himself.

Metatron and the Shekhina are somehow intimately related. Maybe we can use the metaphor of a "hand in glove" to describe their relationship. Just because the glove fits the hand perfectly and fills it totally, nevertheless, the glove is not the hand inside it!

With regard to the Sefirot, a topic which we will discuss in greater detail as we proceed with our discussion of the Masekhet Atzilut text, it is important for us to differentiate between the Vessels of the Divine Light, and the Divine Light itself.

The Shekhina may indeed be associated with the Sefirah Malkhut. But Malkhut and every other Sefirah are not "parts" of God (Heaven forbid to think that God has any "parts"). The Sefirot are vessels for the Light, but they are not the Light itself.

The Shekhina, the Kavod of YHWH is thus a vessel and not the Essence of the Divine Light. This is of vital importance to understand. For the misunderstanding of this has led to some of the worst spiritual disasters of all time.

In the Talmud (Hagigah 15a) we have recorded the ascent of the Four Sages into the Pardes, one of whom was R. Elisha ben Abuya. The Gemara records that while in his Heavenly ascent, he gazed upon Metatron in Heaven, and made the terrible mistake of contemplating whether indeed Metatron was a God Himself, thus indicating that there were two Divine Powers and not just the One. R. Elisha was punished severely for this devastating spiritual crime. But as history has shown, R. Elisha was not the only one to have succumbed to this confusion.

In the earliest Merkava literature, such as the Book of (First) Enoch, there are a number of references to a mysterious angelic entity referred to as the "son of man." These references, most associate with the Angel of the Lord, prior to him being given the title Metatron, which actually has its source in a Greek word, metator, which means "guardian."

This angelic entity is someone special, but he is not God, nor is he to be considered a "son" of God in any literal sense. Do you see where this is heading?

In the days of the Second Temple, there was already talk of a special angel in Heaven close to God. This "son of man" became known as Metatron. But as the Book of Enoch seems to suggest, this entity was supposed to be born as a human being on Earth, and to become God's anointed Mashiah. (See my essay titled, The Secret Soul of the Mashiah, in my book, Aliens, Angels and Demons, page 137). Now, do you see where this is heading?

In the generation before the destruction of the Second Temple, a group of zealot mystics proclaimed that their leader, Yeshu HaNotzri (Jesus), was indeed the incarnation of this special angel in Heaven. It is from this proclaimed association that later Christianity repeated the same terrible spiritual mistake as did R. Elisha and confused "the glove for the hand within it," and thought the vessel of the Sefirah to be the Light itself which it contains. Thus, Christianity began to embrace Yeshu as (God forbid) being God incarnate.

The story of R. Elisha in the Talmud foreshadowed to us the coming beliefs of the Christian Church. History, all too well, has documented the results of this terrible spiritual crime and the sufferings and pain that such a theological concept has brough upon the Jewish people. Rightly then does our text in Masekhet Atzilut speak about the King, the Holy One, blessed be He accompanying the Shekhina to a "faraway place," representing the exile of the Jew from Israel, for fear of what would become of Keneset Yisrael (the Jewish people) in exile. Thus our text says, *"It is also written, "In all of their suffering, He suffers" (Isaiah 63:9)."*

The nature of the relationship between Metatron, the Shekhina, and God Himself is one of the deepest mysteries of the Ma'aseh Merkava. The nature of this relationship, as we see, can become subject to so much misunderstanding and misinterpretation that it is best to continue to conceal the nature of certain spiritual truths, so as to prevent terrible mistakes from being made and repeated.

Even in the days of the Tabernacle, when the Angel of the Lord guided the Children of Israel through the Wilderness, its relationship to the Kavod (Glory) of YHWH that filled the Tabernacle is one relationship best left shrouded in concealment. But even so, we will elaborate more about Metatron, Sandalphon and the Ark of the Covenant in our upcoming commentary.

Scripture (Exodus 23:20-22) records that Moses was warned be careful with regards to this Angel. The two sons of Nadav and Avihu drew too close to the Kavod (Glory) of YHWH, attempting to offer "strange fire" which they were not instructed to do. They paid with their lives because the Kavod was a real energy field which they violated.

Is there a relationship between this tangible energy field, the Angel Metatron, and the Divine Shekhina Presence? I have already said all that can be said, and have explained the dangers in drawing any conclusions. Let us therefore return to the silence of concealment on this matter, and proceed to discuss the rest of our Masekhet Atzilut text. Needless to say, further secrets (those that can be revealed) are waiting for us.

Masekhet Atzilut 11

Secrets of Metratron & Sandalphon

"It is written regarding them, "Each clings to one other; they are interlocked so that they cannot be parted" (Job 41:9). This teaches us that the Princes, Metatron and Sandalphon, each clings to one other, even if they are interlocked with the sins of Israel, they do not break apart nor separate.

Metatron's "sneezing flashes forth light, and his eyes are like the rays of dawn" (Job 41:10). "From his mouth go firebrands" (Job 41:11). "His breath kindles coals" (Job 41:13). This teaches us that he was transformed from flesh and blood to fire. "The coals ignite, in his neck resides strength" (Job 41:13-14). All of these sayings are speaking about Metatron.

"No arrow can put him to flight" (Job 41:20). This is Samael who [acts] as accuser, and who shoots arrows at Israel. "And (s)he plays at the noise of the harpoon" (Job 41:21). This is the evil Lilith.

"Behind him he shines a path" (Job 41:24). This teaches us that Samael and his seventy Princes do not take pleasure from the Light above other than from the backside of Metatron.

"On the dust there is none that rules over him" (Job 41:25). "He looks at all high things" (Job 41:26), meaning that he receives strength and support from Akatriel, who is higher than him, He is king over all the children of arrogance who are Samael and his Princes; for they are arrogant and full of pride."

In our previous section we began our revelations about Metatron. In this section we will continue to reveal more about Metatron and his unique relationships with Sandalphon, Samael, and Akatriel Yah YHWH Tzvaot.

We have already established an association between Metatron as being both, the Angel of YHWH, and the Shekhina, the Divine Presence. In the book Ohel Moed (*32, the Secret of Metatron*) it is written:

"Do not be surprised that Metatron is the Guardian of the Gate, for he is not an angel (God forbid). Rather, he is the tenth attribute [the Sefirah Malkhut, the Shekhina] which includes everything within it, and which [also] receives everything. And this is a feminine function."

The Ohel Moed reveals even more, by challenging the age-old belief that Enoch ascended to Heaven to become Metatron (even as our Masekhet Atzilut states). It is well known that Metatron is far more than just a transformed human being. The Gemara (Yebamot 16b, Tosafot 6) implies that Metatron was with YHWH since the dawn of creation. This makes sense when we identify Metatron in association with the Shekhina, but not when we identify Metatron as being just a transformed human being. The Ohel Moed (*32, the Secret of Metatron*) reveals to us a little-known secret of the Kabbalah:

"Our Sages teach that Enoch was transformed from flesh to fire, becoming Metatron, Guardian of the Gate. God forbid that this be so. Rather Enoch embraced this [tenth] attribute and [came to be] called by its name."

Enoch, the man, seventh generation from Adam did indeed ascend above and was transformed to become a Heavenly entity. Yet the Heavenly entity Metatron already existed (reference Yebamot, Tosafot 16b.6). He was not new. Enoch technically did and did not become Metatron. Enoch did not become a new and detached previously non-existent Heavenly entity. Rather, Enoch upon transformation was absorbed into an already existing collective of beings, who together we call Metatron. It is thus more proper to speak of the race of the Metatrons, as opposed to the single identity of an angelic individual.

As for the association between Metatron and the Shekhina, this also is nothing new. In other Kabbalistic literature, we will often find two different spellings of the name, Metatron. One is spelled in the normal way and pronounced Metatron. The second spelling adds the letter Yod to the name and it is pronounce Mitatron. The first way is to distinguish the angel when he is operating with the lower worlds. The second way is when the angel is serving as a vessel for the Shekhina.

Sefer Ohel Moed adds an interesting detail which is often overlooked. It hints to what we have just mentioned. Metatron is the angel whose body and general service is in the world of Yetzirah, which is associated with the male aspect. And yet the Ohel Moed clearly associates Metatron with the female aspect because of the relationship with the Sefirah Malkhut.

We should not consider this to be contradictory, nor problematic. For Heavenly reality is reflected in earthly living. Just like human beings, Metatron has both male and female aspects within him. Metatron is always male when he reigns and rules over the lower worlds in the Name of YHWH. Yet, Metatron stands submissive and receptive when he serves as the vessel for the Shekhina, as will be discussed shortly. To distinguish between these two functions were the two forms of the name made. Every human being, male and female, has within them the characteristics of the other. As below, so it is above.

A further elaboration upon this this male – female relationship introduces us to Sandalphon, the angel (Ofan) of Asiyah. With regards to the Metatron – Sandalphon connection, Rabbi Moshe Cordovero (Ramak) writes (*Shiur Kumah 79*):

"The primary camps are Metatron and Sandalphon. They are the two governing authorities beneath the Shekhina. The first is Metatron. The second is Sandalphon.

These are the governing authorities of the day and of the night. The secret of the attribute of day governs through Metatron, and the attribute of night governs through Sandalphon.

They are the two "feet" of the Shekhina, the first being the right foot and the second being the left foot. The right is the power of the male that governs the day. The left is the power of the female that governs the night.

These [two] are the shoe and the sandal. Metatron is the shoe, Sandalphon is the sandal, the meaning [of this is that the Shekhina] is cloaked within both authorities together. For the attribute of the night is in the day, and the attribute of day is in the night. Thus we have Metatron, the shoe, and Sandalphon, the sandal."

As we know, the name Sandalphon contains within it the word, sandal, indicating its vessel-like (shoe-like) function. The Name Metatron, however, is often mistaken to itself be a holy name, leading some (specifically those of the Ari'zal school) to refer to the angel as Mem-Tet, thus avoiding its true name. This stringency however is totally unnecessary. Metatron is not a holy name, rather it is a title derived from a foreign language. Rabbi Eliezer of Germiza (*Sodei Razia 2, Laws of Metatron*) has said this outright. *"Know that Metatron is called [by this name] because he is a Metator, meaning a director (or influencer)."*

Now that we have revealed more about the nature of the Metatron identity, let us progress to discuss more about his (their?) function. Our text above states, *"Each clings to one other; they are interlocked so that they cannot be parted" (Job 41:9). This teaches us that the Princes, Metatron and Sandalphon, each clings to one other.* Being that we have identified them as the right and left "legs" of the Shekhina this makes total sense.

Metatron represents the Presence of God (the Shekhina) in the Yetziratic dimension. Sandalphon represents the Presence of God (the Shekhina) in the Asiyatic dimension. Both are active vessels for the Shekhina, and both serve as sheaths of protection, protecting the Divine Presence from becoming overly ensnared by the compromised forces of the Other (Dark) Side, which seeks to siphon off its Life-force energy to be used for their own selfish (and nefarious) purposes. This is what our text above meant when it said that *"Samael and his seventy princes do not take pleasure from the Light above other than from the backside of Metatron.*

Rabbi Cordovero (*Shiur Kumah 55, Galut HaShekhina*) addresses this directly:

"When Israel are exiled from their land, the Shekhina cloaks itself within these powers which are called Ofanim, which is Asiyah, the lowest level of [Divine] influence. Thus it is written, "and behold an Ofan is upon the Earth" (Ezek. 1:15).

Then it is cloaked within the Hitzonim (External Forces), and is thus cast out from the land of Israel to outside the land. And [then] it is cloaked within the External Princes, who are the Seventy Princes, [who are] a portion of the lower Klipot.

Then She (the Shekhina) has no union whatsoever, and the Ayn Sof does not extend itself into the upper Sefirot. Rather, there is a large gap between Hokhma and Binah."

According to Ramak, because the Shekhina is in exile it causes there to be breach between Hokhma and Binah. As we know, Hokhma is intuitive, psychic consciousness, and Binah is rational, intellectual consciousness. How true it is that since the episode of the eating of the forbidden fruit from the Tree of Knowledge in Eden, human beings have lost contact with their intuitive, psychic side.

The whole work of Tikkun (spiritual repair) is to restore the Hokhma-Binah (Abba-Imma) union. This practically means that we are working for the restoration of our inner psychic abilities. Once we can fully unleash our individual inner psychic selves into our rational conscious mind, only then will we have unleashed the necessary mental power for collective humanity to ascend as a whole into the next phase of human existence, which is what we call, the Messianic era.

At present, due to the limited consciousness of collective humanity, the Seventy Princes of this world have the ability to siphon off the Life-force energy from the Shekhina. They prevent human minds from receiving this energy, thus bridling the efforts for human evolution and spiritual growth.

Our present collective human psychic restriction emboldens the Seventy Princes and reinforces their control over the flow of Life-force energy from the higher dimensions. Human beings remain as spiritual cattle, while the Seventy Princes remain the "owners of the ranch," who slaughter, and eat their cattle as they see fit.

Masekhet Atzilut associates Metatron with the Leviathan described in Job 41. This is a rather peculiar relationship. Leviathan, according to the Biblical text is not a Heavenly entity at all. Rather, the Leviathan is described as being what we might describe as an authentic type of physical Godzilla-like monster somewhere here on Earth.

Rabbi Haber, in his Ginzei Meromim commentary to Masekhet Atzilut, following in the footsteps of his master, the Gaon of Vilna, interprets this section of the text in a Lurianic way which is completely removed from the text's original intent and meaning. As we say, *Elu v'Elu Divrei Elohim Hayim*. While Rabbi Haber elaborates on the Sefirotic Partzufim, our text addresses the much more down-to-Earth reality of angelic interactions.

Make no mistake! The terrifying imagery of the Leviathan very well fits the known form and function of Metatron. Also, there truly is a conflict in the realms which we call the spiritual. Our human souls have become ensnared here on Earth. We have been corralled and are essentially being held captive, all the while that our natural portion of Life-force energy is denied us, and has been usurped by others. As long as we tolerate this present state of affairs, these deplorable conditions will continue. It is the job of the Metatrons, acting through the Sandalphon(s?) to address this imbalance, and to work towards its proper realignment.

Metatron in Yetzirah serves as the vessel for Akatriel Yah YHWH Tzvaot. According to the Kabbalistic commentary to the Aggadah of the Gemara, Sefer Otzar HaKavod of Rabbi Todros HaLevi Abulafia, the Name Akatriel is a reference to the Keter of Malkhut. Akatriel and Katriel both derive from the word Keter, which is crown. The crown referenced here is the Keter of Beriah, which itself serves as the vessel for the Malkhut of Atzilut.

So, the Shekhina is the Malkhut of Atzilut, cloaked within Akatriel the Keter of Beriah, which itself is cloaked within the lower Sefirot of Beriah, which are the "head" of Metatron, which itself is attached to the "body" of Metatron in Yetzirah, which is intimately bound with Sandalphon in Asiyah. So, the Shekhina is cloaked in Akatriel, Akatriel in Metatron, and Metatron in Sandalphon. This about sums it up.

Sandalphon is meant to bond with the Children of Israel through their prayers which he (she?) weaves into crowns (Keters) that are to be placed upon the Head of the Holy One, blessed be He (ref. Hagigah 13b).

When we are righteous and moral, we establish this sacred connection. When we act inappropriately, we sever it. As we said above, our mission is to reunite our individual internal Hokhma(s) with our individual internal Binah(s). This is the place of the spiritual, psychic war in which we are presently engaged.

Our Masekhet Atzilut text is teaching us to not view this terrible conflict as merely a philosophical, or psychological affair. It is far more real than this. And we need to take it much more seriously.

Masekhet Atzilut 12

The Hokhma-Binah Union, the Tzadik & Tal

Yeruham ben Yosef opened, "Happy is the man who finds wisdom (Hokhma), and a man who gives forth intelligence (Tevunah)" (Proverbs 3:13).

Come and see, in the place where wisdom (Hokhma) is mentioned, right next to it stands understanding (Binah) and intelligence (Tevunah). This is to teach us that wisdom (Hokhma) and understanding (Binah) are both equal. One never, ever separates from the other.

It is written, "With His knowledge the depths were split, and the heavens dripped dew" (Proverbs 3:20). In the mind of the Holy One, blessed be He the depths of the 50 gates of understanding (Binah) were split, meaning as it says, "From whose womb did the (awesome) ice emerge" (Job 38:29).

"And the heavens dripped dew" (Proverbs 3:20). How [to whom] are the heavens dripping dew? To he who is a Tzadik, who is the Foundation of the world. For it is impossible for the world not to have dew.

And the dew does not stop, meaning, as the Holy One, blessed be He spoke to Israel, fear not for my head is full of dew" (Song 5:2). And it is written, "I will be like dew to Israel" (Hosea 14:6)."

Hokhma and Binah are the two lobes of the human brain, and the two modes of human thought processes. Hokhma is intuitive psychic thinking. Binah is rational intellectual thinking. These two processes are like mirror reflections of one another, meaning that they are like total opposites. But the two of them together form a concentric whole, a unity that cannot be broken.

Intuitive thinking and rational thinking go hand in hand with one another, and both processes operate together like a swinging pendulum. The meditative usage of these modes used in harmonious oscillation is called Sekhel Tenudah (oscillating consciousness).

So now, let us ask the big question, why do we need two modes of consciousness? Shouldn't one be enough? The answer to this is that there really is only one mode of consciousness. This is the consciousness of the singularity which we call God consciousness, or in later Lurianic terminology, Mohin of Gadlut. But our discussion about modes of consciousness is going to take us into lessons about the Ten Sefirot. And it is most fitting that from this section of Masekhet Atzilut to the end of the book, the lessons deal almost exclusively with revelations about the Sefirot.

Hokhma and Binah are Sefirot, and they are also states of consciousness. Therefore, the experience of the Sefirot are themselves states of consciousness. Sefirot, in and of themselves, are energy fields through which we human beings perceive the universe. The Sefirot are the Image of God in which humanity was created. While this section of our text introduces us to sefirotic interactions, it deals exclusively with the Sefirot of the mind. I have written about this topic many times, and in many places in my other works. We will focus here on only a brief review of all that I have already explained elsewhere in detail.

Two modes of consciousness, for one ultimate state of unity consciousness. This is the secret of what the Kabbalists call both Yihud (unity), and Tikun (rectification). While we have many times discussed the nature of these two Sefirotic modes of consciousness, we need to repeat again, why we have two (and not one), and why the two must become one.

In the order of the Divine manifestation of reality, that which we call Seder HaHistalsh'lut, all that came into being did so for a purpose. We understand from the Sefer Yetzirah how reality is meant to be the combination of all possible permutations. Modern science postulates that there may be an infinite number of parallel worlds or universes. Indeed, what the Sefer Yetzirah says and what science postulates might be pointing to the same reality.

As we know from Isaiah 45:7, God is the Creator, Former, and Maker of all things, which include both Light and darkness, good and evil. There is only One Source for all. Being that this is the case, we must ask another important question: why did God create darkness and evil. Why do they need to exist in our universe, alongside us, knowing full well the harm, and suffering that they cause us!

But there is a need for them to exist. We do not need to delve into philosophy to entertain the different opinions as to why evil exist, we just must acknowledge that it does! Darkness and evil are two permutations of the Primordial Force that potentially can, and thus must exist. Like everything in every parallel universe, what exists in one universe does not have to exist in another. So, the measure of darkness and evil in our universe, and thus in our world, is a permutable variation based upon the choices that each of us makes.

Human consciousness is the deciding factor that materializes the good or evil that manifests around us. Consciousness leads to thoughts, which are manifest in feelings, which in turn motivate us to take the actions that we take, be they good or evil. Therefore, what goes on in consciousness at first is vital for the sake of the manifestations of actions that happen last. (Sof Ma'aseh B'Mahshava Tehilah).

As we know, from the beginning the Primordial Force operates in two ways (Hesed and Din) that we can compare to breathing. The Divine Life-force energy (Shefa) extends outwards (and down, Ohr Yashar), and then in turn extends inwards (and up, Ohr Hozer). Exhale and inhale, this seems to be the pattern of the Primordial Divine Force. Now, to where must this Divine Force go forth to?

The Divine Force must go everywhere, as the verse says, "the whole land is full of His Kavod (Glory)" (Isaiah 6:3).

And what is the purpose underlying this "Divine breath"? The answer is to bring about the manifestation of all possible worlds. And of those worlds, some are very far away in shape and form from the original Primary Pattern of Divine creation (A.K.). Some worlds are very different, so different in fact that we may say, as if, that they are the inverse and opposites of the Primary Pattern. Yet, as far removed as these worlds are, they still must exist so that every potential for existence can be made manifest, regardless of how far removed, and different it is from the Primary Pattern.

The furthest away worlds contain within them as little Light and does the Primary Pattern contain within it as little darkness. What is below comes to be the mirror reflection of that which is above. Needless to say, the mirror world below operates oppositely to the Primary world above. As such, what operates above, does not operate below, and what operates below does not operate above. And at the same time, the worlds above and below are intimately joined together as one, in the same way as is an individual and his reflection in a mirror.

So, the Primary Pattern sends forth its Divine Life-force energy. The initial projection outward begins what we call the Right Column of the Sefirot. This initial projection is the Sefirah Hokhma. Hokhma is the projection of the Primary Pattern, thus Hokhma is perceived in our human experience as an internal knowing. Hokhma consciousness is brought about by our looking inwards to see what is already there.

Yet, once I see what is already there, and I look around in my present settings in this lowest of worlds, where darkness and evil are as prolific as they are not in the upper world, what am I supposed to do with my insights into the Primary Pattern of Hokhma? Such insights are wonderful, but so very unapplicable in this mirror reflection reality wherein which Hokhma is next to non-existent, in the same way as it is almost the whole total reality of the higher world.

So, there needs to exist some form of consciousness that is more applicable to the lower world that will enable one to receive Hokhma consciousness and be able to understand what to do with it in a world in which its very existence is miniscule.

And thus Binah consciousness was born! Binah consciousness does not act to look within to receive insight into the Primary Pattern. No, Binah consciousness is the opposite of this! Binah consciousness does not look in to the potentials within the Primary Pattern, rather Binah looks out at the world in which it is in, which in our case, is this mirror reflection lowest world of ours. Binah consciousness gazes upon what is, and seeks to bring it all in through comprehension and understanding. Only when this is accomplished can Binah consciousness then take its next step.

Binah consciousness is the "inhale" to Hokhma's "exhale." Hokhma sends everything down below. Binah, as its opposite, must then send everything back up again. (Ohr Yashar, Hesed and Ohr Hozer, Din). Exhale and inhale, and then exhale and inhale again, throughout eternity, and this describes the Life of our existence.

So, because these lower worlds exist, and the potential of their existence existed long before their manifestation, thus when Hokhma became manifest, Binah had to manifest immediately thereafter, for without the two acting in perfect unity together always, all of existence would cease to breathe. And thus Life and reality as we know it would die!

Hokhma consciousness and Binah consciousness are thus both absolutely integral parts of the Primary Pattern. Life and existence themselves could not exist without them. And there needed to be this dual function operating together, but yet different from one another. For Hokhma cannot perform the "inhale" task of Binah, and Binah cannot perform the "exhale" task of Hokhma. Only the two together form a single unified breath!

Now that we have established why the system exists as it does, let us proceed to discuss its operations.

Binah consciousness gazes out at the worlds around it and gathers in the recognition (understanding) of its experiences and coordinates them with the internal Primary Pattern concealed with the "seed" of Hokhma. When these align, this is called Good. When they digress, this is called Bad (or evil). Binah then gets busy to realign all out-of-alignment realities (Yihud and Tikun).

So, how many out-of-sync realities are there for Binah consciousness to interact with, and to repair? Most likely, a countless number! Being that there are so many worlds to deal with, Binah Itself needs to become very flexible and to manifest itself, and its function in a way that is unique for every existence in which It manifests. And thus we have what we call the 50 Gates of Binah. 50, of course, is a metaphorical number, based on the Biblical model of completion, the Jubilee. Just as the Jubilee is a complete measure of one cycle of time (50 years = I Yovel/Jubilee), the 50 Gates of Binah measures the full gamut of all the different ways in which Binah can manifest.

So Binah becomes the symbolic womb inside of which the "seed" of the Primary Pattern from Hokhma grows. This symbol means that regardless of external circumstances, the outward looking aspect of thought (rational consciousness) still gazes within towards an internal primordial knowing (intuitive consciousness) and is thus able to understand, and can thus define, what is and what is not good and evil. With this clarity in the mind, Binah consciousness then sets out a plan of action that is right and correct for that specific world, in that specific place, and for that specific time.

Our Masekhet Atzilut text speaks about the Divine dew that descends. This dew is the Hokhma concealed within the Binah, as described above. The dew is the Life-force energy that extends down to the lowest of worlds, and thus must be utilized there in these lower worlds in a way that is right and best for both the dew itself, and for the world in which it needs to manifest.

The "place" of proper harmony where dew and world align is called the Tzadik, the Righteous One. This is not at all a reference to an actual human being person, any more than Adam Kadmon is an actual person. The Tzadik is a concept, not an individual.

Now, any human being who embraces the Hokhma – Binah alignment, and acts properly to manifest the Primary Pattern in its correct and proper permutation for that world, that time, and those circumstances, is acting as a conduit for the continued and proper flow of the supernal dew. Any individual who accomplishes this task contributes to the alignment of his world. Such a one is doing the right thing, the Tzodek thing. And thus the one who does what is Tzodek is called a Tzadik.

The role of the Tzadik is thus of paramount importance for all human, and all other types of civilizations, be they in this dimensional reality of space-time, or in any other! The dew must flow! It must be received below (exhale), and then it must be sent back above (inhale). In this way, worlds are realigned with the Primary Pattern, and thus the purpose of their manifestations comes to fruition.

All worlds, however far from the Primordial Plan, are not meant to be destroyed. On the contrary they must exist for the Primary Plan to be complete in its every variable of permutation. Yet, all these permutations must never be disconnected from, or lost to the supernal dew, which is their life and sustenance. Therefore, their realignment serves to manifest within these worlds their inner potentials. When a world becomes properly aligned that world comes to take its rightful place in the family of worlds. And this cycle goes on and on, from world to world, even as the Primary Plan of our blessed Creator has so ordained.

Masekhet Atzilut 13

Wisdom & the Fear of God

Part 1

"Better a little [knowledge of Torah] with the fear of YHWH, than a great treasury that comes with turmoil" (Proverbs 15:16).

Better a little [bit of] Torah and there be with it the fear of God, for one who has [the] fear [of God], goes in straight ways, as it is written, "He who fears YHWH goes in his uprightness" (Proverbs 14:2).

Then he has revealed to him the mysteries of wisdom, as it is written, "but His counsel is with the upright" (Proverbs 3:32). For we have learned, one can do much or one can do little, just as long as he focuses his heart to Heaven.

From great treasure comes turmoil. One who is full of the treasure of Torah and who suffers turmoil therein is because he has no fear [of God]. For then all the days rumble against him.

Woe to him for what he studied, woe to him for what learned, and woe to him that he serviced the Sages. Let this rule be established in your hand, one who has no fear [of God], has no wisdom.

And we learned (Avot 3:17), "if there is no fear [of God, then there is no wisdom. Woe to such a one because of [the] judgment [to come], as it is written, "Behold, the fear of YHWH is wisdom and shunning evil is understanding"(Job 28:28). Thus, even a little [Torah knowledge] is good [as long as it has] the fear of God."

There is much confusion today with regards to a proper understanding of what it means to be "in fear of God," or for one to be "God fearing." First, before we define what exactly it is to be Yirat Shamayim (God fearing), let us dispel some of the prevalent myths with regards to this.

The term for fear is Yirah. As with many Hebrew words, it contains multiple meanings in translation. Many interpret Yirah to mean "awe" as in awesome. It is as if to say, God is so awesome, and I am in awe of God. This popular modern rendition of the term does not capture of the essence of the word. While there is a component of awe contained within Yirah, there is so much more to it.

Yirah means to literally be afraid for one's life. Yirah does not mean being panicked and being terrified. The word for this would be Pahad, also translated as fear, but maybe better to translate it as terror. Mind you, Pahad was the original name of the Sefirah Gevurah and most correctly reveals a secret about its true energetic signature. But we will discuss more about this in the coming section when we discuss the Sefirot.

Yirah means to be in awe, and at the same time it means to be in fear of annihilation. Yirah without this sense of dread and compromised mortality is not Yirah. When we are commanded to fear God, we are not just being told to be in awe of all that He has done, we are also being directed to recognize that if we step out of line, by disregarding the commandments, that punishment will be quick and harsh. This is the fear of annihilation; this is Yirah.

Yirah definitely expresses an emotional component that is focused on the danger to one's self-interests, if not one's very life. One who does not take God seriously, but acts flippantly towards one's service to Heaven, and one's duties to others, most assuredly has what to be afraid of. Only the arrogant fool will deny this, or be blind to seeing it.

As important as Torah study is, even Torah study without the fear of God underlying it is considered to be wasted effort. Being that this is the case, should we not conclude that if one cannot muster up the proper right attitude that is necessary for Torah study that it is maybe best for one to not study at all? No! We do not draw this conclusion at all! Whether or not one has proper intention, one should nevertheless fulfill one's obligations with regards to all things that one must do, especially with the commandment to study Torah.

One of the most important areas in which to exercise a healthy amount of Yirat Shamayim (fear of Heaven) is with regards to the study of Torah. Torah study that is done (lo lishma) without proper motivation and true devotion is considered a waste of effort. Nevertheless, with regards to all commandments, it is better (and required) to perform them, even if for the wrong reasons, than not to perform them at all.

In the Gemara (Sotah 47b, San. 105b), R. Yehuda says in the name of Rav that which sums up matters nicely. He said, *"A person should always engage in Torah and mitzvot, even if he does so not for their own sake, as through such acts performed not for their own sake, one will come to perform them for their own sake."*

Now, let us address the Sod element underlying the relationship between Hokhma (wisdom) and Yirah (fear). In order to be authentic, real Yirah is emotional, it is never rationally based. Yet that which triggers true Yirah is something deep within the unconscious. It is like an irrational fear that one cannot shake. This type of combined awe and dread arises from deep within one's inner sense of knowing. And what is this inner place of which I speak? Obviously, it is one's inner self, one's personal internal Sefirah Hokhma. Thus Hokhma is the source of Yirah. Therefore, one who has no authentic Yirah has no access to authentic Hokhma. Thus the two are essentially one, in that the one (Yirah) is an extension of the other (Hokhma).

Now we can understand why Torah study without Yirah is the same as Torah study without Hokhma. And Torah study without Hokhma is Torah study in the lower realm of Beriah without access to, or insights from the higher realm of the Torah of Atzilut. Such Torah study is disconnected from the Torah's own Source above. As such it is not from Ruah HaKodesh (Divinely inspired). We have all too much of this type of academically-based, non-spiritually oriented Torah being taught today everywhere, and it has misled many from recognizing and embracing the true Torah of Emunah, and the comprehensive, and sincere observance of all its commandments.

We must not only never forget, but we must also strive to experience the reality that as human beings on Earth, our entre existence is insignificantly small when compared to the whole of creation that God has made. The Torah that we have received, regardless of its actual forms of reception is clearly something that is "out of this world." As such, one should never look upon Torah as merely being the surface façade with which we are all familiar.

To this day no human being has fathomed the depths of everything that the Torah conceals. I wonder if we mortal human beings will ever acquire the wisdom necessary to understand the entirety of the Torah.

When it comes to performing the commandments of the Torah incumbent upon the Jewish people, these must be defined clearly and precisely. What to do and how to do it, regardless of all the different interpretations and customs, is still a communal, religious, and national religious imperative. Without an accepted common denominator of forms of Halakhic observance, there would not be any semblance of Jewish community. There is enough chaos in the world; we do not need to add to it, or to invite it into the Jewish community by using rational academic arguments to undermine the very fundamentals of Torah observance.

This is where being Yirat Shamayim comes to play. One whose very soul remains attached to the Torah's origins in the world of Atzilut recognizes deep within oneself an inherent sense, a feeling, and an inner conviction of what is right and wrong, moral and immoral, good and bad with regards to Torah observance.

Those who lack this Atzilutic connection (however unconscious it is) look at Torah Law and seeks to change and pervert it in accordance with any whim of the moment that may arise. This is how the Jewish religion becomes corrupted, all in the name of Torah interpretation that has become corrupted. So true have we been warned that when there is no Yirat Shamayim (fear of God), then there will equally be no true and authentic wisdom derived from the Torah!

Without the Torah of Atzilut (which is the source of internal wisdom) speaking within the recesses of one's personal unconscious, the Torah of Beriah can never be clear and properly understood. These sentiments have already been expressed by Rabbi Eliyahu, the Gaon of Vilna.

In his Even Shelema, Chapter 5, the Gaon of Vilna wrote, *""Whatever is learned according to Pshat must also be in accordance to the Sod. For when the secrets of the Torah are revealed, one realizes that the learnings of his youth are also true and correct. Anyone who does not understand Sod (the secret meanings), even Pshat (the surface meanings) cannot be clear to him."* One must not underestimate the significance of these words.

In modern society, specifically because there is such a terrible imbalance and loss of connection between Hokhma and Binah consciousness, the Torah religious community suffers greatly. There is so much confusion, and so much darkness, all because of a severe lack of Yirat Shamayim. Torah and Torah study is watered down to be nothing more than mere philosophical or moralistic messages. Torah's entire grandiosity is often ignored, if not outright denied.

This terrible state of affairs can never be corrected until there is a communal shift of orientation towards the truth of Torah in general. And then each individual must seek out the Active and Living Presence of the True Divine which is the Atzilutic core of the Torah concealed within its Beriatic cloak. The consequences for the failure to perform this proper rectification is what our text addresses next.

Wisdom & the Fear of God, Part 2

It is written (2 Sam. 23:6-7), "But the wicked are all as thorns thrust away, for they cannot be taken in hand. But if a man touch them, he should be armed with iron and the staff of a spear; and with fire they shall be utterly burned in their place."

These verses speak about Samael and his associates and how they will be burned up, toppled, and destroyed, [they will be] burned in their place (ba'shavet). Do not read [the word] as ba'shavet, but rather as b'Shabat (the Shabat of creation).

There are those who say that on Erev Shabat, his host will be torn [up] in Judgement, "When the wicked flourish like grass, and all workers of violence blossom, only to be destroyed to eternity." (Psalm 92:8).

But we are saved with a single verse, "But, as for me, let my prayer to You, YHWH, be in an Et Ratzon (an auspicious time). With Your abundant kindness, Elohim, answer me with the truth of Your salvation." For then (on Erev Shabat) it is an Et Ratzon (an auspicious time), and the accusers are nullified and concealed in their place. This is what makes it be an Et Ratzon (an auspicious time).

Fear [of God] is so great [a thing] that our teacher Moses (upon him be peace), commanded [us] with regards to it, "And now Israel, what does YHWH your God, ask of you? Only to fear YHWH your God, to walk in all His ways, and to love Him, and to worship YHWH your God, with all your heart and with all your soul." (Deut. 10:12).

All who wish to enter into the [inner] sanctums of wisdom and who have no fear [of God] will lose all that one has gained, as it is written, "The beginning of wisdom is the fear of YHWH, and the knowledge of the holy ones is understanding." (Proverbs 9:10).

Judgment always comes, especially upon those who deserve it the most. And those who have separated the Torah of Beriah from the Torah of Atzilut are targeted by Heaven for special retribution. They are even called "the Satan," and thus equally associated with the accusing angel Samael, himself. For those who disgrace the Torah in the name of the Torah are the very ones who are noticed in Heaven, and who invite down upon themselves and upon others the consequences of their causing a breach between Hokhma (Atzilut) and Binah (Beriah).

It is the job and role of Samael the Satan to bring to light in the Heavenly Court the wrongful behaviors performed by human beings. When Yirat Shamayim is absent, and disgrace towards the Torah abounds, all the more so when such disgrace is done in the name of the Torah itself, then human behavior itself cries out against the ones who do it and makes accusations in Heaven against those who have behaved in such a deplorable manner. One's own behavior comes to serve as accuser, as Satan and Samael, against oneself! Such is the result of a lack of Yirat Shamayim.

Our text here not only addresses the problem, but it also addresses the solution for the problem. This is the secret of the "Et Ratzon," (the Auspicious Time).

There are a number of actual physical times that are considered to be an Et Ratzon (an auspicious time). Some of these include the beginning of the Shabat, Shabat afternoon, and in a lesser way, all afternoons. The list of such times is widely known and available in many places.

But if these auspicious times worked liked magic, then anyone offering a prayer during these times would be assured of one's prayers being answered. And yet, we see from clear daily example that this is not at all the case. Therefore, I think it wise that we surmise that an Et Ratzon is not so much an actual time that is measured on the clock, such as Erev Shabat or Shabat Minha. Rather, an Et Ratzon is actually a stage, or a level of consciousness, wherein which one's heightened state of awareness makes one to be more in sync with supernal reality, and thus in a better "place" to draw down Heavenly energy (blessings) as needed, and desired.

The doorway to Et Ratzon consciousness is Yirat Shamayim! One channels into consciousness the unconscious energy of Atzilutic reality into one's Beriatic rational mind. This is experienced as that feeling of both awe and dread, wherein which one literally feels afraid of the Presence of God. This is an emotional experience, not an intellectual one. Many have tried to copy it, and each time the insincere do nothing other than to aggravate Heaven.

To sum up matters: the fear of God is the unconscious connection that one feels with suppressed Atzilutic consciousness. The realities of the higher worlds cannot be rationally fathomed, but they can be experienced through expanding consciousness. As consciousness expands from the rigid, contracting Beriatic state and into the fluid, expansive Atzilutic state, there is a natural uneasiness that one experiences. After all, letting go of everything that defines for one reality itself is usually a very terrifying experience. Thus it is fearful, and thus begins the fear of God. This is the necessary and true first step along the path towards the Source of Blessings.

.

Masekhet Atzilut 14

Origins of the Sefirot

"It is written, "To You YHWH is the greatness, the might, the glory, the victory, and the majesty. For all that is in the Heavens and on the Earth [is Yours]. Yours is the kingdom, and it is You who is the exalted Head over everything." (1 Chron. 29:11).

We have been taught in the Sefer Yetzirah (1:2) of Avraham Avinu (upon him be peace) that there are Ten Sefirot Blimah. What is Blimah? It is as it is written (Job 26:7), "He suspends the Earth on Blimah (nothing), for therein is no image, nor similarity." Blimah, they are the work of the fingers of God. They are the artisan tools of the Holy One, blessed be He.

For example, an artisan metal-worker has a crucible for [melting] silver, and a kiln for [melting] gold. Even though the crucible and the kiln are both made from clay their names are different. So it is with the attributes and praises of the Holy One, blessed be He.

Why are their names called Sefirot? Because it is written (Ex. 28:18), "sapphire (sapir) and diamond." And it is written (Job 38:37), "who will speak of (yi'saper) the Heavens with wisdom."

And by His artisan's tools the Holy One blessed be He strikes down the boastful, and raises up the humble, one is impoverished, one is made wealthy, this one falls, and this one arises. And if the righteous act righteously and straightforward in the world, and labor in Torah, which is called "a fortress," then the Shekhina says, "If

they would grasp My fortress, they would make peace for Me"
(Isaiah 27:5).

And if the wicked and sinners proliferate throughout the land,
then the world collapses. The Shekhina then cries out, my head is
destroyed, my arm is destroyed.

For life and peace only grow throughout the world when there
are the righteous therein. For the world of the righteous is for life,
and the fruits of evil are for sin."

And now, we introduce the final collection of topics in
Masekhet Atzilut: the Sefirot. Our text begins by quoting the
Scripture verse from which the names of the seven lower Sefirot
have been derived.

Our text references the first book wherein the Sefirot are
mentioned, this being the Sefer Yetzirah. Our text boldly states
outright the ancient tradition recorded in the Sefer Yetzirah itself
that it is originally the work of none less than the Biblical patriarch,
Abraham.

This association of book and author is most definitely
pseudepigraphal. However, who can say how old much of this
ancient knowledge actually is? To the best of my knowledge no one
can clearly show who actually did author Sefer Yetzirah. So with a
lack of any credible evidence, legend ascribes the book to Abraham,
and even later to Rabbi Akiba.

As with all literature ascribed to some ancient personage,
identity of the author is irrelevant. What matters most, and what
we will focus on here, is the nature of the material itself. Our topic
of discussion is the genesis into literature of the Ten Sefirot of
Nothingness (Blimah).

It must be noted from the start that the Sefirot as discussed in
the Sefer Yetzirah have very little in common to their descriptions
found in later Kabbalistic literature.

Our text quotes the verse from Chronicles from where the
seven lower Sefirot are given their names. This association of
names, scripture verse and the Sefirot does not occur at all in the

Sefer Yetzirah. In the S.Y. the Sefirot are never named. They are described, but in the most etheric way. They are called Blimah, which means without form (Mahut). They are said to be ten in number, but never does the S.Y. arrange these ten into the popular present form of the Sefirotic Tree of Life.

To borrow from the terms of the Kabbalah of the Ari'zal, which post-dates the S.Y. by a good one thousand years, the S. Y. seems to be discussing the Ten Sefirot in their original form of Igulim (concentric spheres), prior to their manifestation in the form of Yosher (columns). Indeed, even such a correlation as this one goes far beyond the original intent of the original meaning of the Sefirot in S.Y.

For the S.Y. the Sefirot are the modulating fields of Divine psychic energy that feed into, and thus give life to the twenty-two (22) Hebrew Letters, which themselves form all things in creation. Although the text does not state it outright, the implication is that while the Sefirot are Blimah (without form), the Letters themselves are Mah (meaning, Mahut, form itself).

Our text rightly and clearly declares that the Sefirot are nothing more than tools in the Hands of God. In later Kabbalah, some confusion did set in with regards to understanding the Sefirot as to whether they were (or were not) actually a part of God. Some even speculated whether or not the Sefirot were themselves Divine. This line of thought led some opponents to later Kabbalah to condemn certain Zoharic descriptions and expressions as being akin to idolatry, by saying that there were (God forbid) ten gods (for those who considered each Sefirah to be an actual expression of the Divine).

This type of argumentative banter continues to this day with those radically opposed to Kabbalah study. Little do they understand the Kabbalah that they purport to condemn. And equally small is the amount of true Kabbalah that many so-called Kabbalists study and teach, which gives rise to such grievous errors in understanding the true nature of authentic Kabbalah.

As discussed in the S.Y. the Sefirot cannot be described using any terminology associated with things of this world. The Sefirot are Bli Mahut (Blimah), they are without any tangible forms. They are pure fields of energy, which serve to enliven the 22 Letters of Creation.

The Sefirot, like the Letters themselves, are creations of God, and not an actual part of the Divine. The Sefirot are merely vessels of distinction and demarcation that differentiate the singular Divine Light of the Creator and allows for its manifestation into multiple (if not an infinite number of) forms.

Thus our text makes use of the example of the crucible and kiln. One is used to smelt gold, the other is for silver. However different their names may be, they are both essentially vessels made from hardened clay, each serving a very similar, if not different purpose. So too the Sefirot each serves its individual purpose, which thus gives rise to each ones unique name. Nevertheless, these vessels all come from the same cosmic "clay" created by, formed by, and made by the Divine Hand.

Sefirot are cosmic forces of energy whose interactions form and make space-time as we know it. But is this all that the Sefirot are? Are they just non-corporeal energy fields or do they have any representation of tangible manifestation? No one has seen a Sefirah, they are not material objects subject to the forms within space-time that they themselves create. And yet, the Sefirot are the souls of the material Letters which are the composite forms making up everything in our space-time multiverse.

Throughout our lessons here we have discussed the Kavod of YHWH, and we have identified this to be a tangible, manifest form of energy that is visible and definable here in our physical space. The Kavod of YHWH is also considered to be the Sefirah Malkhut. Now, this is not the place to elaborate on Malkhut. We will do this in our upcoming lesson on Malkhut. But our text here identifies one of the origins of the name Sefirot as coming from Exodus 28:18, and the word Sapir, sapphire.

We all know that sapphire is a gem stone. And a gem stone is not a Sefirah! And yet, Exodus 24:10 relates to us a strange vision experienced by Moses, Aaron, Nadav, Avihu and the seventy Elders of Israel at Mt. Sinai. *"And they saw the God of Israel, and under His feet was the likeness of a sapphire stone, like the very sky for purity."*

They saw YHWH and His footstool looked like a sapphire stone. The Torah text does not say that this was a vision subject to the laws of symbolisms and metaphors. No! Seventy-four people saw the same thing! This was no vision, this was tangible. So, what did they see?

I will not address the issue of what the God of Israel might have looked like to them, or what manifestation it really was. But this something that appears to be like sapphire stone at His feet, this is God's footstool, His Malkhut, and as we see this sapphire-like "whatever-it-is" is something actual and not just visionary and symbolic.

The image of what appeared to be a sapphire stone is the tangible form Malkhut in our Asiyatic space-time. Essentially, it is the Keter of the Malkhut. This is the Kavod, the Glory of YHWH, and we know how dangerous the Kavod is. The sapphire stone is the actual source of life-force energy here in this physical dimension. The sapphire stone seen at Sinai is the fifth element above the four forms of matter: fire, air, water, and earth. The sapphire stone is the Hiyuli Prima-Matter spoke of in Genesis. It is the Even Shetiyah (the Foundation Stone) upon which creation is built.

Throughout human history, in cultures around the world, the sapphire stone has come to be known by many other names. It is the source of life-force energy that today we call by many different names, such as Nefesh, qi, prana, vril, orgone, and kundalini. Being that this "stone" is so powerful, its secret has been sought after throughout history with many claiming to have discovered its power, and then using such power for both the good and the holy, as well as for nefarious, evil purposes. Maybe this Even Shetiyah is the famous Philosopher's Stone of Alchemy.

The sapphire stone, the Livnat Sapir, is the manifestation of the Sefirah Malkhut here in Asiyah. It is the fifth element, the Prima Matter, the Hiyuli, the Nefesh and the Qi. It is the source of Malkhut, and all the Ten Sefirot within it.

All of Malkhut is the world of Asiyah. The world of Asiyah is the world of matter. However, not all matter is visible and tangible within the very limited percentage of Asiyah that we inhabit and know (the Malkhut of Asiyah). There are higher levels within Asiyah itself which are, at present, unknown to us. The sapphire stone is thus not a rock as we would understand a physical object. The Even Shetiyah is not a physical rock on the Temple Mount in Jerusalem.

The sapphire stone is the Even Shetiyah Foundation Stone, but it is not a tangible physical object here in the Malkhut of Asiyah. The sapphire stone represents the Keter of Asiyah, and is thus material, but not by any definition that we can describe. The sapphire stone is pure life-force energy, it is the Prima-Matter, it is the Kavod of YHWH, and it, in and of itself, is very much alive!

The sapphire stone is the conduit connection point between Asiyah and Yetzirah. It is the place where Metatron meets Sandalphon, and where Z.A. meets Nok. The stone is not a physical one that can be picked up and embraced. But the stone may be discovered by identifying its true essence and then seeking it. The sapphire stone is thus the life-force energy that permeates all of creation. One who can tap into this universal energy can, through it, control everything in the Asiyatic world. This is just one of the secrets of the Ark of the Covenant.

The Sefirot in general all act as one. The Sefirot in general interact with one another. Therefore, human activity in its many manifestations, all have influence on the corresponding aspects within the Sefirot, throughout correlating elements in all the worlds. Thus reality as we know it does, in a way, act somewhat mechanical. By this I mean that there is direct cause and effect between what we do, and what happens to us.

This relationship does not have to manifest in any way that we may see and understand within the limited scope of our perceptions of reality. Past, present, future, far, and near are all realities subject to the Divine Eye and Heavenly Judgement. We do not necessarily see how all the pieces of the universal puzzle fit together, but they do!

Destiny, fate, and karma are real! Just as an individual can act in ways to bring about one's destiny, fate, and karma, so too can one act in ways to bring about their nullification. This is the reality of the interactive nature of the Sefirot.

With regards to having the power of this stone falling into the wrong hands, our text states, *"And if the wicked and sinners proliferate throughout the land, then the world collapses. The Shekhina then cries out, my head is destroyed, my arm is destroyed."*

Many have tried to tap into the underlying energy of the universe and to manipulate it. Throughout history, this has been called magic. But there is no such thing as magic, there is only knowledge of manipulating the fifth element in order to influence, and reconstruct the others lower forms of matter (fire, air, water, and earth) that are beneath it. Those who engage in this activity without Heavenly consent, are performing strange and bizarre activities. They are performing strange works. In Hebrew, this is Avodah Zara, which we know better as idolatry. This is what our text is referring to.

This concludes our general understanding of the Sefirot. Let us proceed with our text and understand that our discussion of the Sefirot herein is going to be different from how the Sefirot are portrayed in later Kabbalistic literature. The schools of the philosophical Kabbalah understand the Sefirot as only being concepts to be discussed. They have no real first-hand experience with the Sefirot, and are thus not privy to the truths of their being.

Masekhet Atzilut 15

The First Triad of the Sefirot

"These are them. The first is called Keter. It is divided into 620 paths and beams of light. Regarding this it is written, "and the Ancient of Days sat; His raiment was as white as snow, and the hair of His head was like clean wool." (Daniel 7:9). Therein are the thirteen gates of wisdom and compassion that were referenced in the Torah by Moses our teacher, peace be upon him. Regarding this, they said, that which is too wondrous for you do not seek to elaborate upon it, for you have no business with hidden things.

The second. The Spirit of the Living God, Hokhma. It is divided into thirty-two paths of light. Therein are the depths of hidden wisdom, and perceived wisdom. "For with wisdom did God form the Earth" (Proverbs 3:19).

The third. "For, if you call for Binah (understanding)." (Proverbs 2:3). Therein are the pleasures of the World to Come, and the rest for souls. It is divided into three gates, Hokhma, Binah and Da'at. They are never parted. Regarding them it says, "Has the rain a father, or who begot the waves of dew?" (Job 38:28). Thus, "For YHWH gives wisdom; from His mouth [come forth] Da'at (knowledge) and Tevunah (discernment)." (Proverbs 2:6)."

Keter, Hokhma and Binah form an inseparable triad. Together, in later Kabbalah, they are called the Mohin (the brains). Yet, regardless of the time period or method of explanation, understanding the Sefirot is an internal exercise, and not an external academic course of study. The proof of this comes from the most obvious of places, this being the diagram of the Ten Sefirot themselves, which we have come to refer to as the Tree of Life.

When one looks at the diagram of the Ten Sefirot, one will notice that the diagram is never portrayed as being opposite one, but rather it is portrayed as if it is inside of one. As we know, the Sefirotic diagram has three columns, right, left and center. When someone, or something is standing opposite of you, then its right side is on the same side as your left, and vice a versa. Again, when a person is standing opposite you and he raises his right hand, his right hand is opposite your left hand. When, however that same person is facing the same direction as you, be it in front of you, or behind you (because according to our laws of physics one cannot stand in the same place as you), then when the person raises his right hand, it is on the same side as is your right hand. And so it is with the Sefirot.

When one looks at a diagram of the Ten Sefirot, the right column is always on one's right side, it is not opposite one, as would be someone or something facing you from the opposite side. Learn from this simple drawing arrangement that the Sefirot are always meant to be internalized, and not to be held out in front of one as if they are something external.

When discussing the Sefirot we describe their functions in the form of triads. For the function of Sefirot requires that there be right, left and center, which is the same as male, female, and balance. We may also view the triads as thesis, antithesis, and synthesis. Essentially this means that we begin with a position; the position (whatever it is) gives rise to its opposite. The two opposing positions then merge together in compromise which creates and manifests balance in the whole. Balance is achieved when the polarity of opposites is compromised. While both polarities continue to be what they are, nevertheless, once they merge, they metaphorically give birth to something new, which takes on a life and identity of its own. This is the way of nature and of the universe. Reality is like this because reality is a reflection of Sefirot which underlie it.

The first Sefirah is Keter, which means crown. Keter is the Divine Will. It is the Primordial Pattern. Yet, as a crown upon the head, it is not really a part of the body. Being that all Ten Sefirot correspond to parts of the human body, the Keter is unique in that it does not correspond to any body part at all. Some consider the Keter to be represented by the skull itself. And in the world of metaphors, one set of symbols may or may not be as good as another. We consider the Keter to be part of Active Intelligence, however collective, and unconscious this may be. Keter is certainly not dry bone. Therefore it is best to be aware of the Mohin status of Keter, and to visualize it in your mind's eye as a vibrant, thinking Life-function.

Being that Keter sits on top of the body outside of it, Kabbalists have debated the question of whether or not Keter is actually a part of the Creator, or is it part of creation. This discussion continued to the days of R. Hayim Vital. While Keter is never considered to be part of the Divine, still, it is never counted in the enumerations of the lower worlds. Keter is thus somewhere in between.

In the later Kabbalah, Keter is called Adam Kadmon. A.K. is always portrayed as its own world, one that is above the world of the Divine, which is Atzilut. The Ayn Sof manifested Adam Kadmon, and from A.K. came forth the worlds of Atzilut (and below).

In Zoharic Kabbalah and the later Kabbalah based upon it, we have introduced to us the concept of Partzufim, the Sefirotic Faces. Adam Kadmon is one of these Faces. The Sefirah Keter in Lurianic Kabbalah is divided into four Partzufim. These are Atik Yomin and its Female counterpart, and Arikh Anpin and its Female counterpart. To elaborate on all the Lurianic concepts would require a book of its own. This I have already provided with my book, The Evolution of God. Students interested in more of the academic approach to this topic can reference my work there.

When it comes to prophetic experience, the Sefirah Keter is beyond the grasp of human imagination. Yes, Keter can be conceived, in other words we can, and do, perceive images within our minds that enable us to acknowledge Keter's existence (otherwise how else would we know that it was there). But as for the depths of its being, this is beyond human comprehension. Even the Ancient of Days vision experienced by Daniel is considered to only be a vision of the Keter as it is perceived in the World of Asiyah, or in other words the Keter of the Malkhut. While this is truly a lofty experience, it is still Asiyatic in nature, and Asiyah is the lowest of the four worlds.

The 620 paths are mentioned because the word Keter, spelled Kaf, Tav, Resh is numerically equal to 620. Like with so many other numerical references, this one is also merely symbolic, and not actual. No one has ever enumerated the 620 paths, one by one, and most likely no one ever will. They are a symbol representing the flow of the unfiltered, pure Divine mercy, from the highest Source emanating out to the lowest recipients.

The thirteen gates of wisdom and compassion are associated with two sources in the Bible. The first one is from Exodus (34:6-7), which states, *"YHWH, YHWH, benevolent God, Who is compassionate and gracious, slow to anger and abundant in loving kindness and truth, preserving loving kindness for thousands, forgiving iniquity and rebellion and sin."* The second one is from the book of Micah (7:18), which states, *"Who is a God like You, Who forgives iniquity and passes over the transgression of the remnant of His heritage? He does not maintain His anger forever, for He desires loving-kindness."* Both of these are said to be the thirteen attributes of Divine Mercy. Of course, the later Kabbalah differentiates between them and corresponds the one in Micah with Arikh Anpin, and the one in Exodus with Zeir Anpin (Z.A.). As for why this is so, this is not our concern here.

I have elaborated what we need to know and understand about the Sefirah Keter for our purposes of experiential Prophetic Kabbalah. Keter is the Source, the Kernel, the Seed from which comes forth everything. Keter is the Prima-Matter, the Hiyuli, the fifth Partzuf (and element in Asiyah). Tapping into Keter cannot be accomplished directly, such a connection can only come through both Hokhma and Binah. So let us proceed to discuss their functions in this Primary Triad of Sefirotic Mohin.

Hokhma is the spirit of the Living God. This language is borrowed from the Sefer Yetzirah. Hokhma is the spark or portion of Keter that can be received, and perceived within human consciousness. Due to its sublime nature, the revelation of Hokhma is far too expansive to be congealed into rational consciousness. Therefore, Hokhma is a stream of consciousness all its own. We call it intuition, inner-knowing, and psychic or clairvoyant awareness.

The Thirty-two Paths of Wisdom are enumerated in some places. They are referred to as Sekhelim, which means brains. While in some literature their names are enumerated with very minor descriptions, no elaborated explanations are given of them. What we can conclude from such a list is that they represent subtle shifts in consciousness experienced while gazing into the unknown. I do not consider it a worthwhile endeavor to try to elaborate in any rational sense the differences between subtle shift of consciousness. I consider this to be contradictory.

Like I mentioned earlier with regards to symbolic numbers, thirty-two as a special number has its source in the Sefer Yetzirah, which speaks in Chapter One of the thirty-two wondrous paths. Elaborated there, these paths are the ten Sefirot themselves, along with the twenty-two letters of the Hebrew Alef-bet

Hokhma corresponds to the unconscious in our human experience. We cannot rationally elaborate on unconscious operations because they are supra-rational. They are above rationality. If one wishes to make any rational sense of unconscious Hokhma content, then one needs to proceed outside of Hokhma and into our next Sefirah, Binah. For it is in Binah that Keter within Hokhma can be finally perceived and given some semblance of form.

As Rabbi Moshe Cordovero once wrote, Keter is the "I," Hokhma is the "I Am," and Binah is the "I Am What I Am." This simple statement so eloquently sums up this first Sefirotic Triad of the Mohin. This shows how the three operate as one, and why each one needs the other. The three are a progression of consciousness that begins with "what is" and concludes with the awareness and recognition of "what is." This is the process of human thought and recognition. We are created in the Divine Image, and as the Divine Image "thinks and cognizes thought," so too do we, following in accordance to the Pattern above.

Keter is the Collective Unconscious. Hokhma is the Archetypes of the Collective Unconscious, and Binah is the Higher Self which is the individual and unique recipient of the Collective content specialized for the Individual Self.

The Sefirah Binah represents that realm within the mind wherein which psychic intuitive revelations from above (and beyond), meet and merge with rational, and intelligent information gathered from the outside (physical) world around us.

Binah is the conscious mind. It is the conscious mind of our lower selves existing presently here on Earth in these physical bodies (the Neshama of the Nefesh). It is also is the fullness of our Higher Selves, our Neshama soul, that exists in a higher reality, which our text here refers to as, the World to Come, and the rest for souls. Binah consciousness in the Neshama is the Upper Garden of Eden, which is the domain of the Higher Self.

Now, this Upper Garden of Eden, this World to Come, this Rest for Souls, is not a place of residency. No soul goes to this place, acquires a house (or apartment) there, and resides there (in Heaven) happily ever after. Again, such childish fantasies need to be put aside. This realm of Binah consciousness, the World to Come, the Upper Garden of Eden, is a state of consciousness achieved by the aspiring, ascending soul as it matures and awakens from the sleep in Nefesh consciousness.

Thus, the awakened soul, in an after-life beyond all reincarnations, achieves a level of awareness that enables it to function as the conduit (vessel, Merkava) for the higher emanations coming into creation directly from the Creator. Neshama souls are Beriatic. As such they serve as the Kiseh HaKavod (the Throne of Glory) for receiving the Shekhina (the Malkhut of Atzilut), and then directing its emanations to the lower worlds.

All this happens on both the greater cosmic scale in the universe, and correspondingly on the human scale within our individual minds and consciousness here in these physical bodies, here on Earth.

Keter, Hokhma, and Binah form the Primary Sefirotic Triad of the Mind. As it is above, so is it below. This Triad operates in one grand form in the greater universe, and in a corresponding smaller form within the inner universe of our present human experience. The Pattern repeats itself over and over again, in higher and lower forms. And thus we have Sefirot within Sefirot, and Sefirot within Sefirot within Sefirot, and onwards out to infinity.

Understanding this Triad academically is one thing. But in order for its reality to sink deep within one's consciousness, one needs to witness and to experience the triadic process in operation. This is one of the purposes of meditation. We actually watch ourselves think. We observe how it is that we think, and why it is that we think the way that we do. We pay attention to the subtle impressions being made by unconscious content, possibly coming from our internal Keter (collective content), and we learn how to differentiate those impressions from others emanating from our internal Hokhma (individual content).

We then imagine, and contemplate, and imagine and contemplate some more. Back and forth we move in the thinking process. This is the Sekhel Tenudah, the Oscillating consciousness that, like a pendulum, swings back and forth between Binah and Hokhma, and from Hokhma to Binah. This is what the Sefer Yetzirah (1:4) refers to when it says, *"understand with wisdom, and be wise with understanding."* The one who can perform this function is ready for the next step and this will bring us into our discussion in the next (two) Triads of the Sefirot of the Heart.

Masekhet Atzilut 16

HaGat NaHiY,
the Lower & Middle Sefirotic Triads

The Fourth. Mercy (Hesed) to Avraham (Micah 7:20). This is the attribute of our father Avraham. Water of rest and joy. [It is] called the Right [side or hand] of the Holy One, blessed be He, as it is written (Isaiah 62:8), "YHWH swore by His right hand."

The Fifth. The Fear (Pahad) of Isaac, father of Jacob. This is the attribute of our father Isaac who was bound [upon the altar] by [his father] Abraham. Therein is scorching fire, for YHWH is a devouring fire (Deut. 4:24). [It is] called the Left [side or hand] of the Holy One, blessed be He, as it is written, (Isaiah 62:8), "the arm of His strength."

The Sixth. Glory/Beauty (Tiferet). "And it is his glory to pass over a transgression" (Proverbs 19:11). This is the attribute of our father Jacob. From here was the Torah of Moses our teacher given. It is called the Heart of Heaven, regarding this it is written (Isaiah 44:13), "like the beauty of man to sit [in] the house."

The Seventh. [The] Victory (Netzah) of Israel will not lie. This is the attribute of Moses our teacher, upon him be peace. In his merit did the manna descend from Heaven, that grinds the manna for the righteous.

The Eight. [The] Splendor (Hod) and Majesty of the Holy One, blessed be He. This is the attribute of Aaron, upon him be peace. In his merit there were six clouds covering over Israel in the wilderness.

Regarding them is it written, (Song of Songs 5:15), "His legs are [as] pillars of marble."

The Ninth. [The] Righteous [is the] foundation (Yesod) of the world. This is the attribute of Yosef the Righteous (Tzadik), upon him be peace. From herein comes all the influences of the mercy, grace, and severity of the Holy One, blessed be He. [From here comes] sustenance and support to Collective Israel (Knesset Yisrael). Regarding this it is written (Judges 6:24), "and he called it, "YHWH peace (Shalom)."And it is [also] says (Genesis 28:12), "and its top reached to Heaven."

As can be seen, the six Sefirot (and we shall see even with Malkhut) are not extensively elaborated here in our text. The details given for each one is minimum in comparison to later sources. This has not gone unnoticed.

When Masekhet Atzilut was published within the Yalkut HaRo'im (from where I have taken our text), this section of the text has added to it two extra commentaries in order to elaborate on the subject matter. The two commentary texts are from the Tomer Devorah of R. Moshe Cordovero, and an explanation of the Sefirot authored by the M'har'shal, R. Shlomo Luria. These join the Ginzei Meromim commentary by R. Haber. To give you a flavor of the original, the Hebrew text covering the six Sefirot consists of about 130 words. It is short, simple, and direct. The three commentaries that discuss these 130 words is about thirteen (13) pages long. Apparently, our commentators have a lot more to say than did our original author.

Now, here I am writing my own commentary, and I myself am faced with a question. Should I stay close to the text, and only comment upon what it says? Doing this would be consistent with writing a proper commentary. I could also chose to elaborate on the Sefirot as did my esteemed colleagues before me. What they have written is of great value, and offers a number of contemplative insights. I could follow in their footsteps, and do the same. But I have already done this.

In my books, Yikra B'Shmi, Walking in the Fire, and The Evolution of God, I have discussed the Sefirot in detail. Indeed, even in my book, The Kabbalah of Relationships, I discussed the Sefirot in relationship to personality attributes. I will recommend to my readers to consult my other writings for more elaborations about the Sefirot. So, again, I am left with a decision to make, what I am supposed to write here?

As my reader can see, this is one of those rare occurrences where I am sharing in writing my thoughts as I write them. I am not doing this to waste your time or my own, but rather as my way of introducing to you what I am here now going to share with you about the Sefirot.

This commentary has been written to emphasize the practical, experiential side of our Torah, which we call today Prophetic Kabbalah. Again, the emphasis is on practice, and not just theory, not just talk. Needless to say, here (in short words) I will continue with this method and assist my readers in understanding how to experience the Sefirot moving within one, as opposed to them being mere external cosmological forces of universal energy.

It is very nice that the Sefirot are "out-there." But we need to understand them "in-here," meaning inside ourselves. And with doing this, we must be cautious to not limit the Sefirot to be attributes of personality that one must aspire to embrace (which is the path of the Tomer Devorah). Being that R. Cordovero has done such excellent work along this line who can come along and offer anything of equal value.

So, here, I offer you no elaborate metaphysics or philosophy, and no self-help style psychology. Let's get prophetic, let's go another way, and see if we can learn to sense the Sefirot within us. We begin this journey by my explaining to you how this path was chosen and selected. As I go through my thought process of selection to discern and to differentiate, so too must each of you, my readers. So, learn from my experience, and do the same. And now, let us proceed.

As with the First Triad of Sefirot, the next six form two triads. We thus have three triads of three each. We began with the Thesis of Keter, but it did not divest itself into Antithesis and Synthesis. We will see that our two Triads here do this. But with the first

Triad, the brains, we see a different process of manifestation. We see there the dawn and development of conscious, be it Divine, universal, or in a minute form, human.

Thought went from "I" to "I Am," and finally to "I Am what I Am." And now that this cognition has found itself (in Binah), we must translate cognition into action. In order for this process to occur, the abstract energy of thought must become concrete and directed in order to form action. Action, as we will see is Malkhut. But thought must be energized in order to manifest into action. This energy of which we speak, (and I will borrow the familiar language of the later Kabbalah to help make understanding easier for us) is Yetziratic. In other words, it is sexual!

Masekhet Atzilut does not elaborate on the process of energetic Sefirotic manifestations in this world, or in any other. The one thing that the text places emphasis on is upon identifying each Sefirah with its relative archetypal Patriarch, and is correlative associations within Judaism. And this is about it.

This association of Patriarch with Sefirah becomes an integrated element within later Kabbalah and Judaism. We are all familiar with the tradition of inviting in the Seven Guests (Sheva Ushpizin) during the nights of the Succot holiday. And nowhere in all this symbolism is there any real explanation, discussion, and most certainly no experience of actual Sefirotic energetic interactions.

So, let's change this now. Our first Sefirah is Hesed, it is called God's right Hand. Nice symbol, needless to say, no physical reality to it. Hesed is a moving Force. It is the first manifestation that expresses the thought of the conscious mind. Hesed is the outgoing Force that seeks to manifest the Thought within Binah. And so the Force flows outward seeking its materialization.

But we must remember the nature of Binah. Binah is not an outgoing Force, it is rather an ingathering Force. Binah congeals the outgoing Force of Hokhma. Now, Binah's "child" Hesed expands out, acting like its "father" Hokhma. But Hesed also has a portion of its "mom" within it. As such, as Hesed expands outward, there arises within it its opposite, which is the Force to cease expansion, and to instead contract. And thus Gevurah is born.

With Hesed and Gevurah we now have what we can call Thesis and Antithesis. Both of these Forces, in their primal state struggle with one another, seeking the balance of Tiferet which is to come. Inside of us, the primal Forces of expansion (Hesed) and contraction (Gevurah) are experienced beneath the levels of consciousness. As such they are unconscious motivators, beyond our conscious reach of analytical examination.

In meditation, one contemplates one's thoughts, trying to analyze where they come from, and why one thinks the way that one does. Eventually one comes to a "wall" of-sorts wherein one concludes that one thinks the way that one does because this is the way that one is, with no further analysis or break-down possible. I am the way I am because that is the way that I am. When one has reached this point, one has touched one's inner Tiferet. Tiferet is that internal place, wherein which the Thesis of Hesed, and the Antithesis of Gevurah meet to manifest the Synthesis, which is you (the higher You)!

Hesed and Gevurah are the Supernal Forces above that work within us below. We symbolically call them the Right and Left Hands of God. Essentially, this is how God works within human psychology.

There is the expanding, out-going force that seeks to include all, and then opposite it is the constricting, in-gathering force that seeks to exclude. Naturally and normally, these are supposed to balance in Tiferet, which as we see, is symbolized by Jacob, who becomes Israel.

Thus Israel is Sefirotically defined as the one who finds and maintains true and proper inner balance. I have on many occasions written about the difference between physical Israel (the descendants of all 12 tribes), and "spiritual" Israel, those who like the (archetypal) Patriarch Jacob captures inner control by defeating the enemy who attacks both internally and externally.

Tiferet and Israel is thus the source of the Torah. The Torah is the universal Form of balance. Balance is justice, judgment, law, and mercy all rolled up into one.

Our society today expresses a pathological absence of Tiferet/balance. The Forces of internal Hesed and Gevurah struggle within each one's unconscious. This leads to struggles in world outlooks, political orientations, and social upheavals.

Hesed and Gevurah are the primal Forces of unconscious libido energy. As such they are creative Forces, each in their own way. As creative forces they are sexual by nature. However because they are unconsciously felt as opposed to cognitively understood, they are not experienced as carnal forces, meaning as a desire for any kind of physical sexuality. Yet, they are the underlying energy Forces beneath all types of behaviors that leads towards sexuality and violence, and as we often see, the unhealthy combination of the two.

Without Tiferet to balance them, and to keep them in check, we have nothing but chaos, or as Genesis would say, "tohu v'bohu" (chaos and confusion). This is why the powers that dominate this world seek to block any access to Tiferet, be it in the form of believing the Bible, observing the Biblical commandments, or by embracing Biblical archetypes as role models for behavior.

By removing Tiferet, the "powers that be" can replace Holy Tiferet with a counterfeit Tiferet of their own, and thus siphon off for themselves the flow of supernal Sefirotic energy, using it for their own ends, instead of those of Heaven. And with this insight I have already revealed too much. Yes, there are the Dark Sefirot of the "Other Side." But this is not the place to elaborate upon them. Just let it be known that they exist, and that we do have the internal sensitivity to recognize the counterfeit and to distinguish it from the authentic. And as we say in our Havdalah prayers, Barukh HaMavdil Beyn Kodesh l'Hol.

Tiferet becomes the conduit of identity. Thus it is identified as the Higher Self. In later Kabbalistic literature, Tiferet is associated with Supernal Man, who as we know is Zeir Anpin, the lower reflection (Face) of the original Divine Will of Keter (inside the mask/Partzuf of Arikh Anpin).

Tiferet is both concealed and revealed. It is the place where contemplative meditation reaches one's inner Self. But in order to arrive at this point of consciousness one must first ascend through the lower Triad of Sefirot, which consists of Netzah, Hod, and Yesod, known to us as NaHiY. (I did not think it necessary to spell out that Hesed, Gevurah, and Tiferet are known to us as HaGaT. This should already be clear without having to mention it).

Tiferet is the actualization of Keter. It is the heart of the matter, and thus the place of balance and the center. In order to manifest Tiferet into physical matter (into Malkhut, its physical form), it must repeat the process of expansion, contraction, and balance. This forms the Sefirotic Triad of NaHiY. NaHiY are energetic influences, the likes of which are manifest, and can be experienced, brought into consciousness, and from there, controlled.

Once awareness of the higher Self is touched, there is born along with it an intense desire to manifest it and bring it into manifestation in physical space-time. This force is Netzah. It seeks to impose the Tiferet inner vision upon external reality, reformatting it into alignment with the inner vision.

This Netzah force of imposition is an expansive force, just as is Hesed and Hokhma. This collection of expansive force makes up the right column of the Sefirotic Tree, and is called HaHaN (for Hokhma, Hesed, and Netzah). But as with Hesed above it, Netzah too has limits to its expansion. This then activates the contracting force of Hod.

Hod and Netzah always go hand-in-hand. For Netzah expands outward so as to impose the image of Tiferet, but to what end is this being done? Netzah expands outwards for the betterment of all below. The benefits from above, the rewards, and the beauty thereof, these are Hod. Netzah expands out, Hod contracts in, the two together work in complete unison.

Hod force seeks to build beautiful things, be they physical, or otherwise. Hod and Netzah are like husband and wife. Netzah goes out and conquers. Hod gathers in all that has been conquered and builds something beautiful out of it. Netzah imposes the good of Tiferet so that Hod can manifest that good in a tangible manner.

As the "right" and "left" Hands of Tiferet (Zeir Anpin), Netzah and Hod are the vessels through which the revelation of Tiferet is experienced. As such, Netzah and Hod are considered to be the source of manifestation for prophecy. Yet, before one can achieve clear insight into the Netzah and Hod benefits that Tiferet (one's own higher Self) can provide, one must first gather in the necessary energy and Supernal radiance that originated with Keter, and has now pooled itself, revealed, understood, and focused in the conduit between the physical and energetic universes, this is Yesod.

Yesod is pure and simple life-force energy. It is the energy conduit at the "bottom of the ladder of ascent." As such, in the human body it is found beneath the base of the spine, in that place where the energy emanating from above (on the face side), reverses direction and seeks to ascend above (on the back side, up the spine). In the human body, this place is the seat of biological reproduction, the genitalia.

Sex is such a potent force because it is here in this energy field, and in its corresponding human anatomy that the entire pattern of the Sefirotic Tree converges and seeks to bring into form (birth) that which began in thought. Yesod is pure libido in the form of creative energy. Yesod is the passion to make something, whatever that something is, be it art, music, literature, or any other creative endeavor, including scientific discovery.

Most human beings are oblivious to the higher and subtler energy forces within sexual/libido energy. Therefore, when the urge for sexual intercourse arises, most find themselves incapable of expressing any resistance, and surrender to releasing the energy downward, instead of rechanneling it into a better form of creative expression. This is how Yesod energy is wasted.

Yesod energy is both inside and not inside the act of sexual intercourse. It is in it and above it at the same time. Thus in order for one to collect enough psychic energy in order to attempt authentic Merkava ascents, one must consolidate one's sexual energy, and direct it upwards into more sublime forms than just being released in the acts of sexual orgasm.

This is why sexual chastity is so very important in the Torah tradition, especially in the Kabbalah. One who master this balance is one who anchors the entire Sefirotic Tree of Life and establishes its balance here on Earth. Being that it is the conduit between Asiyah and Yetzirah, one who anchors and balances the energy earn the title of Tzadik, the righteous one, who is always doing the right things.

This is how the Sefirot can be experienced within us through a constant cultivation of personal sensitivity. One needs to not think about what is going on inside one; one needs to feel it. One needs to pay attention to how one feels at any given moment of the day, and to not only sense one's feelings but to also understand them, and their ramifications.

One who cultivates this attention will align one's Malkhut, with one's Yesod, and then with one's Tiferet. Higher than this goes into the realm of the concealed. We cannot see alignment there, but we can indeed feel it! And feeling is what we need to develop.

One last word. When I speak of feeling something, I am not speaking about one's emotions. Emotions and feelings are two very different things. Learn to transcend and see beyond your emotions. Recognize their relative, subjective, and minor significance, and move beyond them.

Seek balance: Tiferet. Calm and balance your emotions. Seek to sense beyond them. This is how we build up Sefirotic sensitivity within ourselves. When this gets accomplished, one can then take the next step, and that is to place the crown (Keter) upon the head of the Queen (Malkhut), as we shall see.

Masekhet Atzilut 17

Malkhut

"The tenth. His Kingdom (Malkhut) is the Kingdom over all worlds. For all of them give radiance and blessing to Her through the attribute of peace that makes peace between Knesset Yisrael and the Holy One, blessed be He.

Therein enter the voices of prayer and supplication. Therein is the reward and punishment of the righteous and justice. It says, "Righteousness and justice are the base of Your throne." (Psalm 89:15).

Therein is the attribute of King David, upon him be peace. Regarding him, it says, "in this I am confident." (Psalm 27:3). "This is from God." (Psalm 118:23)."

Malkhut, is as the song L'kha Dodi says, the final act of creation, which was at the same time, the first thought. In other words, the entire process of creation, and the reason for the existence of the higher dimensions is all for the sake of this physical world.

Malkhut is the place where opposing energy fields, and opposites of all kinds have the potential to meet, interact, and to possibly influence and change one another. We must understand why this is so important, and why this can only happen in a dimension of physical spacetime (and thus the importance of Malkhut/Asiyah).

In energetic worlds, closeness is defined by similarity. Thus the similar can get close, but the different cannot. And the greater the difference, the greater the distance.

In the physical dimension, closeness is defined by physical proximity. Two things, however different, or even opposite, while encased in physical from, can have these physical form vessels draw close to one another, and even touch, all the while that the energies within them remain very distant. But being that their vessels can draw close, the energies within the vessels can also draw close to one another. They can interact with one another, which is something impossible to do in the higher domains. When the two can draw close, then that which was far away can be drawn close, and that which is radically different has the chance to become similar. And this is important, for how else can Yihud (unity) be accomplished?

Malkhut, therefore, provides an opportunity for change, transformation, and the reunion of opposites. The unity that was originally desired in Keter, now has the potential to become fully functional and real in physical form here in Malkhut.

Malkhut is indeed a Kingdom. A kingdom is a unified whole that is controlled by a Single Authority. A kingdom is a microcosm of the world, it has everything in it. The Sefirah Malkhut, in this respect, is no different. Malkhut contains everything within itself. It is thus the final receiver of the influx from all the higher realms.

It is in Malkhut, the bottom, where the energy from on top reverses polarity and begins its ascent back up. Keter manifests Ohr Yashar (descending Light from Keter to Malkhut). Malkhut manifests Ohr Hozer (ascending Light from Malkhut to Keter). Malkhut completes the circuit, and when functioning properly it serves as the anchor to hold together the entire system of creation.

As the Divine energy (Shefa) begins its descent into lower worlds, it begins to shift into its opposite. This is by Divine design so that all possible forms can become manifest (as described in Sefer Yetzirah). The Light of the Ayn Sof is 100% in one way. The Light of Atzilut is 90% this way. Beriah is 80% this way. Yetzirah is 50% this way. Asiyah is 10% this way. All the percentages are only symbolic and approximate. I use this example to help make clear my point.

As Light descends it is lessened in degree by Divine design. By the time the Light reaches Asiyah its manifestation is far different from how it was manifested when it first emanated out of Adam Kadmon and into Atzilut. And now that the Light has reached the depths of Asiyah it can experience the opportunity to become manifest in all its potential forms. The Light now continues its diversification, but only in reverse.

As the Light again become more and more like what it once was, this is called Ascent. So, Malkhut becomes the point where the diversification of Light shifts from outward expansion and into inward ascent. This would make the Ohr Hozer to be Din (contraction as opposed to expansion). This is why in this world, in order to elevate Light, we human beings, who are the conduits for this action, must act in specific and defined ritual ways, be these the observance of Halakha, the maintenance of proper morality, and most certainly the expressions of righteous behavior. These are the vessels that capture the Divine Light and allow it to naturally transform back out of the physical as it ascends into the Yetziratic emotional dimension, and beyond.

Malkhut is properly referred to as "Sof Ma'aseh, b'Mahshava Tehilah" (last action, first thought). Consider Malkhut to be the final extension of an exhale, which then naturally leads its opposite, the inhale. Malkhut completes the process of creation, by providing complete vessels through which all potential manifest forms can actualize, and then interact with one another, regardless of how opposite one another they might be.

The merging of opposites can only occur in Malkhut because Malkhut is at the bottom of the Sefirotic cycle. Thus it originates the contracting Ohr Hozer. This Ohr Hozer (contracting force) exerts influence over the opposites that were each pushed in the direction of their (opposing) polarities by the downward flowing expansive Ohr Yashar. Malkhut exerts the influence of slowing down, and contracting the expansiveness of the original Keter, just like Gevurah performs the same function to its expansive opposite,

Hesed. Malkhut is thus the essential conclusion of the whole process of creation.

We can compass this movement to the face of a clock. As we know the Hour 12 stands at the top of a clock face, with Hour 6 being at the bottom, and Hours 3 & 9 being at opposite right angles (3 to the right, 9 to the left). Using this example, we would say that Light enters into the clock face at Hour 12, the top. It then begins its progression down the right side, from 1 to 2 to 3, all the way down to 6 at the bottom. Once the Light reaches 6 at the bottom, it then begins to ascend the other side of the clock face, until it again reaches 12.

So, using this analogy, the right side of the clock face going down from 12 to 6 is Ohr Yashar, and the left side of the clock face going back up from 6 to 12 is Ohr Hozer. Both sides of the clock face are equally essential. In fact, one cannot have a clock face at all unless we use this cyclical method of representation. On the clock face 6 is not inferior to 12, any more than 3 or 9 are inferior or superior to one another. And so it is with the Sefirot.

Human souls originally volunteered to incarnate in physical vessels (bodies) here on Earth to contribute to the effort of recycling the Divine Light. Human souls emanate from a very high source above (the Image of God within us). As such human souls have the power to incarnate into the Malkhut level without being crushed by the inversion of the original Light that exists here.

The full "weight" of the Tree of the Sefirot falls into Malkhut causing the full permutation of forms, giving rise to what we can call the existence of the twisted and the evil. All souls coming into this plane in order to contribute to the reversal of Ohr Yashar to Ohr Hozer must be able to stand up under the pressure of the descending Light. It can and does crush many different lifeforms twisting them out of their original forms (and into other forms that we call evil).

Remember what happened to the fallen angels referenced in Genesis 6. They wanted to incarnate on Earth with all good intentions. Yet, their souls were not strong enough to tolerate the pressure exerted upon them by the nature of Malkhut. As such they succumbed to the crushing force of Malkhut, and were twisted. Only stronger souls could withstand the force. Those souls are us, and judging from the entire course of recorded human history, our human souls, have had a very rough time at it.

Our present state of human existence is called by the secret Kabbalists, the Shemitah (epoch) of Gevurah. We must understand that the Shemitot are not to be measured on a timeline, measured in years. Shemitot are actually levels of collective consciousness. We are (collectively) going through a cycle of human evolution which requires of us an adjustment period to get used to the crushing force of Malkhut. Thus for us, at this time, we are experiencing all the destructive potentialities that the world of forms can concoct.

Once we have achieved the collective ability to tolerate the Malkhut force, humanity as a whole will be able to get to work, and actively serve as the conduits of ascent, capturing the descending Ohr Yashar, and redirecting its flow into Ohr Hozer.

As this is accomplished, all the opposites that came into being in the Ohr Yashar downward flow can now start to reintegrate with one another. But now, each opposite is wiser from the experiences of their original individuated states. Now, as they ascend, they can recognize the nature of their opposites within their very own selves. Thus the hostilities of isolation (Din) are neutralized, and a reintegration towards unity occurs, this time with each part being aware of, and respectful towards, all other parts. This is the whole of the process of creation, the Sof Ma'aseh, b'Mahshava Tehila.

When collective humanity reaches the point of Malkhut tolerance, then Gevurah will be no more, and from a consciousness point of view we will enter into the Shemitah of Tiferet. We call this time era, the "days of Mashiah." How this will transpire, and what exactly are its details is something that only time itself will tell. In the meantime, we here to perform our righteous deeds, to observe commandments, and to do whatever else it takes for each of us, as individuals, to do in order to establish and maintain proper balance in Malkhut.

And so we have come full circle. Masekhet Atzilut begins with a lesson about the fear of God, and ends with a lesson about the Sefirah Malkhut, which our physical dimension is a part of. (Our physical dimension is the Malkhut of Malkhut, or the Malkhut of Asiyah). The fear of God specifically means that one aligns oneself with the Divine frequency that permeates all reality. Only one who does this here in our physical world can receive the radiating Divine influx from above, and work with it properly for the sake of the universal good.

Divine radiance is the force of Life itself. Divine radiance is itself sentient and intelligent. Not for naught do we call the Divine radiance the Presence of God, or as we say in Hebrew, the Shekhina.

The focus of my commentary to Masekhet Atzilut is not to simply provide my readers with educational information about an interesting topic. My focus is (and has always been) to inspire my reader to pursue spiritual experiences for oneself.

The Shekhina is a real and vital Living Force. The world calls the Shekhina by many other names, one of which is Mother Earth. I myself often use this term so as to make the Presence of the Shekhina to be more understood and welcomed. The Divine Presence is everywhere, and in everything, as it says, *the whole Earth is full of His Kavod*" (Isaiah 6:3).

We know that the Kavod of YHWH is the Divine Presence. We know that the Kavod is YHWH of BEN. We know that the Kavod, the Shekhina is Mother Earth. And we know that the Kavod, the Divine Presence is Malkhut, the very soul and consciousness of our planet Earth.

This is why God is always close. It cannot be any other way because God, here on Earth, is the Divine Presence, and the Divine Presence permeates all things. So as we have said, everything in reality, here on Earth, and maybe elsewhere in the galaxy is replete with what we call "the entrapped sparks of fallen light." And long ago, our human souls came down to Earth to regather these sparks of light and to elevate them back to their source, thus completing the great cycle of movement, or if you will, the Divine Breath of inhale and exhale.

These metaphors all point to the same truth. Each of us has work to do! This work is actual and tangible. And what we do influences multiple dimensions and worlds.

We are not alone. We are never alone. The power and Presence of the Divine is with us always. The Shekhina is the source of every atomic particle and structure that forms us. The Shekhina is the Life-force, the Nefesh, the Hiyuli, the Qi, the Prana, the Orgone, the Zero-Point energy, and the Kundalini. It doesn't matter what name the Presence has been given by the many nations over the many years. What does matter is that Malkhut, the Life-force is alive, sentient, intelligent, as is already (and always) in touch with us. It is now our job to get back in touch with it (Her).

To assist us in accomplishing this task, I have dedicated this commentary to Masekhet Atzilut. Like I say in the Introduction to this commentary, I emphatically do not follow in the footsteps of R. Haber's wonderful commentary, the Ginzei Meromim. His intent was to write an in-depth academic philosophical work, based upon the teachings of his master, Rabbi Eliyahu, the Gaon of Vilna.

R. Haber's intent was to demonstrate how the later Kabbalah of the Ari'zal is the present in, and thus is the correct way to interpret Masekhet Atzilut. I most certainly respect the Rabbi's choice, and highly praise his most esteemed work. But at the same time, I reiterate that one who interprets the past in the eyes of the future, does not see the past for what it truly was. I intentionally have tried to stay true to the original pre-Lurianic, and possibly pre-Zoharic intentions of our anonymous author. I sensed in his work that, like me centuries later, he too wanted to extend within his writing some underlying message of the importance of practice, and not just academic study.

And so, this is my final message that I leave you here with now. In the wise words of the great Sage Hillel (B. Shabat 31a), *"Zil Gamar"* go do it! And also as R. Tarphon said, *"It is not up to you to complete the work, but you are not free to avoid your share."* (Avot 2:16). So, my dear reader, you have work to do. So, get busy. Do it!

My blessings to you all. Shalom.
Ariel B. Tzadok. R. H. (1) Heshvan, 5783 (26 Oct. 2022)

SECTION TWO

THE UNVEILING OF THE VEILED

The Way of Psychic Warfare

<u>Chapter 1</u>

Defense Against Psychic Attack

War is a reality of life! It can never be avoided.

We all live everyday with rumors and threats of external wars. These may come and these may go. But there is another kind of war that is constant. It is not subject to rumor or threat. This kind of war is the most devastating. It is the war that causes the most harm, and creates the most casualties.

This constant war is an internal one.

Once I speak of an internal war, I suspect that most readers will automatically assume that I am speaking spiritually or psychologically about the war that one fights daily within oneself, against oneself. While this war does rage daily, this is not the war that I am speaking about.

There is another internal war fought within our minds that is not the one that we fight against ourselves. This other internal war is the one being fought against the many powers from outside of oneself that seeks to take control of one's mind to control and manipulate one's behavior. It is this war that is the deadliest.

An external threat to one's life, liberty, family, and belongings is often easy to identify. The internal struggle that one faces daily with regards to self-control and self-improvement is also one that is not too hard to identify and to address. But this other war, fought inside ourselves is against an external enemy who cannot be seen, and who cannot normally be detected.

This external enemy does not seek to attack us from the outside, but rather, this external enemy has the power to reach into our minds and attack us clandestinely from within. And we do not see it. Most even deny the presence and the existence of this enemy. And their denials often serve as the cause for even greater perils.

Many are afraid. Many do not even want to consider the possibility. But we are not the only intelligent, sentient race of beings indigenous to planet Earth. And in spite of whatever we may believe, we are not at the top of the food chain. Just like we eat other lower species, other higher species also eat us. It is just that the manner of their nourishment does not come from flesh like with us. Their manner of nourishment is energetic.

To put it simply, these other entities feed off human life-force energy. They literally suck the vigor, livelihood, and strength out of one's life-force energy. Throughout human history there have always been those who were (and are) aware of the existence and presence of these beings. Many interpret them to be evil spirits. But from the point of view of these entities, they do not look at themselves as being evil because they feed off of us, any more than we view ourselves as being evil because we feed off of our lower animals.

These entities are to us malevolent because they seek to control and manipulate us, and to cause us harm. But our harm is their good, so they feel justified to treat humanity in a similar manner to how we treat our animals.

It is easy and preferable to many to deny that such malevolent beings actually exist. But such denials come with a heavy price. Those who deny something obviously refuse to see it. But this does not make that which is denied go away. It only allows it to go about unseen, and to perform its activities unnoticed. And this is exactly what these malevolent beings want.

From the point of view of these malevolent beings, it is so much easier to control human beings who do not believe that they are being controlled. In this way, such people willingly and intentionally remain ignorant and docile. No better way to maintain slavery other than with slaves who believe themselves to be free.

The presence of malevolent beings is not an external reality that we seek to experience. We do not seek to physically enter into their domains, nor do we seek to call upon them to temporarily appear before us. We do not need such blunt verification of their existence and of their close presence.

These beings live right here on Earth side-by-side next to us. The only difference is that they are in a parallel dimension. Normally, they live out their lives in their dimension, and we live out our lives in ours. Normally, we do not seek to breach the barrier separating our worlds, but sometimes, some of us do.

On their side, they have knowledge, possibly natural, or even possibly technological, that enables them to breach the barrier between our dimensions with great ease. They come over here all the time. But the nature of their travel is not physical, it is what we call astral, or psychic. In other words, they project their thoughts and feelings onto and into hapless human beings, and like I said above, influence and direct their chosen human recipients in a similar manner as we would influence and direct animals under our control.

When we look for validation of their presence, we do not look outside ourselves, rather we look within. For not every thought, compulsion or temptation comes to us from within ourselves. Sometimes, such thoughts, ideas, feelings, or compulsions are coming from an outside force that is seeking to direct us from within.

On the outside, there seems to be no proof of such an internal intrusion (but when looked for carefully, some external markers may be evident). This is why the real war is with a hostile external force, but this force attacks us from within (psychically), and thus it is within us that this war must be fought, and won!

When the human mind is filled with confusion, it is easy to manipulate human will (and desire). Generally speaking, average people want to do what is right and good (as this is interpreted to be within their own minds). Thus, the one who can control what people think and how they think will also be able to control how one defines what is good and right.

When the internal workings of a person (or group) is thus controlled, the person or group can be told to act in whatever way that the malevolent ones want. And the individual or group will respond as stimulated and act in accordance to how they have been programmed. The individual or group will embrace and express every kind of wrong and evil behavior all the while thinking that what they are doing is right and good.

The individual or group is thus controlled and comes to act as the "hand" of the malevolent beings, serving them without any awareness of what it is that they are doing, or any realization of their manipulated condition. We have seen numerous examples of this in history on both the national and individual levels.

Now that we have identified the problem, let us consider what it is that the average person is able to do about it. First of all, we have to be realistic with expectations and potential goals. No one individual (or even a group) is going to stop what is happening around the world and what is directed from an interdimensional point of origin. The big picture is in the Hands of God to address. What the individual can address is what is happening in one's own life and in one's personal environment. We cannot change the world, but we can change ourselves.

Therefore, we need to identify and explore the psychic tools that each individual can cultivate in order to help extricate one from the vice-like grip that modern society has upon one's mind.

Needless to say the first step in emancipating the mind from its mental prison is for one to first realize that one's mind is indeed imprisoned. The nature of mind slavery and its many forms need to be recognized and acknowledged as such. No one ever gets free from a prison that one cannot see, or that one denies is truly there. Remember, this war is an internal war. It is fought in the mind, but the battleground also includes one's emotions, one's behavior, and one's place of residence.

You think that you own your own thoughts. You don't. Your thoughts are being influenced and molded by everything to which you are exposed. The entire genre of social information, social media, and entertainment are all designed (in detail) to ever-so-subtly manipulate one's thoughts, directing one to be sympathetic to certain causes, and to equally be hostile towards others. You are not making up your own mind as to what to think, you are being programmed what to think, and you do not even recognize the nature of the mind control.

Mind manipulation is everywhere and in everything. Such manipulation has been in use for decades. Every commercial and advertisement is an attempt to manipulate your mind and to control your actions. Every commercial and advertisement wants you to make use of their product(s). The subtle suggestion made by some sort of pictorial image is that if you use their product not only will you wonderfully enjoy it, but it will actually make you a fuller, more attractive, more desirable human being. None of these subtle promises are true. While we may acknowledge the truths of these statements, most are nevertheless victims of their influence.

One can take a college-level course on the topic of advertising, and one will see how manipulations are taught under the guise of being persuasive. Being that this is so prevalent today, no one seems to notice, and no one seems to care. No wonder why so many have heavy credit card debt because of items purchased that one does not need, and may even never use. This is evidence that many people act without thought and without regard for one's own personal welfare.

Defense against an enemy attacking one's mind is a battle that is fought within one's mind. A psychological operation seeks to instill fear within an opponent's thoughts. Make the opponent believe that he will fail no matter how hard he tries, and indeed, because he believes this, he will indeed fail no matter how hard he tries. You have convinced your enemy that he will be defeated. He believes you. He is thus defeated by his own thoughts. This is true within the context of all psychological battles that we each face daily in life.

Psychological warfare has been an integral part of physical combat since ancient times. Defeat the mind, and the armed resistance completely falls. Human militaries and famous generals have all used (and use to this day) all forms of psychological operations with tremendous success. If human beings can easily manipulate the minds of one another, we can only imagine how easy it is for higher dimensional (malevolent) beings to do the same in the psychic realm.

Psychic attacks follow the same methods as psychological manipulation. Convince the mind and the heart to believe certain things, and the individual thus becomes locked into a self-imposed prison of limited thinking. In order to set the mind free, one must be willing to accept two indisputable facts. Fact one is that indeed one's mind is imprisoned within false and limiting thoughts. Fact two is that one indeed does have the power and the ability to set one's mind free!

We are all subject to manipulative psychic attacks by others. These attacks are always malevolent. Unless they are properly addressed (in the psychic/spiritual domain) their negative and harmful influence can fester within someone like a cancer until it can eventually take one's life. Learning how to properly wield the tools used for psychic self-defense is a necessity for us all. This means that one must learn how to take control of one's own mind.

Real and relevant defense against psychic attack is a twofold process. Step one is that one must block out that which is attempting to come in. Step two is that one must go on the attack and strike back against the source of the psychic aggression. While many people talk about and train to accomplish step one, most are way too timid and afraid to even attempt to engage step two. And without a successful expression of step two, step one will also never be fully achieved.

Blocking out negative and harmful manipulations begins with setting up defensive parameters around the entrance ways that lead to the mind and the creation of its thoughts. These entrance ways are our senses that connect us with the external world. What we allow ourselves to see, and what we allow ourselves to hear are the two most important influences upon thought. One who takes control and voluntarily censors what one allows oneself to see, and equally voluntarily censors what one allows oneself to listen to, will realize that one can no longer be influenced by such external manipulative forces.

Remember this, once an external image or idea enters into your thoughts, higher dimensional (malevolent) beings who operate within your unconscious mind use these images and thoughts as their tools to manipulate your conscious mind. If you deprive them of their tools of operations, then you ae limiting their abilities to control your thoughts from within.

For example, pornographic images can easily influence one to desire to commit immoral sexual behavior. One then acts upon such mentally conceived desires, and performs deeds that may indeed be harmful to oneself and to others. One may feel so compelled to act in this way, as if one has no self-control. This is the result of psychic domination. Remove such images from one's experience by never looking at them in the first place and one will never conceive of the thought to act committing harmful deeds of a sexual nature that negatively influence oneself and others.

Mind you, sex is not bad. Sex is good. But not all sexual activity is good. Some is good, and some is bad. The higher dimensional (malevolent) forces act within one's mind to create confusion, blurring or erasing the difference between the concepts of good and evil. One becomes convinced that good is evil and evil is good, and proceeds to act accordingly, all the while convinced that one is doing the right thing.

The inner boundaries between good and evil need to be reestablished and reinforced. One begins this process by blocking out of sight and thought all those things that can enter in and cause harm.

This is similar to how an alcoholic must address one's relationship with alcohol. One must not drink it even in small amounts. One must remove oneself from areas, or distance oneself from certain people who may seek to entice the alcoholic to imbibe. The alcoholic knows well the battle with one's inner "demon." What the alcoholic may not know is that the battle may indeed be a psychic one against an external malevolent force seeking one's harm, and not just a psychological struggle exclusively under one's personal control.

Psychic attacks involve malevolent beings from higher dimensions who attacks us from within our own unconscious minds. This is why we also reach out into the psychic arena and call upon higher Help to assist us against higher dimensional attack. Like I said above, a strong psychic defense requires a strong psychic offense.

We live in a universe (actually a multiverse) that is entirely built upon and maintained by energy. Even physical matter comes about due to energetic properties and interactions. The original Source of Primordial Energy is that Force which we refer to as God.

By mentioning God here, I want to emphasize that this is not a reference to religion. Religions introduce doctrines, ideas, and beliefs, all of which are constructs of thought within the mind. As such, these thoughts can and do succumb to the influence of the malevolent entities in higher dimensions that seek to control us.

These malevolent entities very often take advantage of religious beliefs and manipulate the minds and the actions of religious individuals. These entities seek to cloud religious people's thoughts, blurring the difference between good and evil, and provoke religious people to act in the most irreligious of ways. This is why we have been subject to so much religious violence over the millennia. The malevolent entities especially love to target religious individuals for psychic attacks because they love to mock their primitive superstitious beliefs about the reality of the Creator, and its true Way.

When we discuss the need to clear the mind from seeing and hearing things that can be used against it in psychic attack, we must include within this group of dangerous things, certain ideas and beliefs that weaken personal resolve, and that seek to create a divide (in one's mind and beliefs) between oneself and our Creator.

Cleaning the mind means opening the mind on one hand to that which is good and positive and closing the mind on the other hand to that which is bad and negative. Only the mind clear of clouded confusion will be able to naturally and intuitively recognize the good from the bad, and embrace the former, while rejecting the latter.

This cleansing is a process. It can only be successfully accomplished by one's drawing to, and bonding with the Creator, the Source of all Primordial Energy. For the Primordial Energy pattern is the definition of balance throughout existence. One who calibrates with the Original will see, understand, and know how other energy patterns either do or do not align properly with the Original Source. And this is why we call directly upon God (and not necessarily upon religion).

There is a Universal Life-force energy that permeates everything in creation. This energy is called by many names which include those which are religious, philosophical, and scientific. Names are not important. What we call the Universal Life-force is not important. What is important is that this Universal Life-force energy does exist, and it alone establishes and defines what is balance and imbalance everywhere in the universe (and multiverse).

This Life-force is itself Alive, Sentient, and Purpose-Driven. The manifestation of the Life-force that we can experience here on Earth is called the "Glory of God," the Kavod referenced in the Bible. But like I just said, names are not really important. For ease of reference, and to make the thought compatible with present human understanding, we can call the Universal Life-force, God. When we say that we call upon God, this has to be understood outside of any specific religious context, and better, more properly understood as an action of energetic alignment with an Active and Real, Sentient Omniscient Universal Life-force.

Such an alignment does not come about simply by wishing it so. It does not come about by becoming or acting religious. As a natural phenomenon underlying all of nature, the Life-force energy field is approached as nature itself has ordained. This is through the natural, energetic modulations of our individual internal energetic bodies. Physically speaking, our internal bodies are made of energy. These bodies are not physically corporeal, and thus we call them spiritual bodies, or astral bodies. We connect with the Divine through these spirit bodies, which serve as the vessels for the true essence of our personal identities, our souls.

Contact with God, and with our own souls, is thus energetic in nature. It is this same energetic property that the malevolent higher dimensional beings crave to tap into. That is why they come after us. They want to control us because in their eyes human souls are a cheap and easy source of nourishment.

This is why these malevolent higher dimensional entities are soul snatchers. They seek to control human beings in order to control the flow of life-force energy that each individually receives. When they intervene in one's life, these malevolent forces cause there to be a break between the individual soul and its Divine Source. Only by removing their malevolent presence and our reconnecting with the Divine Source, and reinforcing the strength of that bond, is what keeps the malevolent ones at bay.

Chapter 2

Aligning One's Psychic Weaponry

Psychic warfare is an everyday reality that is ignored to one's own peril. Yet, knowing about the existence of the war, and being aware of the control and manipulation that is running rampant throughout human society does not alone enable one to assist in the war of resistance.

As with every other form of combat, one needs much training, and needs to acquire many skills if one desires to become a proficient psychic warrior.

Remember, what we call the psychic realm is actually a very fully inhabited parallel dimension wherein the fundamental laws of physics are experienced very differently than how those laws are experienced here on our Earth.

The resident Entities of that higher dimension consist of many kinds. There are those Entities who have no contact with human beings, nor do they have any interest in us at all. These Entities may or may not know about us, but they have other affairs occupying them. Therefore, we leave them alone, and they in turn continue to ignore us.

Then there are other Entities, who by human standards are called "good." These Entities interact with humanity on a regular basis, and often seek to influence human affairs at both the individual and collective levels for the sake of a greater good. The good Entities seek to build and protect humanity. Through their means of unconscious contact, the good Entities seek to inspire human beings to behave in the ways that best calibrates their personal portion of life-force energy with the general Universal Force.

Then of course there are other types of Entities who while residing in the higher dimension are, nonetheless, very malevolent. These Entities are very harmful to us. They look at humanity as a food source waiting to be harvested. These malevolent groups have no care and no regards towards anything human. For them, human beings are just mere food. The malevolent Entities want to keep humanity mentally enslaved, so that their life-force energy can be harvested at any time, as desired.

Malevolent Entities cannot directly access the Universal Life-force energy. In its pure, natural state the malevolent Entities cannot absorb it. This is why they seek to corrupt human behavior. If and when an individual human being fails to be properly calibrated with the Universal Life-force energy, then the amount of life-force within them is lessened. When this occurs, one's life-force energy is diluted and weakened.

The more and more individual human beings wander away from the Universal Balance, the weaker and weaker their individual life-force becomes. The malevolent Entities can thus attach themselves to their chosen victims and siphon off their life force energy. Essentially, the malevolent Entities corral their victims, keep them imprisoned and feed off of them on a regular basis.

Essentially, the universal definitions of good and evil are not to be defined by any human-made system be it religious, moral or otherwise. Human definitions of good and evil are irrelevant. Good and evil are energetic realities that exist in a dimension all their own. Just like there are the realities of space and time and the energetic fields that give birth to them, and which arise from them, so too are good and evil polarities of universal energy.

The definitions of good and evil are thus universal and energetic. Universal human morals exist simply because this is how the universe itself is wired to operate. Those who are in sync with the universe can be called good. Those who are out of sync with the universe can be called bad, or evil.

Good and bad, helpful and malevolent are polar opposite energetic realities. Each individual human being contains within oneself a combination of both energetic realities. A reality of this sort can only exist within a dimension of material physical space. Therefore, good and evil Entities are attracted to, and support those human souls which gravitate more to each's individual side.

One should be realistic, and understand a simple truth, what one attracts is what one draws close to oneself, be it good or evil. And good and evil is not what is decided by the individual, nor by one's religion, and nor by one's personal set of moral values. The Universal Life-force is the objective definition of energetic polarities. As part of this universe, we are all subject to its natural laws just as we are subject to the natural laws of space and time.

Good and evil are natural energetic polarities that are an integral part of the universe. The entire parameters of space, time, thought, and morality are set in each and every universe and dimension. They are universal constants limited only by the parameters of each specific universe. All was designed, by, ordained by and set into motion by the Primordial Source.

Natural law exists, this cannot be denied. Thus, there must be a natural law Giver, this too should not be denied. We call the Giver of natural law, its Creator. Of course, we call the Creator, God. We do not need to expand this understanding too much further. Remember, we are not here to discuss or to promote religion. We are here to understand what is real, and to learn how to experience this reality and to interact with it in a safe manner.

Everything in the universe (and multiverse) is somehow interconnected. This is because the Universal Life-force energy flows through everything. Nothing can exist without the bare minimum of life-force energy. It is the commodity of the universe.

The Sentient, Aware consciousness of the Universal Life-force flows through everything that contains it. The indwelling Universal Life-force energy that dwells within everything we call (in religion) the indwelling Divine Presence (Shekhina). In Oriental philosophy the Universal Life-force energy is called Qi or Prana. It permeates everything, and like I said, it is considered to be a universal commodity.

The good Entities watch over its distribution to affirm that its flow is proper and natural. The evil Entities seek to gather as much of it as they can, exclusively for their own usage. They are very willing to steal it from any place that they can take it. This explains their interest in siphoning off life-force energy from weak-willed and unaware human beings.

Each parallel dimension of the multiverse has its own unique definition and criteria. Each parallel universe operates in accordance to the laws of nature that are the foundations of its identity. And all of them are subject to the overriding Primordial Source of all.

Those who are in greater alignment with the Source energy are in a stronger position to be able to withstand the onslaughts of those who would seek to steal it from them. The strong have the ability to stand against the weak. The weak however, can manipulate the strong, thus weakening them, and thus making them subject to attack, and to defeat.

This is why the Good Entities are in the strengthening business, whereas the evil Entities are in the weakening business. And remember, the evil Entities always attack the thought processes of human beings in the attempt to confuse the difference between the natural and the unnatural, between the good and the evil, and the right from the wrong.

All these definitions can never be proven or validated by thought alone. These energetic presences need to be felt and experienced in order for their realities to be realized and normalized within the individual. It is this process of acquiring naturally experienced energetic flow in alignment with the Supernal Universal Life-force that gives one the ability to withstand any type of psychic attack that emanates from the evil Entities.

So, how does one align with the Supernal Universal Life-force? Obviously, step one is that one must acknowledge that this Supernal Universal Life-force does exist. Step two is to acknowledge that one can have experiential access to it. And step three is to take the necessary steps to implement step two. This is what we need now to address.

As I have said above, the Supernal Universal Life-force energy is what we have come to know as God. As for what is the nature of God and what are the details of Divine existence, who can say without a direct experience of these things. It is important that one's search for God and one's approach to God not be tainted by beliefs in religious dogmas and doctrines. Once we begin to say that God is this way, or that, or that God did this thing or that, we limit our minds from understanding (as best as we can) what God may really be all about, at least from within the context of our limited ability of perception due to our present human forms.

God is the Source of the Supernal Universal Life-force. God is the Law Giver of all natural laws. God is sentient, and aware, and the Divine Presence can be experienced personally. Throughout history those who have achieved this have been called holy persons (male and female). Such holy individuals transcend normal psychic development and seem to go far beyond it.

Some would say that holy people, when they are truly accomplished in the field of holiness become, for lack of a better description, "super-psychics." They have become renown as miracle workers, and master "powers and abilities far above those of mortal men."

All of these abilities do not flow through them because of a power of their own. Rather, their abilities flow through them because of their intense and absolute bond with God that enables them to become living conduits of the Supernal Universal Life-force energy here on Earth.

These individuals are not masters of the human race but rather they are the humble servant of the Living God. I am sorry if this sounds too religious for some, but we must get past personal religious prejudices if one is going to be able to experience this reality on a personal basis.

Psychic offense (and defense) is only possible because one is bringing onto the psychic playing field a power and ability greater than the one that is being used against one.

Psychic warfare is not defined by the limits of human imagination. Psychic warfare (like physical warfare) is subject to the natural laws that defines the parameters of physics (in each and every individual universe and dimension).

Tapping into the One Source energy that rules them all grants one the ability to successfully interact with the natural laws of each universe and dimension based upon the direction and the strength received directly from the Supernal Law-Giver.

All of reality is energy based. Energy is a force that is subject to the laws of its created parameters. Energy is science. It is not religion or philosophy. Therefore, when we recognize that the Supernal Life-force energy underlying all of reality is what we call God, then finally we can realize that the reality of God belongs to the realms of science, as much as it does the realms of religion or philosophy. After all, God is the Creator and Law-Giver of Universal Law.

As such, God is the ultimate Source of science, and its goal. Science seeks to know what reality is all about, and how it all actually works. Being that God put it all together, one who studies the Universal blue-prints will discover how the entire apparatus of existence is meant to operate in its peak and proper conditions. Yet, without the blue-prints, all continuing discoveries are minor and are only unconnected parts of the whole. Without awareness of the whole, one lacks the proper awareness of the operations of what appears to be individual and isolated parts.

This is where scientific knowledge is today, both here and elsewhere. Whenever there is a lack of awareness of the Singularity of the Supernal Life-force energy, then here is equally a misalignment with it. As such psychic defense and offense begins with the individual seeking to align oneself with the Singularity of the Supernal Life-force energy of all existence. This Singularity is God.

The proper alignment between the Singularity and human beings living at this time on planet Earth is that power which we call holiness. Holiness is the alignment of Universal Life-force energy within the human spirit, mind, and body.

Holiness is not a concept of religion or philosophy. Holiness is an energetic reality. Like with all other scientific matters that are subject to identification and measurement, with regards to holiness, one either has it, or one does not have it. And if one does have it, like energy stored in a battery, its charge is subject to fluctuation and modulation.

Psychic defense and attack begins with the individual human being cultivating the Universal Life-force energy of holiness. Again, this is not a statement of religion, but rather one of energy! One's thoughts, feelings, and behaviors all either channel holiness within oneself, or repel holiness outside of oneself.

Psychic defense and attack begins by one channeling holiness into one's thoughts, feelings, and behavior. This type of activity is not subject to one's personal interpretation of what this means, or how one's believes it is to be done. Being that we are dealing with energy we can easily see and measure an individual's level of holiness by careful observation of one's thinking patterns, one's emotional stability, and one's righteous and naturally proper behavior.

Now, remember this! Psychic development of the powers of the mind and soul do not necessarily afford one any greater ability of psychic defense or offense.

There are a great number of Entities out there, surrounding us all the time, who because of their ease of flow in the higher dimensions have easy access to human souls through the subconscious and unconscious content of the individual human mind. Just because a human being can enter among these forces and learn to interact as they do, does not afford that individual any greater force of holiness. On the contrary, it usually leads to a weakening and loss of holiness.

This is why those individuals who walk the path of psychic development that is not centered upon the Singularity of the Supernal Life-force energy of God, the Creator, most often become absorbed (possessed) by the higher (malevolent) Entities in the higher domain, who view such souls as nothing more than as a simple snack to quickly digest.

Psychic development is a vital and important thing, but just like scientific progression, one must proceed with caution and with wisdom. How many scientists have caused explosions leading to serious harm or death all because they were not careful (or aware) of what it is that they were doing. So it is with psychic development.

One must align with the Singularity in holiness, manifesting proper changes in one's thinking, emotions, and behaviors. Only once these are clearly manifest can we say with certainty that some holiness exists. At this point one then continues the process of realignment with the Universal Singularity (God).

As this process continues one develops greater and stronger tools that one can use for psychic defense and offense. This is the Way of things. It is not subject to interpretation or personal beliefs any more than are the laws of gravity or electromagnetism.

The one who cultivates this energy cultivates the abilities for psychic defense and attack. The one who does not cultivate the energy of holiness is left wide open, and regardless of one's beliefs to the opposite, one will remain an open psychic target.

Again, this is not religion or philosophy, it is the Way of reality, and is subject to testing and verification. Only the one who works with real energy will know of its power. All others are simply like young children playing with toys making believe that they are the real things. Needless to say, children need to grow up.

Chapter 3

Overcoming Delusions, Fighting Psychic Attackers

For each individual there are always two types of reality. There is the reality that one perceives to be real, and then there is a truer reality that lies beyond personal perception blocked from sight by illusions of deception. These illusions are the weapons of mind control used by attacking psychic soldiers.

An individual's perceived reality is derived from one's personal experiences at any moment, and one's personal interpretations of those experiences. Each of us filters the reality around us through our individual minds, which are filled with our own ideas, fantasies, and beliefs. We may experience one thing in life, and then interpret it to mean something very different from what it actually is. This creates for each of us a unique set of illusions that cover over our reality like the hard shell over a walnut. Needless to say, one must recognize the existence of the shell before one can go about making the efforts to break it.

The shell of illusions that covers over our perceptions of reality is always self-made, but not always self-imposed. Not everyone wants to see reality from only one's personal point of view. Some really do want to expand their horizons and see beyond the limits of one's own personal perceptions. But such insights do not come easily. Granted, another person can always share a different point of view, and provide insights unseen at first. While this is often a good and beneficial thing, it also does not go deep enough into one's subconscious to unravel all the twisted knots of unresolved emotions, and the convoluted, prejudiced thoughts that come forth from them.

The hardships in life inflict serious damage on the human psyche. The wise and the strong eventually come to recognize this, and then seek to heal themselves as necessary. Without even realizing it, the more one heals oneself of all subconscious conflict, the greater one's natural psychic self-defense becomes.

Of course, the opposite is also true. The more one allows an internal buildup of unresolved internal conflicts, the greater one's personal shell becomes. This shell more and more separates one from a clear perception of one's surroundings. A malevolent higher dimensional Entity can then come and take advantage of such a one's psychic isolation.

This Entity will proceed to seed one's subconscious with fears, doubts, and insecurities about everything in life, that then reinforce one's shell, strengthening it. From this place of influence, the Entity can then proceed to serve as an internal source of negative persuasion that easily influences one's feelings, thoughts, and actions. One's shell of delusions is thus made hard, and permeates all of one's personal perceptions of reality. One has thus become a casualty of psychic attack.

One who defines one's own reality in accordance to one's own rules and one's own personal perceptions defines right and wrong, and good and evil in accordance to one's own personal beliefs. One who is out of sync with the outer reality lives in an illusion of one's own making. The big problem with this is that each individual who lives in one's own little bubble always comes into contact with other people who are each living in their own little bubbles. When the two meet, their perceptions of reality collide with one another. This is what causes strife, conflict, and violence in human society.

Bubble attacks bubble. Shell attacks shell. And the confused and delusional human beings inside those bubbles and shells fall victim to forces which are sometimes of their own making. Again, now more than one has become casualties of psychic attack.

The only solution to this horrible cycle of mind and behavior control is for the individual to pop one's bubble, and to break open one's shell. And while these words are easy to write and to read, putting them into actual practice is often a very difficult enterprise. After all, who is really willing to make the efforts to undo what one has done? Who is really willing to fight the psychic fight and go on the attack?

Remember psychic self-defense and psychic attack go hand in hand. One cannot have the one without the other. Before one can actually fight off malevolent higher dimensional Entities, one must first recognize their presence inside one's own mind, and first expel them from there.

The psychic battle includes the psychological battle, but is not limited to it. Therefore, the two are not the same. The psychic battle begins with addressing one's inner psychological and emotional turmoil. Only once this is addressed successfully can one crack this portion of one's shell. One then proceeds into other areas of the mind to challenge one's perceptions of reality.

So, how is one to accomplish this great task? Where does one begin? How does one who is lost discern which path to follow that will lead one to one's personal liberation? After all, if one's internal personal perceptions are compromised, how does one know what to believe, and in what to place one's trust? True psychic self-defense begins with the answers to these questions.

And to provide for you the answers to these questions has this book called, The Unveiling, been written. Herein are contained many truths and secrets of life, of living, of higher realities, and of this reality. Herein are revealed for the first time many of the deepest secrets of the experiential, Biblical, prophetic Kabbalah, exposed raw, without their garments of metaphors and symbolisms.

All the revelations and insights exposed in this book will require of you, the reader, one thing: As you contemplate these words within your mind and heart you must come to know them as truth, and not just to believe them intellectually. You do not need more things to believe. What you need is to have a knowing, one that arises from within you, and echoes in your mind that these ae truths that you have always known, but had maybe forgotten. It is time to remember. It is time for the sleeper to awaken, and thus experience, The Unveiling.

Blessings to you all,

Ariel B. Tzadok
14 March 2023

SECTION THREE

ECHOES FROM THE VOICE

Sihot: Words of Revelation, Insights & Prophecy
January – April 2023

CONTENTS

NEW SIHOT

Sihot: Words of Revelation, Insights & Prophecy

These are the words that were spoken within me by the Echo of the Voice, which is the "still silent voice" that I have learned to hear. It speaks to me so that I may speak to you. And so, I pass on what I have learned, even as I have been instructed to do.

These Sihot came to me in the period of time from January through April 2023. I relate their dates so as to provide for you insights into the flow of consciousness as it progresses. Those who contemplate this will discover the hidden truths therein.

The deepest secrets of the Ma'aseh Merkava are a reflection of our souls. As we are below, so are we above. Our mission is to reconnect consciousness below with consciousness above. This can only be done within a mind that is unhindered by unnecessary blockages. This is why I have related the truths herein in the most direct and straightforward manner. These words need to be contemplated in one's heart, and not torn apart by the turbulence of unsettled intellect. To embrace these words, one needs more than understanding, one need wisdom. The deepest secrets of the Ma'aseh Merkava are revealed to the open heart and the wise mind.

There are 73 separate selections in this work (the numerical value of the word, Hokhma, wisdom). While each one was written consecutively, they do not need to be read as such. Each one stands alone as its own message, with each having its own meaning.

The proper way to approach this material is to simply flip through the pages at random. Stop and read whichever one (or more) of the selections that you may desire. There is no right or wrong choice here. You can read as little or as much as you may desire.

Once you have read your portion, do not read any further. Stop and pause, think about what you have read and what it really means. You may be surprised by the nature of the thoughts that will pop up into your head. Open yourself to what comes into you from our own Higher Self. This is how one becomes a Merkava.

These words are meant to speak first to your heart, and only then to your head. Follow the proper path. May they be a blessing to you.

1. Tricks of the Mind

Jan. 04, 23

Desire, the Choice of Thoughts, and the Creation of Self-Imposed Illusion.

Thoughts are things. Desires are things. What we desire and what we think can take on a life of their own inside us, and create for us a perception of reality which defines for us our world.

Yes, every secret desire that lies hidden somewhere in one's subconscious mind motivates many forces in the psyche to bring it forth into manifestation.

Sometimes one's subconscious desires may be for things that are not acceptable or good. Fulfillment of such desires is met by a strong wall of blockage from thoughts and mind. The subconscious says, "I want." The mind says, "No, that is evil, or wrong."

The subconscious does not take such rejection lightly. It seeks to circumvent the mind. If the mind will not allow the subconscious to act out its inner desires, it can at least flood the mind with imagery and desires about said behaviors, forcing the mind to have to address the thoughts.

And then something most devious often happens. The subconscious knows how to get the mind to focus on its desires in a way that the mind can find acceptable. Instead of thinking about embracing the forbidden desires, the mind is tricked into thinking about all kinds of ways to combat the forbidden desires, to contemplate the forbidden desires so as to explore new ways in which such desires can be fought and eradicated.

Essentially the mind becomes obsessed with the forbidden desires, however thinking itself to be fighting them, and not even realizing that it has fallen under the influence of the subconscious.

One may find oneself believing that one is actually on some sort of crusade against the evil that one's subconscious desires represent. And inside oneself, one does not recognize that the very desires that one seems to be fighting on the surface, are the very ones that one subconsciously embraces and loves, but the wall of the mind will never allow this insight.

It is often the case when an individual is so focused (obsessed?) on a course of action against something that there is a deeply concealed subconscious motivational factor behind it. This factor is what structures one's perception of reality, and creates around one a husk or a shell of one's own making.

This is how illusions are born and thrive. It all begins within the murky inner recesses of unresolved psychic, psychological content that resides within each individual's psyche.

Essentially, we all lie to ourselves. We then present to others a picture of ourselves which essentially expresses our own individual untruths. And the more we get others to believe our untruths, the more we ourselves become convinced that our untruths are true.

So, how much of the world around is seen as it truly is, and how much of the world is seen through the limited eyes of personal perceptions? The answer is that as long as each individual subconsciously interprets the events surrounding one, there is very little real truth getting through to an untainted rational mind.

2. The Way of Psychic Images

Jan. 08, 23

Focusing on the positive is always a good thing.

But be warned, whatever image that we form in our minds to represent what we consider to be good and positive is, in and of itself, an artificial construct of the human imagination.

No one, regardless of how mentally and psychically fit one may be, is free from this layer over perception that exists simply as a byproduct of the human physical condition.

This is why we seek to interpret experience through sensation and feeling and not by how something looks, or sounds.

Seeking an experience that begins within the imagination and then goes beyond it is not too hard a task to accomplish. Yet, such experiences are almost always misunderstood because one pays attention to the images of the experience, as opposed to their actual internal intentions.

Learning how to sense beyond the imagery requires one to first be emotionally detached from the imagery. One's mind reacts to imagery as if the images were of something real from this physical reality. This immediate reaction is the first thing that needs to be dismissed as having no value.

The imagery is symbolic, thus there is no place for any emotional response that one may feel as if the imagery were not symbolic. Dismiss the initial emotional sensations. Now, recognize the symbolic nature of the imaged images. If one's mind is calm one should not feel any sense of alarm or disturbance. One looks at what is popping up in one's mind with detachment and curiosity. One asks oneself, why am I seeing this set of images? What are these supposed to mean to me?

And now, instead of using the intellect to break down and analyze the images, pause, and pay attention instead to how the images are making you feel at the moment. Try to sense what thought pops into your head at the moment. Try to be sensitive to any inner insight, or flash of revelation that might just pop up into your consciousness and memory.

Sometimes something can pop up in a flash and leave a deep impression. Other times, one may not feel anything deep whatsoever.

Still, it is possible that one's mind received a communication that circumvented consciousness and planted itself directly within one's unconscious. Such planted thoughts can be rightly compared to an information download into the operations system of a computer device. The info does not need to be on the desktop (consciousness), it is stored deep within, and will be retrieved at the right time, and in the right way by operational forces that are beyond the comprehension of our conscious minds.

Rather than look for results, be they conscious or programmed, one should instead continue to allow the mind full access to its imaginative abilities, and to drift off into daydreaming consciousness, or deeper trance consciousness all the time.

The more that one is open to receiving, the more one will indeed receive, be it knowingly or not.

Thus always focus on positive things. Think positive thoughts. Project positive feelings. Seek to contemplate only on positive imagery. If this is what you can out to, then this is what will respond to you.

3. Limited Awareness in Perception

Jan. 09, 23

One who is in the middle of a thing cannot see the whole of the thing.

One needs to be outside of a thing, and then at a distance from it in order to see the thing. Only then one can begin to use one's power of observation and analysis to help define what it is that one sees.

And just because one can see a thing does not mean that one will properly understand what it is that one sees. One may observe a thing and conclude that it "looks like this," or that it "appears similar to that." And while in the mind of the beholder the observed thing may look one way, the thing itself in reality may be absolutely and totally different from how the mind of the observer describes it.

But the observer, without any ability of further exploration, is left with the most flimsy of descriptions that may actually take away from an actual understanding of the thing.

Limited knowledge is what it is: limited. No one can make an assessment about the whole of a thing based on having only 1% or 2% of the information about the thing, and this is especially true when even the 1% or 2% that is believed known is itself subject to deeper analysis.

What information rational analysis provides is limited, faulty, and subject to many different external influences. As unsettling as it may sound, but all perceptions that each of us experience is only as real as what our individual minds are capable of grasping at the moment.

Inside the middle of a thing clouds one's eyes from seeing the whole of a thing. And even when outside of a thing, and at enough of a distance to observe it carefully, one must still be cautious and recognize one's overall limitations of perception and analysis.

4. Dulling of the Mind & its Resharpening

Jan. 09, 23

The modern era of social media, particularly all kinds of video-based entertainment including television programs and movies, are the single-most guilty culprit in deadening down the human mind from independent thinking.

All the while that the human mind craves images upon images of constant mental stimulation the mind grows less and less able to cultivate and then process in-depth independent thought.

This was decades in the making. And now it has become very clear. What people see in the entertainment industry tells them what to think. For the most part no one any longer has the ability to think critically and independently.

No one knows any longer how to think. All thought is controlled by and dictated by emotionally-based and easily manipulated public opinion. This is the true definition of a "brainwashed" or "mind-controlled" society.

And if one tries to raise this very subject and to publicly address it, such a one is immediately met by the minions of society who, in mindless union, cry out in derisive laughter, insulting and mocking the voice of opposition, and calling for its comprehensive repression, and destructive end.

As in times in the past, the minions of the masses follow their orders doing as they have been told. They will continue to do so, wreaking the havoc and destruction that their kind cannot avoid but do. They will continue until they destroy everything around them, including themselves.

The power-brokers who own and control society have successfully taken over almost the entire world. They control the minds and hearts of the clueless masses.

There is no human power on Earth that can fight them. Be this as it may, it will only lead to the rise of another kind of power that will eventually topple them. And when the great world order is toppled, all its minions will fall alongside them, never to be raised up again.

For those struggling against this mindless society, the only way out of it is to disconnect from it. This means that one must change one's ways of interaction with society and first and foremost disconnect from the entertainment media, and the ways and means in which it operates.

Hundreds of years ago, an educated individual was one who read books. One contemplated ideas, and allowed one's imagination to expand and express itself independently outside of external control and manipulation. Such well-read individuals became known as the educated and the elite. They were the ones who taught others how to think, how to question, and how to inquire.

For the educated, an artist would paint a painting or sculpt a statue that was worthy of awe. One could look upon these magnificent works of art with wonder, and contemplate them for great amounts of time, discovering within them the wonderful nuances of their being.

We no longer have such art, such artists, or the minds of patrons who can think deep enough to appreciate any of this.

The only way out of the present quagmire of mental degeneration is to go back out the way that we came in. We need to return to the written word, and read it! We need to turn off the pictures! We need to stop looking at comic-book level social media with all its attractive videos. We need to pay attention to the essence of a thing, and not the wrapper and package it comes dressed in.

No more fancy videos and pictures. If this is what grabs one's attention, it is best to let such a person go! Those who are attracted to pictures and videos, and who lack the attention span to stay committed to a full investment of one's mental energy is clearly an unworthy candidate for further in-depth studies.

Let the children return to their comic-books, and open the doors only to qualified and educated adults who wish to continue to distance themselves from the mindless masses of today.

Don't make things easy on a person. On the contrary make it hard. And not only make it hard, but make it harder and harder. The truly challenged are not interested in easy successes. The truly challenged want to earn their accomplishments.

Those who complain how hard things are should be dismissed and turned away. Let the little children cry over their wounded prides. Put the babies to the side, and make room for the real adults who are ready, grown up, and mature enough to make the efforts to succeed.

With every step create greater and greater hardships. Let each and every obstacle become more and more difficult to overcome. With great effort will come great accomplishment. And this is how true and strong leaders are molded in the fires of purgatory.

Push forward without mercy. Overcome every adversity. Be stoic in the face of pain, setback, and opposition. Learn how to overcome. Fight and win.

And there is no final victory. All victories are temporary. The next challenge is there right now. Do not keep it waiting.

Babies belong together in the playground. If that is where you belong, then go there, and stop making believe that you are a grown-up.

Adults stand where only adults can go. Adults go to the school of life, and they learn life's hard lessons. They do not cry, they do not wallow in self-pity, and they never accept any excuse for failure!

Move forward. Reclaim your mind. Recognize the children's playground on the modern social entertainment industry. It has enslaved your mind, and has captured your vision. Free yourself from its disgusting clutches. And move forward (by moving back) to the state of self-mastery and independent thought.

Turn off the internet! Read books! Learn again about what is important and what is not! Reclaim your rightful adulthood!

Stop acting and whining like a spoiled child. It's now or never. As for me, I chose to no longer babysit the infants who refuse to grow up.

As for me, I will surround myself with adults; adults who prove themselves with their accomplishments. If you are such an adult, then you are welcome. If you are a child, go away little one, what I have here is not for you!

5. Two Worlds, One Reality

Jan. 10, 23, morning

Which is more important, placing focus on the everyday affairs of this world, or to withdraw from such affairs and to instead place focus on exploring higher realities and our relationships with them?

Think about this question before you rush to answer it!

Each of us comes to Earth from a place and domain that we call a higher dimension. We do believe that we have all been here before many times over (reincarnation), and yet in the vast majority of cases, all such previous memories are wiped clean allowing for the creation of a brand-new Ego (Nefesh) identity which then leads a life of its own.

This brand-new Ego (Nefesh) identity lives its life, learns its lessons, and upon the death of the vessel of the body it returns to a higher dimension to inhabit whatever place and to perform whatever role it is to do in that place.

Our time here on Earth is always severely finite. No human lifespan, no matter how long, is anything more than a blink of the eye in the greater scope of cosmic time. We come and we go, and that is the truth of things.

And yet, we are always coming and going, back and forth. Each time, we develop a new Ego (Nefesh) identity, and each time, the Ego identity is vacated, and left behind to merge into the greater collective memory of combined humanity.

And so, back to our original question. We come here to Earth. We get involved with our everyday affairs. We devote a lifetime to build, maintain and support that which we build. And in the end, everything that we have passes on, into other hands. This again is the way of things.

All our efforts and ventures here on Earth no matter how seemingly permanent are as temporary as is human life. And yet, we continue to place all emphasis on such building and maintenance. For without our efforts, human civilization as we know it would come screeching to a halt. And so we focus on this temporary world and upon the illusion of its permanence.

Is this what life is all about, to completely, however temporarily lose focus of our higher dimensional origins while we focus on the illusionary of the moment?

Seeing how everything that one builds never seems to last, one may indeed contemplate how much of a waste of time it all appears to be. And nevertheless, even such contemplative thought will not hinder one from moving forward in the illusionary to build as if there really is some semblance of permanence.

And what if we were to withdraw from the illusionary and spend all of one's time to reestablish one's connection with the higher dimensions of one's origins, and to equally reconnect with one's higher (and truer) identity (one's higher Self, Neshama), what then?

What is the purpose of such an endeavor? After all, given time, everyone will reconnect in one form or another with the passing of the temporary body of flesh. And so again, should one focus on the illusionary of this world, or should one try to reconnect with the permanence of the higher realities from which we come?

Before we offer an answer to this question, there is one other question that may indeed need to be answered first. Being that this world is so illusionary and temporary, why on Earth (on Earth indeed!) do we come here in the first place?

We believe (and even deeply sense) that the universe operates as it does with profound intelligence, wisdom, purpose, and direction. If we keep coming here over and over again, it is not by accident, but rather it is by design. So, why do we keep coming back here? Why do we spend so much effort to build new Ego (Nefesh) identities only to have them cast aside in the end?

Before we decide to dismiss all interest in Ego (Nefesh) building and to place all our emphasis upon remembering our higher realities, we need to understand why our higher Selves (Neshama) continuously allows and maybe even dictates that a part of itself repeatedly comes here to Earth. We cannot chose to focus on one or the other because maybe the very choice of difference between the two is itself part of the illusionary nature of life here on Earth?

Coming to Earth and building the temporary life here seems to have a very important purpose all its own. Spending time here upon Earth to expand consciousness to gain a glimpse into the higher realities of our origins also seems to be an important part of this temporary life.

So, the answer to our question of which is more important is that they both seem to bear equal importance, each within their domain, and each with their own purpose.

We are here for a reason. Something programmed deep inside of each of us drives us forward on the quest to discover our individual purpose and meaning. As much as we build this illusionary world, we each also deeply desire to return home (however the concept of "home" may be imagined).

There are some individuals who bear almost no interest whatsoever in discovering higher realities, be they inside of one, or elsewhere. Then again, there are other individuals who care so little about the illusionary nature of this world, and seek to discover and then to share the nature of the higher realities that surround us all. Each individual seems to fit in as one does and each individual performs one's task for some greater unseen purpose. And life goes on!

Some seek and discover higher realities. Others couldn't care less. Yet, one thing all share in common. We are born. We are here. And we remain here until we leave. And we all leave. And whatever is left behind rarely survives.

Some things that remain last a very long time, but these things usually represent ideas, and values that speak deeply to the higher parts within each of us. The fact that these things survive is itself a reality worthy of contemplation in its own right.

Maybe such insights may contribute to our understanding about why we keep coming back here to Earth over and over again. There is, of course, a purpose to it all. This too is one of those things that is worthy of our contemplations.

6. The Way of Freedom for the Mind

Jan. 10, 23, evening

The realities of this world are both true and false at the same time. One way or another, whatever it is that we experience on a daily basis is the same exact things that those who came before us experienced, each in their own way.

There truly is nothing new under the sun. With this being said, we still need to address the issue as to why we keep coming back here to Earth over and over again, seemingly repeating very similar type lives every time.

The secret is in the unity of our two worlds. As we are born a new Ego (Nefesh) identity is born. But as it grows and matures in this world, it is not meant to drift further and further away from its preborn higher reality which dwells securely within one's individual conscious mind. On the contrary our purpose being here on Earth is as the proverb says, to bring Heaven down to Earth.

What this means is not something merely metaphorical, there is to this an actual tangible and real component. The part of Heaven that we bring down to Earth is that part of our thinking process that is designed for higher dimensional interaction. We do not need to introduce our wiped memories of our higher existence to life here on Earth. For the most part, such memories can serve as a big distraction to everyday living. Nevertheless, it is the way that we think that needs to be elevated and expanded.

We all too often think using only the rational intellectual side of the mind and we surrender all perceptions of reality to the filter of this mental faculty. This is where we fail our purpose for being incarnate on Earth.

We come to Earth to learn to see Earthly living from the perspective of the intuitive psychic mind. The rational and the intellectual have their place, this is true, but that place is secondary to that which we call the spirit.

For it is the spirit, the psychic intuition that should reign supreme in the mind of the one who wishes to live life on this Earth in accordance to the higher reality of the greater universe from which we come, and to which we will eventually return.

While we live here on Earth, in order to avoid mental enslavement to the domineering, oppressive culture in which most of us live, one must learn to channel one's inner higher Self and to allow its psychic intuitive essence to flow through the material form of the physical body and conscious mind. This alone is the true definition of freedom. All who have not yet learned to live in this way are still mental slaves to a false system of perception that seeks to strengthen itself more and more, further enslaving human minds.

Freedom comes when one follows one's own path, and as we say marches to the beat of one's own inner drummer.

This will indeed put one into direct conflict, if not outright confrontation, with one's surroundings. But this is why we come here to Earth. We are here to try to set free enslaved minds.

One who walks this path in the freedom of choice may indeed act in ways that others cannot understand, and that others will indeed many times condemn. But the aware mind cares nothing about the condemnation of others. Indeed, the opinions of others, be they pro or con, have no value to the aware soul.

One who hears the inner voice and who lives by it already knows what to do and how to do it. One simply follows the inner knowing and lives in accordance to it. Heaven speaks into one's Earthly mind, and the free mind hears and knows what to do.

One who lives in this way brings to Earth a knowing about the true natural way of life, and lives it to the fullest. No explanations are offered. One just does, and that's it. Some may consider such a one to be crazy, and yet such a one couldn't care less about what others think. Sometimes to be a little crazy (in good way) is not a bad thing at all.

7. Are We Heard?

Jan 11, 23, morning

It is all too unfortunate that we have no direct and visibly overt Divine intervention to help combat the infestation of lies and evil that have so corrupted human society today.

More and more lies abound. More and more hatred grows against everything that is moral, righteous, and holy. The attacks are never-ceasing. The number of enemies are just too overwhelming to fight. It seems as if the powers of righteousness, morality and holiness have already lost the battle for the hearts and minds of the masses.

We have seen in the past what happens when the masses are turned towards evil and then let loose to unleash their violence and their hate upon innocents.

Is this our future? Will history repeat itself? We all want to remain optimistic and believe that all will be well. But everything is not well! Everything is not getting any better, it is not even staying the same.

Things are getting progressively worse. It seems, regardless of all denials to the opposite, that we are indeed heading straightforward into a repetition of the past, where wanton violence and worse than animal-like depravity will reign in the hearts, minds, and actions of the masses.

Where is Divine intervention when we need it? Can one wonder why the faithful are deeply shaken to their very core? All their prayers and all their righteousness seems to go unnoticed by Heaven.

8. Reminiscing

Jan. 11, 23, evening

One of our greatest mental assets is that those of us who are old enough can reminisce about older and better times. We can reminisce about the innocence of days long gone by. No, those days were by no means perfect. They certainly were no utopia. But what they were is better than the days today.

Moral values were more widespread. What was wrong was admitted to be wrong, without anyone trying to justify it to make what is wrong look right. When one did wrong and got caught, one was sincerely ashamed of one's bad behavior. One had a sense of remorse. One had a conscience. How so very different are things today when the very foundations of innocence have been stripped away and replaced with a quagmire of moral filth. It is no wonder why those of us who can want so desperately to reminisce about older, more noble days (however imperfect that they were).

Of course the danger in reminiscing too much is that one can become lost in the memories of the past to the point where the present becomes ignored. While one can sympathize in this escape from disgusting modernity, nevertheless, the past is not a safe haven for the mind to seek refuge. While it is good to remember the good of the past, it is an even better thing to at least to try to share the older values with a modern generation that is so lost and disconnected from anything moral.

9. Secrets of the Torah

Jan. 12, 23

For a very long time there has been a body of knowledge known as the Secrets of the Torah.

For centuries now, these secret teachings have been given the name of Kabbalah, and many books are associated with it.

For centuries many study these books of Kabbalah learning about philosophical and metaphysical ideas and beliefs, and all the while these students are convinced that they are the students of, if not the masters of the Secrets of the Torah.

Granted, while many students of this path do become scholars of the material that they study, still, nevertheless, all that they are studying and the books which form the basis of their beliefs, have nothing to do with the real and authentic Secrets of the Torah.

Essentially what is today publicized as Kabbalah is a bait-and-switch with the real Secrets of the Torah. The true Secrets of the Torah remain properly concealed as they have always been.

It is a well-known law that the true Secrets of the Torah can only be received one-on-one from master to student in private, oral learning and practice. And thus the ancient Secrets remain secret from the masses, and remain wisely concealed in the hearts and minds of those who have truly received the ancient instruction.

There is one thing that can be revealed, and that is that the authentic Secrets of the Torah are not written in any book, nor can they be written in any book. All that can ever be written are signposts that point the way along the path, but the path itself and its goal is private. It can only be walked by one, not two.

So many today pursue so many modern golden-calves while thinking that each one has a truth and a value to it. This is what happens when individuals convince themselves that something is real, all the while that it is not.

And when the blind lead the blind, then there is only reinforcement of a modern day golden-calf, with many gathering around it proclaiming, "this is your god, Israel."

This is why so many seek to know Heaven, and almost none of them have even a clue as to what Heaven is really all about.

Many indeed seek an experience of God, and in their childlike naiveté convinced themselves that some sort of an emotional high is what it feels like to be closer to God.

This is what happens when the blind lead the blind and convince the blind that what is false is true.

Drawing close to Heaven is an experience of expanded consciousness. It does not come and go; it is not subject to emotional expression.

One who draws closer to Heaven can see things that the Earthbound cannot. This is why one who is indeed closer to Heaven can see inside the minds and hearts of other human beings, can communicate with other non-human lifeforms, and can penetrate the veil of the illusions of this world and gain a glimpse at the hidden, truer reality.

So, one who claims to be closer to Heaven, or who is believed to be closer to Heaven can be seen to be either true or false all based upon who the person is and what the person can in actuality do.

Those who are believed to be closer to Heaven are in many cases, just modern day golden-calves or those that worship one.

The masses have no idea about the truth of things. They carry on living in their little illusionary world, oblivious to the untruth that all that they embrace as sacred is essentially false.

They don't know it. They don't want to know it. And they will take many steps to repress any attempt that would even suggest revealing the truth.

And so the worship of the modern day golden calves continues, all the while that the masses proclaim louder and louder, "these are your God, Israel."

And Heaven sees all, and those who safeguard the authentic Secrets of the Torah withdraw from them further and further, from even the possibility of prying eyes.

There truly is a famine for the living Word of YHWH. All are deaf, and all are blind.

And this is the way it shall remain until Heaven decides to intervene and to again destroy the modern golden calves, even as the first one was destroyed a long time ago.

10. Religion Drug

Jan. 13, 23

Religion truly is like a drug. It fills its believers with all kinds of ideas, beliefs, and feelings that they cling to with utter disregard to objective analysis. Regardless of what nature itself dictates, Religionists adamantly insist that their faith is right, and seek to justify those things that defy justification.

It is truly an act of desperation to try to look at that which is bad and then make any and every attempt to make it look good. This is an evil thing to do.

11. Perversion of Righteousness

Jan 14, 2023

Sometimes the evil deeds of people are told "like it is." No cover-up. No justification. No white-wash. No reinterpretations. This is raw truth. And this alone is what we can call, the Way of God. Truth, honesty, and integrity are all necessary ingredients for one to live a righteous life. And there is nothing more important on Earth than righteousness.

Righteousness makes human society to be balanced, and thus in harmony with Heaven. Righteousness at the individual and at the collective levels leads to a life of prosperity and peace.

When righteousness is perverted, then society as a whole becomes corrupt. It will not escape its inevitable destruction. The individual who acts evil, and who makes every effort to justify one's behavior, and even to be looked at as righteous, such a one is the worst of the worst. This type of evil, lousy hypocrite should be shunned and cast out with every due bit of force and rigor.

When a person is righteous, then the person is righteous. When one is struggling to lead a righteous life, then one struggles. We make every effort to assist one in making righteous choices all the time. When, however, one acts unrighteous and seeks to justify one's behavior using some form of manipulative religious argument, this is the definition of an evil person (Rasha), the likes of which should be totally shunned.

12. The Flow of Energy

Jan. 16, 23

To simplify matters, consider this, energy flows in one of two ways. It either flows in, or it flows out. Now, remember, this is just a symbolic metaphor, so do not apply the actual laws of physics to this subjective example. Understand it as it is given over to you to understand.

And this is my meaning. Energy flows into an object and congeals there (stays there), or energy flows through and out of an object, not staying still, but rather remains in constant movement.

These two states of energetic flow are what underlie the two human behaviors that we know all so well as righteousness and wickedness. Yes, the one who receives and gives is called righteous. Whereas the one who receives (or takes) and gives or shares nothing (or very little) is called wicked and evil.

Now, understand this outside of the context of morality and understand it within nature itself. Nature is ever-moving, vibrant, and changing. This is the natural way of life. In order for life to be maintained, there needs to be a constant flow and movement of energy.

When, however, the flow of energy becomes stagnant, or stuck, then the entire system suffers thereby. It becomes essential for nature to unblock the blockage. However much effort is needed to be used to unblock the blockage *is* used, until normalcy and natural flow is restored.

Human energetic systems (behaviors) are part of nature. When human behavior (at the individual and collective levels) are in sync with the flow of nature then everything naturally flows in abundance. This state we can call a blessing.

When, however, the natural flow becomes stuck because human behavior becomes selfish and corrupted, then human beings (be it the individual or the society) grow more out of sync with the greater body of the natural world. This state is what we call being cursed.

The individual(s) who embrace this course of action are acting like cancer cells in the body. The more that they grow, the greater the threat to life itself. Nature therefore intervenes and makes every effort to remove the cancerous cells (wicked individuals or societies) from its body. Once cleansed, the body of nature heals itself, and life goes on as intended.

Everything is energy. Nature is energy. Human beings are energy. Human society is energy. Morals and behavior are energy. And yes, even righteousness and wickedness are energy. We always observe and judge others by their individual energy signatures.

Any individual who embraces evil and unnatural ways is by definition out of sync with nature. And nature will respond. For those who seek to walk the natural path and to be naturally righteous and moral, such a one should make every effort to distance oneself from those individuals who are cancerous members within society. No good can came from out of sync individuals. The wise therefore proceed with wisdom and separate themselves from those who bring harm to themselves and others. This is done naturally in righteousness, with morals and dignity (and not with expressions of emotional disdain).

Natural energy must flow. Righteousness must prevail. Every one of us is either part of the problem, or part of the solution. One is either a taker, or a giver. Yes, in reality there is a bit of both in each of us, but I am not talking about day to day behaviors, I am talking about the natural flow of energy through the individual human system.

Some by nature seek to take, to keep, to hoard, and not to share. This is the evil one. Others by nature seek to give, to share, to help others, and work for their betterment. This is the righteous one.

Yes, we each have some of both within us. And this is why the great natural battle resides within the individual. In the end the great separation will occur, and one will be found to be either disease or cure. And then one's future will be determined as to what lessons one will have to endure in order to realign and to come back in sync with the natural way.

Everything is energy, and energy can be felt. Sensing the natural way becomes all the easier when one returns to a natural environment and feels from nature itself what is and what is not the natural way. That which we call the Hand of God is what moves nature. One who seeks to bond with God will only find God in the natural way. For here is where the Way of God is to be found.

13. Psychic Being

Jan. 17, 23, pre-dawn

For those who seek to develop the psychic powers of the mind, know that such a pursuit is built upon a lie. And this is why no one who seeks to walk this path succeeds in finding one's goal.

The lie is subtle and easy to expose. Psychic development has nothing to do with the expansion of the rational, intellectual faculties of thought. You can't think psychically. To be psychic and to think are on opposite sides of the spectrum of the mind. Indeed, we have to stop thinking of the mind as being an exclusive tool for rational, intellectual thought.

Psychic mind is an expression of psychic energy. Psychic energy is biological, and it is very overtly (in its own way) magnetic. We call this psychic magnetic energy sexual.

Psychic energy is sexual energy. Sexual energy is the function of the mind (yes, mind) that we call the heart, or feelings, or sensations (as opposed to simple everyday emotions). Thus the way to develop psychic abilities is to cultivate and manipulate sexual energy.

And no one can gather sexual energy while one is wasting it, and dissipating it by promiscuous sexual activity. This is why one finds in all ancient (authentic) spiritual (psychic, prophetic) training programs there was always a strong set of rules with regards to the right and wrong ways of expressing one's sexuality.

None of these systems were celibate, and equally on the opposite end, none of them practiced debauchery. There was a healthy and proper balance of sexual energy that matched and calibrated with the Earth's and the universe's natural balance and harmony.

Without this natural balance and harmony any and all sexual practices, be they for spiritual purposes or merely for physical gratification, will still contain a higher energetic, magnetic component that by nature attracts to every participant an equally psychic, sexual, energetic force.

This is why and how improper sexual activity opens the participant up to attachments to, and involvement with higher dimensional forces that view one's waste of sexual energy (through intercourse and ejaculation) as an easy source of psychic food.

The more that one is promiscuous, the greater the feeding frenzy one creates with one's actions. The more promiscuous that one is the greater the number of entities that feed off the one.

Such a one becomes a source for psychic feeding, and the results of which are that the individual is left without enough psychic (life-force) energy for oneself. When this results one sees that such infected individuals suffer from a long list of emotional and mental health problems, usually with negative social implications. In almost all cases, physical illnesses eventually manifest.

Unless there is a comprehensive change in one's life style, such an individual usually becomes very self-destructive and seeks to harm oneself (and others) in many different ways. If and when such an individual seeks to involves oneself with any kind of spiritual or religious pursuit, it becomes quickly clear that the expressions of choice that the one embraces only reinforces one's negative state, and then (like a virus) one seeks to propagate it in others. This is how religious cults, and bizarre beliefs and rituals are born. They all reinforce the psychic feeding frenzy of higher entities feeding off of the souls of imbalanced blind fools.

Those who walk the natural path bond with a partner of the opposite sex in a proper monogamous relationship. This relationship may be temporary or permanent. The greater the longevity the greater the natural flow of balanced and harmonious Earthly and universal energy that is generated between the two and flows naturally through them.

In this state of natural and harmonious energetic alignment, there is no waste, and thus no opening for external entities to enter in and to seek to siphon off any waste.

In such a state of energetic balance, one can feel one's internal state of balance, and use this feeling as a guide towards feeling beyond it into higher dimensional realms where revelations and insights come to one's mind through the feeling sensation as it is experienced through the imaginative faculty.

In essence, one sees something imagined within one's inner vision, and one's internal energy senses the truth of it and embraces it as such. With greater energetic focus, one may even become aware of the meanings underlying obtuse images that permeate one's inner vision during such visionary experiences.

This is how psychic seeing and prophecy works. It is not thought, it is felt. It is not conjured by an act of concentration, rather it is received by an act of imagination. Everything thus revolves around the proper flow of universal energy.

14. Never Extreme

Jan. 17, 23, post dawn

Never be extreme! Every swing of the pendulum creates a force for movement in the opposite direction.

This is the rule of natural law in this physical domain. And this physical law is only a local manifestation of the same principle that operates in higher dimensions in accordance to the laws of physics that dominate there.

Everything is always in movement. Right and wrong movements are defined by natural laws in each dimension and world. That which is right and normal is universal and is applicable everywhere, but with this being said, the nature of its application will be unique. But being unique does not mean that such movements will contradict or act in opposition to natural norms.

The natural law of energetic movement is what defines what is normal and abnormal, and thus equally defines what is right from wrong, what is moral from immoral, and also defines the difference between righteousness and wickedness. All these human concepts are not subject to human definitions. They are already predefined, and prescribed by nature and natural law.

It is however true that human beings, the more and more that they embrace unnatural ways of thinking and behavior, create a growing unnatural push of the proverbial pendulum. And the laws of physics dictate, the greater the push into the unnatural, the greater is the force generated to push in the opposite direction in order to restore balance.

These natural forces look at human beings and the energetic movements that their behaviors generate as being part and parcel of the energetic whole of things. Thus when human behavior generates unnatural energetic waves, creating extremes, nature and natural law responds (in its own time) and restores balance.

From a human point of view, the restoration of balance may manifest in the collapse of a civilization alongside the deaths of millions (or billions). Nature and natural law simple doesn't care. It is operating in accordance to higher natural principle and natural laws which have their origins with nature's proverbial Law Giver.

So, those who think that they can live unnatural lives and at the same time call upon their Creator to maintain and even bless their unnatural lifestyles are in for a shocking awakening. All the more so those who embrace the mentality that there is no Creator, nor are there any natural laws to which one must submit and comply, they will also find themselves and all that they built swept away under the force of the opposite movement of the natural pendulum, itself caused by their own pushing it into such extreme imbalance.

15. Knowing & Doing

Jan. 17, 23, evening

It is never enough to merely agree with something. One must then implement a course of action to enact that which one embraces. Talk is cheap. Only actions speak.

Those who engage in extensive academic reviews waste their time if they do not seek their answers from the higher dimensional realm from which all answers come.

One must recognize the limits of the academic approach. Reality is far more than material and physical. Everything manifest in this universe is only a part of its greater whole. We do not see the whole. Indeed, we blind our eyes to anything from the higher dimensions. We arrogantly proclaim there are no such dimensions, and that they cannot possibly dictate and control one's life. But they do!

The higher dimensions are all around us, inside us and are very much an integral part of us. Those who lose contact with this reality will experience life as being similar to a puppet on a string, with no control and no power of direction.

Only those who sense out and feel the higher dimension and the power of its pull over everything both here and there will be able to make some sense out of one's life and the experiences that one seems destined to experience.

One must unlearn all that one has learned, and to start again from the beginning to seek out the true meaning of life, living, and the world around us. One who continues to walk the academic path, demanding that all make sense, and that all reality submit to one's limited perspective and intelligence will continue to walk in darkness, and reinforce darkness wherever such a one goes.

One must unlearn the rigid and learn the fluid. One must learn from the reception of consciousness that comes from higher dimensions what are the proper parameters and boundaries of all things.

How much is too much, how much is too little, how much is right, how much is wrong, what is the right balance for all things, both seen and unseen; the academic mind can never discover the truths of these things. These things are known in the higher dimensions, and only the reception of revelation from these dimensions will give one the inner knowing that gives one truth, balance, and wisdom.

Do not agree with these words and then do nothing. If these words speak to you then inside your heart you know the truth of them. It is never enough to simply agree, one must then proceed to implement a course of change. And all change begins within, but never stops there. One's life, one's place, one's lifestyle must change in order to bring one into proper alignment with the ways of the higher dimensions that truly control all things around us.

Start by unlearning. Close your books. Silence your mouth from questions. Still your mind from contemplation. Sit still and silent in the midst of the natural world that is our Mother, and listen! Learn to receive, not to take. Be open to movement. Be willing to change. Allow the wind to blow where it will, and to blow you to where you need to be. The knowing of the higher dimensions will guide your path, but you need to be open to surrender to it, and to not stand as an obstacle in its way.

Enough words for now. Contemplate them, but not too much. Allow your mind to drift off and to wander. Ask Heaven to guide both your feelings and your thoughts. When the knowing comes, you will know it.

16. Mob Mind-Violence

Jan 19, 23, predawn

Any intellectual position that seeks to justify itself based upon emotional outbursts and tirades is a position that most likely has no intellectual honesty to it whatsoever.

Be very careful of believing a thing because of how you feel about it. Just like your feelings are subject to manipulation so too is what you think. When an outside force can manipulate how you feel about a thing, then one's emotions overwhelm one's intellect and convinces one that what one feels is logical and right, and therefore what one thinks is equally logical and right. One then feels justified, and even motivated to act upon what one feels. This is how people are manipulated into performing acts of evil and terror.

Mob violence comes in many forms. Mob violence is when a manipulated group is unleashed upon another group (or individual) who the mob has been convinced is a source of evil and is a danger. The group-think of the mob shows that there is no longer independent intellectual thought possible on behalf of the individuals within the mob. The individual has been lost, and one's identity is absorbed into the greater group. The loss of Self and the absorption of Self into the mob is the clearest definition of mental slavery.

Another term for such mental slavery is mind-control. Mind control begins with emotional control. Emotional control is a form of programming wherein the individual is constantly bombarded with imagery, words, impressions, and social pressure compelling the individual to submit to the mob-mind.

Most individuals are not astute mental thinkers. Most do not even see the creeping specter of mob-mind seeping into their consciousness. Most are so oblivious that they lose their individuality and become absorbed into mob-mind without even being aware of it happening. This is how mindless masses are formed. And history has recorded all too many times when the mindless masses are unleashed leading to destruction and the deaths of millions.

Death and destruction come, and the first casualty is always the individuality of the person. The intellect is made subservient to swaying, manipulated emotions. And the emotions of the mob are manipulated by the puppet-master, who is pulling the strings from some concealed position. There is always (at least) one who fires up the mob, brainwashing them, manipulating them, and then like a primed time-bomb unleashes them upon whatever target that the hidden puppet-master has chosen for attack and destruction.

We can look to history and see these events in episodes like the Crusades, the Pogroms, and the Holocaust. There are unfortunately countless other examples. But even with an historical review, most in present times, cannot see how the forms of manipulation used in the past are equally being used in the present in an attempt to seduce modern masses, turning them into a mob designed to mindlessly act and wreak havoc on behalf of some modern hidden puppet-master. And as in the past, people today lose their individuality and find themselves absorbed into today's slavery of the mind, with all the social control that comes along with it.

Today the world wide web, social media, and the general trends in society have all been weaponized and used to destroy individuality. The new message is that the individual is a danger and a threat. The new morality is that independent thinking is harmful and wrong. The proclaimed solution to all our problems is that each and every one must submit to the greater whole and to be absorbed into it. Only when the individual no longer exists can the mob rule supreme. And thus we have mental slavery and mind control, where the masses have no idea as to what has happened to them, and have no desire for change.

Today it is the world wide web, social media, and the general trends in society that manipulate the loss of Self and the absorption into the mob mind. All those who embrace and interact with the world wide web, social media, and the general trends in society will not escape being tainted by their foul and contaminating grip. One cannot come into contact with mud and not get dirty.

There is only one defense against the onslaught against the Self that most face today. One must lessen one's emotional reaction to things, and learn to think slowly, carefully, and cautiously before one decides what one chooses to think. Clear thought can put one in touch with one's inner Self, the Source within us that knows to be above manipulation be it emotional or even intellectual. Only by not succumbing to mob-mind can one resist its ceaseless onslaught. And the only way to not succumb to mob-mind is to make every effort to maintain one's individuality, and one's independent thoughts.

However, there is a danger. One who stands up to mob-mind will be noticed as different. For the mob that which is different is bad, evil and a threat. One who thinks for oneself will be recognized, targeted, isolated, and eventually condemned as the enemy. What will happen next is not a course of action that any rational individual wants to see. But the mob wants to see it, and indeed participate in it, if not outright instigate it. This is the example of history. Based upon the present, this is our fear for the future.

17. The Right Time

Jan. 21, 23 After Sabbath

Everything has its time. Everything has its own pace. We often use the term "right time" to describe something that happens at a time that manifests certain positive conditions. And we use the opposite term, "bad (wrong) time" to describe something that happens at a time that manifests certain negative conditions.

But how is one to know in advance what is the right time or what is the wrong time. Are not both understandings of time only clear in hindsight, after an event has occurred, and the results of its occurrence observed? Those who are disconnected from time itself may indeed believe such to be the case. But for those who understand "the times" that which is right and that which is wrong is sensed and known long before the manifestation of the time in material space.

In energetic reality all things are in constant movement. As such it can be known when certain energetic realities will become manifest in physical space-time, and also when their manifestation will cease. Many might wish to view this movement as being mechanical. As if one could measure the speeds and directions of certain energy fields, and thus forecast when they will intersect with material space-time and accordingly manifest therein. But such mechanical calculations can never be properly made while one's observation is limited to material space-time. Therefore, those who are limited by the confines of their own thought-patterns are not capable of seeing or knowing the reality of energetic movements.

Each of us exists (right at the very moment) in higher dimensional realities. Our physical brain is hardwired to draw our attention to only those things of this material space-time dimension. Awareness of the higher dimensions (while always present) is repressed into a part of ourselves that we now call the Unconscious Mind. Unconscious means unaware. It is a part of ourselves that we are not aware of due to our focus on external material space-time at the reality that it creates.

When one diverts attention away from the forms and attractions of external material space-time, one is able to walk an internal path back towards one's higher consciousness.

Along this path one learns to unlearn. Along this path one learns to let go, rather than to hang on. Along this path one surrenders one's connection to the outside world, and allows the higher reality of one's being to permeate one's conscious mind bringing to it a knowing that transcends the boundaries of material space time.

In this knowing one is able to experience the energetic realities of the higher dimensions. In this knowing one is able to interact with the energetic realities of the higher dimensions. And in this knowing, one may very well indeed be able to influence the energetic realities of the higher dimensions. And one who can influence a thing can participate in its energetic manifestation in physical space-time. One can indeed influence and even change the times.

18. The Seer

Jan. 22, 23

Some things exist above and beyond space and time. And yet due to the natural modulations and movements of these things, they can every now and then descend and manifest in this physical dimension. They will simply come and go. They enter and they exist. They descend and ascend again.

As they come closer to this physical dimension their presence is sensed by those in this dimension who are sensitive enough to sense their approaching manifestation. Often those who are sensitive enough to sense what is coming will make this coming manifestation known to others in this physical dimension.

Yet those others here who have no sensitivity to anything in the higher dimensions do not and cannot see that which the sensitive do see. They therefore look upon the sensitive with skepticism, and often with scorn.

These same sensitive types we call by different names. We can call them seer, prophet, or psychic. Granted many will call themselves by one of these names, and of the many who claim the title only a rare few are really ever sensitive enough to earn it.

Many sense many things but do not see clearly into the higher dimensions to see what it is that they are sensing. As such their sensing abilities are clouded and unclear. This is almost always due to the individual's energy signature which itself is a byproduct of one's personal actions, feelings, and thoughts. As long as one embraces that which is unnatural, untrue and out-of-sync with the fluctuations of the higher dimensions, one's sensitivities to the higher dimensions will remain cloudy and unclear.

Thus when one like this attempts to forewarn of a coming interdimensional interaction, what they visualize as happening may or may not come to fruition. This is why many who are sensitive to higher dimensions are not sensitive enough. They in turn become known as false prophets.

Higher dimensional realities have a life of their own. They fluctuate and move in accordance to the nature of their own innate beings. They will come and go, rise and fall, grow and shrink, all in accordance to the nature of their being as ordained by higher law.

Sometimes human interactions can have an influence upon them. Sometimes human energetic signatures generate their own fields which will interact with the higher realities.

When this occurs, these autonomous higher realities are influenced. Their modulations and movements are affected. This will influence their interaction with physical space-time, making such an interaction to be either more or less intense. All human behavior has this energetic influence. While some may seek to use their awareness of the higher dimensions to influence the movements of things therein, they may or may not be hindered by the energetic signatures of the rest of humanity.

Sometimes, some individuals can (and do) intervene to influence the manifestations of higher realities into physical space-time. Sometimes those who can influence, and who seek to do so, are not able to do so because of the overwhelming energy signatures of the rest of humanity. This happens quite regularly. When it does, what manifests will manifest, and it will interact with everything in this physical space-time dimension (and those that dwell here), each in accordance to the specific interaction of the energy signature of the individual with that which manifests.

The results of these interactions may bring blessing or curse, help or harm, salvation or damnation. It all depends on many different things.

This is why those who are properly trained to be sensitive to these comings and goings also seek to make the interactions to be most beneficial for those who dwell in this physical space-time reality. Sometimes the sensitive succeed and sometimes they do not.

They always see what is coming. Whether or not they can influence what is coming is always subject to numerous variables, the likes of which no one on Earth can completely control.

The sensitive who are called seer, prophet, and psychic share their message. But who listens? Most often the seer, prophet and psychic are condemned and insulted. Only too late is it realized just how true they are.

The movement in higher dimensions can be symbolically compared to the roar of a ferocious lion. All in nature who hear the lion's roar know to fear and to take precautions. The true and sincere seers, prophets and psychics hear the lion's roar, and advise all of the coming lion. They themselves take precautions. As for the rest, nature must take its course.

The lion will find its prey. And life will go on. That which is above will manifest below. It will stay for its time and ascend above all in accordance to its nature and the nature of its interactions. Those who cultivate sensitivities to the higher movements will know and understand. As for the rest, what else can be said, or done?

19. Where You Think

Jan. 23, 23 predawn

Make no mistake! One's reality is built upon the very thoughts that one allows to enter into one's mind. If one allows oneself to be exposed to negative thoughts, then the imagery of those negative thoughts will cling to the inside of one's mind.

These negative images will implant themselves within one's subconscious, waiting for a trigger to occur to arouse them from the depths and to rise and to haunt one's conscious thoughts. Such negative thoughts and images can never come into one's conscious mind unless one allowed them access in the first place.

Where one thinks is where one is at! What one thinks influences one's emotions and one's behavior. What one thinks about oneself and about the world surrounding one is almost for sure faulty and wrong. No one can see all reality in the truth of its being. We always see what is through the veil that covers the eyes and that clouds the thoughts. As such, one's thoughts always cloud one's perceptions of reality. Thus where is one at? One resides in a place that one cannot see clearly. Essentially, one's thoughts, due to the limitations inherent in their nature, create for one a perception of reality that is not real.

Before one can attempt to approach a perception of higher dimensional realities, one must first address the improper perceptions that pervert one's perception of the reality of this physical space-time dimension. One who cannot see the reality underlying this dimension will certainly not be able to see the realities underlying any other dimension (be it higher or lower).

Clouded vision is clouded vision. It will affect everything that one sees and perceives regardless of what it is (or where it is) that one gazes. No one will see a clear vision of Heaven prior to one having a clear vision of Earth.

The human subconscious mind is that domain which sits between the conscious mind that views and interacts with this physical space-time dimension, and the unconscious, which is one's higher Self, residing as it is presently in higher dimensions, as it interacts with its domain of higher realities. The subconscious mind is a barrier, a husk, a shell that separates between realities and realities. Unless the individual can penetrate into one's personal subconscious and clean it out, one will forever be tainted and haunted by its contents.

Cleansing the subconscious is a doable thing. For some it may be more difficult than for others. But as it said, the amount of reward (that comes out of a thing) equals the amount of effort (put into it in the first place).

One must contemplate one's own thoughts and seek to understand them in depth. One must not only ask what it is that one is thinking, but also, why it is that one is thinking these thoughts. What is it about a certain set of images that makes them pop up out of nowhere into the conscious mind?

One must gaze upon one's own thoughts and observe their comings and their goings. One must observe and understand how these thoughts make one feel, and how they motivate one to act in one way or another (for either good or evil).

The observation process may take one a long time, but again, the more effort one puts into understanding one's self, the greater the reward of clarity of thought, and the greater clarity of seeing the deeper reality of the world both inside us and surrounding us. Only when this procedure has brought about significant results in cleansing one's subconscious can one begin to walk the path of connecting with one's unconscious and through it begin to experience (along with it) the higher realities in which we live, but are oblivious to.

Where one thinks is where one is at. Every individual has the ability to change. Every individual can move one's thoughts from a bad place to a good place. Yes, effort is involved. But the rewards for such effort will be self-evident.

Every hell-on-Earth begins in the mind of the individual. Every redemption and salvation begins within the same mind. There is great power within the mind of the one who chooses to confront and to cleanse one's personal subconscious. One's own higher unconscious Self is always present inspiring the conscious mind to clean up its mess.

This is indeed a long and arduous process, but it is a necessary one. And now is the time for one to get to work doing this; for if not now, then when?

<u>20. Guarding Secrets</u>

Jan. 24, 23 morning

Information is both a commodity and a tool. Tools are used for many different things, both for building and for destruction.

A hammer is a tool. It can be used to either build a thing or to tear it down. Yet, one thing is certain, tools are not toys.

One would not give a small child a hammer to play with. Indeed, the child might be hurt severely, and the one to blame would be the one who gave the child the hammer in the first place. The child does not understand the dangers inherent in the misuse of the hammer, whereas the adult does know this, and is expected to act accordingly with an adult's understanding of a child's limitations.

Information is a tool. Information can be used to build or to destroy. Like the hammer, certain information does not belong in the hands of the one who is not properly able to use it. Just like the child must be safeguarded from the hammer, so too must the unprepared be safeguarded from information that can prove to be harmful to them.

In order to safeguard information and in order to protect the unprepared, secrets are made, and kept. It is not only wise, but also necessary that certain information be kept secret from those who are unprepared to receive it.

Revealing secrets to those who are not prepared to receive the information therein is rightfully compared to giving a young child a dangerous tool to play with. A hammer is a dangerous tool. Without even realizing it, a child can swing the hammer in fun, and strike another child, causing severe bodily harm, and maybe even death. Information in the wrong hands leads those who possess it to act in ways similar to the child, by reacting or responding to the information in ways that is harmful to oneself and to others.

The one in charge is therefore responsible to make sure that no harm, and no damage occurs. This is why secrets are properly safeguarded, and even their existence remains secret and out of the hands of those not ready to receive them.

There are many secrets. Rightfully are they safeguarded. Although the child might whine and cry demanding to play with a new toy, the wise adult does not succumb to childish whining. Secrets will remain secret. Information will be withheld. This will continue until the individual child grows up and proves oneself to be an adult. Once one proves oneself to be mature and responsible, only then can such a one be trusted with that, which they could be trusted with before.

This is my message to all those out there looking for secrets. Grow up! Stop being a child. Stop acting like a child. Once you prove your maturity and your ability to properly use a tool, only then will you be entrusted with it. So, the burden of growth and maturity is upon the individual. Once you are an adult, and act like one, only then will you be ready.

Becoming an adult is not about biological aging, it is about psychological aging. We have many biological adults who still act like little children. Temper tantrums and emotional outbursts are what is expected from children. Once one matures, and grows up, and learns how to handle one's internal affairs, only then can we say that the biological adult is also a psychological adult.

Due to present affairs, and the proliferation of adult children, secrets will remain secret for a long time to come. It is such a shame that there is such a proliferation of adult children, for this diminishes the number of builders that society could have. But it is better that there are less builders than to have an overwhelming numbers of destroyers.

Society today has enough adult children who serve as destroyers. To keep away from them any tools that will contribute to their destructive behavior is a very good thing. And thus secrets will remain secret, and the children can whine and cry all they want. In this way, life, and the world itself, remains safe. Good!

21. Layers

Jan. 25, 23 predawn

To everything there are layers. Layers upon layers, one covering over another, one concealing another. Nothing ever is as it seems. This is a fundamental truth in all applications.

So, why is this important? Why must we know that there are layers to all things? The answer is clear to those who seek answers. The wise know that everything that they see and experience is only the surface level of the truth that confronts them. The wise and the observant recognize that what they see and what they perceive is really only the first of many causes.

To understand why something is the way that it is; and equally to understand why something acts the way that it does, one must delve beneath its superficial surface and look for underlying layers of influence that are creating the combination of effects that manifest as the way that a thing is, or the way that it acts. Without such insight nothing can be properly understood.

To understand a thing requires a thorough perception of all its parts and how each interacts with one another to cause and to manifest that which is. And herein lies a problem. Unless one investigates beneath the surface of a thing, and then investigates even deeper levels, and again ever more deeper levels, one will not come to the ultimate understanding of the how and why of anything. One may indeed tire from such intensive penetrations, but without them full clarity cannot be achieved.

Understanding is a product of the intellectual mind. Understanding requires clarity of consciousness. The mind must expand consciousness in order to expand understanding. And an expansion of consciousness comes from a source of thought that itself is hidden under layers upon layers of concealment.

To acquire understanding one must learn how to peel away one's internal layers of confusion that cloud the mind, inhibiting clarity. For whatever thoughts that one may think, there are deeper reasons, deeper meanings, and even deeper thoughts.

As one thinks one must ask oneself why does one think the way that one does. When one gazes out upon the world, one sees what one sees. And yet one must ask why is it that one perceives things in the way that one does.

Essentially, rather than judge what one sees at face value, one instead questions oneself to ask, am I seeing what is before me correctly? Is there more than meets the eye concealed before me now, hidden from my present perception? The answer to this is most often always yes.

Therefore before one draws conclusions that will serve as the reasons for one's actions, one must pause and look carefully for that which cannot be seen, and for that which may be hidden. For the concealed and the hidden may reveal vital information that will completely change the conclusions that one will draw, and thus change the way that one will react.

A wrong reaction usually comes about from wrong perception, and wrong perception comes about from a lack of understanding, and the lack of understanding comes about because one does not look deeply enough to properly understand a thing in the first place. Shallow thinking and shallow perceptions lead to wrong conclusions and thus to wrong actions. Wrong actions cause great harm and should be avoided at all costs.

Expanding consciousness thus requires expanded understanding. And as one explores deeper understandings one will discover within oneself, within one's mind, an inner guide that will steer one towards the insights that one seeks. This inner guide is Wisdom.

Wisdom speaks with a soft, almost silent voice deep within one's thoughts. Yet, once one senses it and cultivates its growth, its voice grows loud and clear, granting deep and profound understanding that can prove itself under the tests of contemplation and analysis.

Wisdom guides one to understanding and understanding brings one to clarity. Clarity, in turn, calms the turbulent heart. And once the mind is clear, and the heart is calm, one can then know how to act, and what to do that is right and proper for the moment.

To everything there are layers upon layers of hidden truths. One who sees only the surface of a thing sees only the façade and not the truth concealed underneath it. One who embraces the shallow façade and acts upon it understands little, if anything at all. The actions of such a one, because of a lack of understanding, may indeed prove to be harmful and dangerous.

The way to depth is the work of the mind. Wisdom and understanding work together to bring revelation. This is the path towards progress and growth. Without wisdom and understanding the mind remains primitive, blind, and essentially dangerous. Yet, this is a danger that can be avoided and overcome. All one has to do is to seek deeper understanding, and to allow the calm heart and wisdom to internally guide the way.

22. Words of Power

Jan. 26, 23 morning

Remember! Words in the pages of a book are just words! Their message and meaning only have power in the mind of the reader.

Some words speak with a voice louder than others. Some words, spoken or written, come from a source beyond the speaker or writer.

Words like these have a power to them, a power to motivate and to inspire. Words like these speak not only to the rational mind, but also to the feeling heart. Words like these inspire action. Words like these compel one to act, and to bring about some sort of change that the words motivate.

Some words do indeed have this power. But not all words. Most words have very little power, if any power at all.

Words in a book are dead, unless the reader choses to bring them to life. And raising the dead requires of one more than just reading.

Words of power have a life of their own. When one reads them, their dead forms on the page of a book send forth their spirit. The spirit of the words then penetrates the mind and the heart of the reader. Within the inner recesses of the mind of the reader the spirit of the words, like seeds, take root and begin to grow. Influence is thus born. Influence can lead to many forms of manifestation, be these for good or for evil.

One must always be aware of the spirit of the words that one reads (or hears spoken). For the spirit turns dead words into living ones. And the living word is an immortal being whose influence spans both time and language. Know and understand the power of the living word, and distinguish it from the word that bears no such power.

The living word survives because the spirit within it lives on. Dead words die because once read (or spoken), there is not enough spirit within them to take root in the minds and imaginations of those who read (or hear them).

Beware of words that are important to some but not to others. Some see in some words a power that only they can sense and feel, whereas others feel and sense no such thing.

Some words are interpreted to say things that they do not say. Some words are understood to mean that which they do not mean. When this occurs, some apply to words an understanding and a power that is not truly there. When this occurs, dead words are presented as alive, and instead all that we have is an animated corpse.

Such words become monsters in their own right, frightening others to comply with their intended meaning, and threatening those who do not comply.

Beware of dead words in the minds and hearts of those whose spirit is dead. For such souls are the blind who seek to lead the blind and to promote more blindness. For in the darkness of blindness dead words proclaimed to be alive appear to be actually alive. No one sees the monster for what it truly is. And this is how the monsters of deception grow and prosper.

When another tells you that such are words of power, but you do not sense such power, do not succumb to the mindset of that other. Always let your truth be yours.

Do not accept the truth of another simply because you are being told that this is the right thing to do! If you do not sense the life in living words, then those words are not alive. Do not seek life where it is not.

The spirit of life in words needs to speak to the spirit of life within you. If there is no communication of spirit to spirit, then there is no life in those words for you.

What life another may sense in such words is for that other to decide. But for you, dead words will plant no seed within your mind, and will inspire no imagination to have you soar to higher heights. Leave such dead words in the graves of the pages of the books in which they are printed.

And if another comes to tell you how alive such words are, and that it is you who is dead, and not the words; do not be deceived by such a manipulative argument. Simply walk away. Monsters are born when the dead are raised without true life. Do not contribute to this effort, especially when others are pushing you to do this very thing.

23. Blindness

Jan 26, 23 evening.

How foolish we all are. How blind are we all that we cannot see even the simplest of truths standing right before our eyes.

Our reality is so much more than the material forms that we see. Our material forms are nothing more than shells. They contain a part of our consciousness, and at the same time entrap that part, and disconnect it from our greater, whole selves.

We are entrapped in a material world in which we are aware of only the smallest portion of ourselves that is imprisoned here.

Each of us is far more than our material forms. Each of us exists in multiple places, and in multiple forms simultaneously. Right now, at this very moment, we are aware of the part of us that is here and now reading these words. But there are other parts of us that are right now doing other things in other places. Each of these other parts of ourselves is as real as the part that we recognize as ourselves in this material world.

Many times other parts of ourselves influence the part of us that is here now. We may or may not be aware of this influence. But because all parts of us are an integral whole, it is no wonder that one part influences another, even if and when we are unaware of the source of influence.

24. Simplicity

Jan 29, 23

The greatest secrets are always concealed in simplicity. This is why they are rarely discovered.

The more simple something is the greater the sublime that it conceals. But such revelation can only come about upon contemplation. When one gazes upon the simple, the rational mind is offended by the simplicity and often refuses to entertain the thought that there is hidden complexity veiled under a thin façade of simplicity. The arrogant mind therefore deceives itself, and limits itself from experiencing revelation.

Indeed, when one sees that which appears complex one is attracted to its complexity in the same way as the moth is destructively attracted to the light of fire. The human mind can only understand the complex to a point. Beyond this point, the rational intellect must consult its own inner intuition for further insights and revelation. Every scientist and artist knows this truth intimately. The intellect can only proceed so far before it runs into a brick wall of not knowing any more, and not having any access to further insight or knowledge. This is when one's intuition seeps into the mind and provides further hints along the way, enabling the intellect to continue its pursuit of truth.

As revelations come, the mind gazes upon what appears to be simple and begins to see "around its edges" signs and hints of further realities that were not seen before. And thus the mind, with intellect combined alongside intuition seeks to reappraise the simple. By exploring the simplicity of the simple one comes to revelations about the nature of simplicity that reveal the most intensely complex and the most intensely simple are actually one and the same.

This insight cannot come to be through rational thought alone. One must be shown this! And the one who shows this to oneself is none other than one's own higher mind (soul) that speaks the language of intuition (wisdom) into the rational thought of intellect (understanding).

Thus the greatest secrets are not found in that which the mind finds complex. Rather the greatest secrets are found in that which the mind finds simple. But since simplicity is not attractive to the complex mind, its hidden wisdom remains hidden.

Philosophical speculation is an entertainment for the complex intellect. As such it serves as a distraction preventing the inquiring mind from discovering the simplest of truths. The mind that seeks to make the simple complex is working in the direction away from revelation and not towards it. The philosophical mind looks to make connections between those pieces which it believes fits together.

The philosophical mind is so severely limited (a limitation which the mind itself strongly denies), that it builds complete constructs (of thought) that it is convinced (by its own rationale) to be are valid. The simple mind (on the other hand) led by intuition can clearly see beyond all the façade of philosophy and recognize the illusions and delusions that the philosophical mind has created for itself, and imprisons itself within.

And so the more rational and intellectual the mind, the greater its distance from spirit and intuition. The only solution for this self-imposed blindness is for one to unlearn what one has learned. One needs to stop being theoretical and learn to be actual, to learn from experience, and not from theory.

Simplicity is the key to revelation. Experience is the validation of knowing. The wise seek understanding through wisdom, and know that wisdom and understanding go hand in hand. One will not have one without the other.

One who seeks wisdom will find it in simplicity. One who seeks wisdom must learn to close one's books and to instead open one's heart. Instead of seeking the complex, one must return to simplicity. One must give up one's addiction to complexity and return to the natural way. Only in the experience of this will one understand (through) wisdom the validity of the experience. This is how secrets are revealed, communion is established, and wisdom received.

Do not think about this, but rather seek to feel its truth. If you do, only then will you experience knowing.

25. The Living Universe

Jan. 30, 23 morning

The universe around us is alive and it has a mind (soul) of its own. We are aware of the laws of nature that define for us the operations of the reality that we perceive. Yet behind all of natural law stands a natural Will, and the presence of a natural Will reveals the existence of a natural, universal Mind. Natural laws must have their source from somewhere or something. Let us call the source of natural law the natural Law Giver.

The universe is alive. It has been formed and made into the way that it is today. We human beings understand very little about the nature (the true identity) of the universe. We observe only the smallest part of the whole. And only the fool and the arrogant will make statements about the whole based on the limited knowledge of only a small portion of the truth. The one who looks upon the universe and who does not see it alive is oneself both blind and dead.

The human race and every member thereof, is part of nature and is thus subject to nature's natural laws. Human beings are thus subject to, and subjects of the universe's Law Giver. Human minds are subject to the universal Mind. Human will is subject to the Will of the universe. When human beings are properly aligned with the greater universe around them, then all is at peace. When however, human beings violate their own internal natural law, the universal Law Giver senses the disruption and the imbalance. This is true not only with human imbalance, but it is also true with regards to any place or source of imbalance anywhere in the universe.

Any human being seeking the meaning of life needs to contemplate the way and flow of life itself. For life itself manifests the Will of the universe's Law Giver. Proper life and proper living is the Way of the universe's Law Giver. The Law Giver is the singular source of all things, including the two powerful Forces, creation and destruction.

As we can see from clear observations, the universe will often unleash a power that brings with it death and destruction. But this destructive force is not a negative thing. For this destructive force destroys so that new life and new forms can be born. This is destruction for the sake of construction. One thing is broken down so that another (better) thing can come and take its place.

26. From the Mountaintop

Jan. 31, 23 predawn

What is wisdom? Why do we crave revelations and insights?

Wisdom is a higher knowing. We crave revelations and insights because we know deep within ourselves that there is more to everything than the mere shallow façade that we each experience daily. It is the inner truth of a thing that creates for each of us a hunger and a thirst that cannot be quenched.

We presently exist in a world of lies. Everything that we see and know is only the uppermost layer of many layers of deeper, hidden realities. This truth does not only describe that which is outside of us, it also, by all means, describes the reality inside of us. As such, we each experience and know that all that we see and hear is merely the surface layer of truth. And this surface layer is itself very, very different from the greater truths that are concealed within.

Those who allow themselves to be distracted by the false realities of this world become enslaved within them for lifetimes to come. So many today refuse to truthfully gaze beneath the surface of things. And yet, they will claim that they indeed seek wisdom, revelations, and insights.

But let the truth be told! Shallow people seek only shallow things. Those who embrace the façades and lies of this reality only seek inner depths that will reinforce their lies. They do nothing to expose such lies. They resist with vigor any attempt to expose their lies. They love their lies, and their lifestyles of distraction, and will fight to maintain the veils over their eyes. They create all kinds of arguments and philosophes to justify their foolish embrace, and arrogantly proclaim their way to be right!

Thus it is with fools and their foolishness. There is no talking to them. They have ears but cannot hear. They have eyes but cannot see.

The truly wise know where to best invest their efforts. The truly wise see the shallow ones, those who revel in the lies of this world, and remove themselves from their presence. The wise know that true wisdom can only take root within the minds and hearts of those who reject the ways of this world, and who refuse to allow themselves to be distracted by them.

Know and understand a simple truth. What you cling to, in turn clings to you. The thoughts that you think create for you the reality which you experience. The more one clings to the façades of truth, the more and more shallow one becomes. The greater one revels in lies, the more convincing those lies become. There is no greater lie than the one that convinces one that one is righteous, when in reality one is very far from righteousness.

Many claim that they seek the higher wisdom. But the higher wisdom begins only when lower wisdom ends. This is only natural, but who today can see the natural through the many layers of the unnatural which we embrace and cloak ourselves within. Lower wisdom ends first before higher wisdom begins.

One who interprets emotional sensations as wisdom is a fool! Wisdom begins only when emotions are calm, balanced, and at peace. Wisdom is like a breath of fresh air, a soft refreshing breeze that moves over the turmoil of the waters of emotion. Wisdom calms. Emotions create turmoil, the opposite of calm. One who seeks true wisdom must know the meaning of the ever-beating, but always still heart.

Lies come and entertain one's mind with thoughts that makes one feel good. Lies come and elevate one's emotional state, giving one a sense of a high. One likes this sense of being high, one enjoys the entertainments of the mind. These make one happy, and then one rejoices in this happiness, and believes that such rejoicing is itself a higher state of being and consciousness. And so the blind remain blind, and lies serve to reinforce themselves. Those who cling to the façades of truth will never go beyond them.

All façades and all lies eventually come to an end. When it is their natural time to die, those that cling to them will often die along with them. Being that the shallow have chosen nothing but shallowness, they have no deeper roots to withstand the storms of change. Circumstances and situations arise in the world which leads to their recycling. Those who cling to this world pass away with this world. And to this world they return over and over again, all because they refuse to let go of the façades. They cling to lies, and in turn lies cling to them. This is a repetitive process and takes many lifetimes to change and to cleanse.

For the wise, it is a tiring burden to gaze upon the fools of façades. The wise thus chose not to engage them. The wise respond to the fools of façades with a façade all their own. The wise put on a friendly face, act humbly, conceal their wisdom, and their inner knowing, and move (when necessary) among the fools of façades with the least amount of notice. The wise do not cling to the fools of façade for fear that their foolishness might attempt to cling to them.

Remember the great rule: anything that holds you down, prevents you from rising up. The wise know this and act accordingly.

And so now, what more can I say? What more is there to be done? I, myself, the author of these words, must confess that in truth, while I am the one writing down these words, the words themselves are being spoken into my thoughts as I write them. They come to me from deep within, from the higher domains to which I cling.

What I see, I see with a vision of insight that most others cannot see, and thus do not share. It is foolish and in vain to try and convince another to accept that which I see, but which they cannot. All I can do is to say and proclaim that there is more to see for those who wish to see. All I can do is to point the way to the mountaintop, and say: climb! And when you reach the top, you too will see, and thus you will know, even as do I.

I have struggled to climb to the mountaintop. I have let go of the façades and the shallowness that holds one down. I have surrendered all that weighs one down, so that that can move about with greater mobility and ease. When you chose the same, you will accomplish the same.

One may be surrounded by the things of this world without the things of this world clinging to one, holding one down. This is indeed a difficult balance, but it can be done.

Detach, let go, and at the same time, fulfill your responsibilities. Cast off and reject the façades and the shallowness. If you wish to walk the path, it lies before you, open and welcoming. But the rules are the rules. The natural ways must be respected. You cannot take the shallow into the deep. You cannot take the things of this world into the higher domains. You must let go of the one, in order to pursue the other.

And so the wise continue to be wise, and the fools continue to be fools. From the mountaintop we shout down, and show those below the path to ascend. Those who look up will see. Those still playing with their distracting toys will not!

And so the Voice continues to cry out every day. Deep within us all, the Voice creates its ripples underneath the surface of consciousness. Those buried under the façades of foolishness make every effort to repress the inner Voice, and to ignore its call. But the Voice will not cease, now or ever. The Voice has its Way, and its Will shall be done. And there is no more to say than this.

I am returning now to gaze out from my mountaintop. The rest is up to you.

27. The Light of the Moon

Feb. 1, 23

And so it begins! Or does it? Consciousness operates in cycles. Like a spiral staircase consciousness expands by going around and around in ascent.

Consciousness expands as the contemplative mind gazes out to glean insights from all things, be they good or evil. For all things that occur in this space-time reality happen for a reason. If one gazes upon what happens and seeks to understand it in all its complex parts, one will discover underlying it (and underlying all things) that there is a singularity of simplicity.

And so it begins! Or does it? Expanded consciousness dawns within one's perception of reality. And one believes that this is the beginning. But it is no such thing! That which may be new to us is not new unto itself.

Consciousness has no beginning even though there is a point of its beginning to dawn within our individual minds. We must realize that there is nothing new under the sun, and allow your consciousness to know that there is nothing new over the sun as well. Be it under or over, higher or lower, greater to lesser, this dimension or another, all are part of the greater whole. We too are part of this greater whole.

Within every part of the whole there exists in miniature the sum total of the whole. Therefore, rather than seek to gaze outside to grasp a glimpse of vision of that which no external vision can grasp, the wise know to invert their vision and to gaze within. For the whole of all can be gazed upon by seeing the miniature of the whole that is within each and every part of us (and of all things).

It is this manner of internal contemplation that provides for one the birth of expanded consciousness. And this birth is a no-birth. For although consciousness is born into the mind of the individual, it comes into mind with all its parts and form intact. Like a child that comes forth from the womb of its mother, consciousness is born, both anew and not new.

Just like the newborn child that is born to live again, so too consciousness that dawns into the mind of the individual has been in the minds of others previously, and was to those others like their own child, just like the ideas of expanded consciousness are like the children of those who perceive them now.

Indeed, the thoughts that you (and I) are thinking now have been thought of before, in the minds of many others. And so it begins? No! And so it continues! Life and consciousness always recycle (reincarnate), for thus is the Will of the Mind behind the universal Way.

The one who clears the mind of thought creates an empty space. It is in this empty space that new thoughts of expanded consciousness can enter in, and fill. So, the beginning is not the reception, but rather it is the removal of the old to make a place for the new. Reception begins by first making a place in the mind for the reception to be received.

The womb is cleansed of the old before the new can grow within. Every woman knows this within the secrets of her own flesh. Gaze within a thing to understand a thing. Even the natural way of the monthly cycle of women teaches us the secrets of the reception of expanded consciousness. Let go of the old, cleanse the receptacle, and then the new can penetrate within, and bring with it the creation of new life, that is in reality old life that now comes in new form.

Consciousness grows in just this way. The older form of consciousness in the mind and experience of one is reborn into the mind and experience of another. The kernel of consciousness is like the father, the new forms in the new mind are like its mother. The old and new combine, and thus consciousness is reborn, now in a new form, higher up on the spiraling ladder of ascent.

This is the way of expanding consciousness. Father unites with Mother in the properly prepared womb. Know this secret! Understand its truths by gazing within. When you see the truth of it, you will know what to do, and how to cleanse your mind even as the body of the female cleanses itself every month.

The Light of the Moon is a reflection of the Light of the Sun. Know the secret of the Moon, and your will see the Light of the Sun shining upon you.

28. Naturally Wise

Feb. 2, 23 midnight

There is a time for noise and there is a time for silence. There is a time for movement and there is a time for stillness. There is a time to look outside of oneself and there is a time to look inside of oneself. There is a time for childhood and there is a time for childhood to end.

One with wisdom understands that the child within needs to grow up and become an adult. One without wisdom seeks to remain a child and refuses nature's call to grow up and mature.

As we can see there are many paths before one. One path, the path of noise, movement, and external observation is the path of the child, the one who has not yet learned wisdom. The other path is the way of silence, stillness, and internal reflection. This is the path of one who has matured into wisdom.

The child knows only one path and thus goes through life making lots of noise, running around erratically, and always looking outside of oneself for the next stimuli for excitement.

The mature adult knows many paths, and knows that alongside silence, there is still a time for noise; alongside stillness, there is still a time for movement, and alongside internal contemplation there is still time for external observations. All these things the wise know, and they know them in moderation, and in balance. They recognize the differences between the times for the one, and the times for the other.

This is what separates the child from the adult, and the one without wisdom from the one with wisdom. The child has no wisdom and thus cannot discern the different times. The child acts upon its whims. It does what it wants. It cares not for any consequences, because the child is usually oblivious of their inevitable manifestations.

The wise on the other hand act upon what is right and good. The wise understands the times and the moment. The wise know what to do, how to do it, and when it is right (or wrong) to act. The child knows none of this, and thus creates chaos. The wise know all of this and avoids chaos, and instead creates peace, harmony, and balance.

In order to acquire wisdom the child must follow nature's course, and grow up and become an adult. But far too many physical adults remain immature children within themselves. We can see many who have grown up physically, but who remain adolescent, immature children within. These adult children are the source and cause of many of life's troubles, both for themselves and for others.

Individuals in positions of power and wealth are often adult children. The rich, famous, and powerful are often compelled to succeed in their fields of dominating others simply because of their childlike attitudes of always wanting to be first.

Throughout history we have always seen that it is these people of wealth, fame and power who manipulate others to submit to their will. And if their will is violated, they usually throw childlike temper-tantrums, and lash out with anger and violence against all those who oppose them. This is so similar to how little children play and fight with one another, crying and raging whenever they do not get their way.

When a child misbehaves and refuses correction, it is the job and role of the parent to execute discipline. The right form of discipline is the one that works to educate the child, to convince the child not to repeat their chaotic behavior.

Adult children are rarely disciplined. This is why their behavior is out of control, and why they bring so much chaos into the world.

The wise embrace discipline and seek its guiding hand. The wise want to grow up and be mature. The wise seek to know and understand all paths, and to walk each path as is necessary, but not for any longer. The wise know when to turn right, or to go left. The wise know when to pause, and when to proceed. The wise know when to speak out, and when to shut up. The wise know when to engage, and they know when to disengage. The wise know when to stay, and they know when it is time to leave.

The world is in trouble because of all the undisciplined children in adult bodies. Even the wise cannot admonish the wayward children for fear of their violent reprisals. So the wise look within, and seek out the Force of higher realms.

The wise know that there is a Guiding Hand upon us all. If the wayward children will not tolerate the admonishments of the wise, then they will become subject to the spanking given them from the higher Guiding Hand. One way or another, wayward children will be disciplined. It is only natural, and it is etched into the very fabric of the natural laws that operate the universe.

The wise see the movement of the Guiding Hand. They know how to complement it, and when to get out of its way. As for the wayward children, they need to grow up. Childhood's end is at hand. The wayward children will either mature willingly and naturally, or they will face the spanking from the Guiding Hand. This too is also only natural, and it is only a matter of time. And so, it will be.

29. The Call of YHWH (God)

Feb 5, 23 midnight

Only a prophet hears the Voice of YHWH.

Only a prophet knows the Will of YHWH.

Only a prophet knows the Way of YHWH.

Only a prophet knows the Plan of YHWH.

When prophecy ceased, so too did direct knowledge of YHWH.

When prophecy ceased, YHWH was no longer known to the people.

Before prophecy ceased, the prophets foresaw what was coming, and knew what to do.

Before prophecy ceased, the prophets consolidated the Torah of YHWH and concealed the secrets of prophecy within their books.

All that one needs to know, all that one needs to study can be found within these three collections: the Torah of Moshe, the Prophets and the (other) Writings.

Prophecy comes to teach us about the truths of life.

Prophecy comes to teach us about the truths of all things.

One who connects with the Living Word connects with the One who spoke the Living Word.

The Living Word brings clarity into the place of confusion.

The Living Word brings simplicity into the place of complexity.

The Living Word binds the broken heart, and heals every wound of the soul.

All other books serve their purpose and have their place, but the three collections that are now one teach all lessons and are for all peoples, in all places.

YHWH is experienced through prophecy. Prophecy is found in the three collections that are now one book.

Only the one who returns to the Words of the Prophets will discover their secret.

Only the one who returns to the Words of the Prophets, receiving them and taking in their wisdom, is the receiver of the original ancient wisdom.

Only such a one truly receives (Kabbalah), and thus only the one who receives the Word and Wisdom of the Prophets is the one rightfully called a Receiver (Kabbalist).

One who wishes to hear the Voice of YHWH must return to the Prophets.

One who wishes to know the Will of YHWH must return to the Prophets.

One who wishes to know the Way of YHWH must return to the Prophets.

One who wishes to know the Plan of YHWH must return to the Prophets.

The time has come for the return of prophecy. In order for true new prophets to arise, there must first be a return to the Words of the old prophets.

Many deluded souls will continue to walk in darkness, and embrace it from both inside and out.

But the wise, who know the Way of the Prophet discerns between the sacred and the profane.

The wise stay away from the words of blind men, and seek only the Living Word of YHWH.

Those who seek YHWH clear their minds of speculation, questioning, confusions, and doubts.

Those who seek YHWH embrace the Fear of God first and foremost.

Those who seek YHWH know the meaning of obedience, and submission.

Thus those who seek YHWH are called His servants.

Return to the Source, to the original teachings of the Torah of Moshe, the works of the Prophets, and the (other) Writings of the Men of Divine wisdom. All that you seek is to be found therein.

There is nothing more to be said, although there is much more to be done.

Close your books, open your heart and mind. Seek YHWH and find Him.

It is time for the children to return to their fathers, and then the fathers will in turn return to their children. When this psychic unity is achieved many great things will happen.

Come back to YHWH in the original Way, for herein will be discovered and unleashed the true redemption. Amen!!!

30. A Visit with my Father

Feb. 6, 23 (Tu B'Shvat) predawn

Revelations. I saw it. The wedding preparations are well under way. The time has come. It is upon us now. We only have a couple of hours left.

But as dreams and visions go, their symbolic language, as always, needs to be understood. And, in this case, I did understand.

I was heavily involved in the preparations, very aware of the amount of work being done, and what was left to be done. But everything was under control, there was no chaos, no sense of stress.

And as I was doing my chores, after so very much a long time, I encountered my father (upon him be peace). I was only 19 when he passed away at the young age of 56. He looked like he did in life, conservative suit, and tie. I saw him as I knew him.

We walked and we talked. He observed how I was assisting in the wedding plans. As we walked, I wanted to introduce him to my family, but they were nowhere to be found.

Then he asked me about my life. I wanted to answer him, but as I tried, I could sense a number of things in my life that were more difficult than they needed to be. Mistakes? Perhaps! But it didn't feel that way. I did not feel any guilt. I just felt like I had made choices that made my life more difficult than it needed to be. And I told him that I was embarrassed because I had made things more difficult than they needed to be. I wanted my family to be there to help explain to him things, but they were not to be found.

As my father and I walked, he did something that I do not remember him ever doing in this life. He took me by the hand, and we walk together. For a brief moment, as our hands joined, I could see the form of a child's hand being held by the adult parent. But I could not tell in this case if it was my hand that became the child's or my father's. I awoke after this.

I am now 65 years old. My father passed away 46 years ago. In all these many years, I have not seen him much. I knew that he was busy elsewhere helping my siblings in their lives. My father and I were never very close in this world, and he died before we could build an adult relationship between us. This was the first time, in all these years, that I could be with my father, man to man, with respect and very clear intimacy. It was a very nice experience.

As I said, the wedding plans are almost finished. We have maybe only a couple of hours left, and that is all. Some may want to interpret the symbol of the couple of hours in some literal symbolic fashion, as some in the past have done. In this case I did not sense that an hour represented 42 years. I did not get the feeling that we are 84 years (or so) from the great wedding. I got the feeling that things are much closer than this. The time is imminent. It is just not immediate, there is still time to get other work done.

I understood the meaning of this message. I understood the times. Great preparations are going on all around us. But we still have time for each of us to get ourselves a better outfit to wear to the coming feast. But beware, while we still have some time, we do not have a lot of it.

This was not my first dream of the night. In my first dream I saw things that few human beings are allowed to see.

I saw a relationship between a secret group of human beings and Others whom I will not describe. I saw the humans being given a tour of the domain of these Others, and how their domain was one of deep darkness. As the humans passed from one place to the next, they tried to shine some light on their path, but the Others only let their light penetrate to guide their next step. The humans could see the deep darkness surrounding them but made no effort to shine any light therein. The humans observed and did not realize who it was that they were dealing with.

The Others were clearly being deceptive, and concealing the truth of their domain. I tried to warn the humans to do everything that they could to avoid the darkness and to bring in floodlights and to illuminate that domain showering it in brilliant light. In my vision, I did not see them heeding my warning. But as I awoke, I said a prayer to God asking Him to please shine light into these domains, and to free those who were ensnared within the darkness.

There are many secret parts of this vision that I am not allowed to reveal. I cannot reveal to you the identity of which humans I saw, (but I knew them), who the Others are (I knew them too), nor the location of their domain (which is very physical and known to all). All I can reveal is that there is a war going on between us and them. And they have the upper hand because "we" refuse to admit who and what it is that "we" are dealing with. More than this I cannot reveal. In conclusion let me say that flooding their domain with light, leaving no darkness whatsoever is the only way to resolve the deception that is ensnaring us.

And these are the visions that were shown to me this night, Tu B'Shvat (the 15th of the month of Shvat), the night of the full moon, as the spark of life came down to Earth, to revive those who sleep in the ground during winter's rest.

31. Consequences

Feb. 7, 23 morning

I awoke this morning with a single thought piercing my consciousness: Consequences! I knew that it was time to address this most serious reality.

Long ago, in many different words and forms, we were taught, what one sows is what one reaps, and that in accordance to the effort comes the reward. Of all the lessons lost and forgotten in today's darkness, the consequences for forgetting this will soon become devastatingly apparent.

One cannot walk through life, acting however one wishes to act, and not expect there to be consequences for one's actions. What goes around comes around. This is a law of both nature and morality. Try as one will, the law of the universe will be upheld. No one shall escape it!

We live in the delusion of a monolithic materialistic world, wherein which we believe (falsely so) that all reality is what we see and experience, that there is nothing more, not above, not below, and not anywhere else!

The fool is the one who walks in blindness and proclaims in arrogance that he can see. The evil person is the one who walks in blindness, proclaims vision, and then proceeds to intentionally blind everyone else, and to force them to stumble and fall.

More than this, the evil person convinces their blind followers that to stumble and fall is in actually to walk tall and proud. And being blind and deceived, the fools accept what they are told. And in spite of every reality which declares the opposite of their beliefs the fools and their evil masters walk boldly forward off the edge of the cliff, and fall into the pit of fire and torment. All too late for them! But even in their torment and suffering they refuse to see the truth, and to change their ways. And so they burn! Consequences!

Those who seek to blind others with their deceptive arguments and their lying words are evil monsters. They are the eternal enemy. All who engage them will not escape unscathed. Consequences!

There are those who seek to destroy for the sake of rebuilding something better. This has its merits, and indeed this is the natural way. But beware! Do not allow this truth to be twisted by deception and lies.

There are those who seek to destroy, but who have no plan, no desire, and no ability to rebuild. There are those who seek to destroy for destruction's sake. They revel in the destruction that they have caused, and they rejoice in the suffering that they cause for those who follow them.

Indeed, they are evil monsters! They destroy for destruction's sake! And their blind minions follow their lead, falsely believing that they are destroying in order to build something better. But something better never materializes. Only something worse comes.

And the something worse that comes entrenches itself and lingers for as long as it can be maintained. The destruction feeds off the life of those it has deceived and enslaves them, body and mind, to live in squalor, filth, shame and despair.

And why is this so? Because the fools chose blindness, walked in arrogance, and destroyed both the bad and the good, leaving themselves with nothing. All the while the monsters laugh at them and mock them. This is what the fools sowed, and this is what they reap. Consequences!

The blind fools receive their just rewards be it in this world, or in this dimension, or in any other. They proclaim that there is no other world, and no other reality. And thus to the worlds and dimensions that they deny exist, to there are they exiled, to face the consequences of their actions, not limited to the conditions of this finite physical world. Consequences!

Nature will not be denied! Natural law will be obeyed. Those who embrace the monster will be devoured by it, over and over again, in accordance to higher laws that the blind fools deny, and continue to deny, even in the midst of their suffering and pain. Consequences!

My reader, pay attention! No one escapes the consequences of their actions. Choose your course with wisdom. Pause before you act. Think clearly, beforehand, and attempt to foresee what can result from the actions that you ponder doing at this very moment.

This is the path of wisdom. It requires thought, and forethought. Look ahead upon the road you wish to travel. Study it with care before you embark upon your journey. Be prepared for what is to come. Avoid pitfalls and bumps in the road before you encounter them. Gaze ahead and act with calmness. Never, ever act rashly!

Never ever allow your emotions to push you forward into the realms of consequences, with no return. Head over heart, and let the two together lead you to greener pastures, where you will know peace and calm, and where you can remain safe from the evil monster and its blind and arrogant minions who seek to devour you, and to turn you into one of them.

Remember, to all things there are consequences! As you bless, so are you blessed. As you curse, so are you cursed. Choose then that which will bring you the consequences of blessings.

32. How False Beliefs are Born

Feb. 9, 23

What is out there beyond where you can see? What is the reality of other worlds and dimensions the likes of which you cannot personally experience?

If one were to tell a blind person that red is blue, and that blue is red, how would the blind person know the difference? If the blind person was born blind and had never seen either blue or red, how could such a person be expected to know a thing beyond what such a person could experience?

There are many things taught about other worlds and other dimensions, and those who dwell there. And those who have no access to these places lack the ability to verify or to disprove all the claims that are being made. One who is blind does not see, and even if one claims to have vision, it is easy to put such claims to the test to verify or to disprove them. For we have access to the blind person, and can easily administer a test for blindness. But this cannot be said about the realities beyond our material and materialistic world. With regards to the realms beyond, almost everyone is blind.

Emotional manipulation is accomplished when one motivates another to feel in a certain way. One then convinces another of what is and what is not the truth based upon emotional convictions, and not based upon experience, and rational analysis. And once one is emotionally convinced that something is true, the mind is shut off, and all conversation about the truth of a thing is silenced.

When one wants to convince another about the realities of other worlds, realms and dimensions, places that one cannot access or directly experience to ascertain the truths of such places, all one has to do is to emotionally convince another about the truths of these places, and without any evidence, and without any experience, one will be convinced about the reality of such places, regardless of the fact that one is indeed blind to such realities.

This is how falsehoods and false beliefs are born. Indeed, this is how false religions grow as well. One is told what to believe about other realms, and then one is emotionally convinced to accept such beliefs as truth. And once emotion steps in, analytical analysis steps out. And so falsehoods grow, all based upon emotional manipulations and intellectual repressions.

All of us, together, live in a world of lies! Even what we see and understand about our material world around us is so very limited. Based upon observation many draw conclusions considering that what they see and experience is all that there is to see and experience.

And once a conclusion is set into one's mind, one's emotions kick in and convince one that one is right, and that any other information or evidence to the opposite of what one now believes to be true, is itself false. Deception, therefore, is self-reinforced.

But there is far more to this material world than what meets the eye. We do not yet understand the realities of the world round us, all the more so the other worlds, realms, and dimensions that surround and permeate this material world. But never has a lack of understanding limited the closed mind from believing whatever it is that it wishes, regardless of whatever contrary realities that it may encounter. Deception, therefore, is self-reinforced.

Deception can come about by accident. A person cannot be blamed to forming beliefs in the absence of experience. Yet, once experiences arise, how does one respond to them? Is one open to learn new things from one's experiences? Or does one deny the clarity of one's experiences, and seek to reinterpret one's experiences in order to make them compatible with what one already believes? And so, while one may be living in a deception, one may be able to rise out of it, if one so chooses. Or on the other hand, one may choose to reinforce one's deception, thus adding layer upon layer of deception on top of one another. It all depends upon one's choices, and one being able to stand up to the emotional manipulation of others.

Are you searching for truth? You don't have it, regardless of all that you believe! None of us has the truth. All we have are bits and pieces of it.

What we do have are the necessary tools to help train ourselves to be able to recognize truth, and to separate it from speculation and from falsehoods. Those who make use of these tools free their minds from the deceptions laid upon them by others.

Emotions are important and valuable, but they do not stand alone. The thinking mind must be part of every decision-making process. And the thinking process must gain access to, and accept insight from one's own inner resources of intuition, wisdom, and higher awareness.

Yet, these alone, without clarity of rational thought can lead one to feelings and beliefs that have no foundations in truth. The psychic mind and the rational mind must work together in harmony to guide one towards seeing and experiencing higher realities. Expanded consciousness only comes about through experience, and not through speculation. But then again, speculative imagination is the doorway to higher psychic experience. Speculation must lead to experience, or otherwise it too remains in the darkness of blindness.

Inside each of us there is a still soft voice that speaks and guides our conscious minds. Only a still and silent mind can hear it. It doesn't speak words, but it can put words into your mind, and into your mouth. Learn to become silent within. Learn to see in the dark. Learn to experience. As you learn these things, you will learn how your own mind deceives you, and how your own emotions lead you astray.

You will learn to overcome. And you will learn how to set yourself free. And in the freedom of your being you will see and experience that which those who walk in darkness cannot see. They believe that they know what is blue, what is red, and the differences between them. But you will know the truth of these things. You will see for real what the others believe that they see. And you will see who is and who is not in touch with real truth. All these things await the awakened mind.

33. Searching, but Not Finding

Feb. 10, 23, predawn

Many seek to discover the hidden secrets of our true reality, and of the universe itself. But most often such seekers fail miserably to find the truths of that which they seek. Such a failure may indeed not be due to their own faults, but rather due to something else, something nefarious.

How can one expect to find something if one is looking for it in all the wrong places? If one does not know how to truly recognize that which one seeks one could indeed encounter what it is that one seeks and not recognize it. In such cases, one passes by the long-sought-after truths, paying them no mind, simply because one does not recognize what they are.

And why does one not recognize one's long-sought-after treasure? There are two reasons for this. Reason number one is that the reality of the long-sought-after treasure has been deceptively concealed. There are powers that be in this world (and maybe even in higher worlds as well) that outright deceive one into believing that the secret treasures of hidden truths are one thing, when in fact they are entirely something else. Thus one sets out of a journey seeking truths that are no such thing, and the actual truths that one desires to acquire remain unimagined, and thus unidentifiable. And this leads us to reason number two.

Even though one has been deceived about the true nature of hidden truths, one might expect that there still remains deep within one a spark of intuition that may assist one in discovering the long-sought-after truths. However, while such a spark does exist within each of us, it has been buried under so many layers of deceptive lies, that almost no one can any longer hear the still soft voice that speaks from within.

Thus we find that our inner voice is silenced by a never-ending assault of outside noise. And the identity and nature of truth itself is deceptively concealed. All who express an interest in seeking it out and discovering it are fed a pack of lies as to what to look for. One sets out on the right journey along the wrong path, seeking lies that one has been told are truths. And one's inner compass is securely silenced so that one has no inner recourse to correct one's way.

And thus lies and deception reign supreme. And truth remains hidden, barren, cut-off, abandoned, and emasculated. And it is the "powers that be" that have made this to be so. This is the way that they want things to be. And by their power and might, they have made things to be this way. And the vast majority of souls care little or nothing about this, and remain the happy and dumb sheep that they are.

And so what is the deaf, dumb, and blind soul supposed to do? It seems like the universe itself conspires against the one who craves and desires to seek out its hidden truths. But is this conspiracy really true? Is the universe itself out to keep us crippled and weak? We may indeed feel that this is so, but this too is an incredible lie! We must never entertain the thought that it is natural or normal for us to be psychically weak and emasculated. We must never accept the deception, the delusion, that the material world of what we see with our physical eyes is all that there is to reality.

Step one in healing this crises of conspiracy is for each individual to start peeling away the multiple layers of garbage that inundate us from the outside. Stop listening to what others are telling you is truth, and cultivate your own inner sense of awareness and recognition. As long as you try to see what others are telling you to see you will never see that which is there for you to see inside yourself.

Do not argue or debate with others. Remain silent, and share nothing with them about your internal explorations. The path to discovering inner truths is an individual one. Sharing it with many others only invites their intrusions of ideas, doubts, and disbelief. Do not accept these! Do not solicit them, do not entertain the thought of these things at all. Doubt and disbelief are poisons that will kill your soul within you. Do not accept their presence within you. Do not accept them from others who offer them to you, or who throw them at you. Seek out your inner truth, alone, and stay faithful to it, in private and in silence.

Once you have begun sensing an awareness of your inner spark of psychic reality, you must nurture it, and coddle it to grow and to blossom. In order to do this correctly, do not look outside of yourself for direction! Do not read books or seek out academic information about how this is to be done. This entire genre of information is intellectual, and theoretical. It will from the onset misguide you and send you off along the path of discovery in the wrong direction. You will waste your time and energy and accomplish nothing. You will end up being frustrated, defeated, and depressed. Avoid the academics. Avoid those who take the realm of spirit and squeeze it into the realm of the intellect. This is where the right goes wrong.

Separate yourself psychologically and physically from those who seek to deceive you. They are the blind who seek to lead the blind. They themselves do not know that they are blind. They think that they can see, and they think that the darkness that they experience is light. It is this darkness that they will tell you is light, and unless you can see for yourself, to know better, they will convince you that their darkness truly is light. So, stay away from their influence. And do not announce what it is that you are doing. And tell no one what it is that you have discovered, and what it is that you truly seek.

Truth is out there to discover. It will be discovered through experience. Truth will be discovered by the one who seeks it out in the right places and in the right way. Separate then from the wrong ways. Separate from the outside influences of lies, deception and darkness.

Isolate yourself, psychologically, and perhaps even physically. Seek out your own buried spark. Dig it up from inside yourself. Cast away the many layers of dirt, filth and lies that modern society and its teachers and leaders have buried you under.

If you begin the right path in the right way, in time, and with effort, you will begin to discover the right things. And once you do, if you proceed with tenacity, there will be no stopping you. Then you will see the universe itself opening to you, and welcoming you back to the place where each of us rightly belongs.

34. Discovering True Identity

Feb. 11, 23. Motzei Shabat

Will is the existence of Self prior to the cognition of Self. Understanding of Self comes about through the observance of what is cognized. First there is Will, then there is Self, and then there is Understanding. Together this triad gives birth to that which we call by many names, but we shall call it, Identity.

There is Will and there is Identity. The one gives birth to the other. And the other is born from the one. Will and Identity are the conscious and unconscious faces of the Self. This is true both above and below.

One who understands one's self will open the doorway of inner awareness to thus come and know many things. There can be no knowing prior to the knowing of one's self. For how can there be knowing if one does not know who is doing the knowing?

Awareness may enter in, but into where is it going? Unless one knows the answer to this, one will surely not know the answer to anything else.

All knowing begins with the knowing of self. Knowing of self is the knowing of one's true Identity. Knowing one's true Identity comes about when one understands one's higher Self, and sees within it, the origins of Self, which is the individual, unfathomable, and pre-cognized Will.

When there is a Will there is a Way. When there is no Will, there is no Way. Unless one taps into the unknowable Source, one will have no direction in the realms of the knowable and the known.

Those who do not gaze within, cannot see anything right and clear in the outside world. The one who does not gaze within is blind in the outside world. Such a one has eyes but cannot see. And all that one sees with one's physical eyes contains within it layer upon layer of concealed truths, the likes of which cannot be seen, all because one is blind (often by choice) to all these other realities.

Contemplation of one's inner Self is the beginning, middle and end of the Way of enlightenment. For the inner Self is a reflection of the Will above. And as it is above, so too is it below. The pattern of the terrestrial self reflects the pattern of supernal Self. Human beings below are considered to be the children of the One Human Being above. Knowing the self below guides one to understanding the Self above.

Do not over-think this. No books can help one understand this. The deeper one tries to analyze this, the deeper one will fall into confusion, and the further away from one's Self will one move.

Contemplation is the act of observing one's inner Self by gazing within and seeing what there is to be seen. This is an experience that is often visual. It is the awakening of inner sight, which some consider to be like a Third Eye. Two eyes gaze outwards into the world, one Eye gazes inward to discover and explore that which the Will manifests within Identity.

Silence your tongue. Ask no questions! Do not seek to comprehend through rational thought. For what is rational here below is irrational there above, for those above do not see things in the same way as do those below. Mirrors reflect; they are not windows.

Explore your Identity. Know who you are, and who you are not. Experience your own inner parameters. Know what it is that makes you an Individual. And the more you know about what it is that makes you to be you, the more will you come to understand many things.

Turn off the outside. Turn on the inside. Contemplate who you really are, without the voices of others attempting to define this for you. They are not you. Only you are you.

Discover your true Identity. Know your true Self. And you will come to know the Way of things, simply because you are in touch with the Will. The Will and the Way, and the Way and the Will are one. Know the one, and you will know the other. There is no more important knowing than this. Now, go know it!

35. Finding the Secrets of the Kabbalah

Feb. 12, 23 morning

For those who seek the secrets of the Kabbalah, knows these things:

The secrets which you seek are only spoken about in books, but they are not to be found in books.

The worlds of the Kabbalah are outside and above this world, therefore nothing in this world contains their secrets.

This world and everything within it are only a reflection of higher truths. One thus studies the ways of this world to discover the secrets reflected (but not present) within.

Only the inner eye can see inner truths. The intellect is of this world, and can only see things of this world.

The imagination can see beyond, but only if it is unleashed from the limitations placed upon it by the intellect.

One must close one's outer eyes in order to see inner truths.

One must leave behind the ways of this world in order to discover the ways of the higher worlds.

The secrets of the Kabbalah are never learned! They are experienced!

The secrets of the Kabbalah are never taught. They can only be received.

The secrets of the Kabbalah can only be received by the one who is open to receive them.

In order to be open to receive, one must first remove all that which blocks the reception.

The intellect and its thoughts are what block the reception of experience that is triggered by the imagination.

So, close your books. They are only shadows.

Open your hearts, and allow the inner truths to shine into your intellectual minds.

The secrets of the Kabbalah are not words on a page, they are not thoughts for your mind.

The secrets of the Kabbalah need to be experienced in order for one to know them.

Close your eyes, block out all external influences, for they are all distractions.

Gaze within. Call upon The Name, The Only Name. Call upon The Only Name in its right form and way.

As you call upon The Only Name, The Only Name will hear you, and call back to you.

But are you listening? Silence your mind from thoughts. Allow your imagination to bring into your awareness the Presence of The Only Name.

Do this, and the secrets that you seek will pour into you. No books needed. Indeed, the books impede this!

Know The Only Name, and it will know you. This is experience. No words can describe it.

When you know – you will know – and there will be nothing more to say.

This is the secret of the reception of secrets. Now, go do it!

36. On Making Decisions

Feb. 12, 23 evening

One who makes decisions based upon insufficient information will be proven to be psychic if one's decisions turn out well, or proven to be a fool if they do not.

All too often one runs to draw conclusions and to make decisions based upon what one believes to be true. But what one believes to be true may not be. What one believes may not even be close to the truth. When this is the case, the conclusions drawn and the decisions made can end up causing more harm than good. These are the consequences for short-sightedness.

One sees only a little, but there is a lot more to see. One knows so little, when there is so much more to know. Under such circumstances, the wise know to withhold judgement and to wait patiently and watch. The wise know that in their patience, things can happen that will reveal more of what needs to be known. The wise know not to rush to conclusions. The wise know to seek inner counsel, for that is where one taps into higher knowing that comes from a higher world.

37. Emotions & Thinking

Feb. 13, 23

That which attracts the attention of adults is not that different from that which attracts the attention of children.

One who understands the way that people think is able to manipulate and control what those people think.

Influencing emotions is a sure way to manipulate behavior. Influencing emotions is a sure way to shut down independent, rational thought. Influencing emotions is a sure way to hijack the spirit and to direct it in malevolent ways.

It is not hard to persuade the masses to commit mass evil. All that has to be done is to capture their hearts and the rest of the mind, spirit and body will follow.

Create emotional need in another, and then fill it. Create the need to be what you want it to be, and then fill it in the way that you wish. You will have created a faithful and loyal following of those who will be addicted to you, and who will follow you anywhere. How many times in history have we seen evil dictators (and cult leaders) do exactly this, manipulating masses, and then leading them on a course of self-destruction.

The human mind craves to think. If the individual does not use one's own mind to think independently, then one's mind will find, welcome, and receive another (outside) force to think for it. The mind thinks; this is what it does. It will either think the thoughts that one puts into one's own head, or it will think the thoughts that another puts into one's head.

Sometimes, it is hard to tell the difference between thoughts that come from oneself and those that come from an outside source. One way to help discern the difference is the amount of emotion associated with said thoughts. Another way is to gauge one's personal reaction to thoughts which contradict or disagree with those thoughts which themselves rouse deep emotion.

Think a thought. This should be easy. It does not matter what the thought may be. Consider a thought about something wrong, disgusting, and even evil. Consider a thought about something that one would never, ever do. Once this thought crosses one's mind, one's immediate reaction to it is, no! One says, "not me, not interested," and then naturally and normally one moves on to think other thoughts.

But what happens if such a thought, however briefly thought, sparks an emotional explosion of feelings. What if such a thought, once entertained in the mind, cannot be let go of? What happens when such a thought haunts one's mind, and one cannot dismiss it, forget it, and move on to something else. If this occurs, and it often does, one has discovered an emotional attachment that one may not have known was there. If this occurs, and one cannot let go, one needs to pause and contemplate what it is that one is thinking, and not only what one feels about such a thought, but why such a feeling is associated with such a thought.

Some emotional associations with certain thoughts are normal and natural. Thoughts and feelings of sadness are normally associated with sad events, and thoughts and feelings of happiness are associated with happy events. This is easy to understand. But not everything is this easy to understand.

Some thoughts solicit deep emotion, without them being connected to any kind of personal event or experience. Some thoughts arouse deep emotion for no apparent reason whatsoever. These emotionally charged thoughts, that are filled with baseless impersonal passion, are the very ones that are suspect as coming from an outside source.

When one's mind does not think for itself, and another comes along to do the thinking for one, the other imposes it's thoughts within the other's mind through the imprint of emotion. The other gets you to feel a certain way, and thus you will think in a certain way. And this, needless to say, gets you to act in a certain way. Emotional manipulation is the key to mind control.

Mind your thoughts! Observe what you think and feel about a thing. Consider why you think and feel one way, and if you are even open to consider any alternative line of thinking. If you discover that your feelings are what is blocking you from entertaining any alternative line of thinking, then the chances are you have been influenced by an outside, external source. What you will choose to do about this is entirely up to you.

Clear thinking is rational, analytical, and critical. Clear thinking takes its time to consider and to contemplate. Clear rational thinking always takes council from one's inner intuition. For one's inner knowing helps guide the thinking process and exposes emotional influences, be they from outside of oneself, or from within.

We are all emotional beings, but as each individual matures, and develops the power of thought, the pull of one's emotions takes a second seat to the driving force of rational thinking, which itself more and more includes intuitive insights. This is what separates the mind of an adult from the mind of a child. Children throw temper tantrums, mature adults do not!

Those who seek to manipulate others first seek to revert them to a childlike mentality of emotions first, and thinking second. In this way, such adult children are easy to control. This is the reverse of the natural, normal way for the adult.

If society is in chaos, it is because the individuals therein are all chaotic. The solution is simple. Introduce order to replace chaos. And order will come to one from within oneself, or it will be imposed by an outside party. And mind you, the agenda of the other party might very well contradict one's own best interests. Salvation comes to those who are adults, internally and psychologically.

38. Distractions

Feb. 16, 23

Distractions! They are always there. Distractions are like annoying flies always buzzing around one's face. They seem to always be there, and are always annoying.

Distractions, more than anything else, are what take away our focus from the more important things in life.

But this does not have to be! Indeed, it must not be. Distractions are what they are. Yet, how each individual perceives the distraction and deals with it decides whether or not a distraction really is (or is not) a distraction at all.

The great unexperienced truth is that all is One. Whatever we experience, what is out there, or inside us, is part of the greater Whole. And the greater Whole is One, and acts as one. While many can agree with this concept, few actually achieve a level of consciousness to experience the One for oneself.

Outside of the experience of the One, everything appears to be separate and distinct. The world inside us and around us appears to be in constant chaos. There does not seem to be any order, or any arrangement. Reality appears to be hostile and confusing to the one(s) who live in the illusion of separation, division, and strife.

From time to time an individual will seek refuge from the outside, hostile world. One will seek to sink within oneself for a period of solace, and rest. And yet, just as one enters one's internal state of inner peace, along comes some external distraction and drags one out of that escape, and back into the outside chaotic world. How annoying, and frustrating.

Yet, this separation between inner peace and outer chaos is only a mirage! In reality it does not exist. There is no such division or separation. Only the only who lives in the perception of separation sees separation. Whereas the one who lives in the One, in the Unity, sees the peace within, and the chaos outside, as two sides of the same coin. Such an individual is always in a state of inner peace and unity.

Thus such a one enters into the outside chaos already in a state of inner peace. Such a one thus imposes one's inner peace on the state of the external chaos. Instead of contributing more to the problem, one with inner peace contributes to the solution of the problem, and to the cure of the disease.

Perception is everything. Each individual has a choice. While no one can dictate what happens in the outside world, one can dictate, and be the master of how one chooses to respond to everything that happens to one from the outside world.

All things come from the One. All things happen for a reason. Yes! Even distractions come from the One, and serve a purpose. Distractions are not really like annoying flies taking away one's attention from more important matters. Distractions are part of the puzzle of life. They happen for practical reasons, and each distraction has within it a hidden internal message. One who sees life within the Singularity of the Unity of the True One sees distractions as an opportunity for further insights and growth.

When a distraction arises when one is in a deep state of contemplation or meditation, one may indeed have to open one's eyes and to immediately address some issue that seems to be in contradiction with one's inner state of peace. But there is no such contradiction. There are no real separations (only apparent ones, but no real ones). Within all chaos there is Order for those who can see it. And this is why distractions come to the individual who resides within the consciousness of the One.

Meditation and contemplation is not something to be done with one's eyes closed, and detached from the world and its outside chaos. No! One must engage the world and its chaos in one's inner state of peace. One must gaze upon the distraction, and realize that it has come for a purpose. It has a reason to be.

So, the wise engage the distraction and address its issues, all the while performing their physical tasks, and at the same time seeking the meaning of the moment, and maintaining one's inner peace and higher awareness throughout.

Growth does not come easy. Growth does not come without its challenges. Growth requires change. One changes oneself from a consciousness of separation and into a consciousness of Unity. In the Unity the meditation and the distraction from meditation are one. One continues one's meditation throughout all distractions. One meditates in all places, at all times, and in all ways. One engages the outside world from one's place of inner peace and Unity. One sees, and knows.

Whatever comes into this material world comes for a reason. Whatever happens in this world happens for a reason. The wise seek understanding in all things. For the wise, distractions are opportunities for contemplation. For the wise, distractions enable them to expand their domain of inner peace into greater portions of the outside chaotic world.

Do not be dismayed by distractions. The One is in them, and the One is in all. Those who seeks the One will see the One, not only within one's own inner silence, but also in the chaos and noise of the external world. And in this, the secret of Unity is reinforced. There is only the One. There are no real distractions, only perceived ones. Rise above the deception and see the truth for yourself!

39. True Happiness

Feb. 17, 23 predawn

The secret of true, continual happiness has nothing to do with one's emotional state. Happiness is a state of being, not a state of feelings. Those who seek to feel happy all the time will never achieve their goal. Those who claim that they feel happy all the time are either liars, self-deceived, or most likely, both!

The ignorant masses associate happiness with a state of enhanced emotional well-being. But these types of states are never permanent. Many times such emotional highs occur within a person due to some type of chemical interactions in the brain. Needless to say, a lot goes on inside the brain. Most people have no idea how much of their feelings, and compulsions are stirred by mere chemical activity in the brain, without there even being an external stimuli involved.

True happiness really means that one is accepting and embracing of one's condition and circumstances in life. This is how certain people can be happy even in the most dire of circumstances. It also explains why some people are never happy, regardless of how good their portion may be.

Those individuals who isolate their souls from the greater, higher reality look at themselves as being in competition, and conflict with everything around them. For such isolated souls, every interaction is a struggle for dominance. Such lost souls only feel good about themselves when they can conquer all circumstances around them, and be in control of (and rule over) their reality.

Such lost souls are suspicious of everything around them. Such lost souls continually look around them for threats. Such lost souls never know any peace. Such lost souls seek security in being in control of everything around them. But even when they are in control, and even if they acquire much wealth and power, inside of themselves they are still isolated, and lonely. Whether known or unknown to their conscious selves their level of internal torment is great.

True happiness comes when the individual soul remembers that it is part of a greater whole. The soul remembers that it is alive and living, both before it came into its present body and once it leaves its present body. The happy soul knows how temporary and transient life is here on Earth. Therefore the happy soul is also a wise soul. It spends its time seeking out and embracing those things in life that are long-lasting and permanent.

As for the other transient things of this world, like wealth and power, these are not pursued for their own sake. Thus the one who has wealth and power does not have increased happiness because of it, and the one without one wealth and power does not have decreased happiness because of it. Being that one has oneself, and recognizes one's soul, and one's place, and one's mission in life, these are the sources of happiness; these are permanent, and stable.

There is nothing wrong with the acquisition of the things of this world, as long as these things (their presence or their absence) do not become a source of trouble for one.

All too many fools associate happiness with worldly acquisitions. But those with more do not have more happiness. Just as those with less do not necessarily have less happiness. There are many happy poor people, and many miserable wealthy people. One can take solace in one's wealth and power, all that one may wish, but one will remain empty and alone inside, and all such souls know this to be true, regardless of however much it may be denied.

Seek true happiness where it is to be found and one will discover it there. Happiness is key to life. Therefore, this sacred key must be sought and found where it is, and not where it is not.

True happiness is of the soul, and never of the body. Brain chemistry creates all kinds of emotional states, including elation and depression. Brain chemistry is thus an up-and-down roller-coaster. Those who seek happiness there will never find it.

True happiness is of the soul. The soul knows the ups-and-downs of the body it inhabits, and chooses not to identify its state of wellbeing with the state of the temporary physical flesh. While the body is itself sacred and important, and its needs must always be met, still, nevertheless, physical fulfillment and true happiness of the soul are two very different things.

Gaze within. Discover yourself. Know yourself. Know your purpose and your mission. Pursue these with all vigor, with or without wealth and power. When you are true to you, then you will align with the greater reality. When you are this, you will know the knowing of truth; you will know the knowing of true happiness. Indeed, you will be forever happy. It will not manifest as a state of emotional elation, but rather as a state of deep internal contentment, and peace. This state is worth more than all the material wealth and power that this world has to offer.

Observe the wise, for they are the happy ones; the ones who are satisfied with their portion in this temporal world. Happiness is the state of their being. And so it should be for us all.

40. The Lifespan of Consciousness, 1

Feb. 18, 23 Motzei Shabat

Consciousness, it expands or contracts in accordance to a multi-dimensional evolutionary scale that is engrained in the fabric of natural reality.

That which we call human consciousness is the awareness of the identity of self. But just as there are many levels of consciousness, so too are the many levels of self-identity.

Every place in space and time, in every dimension, in every world, and in every universe generates its own unique expression of individual consciousness.

One soul can have many identities; one soul can be conscious in many different places in space and time simultaneously. And of all the identities, and all the separate expressions of consciousness, the consciousness that is present in the physical human body is the one cut off from all the others. So many different worlds, so many different realities, and the awareness and experience of them all is blocked out of mind by the consciousness associated with the human body.

The human body is the natural form that is indigenous to this physical world. The physical body generates its own consciousness model that cloaks one's true identity all the while that one remains in prison within the body.

The consciousness associated with the body conceals within itself all the higher levels of one's greater Identity. This concealment, for the most part, is unknown to the consciousness associated with the body, and for the most part, the consciousness of the body denies the reality of any higher Identity. This defines why the portion of one's identity associated with the physical body is considered entrapped in a prison.

With the death of the physical body, the identity associated with it cannot immediately reabsorb back into its own higher Identity. All during life in the body one remained ignorant or in denial of the higher reality. Now with the passing of the body, reabsorbing consciousness is not a guaranteed accomplishment.

When the isolated consciousness once associated with a human body can no longer reabsorb back into its own true greater Identity, it remains cut off, and thus lost to its own Self. This situation best describes the vast majority of human souls today. Most are simply isolated individual parts of a greater whole with whom they have lost conscious connection. Yet, while the individual isolated parts cannot see their way back into their greater Identity, the greater Identity still sees each of its lost parts, and works with each one of them to reintegrate them back into the greater whole.

The greater Identity, which is also called one's higher Self, interacts within multiple dimensions, times, and worlds simultaneously. It sees each of its lost and isolated parts, and knows how best to work with each one in order to set them along the path of reawakening and reconnection. One's greater Identity directs each of its wayward parts into whatever scenarios that are deemed necessary for each wayward part to experience, and to therein learn specific lessons that will help bring about its reintegration.

Each scenario is an incarnation into a body of whatever sorts, in whatever world, at whatever time period that it deemed necessary. This process is the recycling of souls that is popularly known as reincarnation. Souls will go from one body to another, and to another, with each experience designed to teach one the appropriate lessons about reintegration. Some souls learn their lessons well and progress. Other souls refuse their lessons and reinforce their isolation, becoming more and more isolated. The process of repair continues.

The process of repair and reintegration contains three steps of concentric expanding consciousness. These three steps are well known in many systems found on this Earth. They are called by many different names. Here, we will avoid using what may be common or popular symbolic references to focus on the truth of these things, without getting caught up in metaphorical descriptions. *To be continued...*

41. The Lifespan of Consciousness, 2

Feb. 19, 23 predawn (Part 2 of 3)

The individual human soul is only a small part of its own higher Identity. The higher Identity exists in many times, and many places simultaneously. It experiences many different realities all at the same time.

When an individual soul incarnates into human form here on Earth, somewhere along the timeline, it has no choice but to submit to the natural forces that are inherent presently on this planet. These natural forces place layer upon layer of material influence upon the soul. It is these very same layers of natural influence which cause the soul to lose sight of its origins in its higher Identity. It is thus born anew in a body, stripped of its previous identity.

Now, one's true Identity is not torn away or removed, rather it is just buried deep under layers of material influence. As such, one's true Identity, while blocked out of consciousness is nevertheless still there in a place which in modern terms, we call the unconscious. It is from within this unconscious realm that one's true Identity can lead, guide, and direct the isolated part of itself into a remembrance of its forgotten Self.

The reintegration of the isolated parts of Self follows a specific path of expanding consciousness. This is a path that must be traversed by each and every isolated human soul in order for it to again remember it's true Self, to reintegrate with it, and to thus properly digest and integrate all the lessons for which it came to this Earth in the first place.

Upon birth here on Earth, the consciousness of the isolated human soul is not too different from any of the other life forms on the planet. Without guidance and training many isolated souls remain fixed in this level of animal consciousness. Human souls are more intelligent than most (but not all) animal species on the planet. Human beings use this intelligence to build their societies. Yet, as history has clearly shown, human consciousness is not too far away from the animal. Human violence and savagery is all too well known amongst us. The reason for all of what we call immoral and violent human behavior is because of the animal level of consciousness that permeates the reality of these isolated souls.

One's individual higher Identity guides each isolated soul through a number of experiences here on Earth (while in human form and otherwise) in order to jar the animal consciousness and to push it to expand and to experience a higher state. We can call this the first stage of human consciousness, which as we have said, there are three.

Human beings will suffer from lifetime to lifetime experiences of the ravages of animal consciousness. This continued suffering awakens within them both the thought and the longing for something better. It is the power of this longing for something better that awakens the first stage of human consciousness. In this phase the isolated soul realizes that there is more to life than merely being an animal.

Human souls also have the capacity of understanding and through this understanding one can (and does) tame one's world, transforming it into a better place. Yet, in order for this to happen, human souls need to cooperate with one another, and work together for the common good. Even animals are aware of this, but when humans become aware of this, and work together in peace, their accomplishments can be amazing.

So the concealed (unconscious) higher Identity works to awaken within the isolated souls an awareness that each is not alone in (what appears to be) the struggle for life. A number of isolated souls thus awaken simultaneously and decide to work together for a common good. This is the beginning of civilization.

As human souls begin to work together, conflicts are inevitable. However, rather than settle conflicts in animal consciousness with a fight to the death, the awakening souls create for themselves laws and surrender themselves to be under their authority. This is the beginning of law and order, the awareness and practice of a single higher authority.

One's higher Identity, which is one's true inner single higher authority creates a shadow of itself in the minds of the isolated souls. This shadow becomes the structure and form of government. The isolated human souls have become aware of, and accept the concept of there being a higher authority. This is an awareness not existent in animal consciousness. The first stage of human remembrance is thus accomplished.

This first stage of developing human consciousness always includes within it the awareness of a higher authority. Now, no body of human beings can declare itself superior over others by its own rights. Such an attitude is a leftover from animal consciousness. When any group of human souls tries to rule over others by sheer force of will or arms, this creates resentment and hostility and the resurrection of animal consciousness, which leads to violence, wars, and savagery. Therefore, in order to secure the awareness of a higher authority, there must be an awareness of, and surrender to, an authority which is higher than anything human.

At this stage of developing human consciousness, the isolated souls still cannot conceive of each one having within oneself a higher Identity which is guiding and directing all. Therefore, if the higher Authority is clearly not inside themselves, then it is equally clear that such Authority is outside of themselves.

This higher Authority is not human, and therefore must be a god. Thus religion is born built upon the awareness of human submission to a higher Heavenly Authority. Again, this is guided by one's higher Identity. Primitive religions thus place in the minds of isolated souls an awareness of a higher Force and the need to submit to this higher Force for the sake of the common good.

At this stage, step one in expanding consciousness is complete. When this occurs, the higher Identity slowly nudges the isolated souls (possibly over many lifetimes) to mature again, and to grow. This growth comes about through a development of moral and righteous human behavior, and this is complimented by a deepening sense of the Presence of the Divine God.

At the early stage each group of isolated souls develop their own concepts and ideas about authoritative higher gods. Needless to say, as groups interact, so do their ideas and beliefs. Being that animal consciousness has not be completely purges out of the human soul, when groups come into contact, they often fight, whether it be over resources for survival, or because of their differences of beliefs over whose god is stronger.

In order to overcome the residuals of animal consciousness, stage two of expanding human consciousness is now guided into the understanding that there is a singular God that rules over all. The idea of multiple gods, one for each isolated group must itself be outgrown just as human souls must outgrow their residual animal nature.

Isolated souls learn to stand together as a united whole, and recognize that this united whole is the right and proper way to be. But this learning curve does not come easy. The multiple layers of material influence inflicting human souls have not gone away nor has it dissipated in the least. There is always a constant struggle between the natural forces that one feels, and the lofty ideas and beliefs about unity that one thinks. Isolated thoughts are as unstable as isolated souls. Even belief in a singular higher God is not enough. Such beliefs can be challenged and even destroyed, leading to the return of animal consciousness, and the need to restart the whole building process from scratch. This has happened many times in the ancient, and not-to-distant past.

Beliefs and ideas by themselves are no substitute for the experience of the higher reality itself. *To be continued....*

42. The Lifespan of Consciousness, 3

Feb. 20, 23 predawn

The human experience on Earth is a growth experience. It is school, where the individual and isolated parts of the greater Identity come and learn how to be part of a whole instead of continuing to experience their isolation.

The maturation process follows what we can describe as three basic phases. These three are childhood, adolescence, and adulthood.

In childhood, the human soul is focused on its own separate identity. In its infantile state it interprets the perception of its isolation as a conflict for survival. And thus the human soul acts like the lower-consciousness natural animal, who lives in the wild, and must struggle with nature in order to survive. This animal consciousness is the infancy state of developing human souls.

In the adolescent stage of developing consciousness the human soul begins to awaken to a reality wherein which it realizes that its isolation is also the case with many others who are equally isolated. The lesson is learned that there is strength in numbers. And so many isolated souls band together to pursue (however unfortunately) the same goals that were pursued by the individual (infantile) isolated soul.

Now, instead of individuals seeing each other as in a constant struggle for survival with one another, each group can now embrace this identity. Group fights group. Thus we have the conflicts between nations, cultures, and religions. Ultimately, after much struggle, the individual groups mature a bit and realize that there must be a unifying factor to unite them all. And so groups seek to unite and to forge alliances. Each individual isolated soul begins to embrace the awareness that even in its isolation it can, if it so chooses, become a part of a great whole. Of course, while this happens, the identity of the individual remains isolated. Awareness of the reality of all individual isolated souls being part of an actual integral whole has not yet arisen.

Remember, all human activity, be it on Earth or elsewhere (and there are many "elsewheres"), is guided from a higher reality in which there is a singular Identity of which all human souls are a part of. In religious and mystical literature this higher Identity has been called Supernal Man (but do not make the mistake of thinking that anything manifest here on material Earth actually has any semblance of physical resemblance to its energetic source in higher dimensions).

The ultimate goal of the human experience is for all isolated parts of the whole (which are individual souls) to recognize the state of their integrated unity. This unity is not one that is imposed from the outside with a gathering of souls into nations sharing a common identity. Rather, the awareness of the unity must arise from within and bring with it into consciousness a knowing that cannot be dictated from outside, nor for that matter challenged or contradicted by anything outside. This internal dawn of unity consciousness is the third and final stage, which is human (energetic, psychic, or spiritual) adulthood.

This third and final phase of the human experience here on Earth comes about as the higher Identity guides and directs human activity to create an external mirror of unity that is the reflection of the internal, however yet unrealized state of actual unity.

In order to be complete in all of its parts, the greater Identity (of Supernal Man) spreads forth is multiple parts to experience all kinds of reality under all kinds of different circumstances. Parts of the higher Identity thus come to experience life here on Earth, for it is necessary to absorb the lessons of life on Earth into the awareness of the whole.

Yet, as they come here, the parts of the whole (individual souls) become subject to the layer upon layer of materialistic forces that dominate this space-time reality. These layers are what cause the loss of the original awareness and create the illusion of isolation. The lesson that the souls come here to learn is that there is no such thing as isolation, and that no soul is in reality lost or disconnected.

Under the many layers of Earth's materialistic influences the individual souls lose the sense of unity with one another and therefore, like the animal, struggle to survive, one against the other. Yet, the higher Identity sees and knows all that transpires in each of its individual parts. While the individual souls sees themselves as isolated and lost, the greater Identity sees no such thing! It navigates each isolated part of itself and guides it from lifetime to lifetime bringing it successively along the path of maturation from childhood to adolescence, and into adulthood.

Once reunited, the individual souls are restored into their natural collective now with the greater awareness of what it means to be isolated and lost. The individual souls also have learned how to navigate the crushing forces of materialistic energy that dominate here on Earth, and how to not be crushed by them.

In the state of restored collective consciousness, each individual soul maintains its own unique identity, but instead of being isolated, alone, and in a state of struggle with all others, it realizes that it is part of a greater "body" and serves its unique function within the body for the sake of the good of the whole, which is by definition also the good for itself as well.

This awareness of higher unity cannot be imposed on the soul from the outside. No one or nothing can tell the soul that this is the way things are. The soul needs to know this to be true from dawning inner awareness, and from direct personal experience. The soul needs to experience and live the reality of unity; it cannot just be told about it. Each individual soul is thus the higher Identity, and the higher Identity lives and is aware within each and every part of Itself. Awareness of the whole is now complete in each of its parts.

And thus school on planet Earth is complete. The higher Identity of us all is now free to explore new life forms in new worlds, and to learn from them all the lessons that are to be learned. In this way the higher Identity continues the cause of creation, which is to be everywhere, and to know everything. And thus life grows and grows, as is its way.

43. From You to You

Feb. 21, 23 morning

Will, wisdom, and understanding. Flexibility, rigidity, and balance. Expansion, contraction, vibration. All of these together, when in proper alignment with one another, give rise to Form, that is complete and whole.

In the beginning there is that which is. At first, sometime after the beginning, that which is becomes aware. Thus an idea is born. The idea is contemplated, and thus grows into a mature and well-conceived thought. The thought is complete in all its parts, but yet it is only a thought. It has not yet become manifest into being.

Seeing the thought bereft and formless, that which is from the beginning is aroused with passion. Emotion is thus born, along with its place, the heart. Heart gazes upon thought and arouses its forces of flexibility and rigidity, of expansion and contraction, and works to manifest the balance of thought through the force of vibration. This process of movement continues until it reaches its conclusion, and form is born.

We begin with what is, which reveals an idea. This gives rise to a thought, which is then acted upon. Action continues until the thought is manifest in full form, complete and whole. And thus the unmanifest becomes manifest, and the concealed becomes revealed.

What once was, now is. That which was above is now below. That which was only potential is now actual. In the beginning there was will. In the end there is complete form. This is the Way of Life. When there is a Will, there is a Way. When there is no Will, there is no Way.

Will, heart, vibration, and form. This the Way from above to below. Will works though wisdom and understanding. Heart is balance that works through flexibility and rigidity. Vibration works through expansion and contraction. All together contribute to the final form. All together are the Way of the Will.

Contemplate this internally. Sense its truth within yourself. See its reality within your own being. If you do this, and follow the Way. You will come to knowing. Knowing is the being of the known. This will not be outside of you. No one will give this to you. This will be inside you. You will birth it. But what you birth will not be a child of yourself, but rather you will birth yourself!

Do you see this? If yes, then you have understanding and wisdom. If no, then your birthing is not yet complete. Return to the beginning, for it is only from there that you can reach the end.

In the beginning, there is you. In the end, there is you. The Way of the Will traverses the Path from you to you. All this is brings about the you, which is your identity. Enough for now. Go! Do it.

44. Punishment

Feb. 23, 23

When God wants to punish a society the first thing that He does is to take away its wisdom.

When God wants to punish a society, He allows foolishness to lead it to insanity.

Insanity is defined as behavior (feelings and thoughts) that when subject to natural, rational, and logical analysis are clearly delusional, out-of-touch with reality, and thus harmful, and self-destructive.

When God wants to punish a society, God just removes His Presence, which is His subtle influence for good, and allows nature to take its course.

Ultimately, God does not have to intervene in any supernatural way. God just allows human arrogance, foolishness, and insanity to bear its fruits.

God then does not intervene to save an evil society from itself. Nature take its course. The society self-destructs.

What comes next is decided by the people themselves. Either they learn the lesson to submit and surrender to the Will of Heaven, which means to live righteous and moral God-centered lives, or to reinforce the ways of arrogance and foolishness, which will again lead down the path to even more destruction.

When we see insanity in place of normalcy; when we see perversion in the place of morality; when we see evil in the place of good, then rest assured judgment is near.

Insanity, perversion, and evil are all negatively-charged forces of energy. They will run their course, and bring destruction, because this is what they do!

The wise, those who understand the ways of Energy need to pay heed, and not submit to public influences that seek to blind the eye from the truth.

But the arrogant and the foolish pay no heed. Many consider themselves to be religious, and believe that their religion will save them. This is one of the greatest concepts of misguided faith.

Like in the past, God judges who is and who is not faithful to Him based upon criteria that mortal human beings do not understand.

Only the one who submits and surrenders to the Will of God will be guided out of judgement's path.

Now is the time to change the course of one's life, while one still can.

Reject and renounce the values of this evil and wicked secular society. Uphold Biblical values! Distance yourselves from those who reject the Sacred Truths.

If you tolerate the evil around you, it will penetrate you and become part of you. You will become the fool; you will become arrogant. You will mock and not believe, until the moment of no-return arrives and nature takes its course.

Seek out the Face of God while there is still time. But do not cry out to hear the Divine Voice unless you are committed to listen to what it tells you. Judgment falls first upon those to whom God speaks but who chose not to obey!

These words are what they are, a simple message of simple truths. Return to God in simplicity. Reject all unnecessary complexities. Seek out the Face of God, and surrender to the Divine Will. In this there is blessing. Outside of this there is judgment.

What you do defines your destiny. May the blessings of Shalom be with you.

45. Salvation

Feb. 24, 23

The blessings of salvation can only come to the one whose mind can think clearly beyond the turmoil of emotional instability.

The enlightened mind is the one that is strongly rational and openly intuitive, both at the same time. For in order for there to be understanding, there must first be wisdom. These two, understanding and wisdom are Mother and Father to us all.

Only the faithful child will grow up and become a true Man; he whose beard descends down his face to embrace his heart unto his navel. This is the Man above. He is the source of Identity for all men and women alike. And remember, this is symbolic language! Never confuse the literal with the metaphor.

The Man above resides within us all, within both men and women alike. Long ago we were advised that in a place where there are no men, strive to be a Man! This is a true lesson for both men and women today.

It is unfortunate that today we have many males who have not succeeded in becoming men. And indeed, we have many females who have succeeded in becoming men. This can be either a blessing or a curse. It all depends upon the individual and one's alignment with the natural Way.

A Man is the one who unites Heaven and Earth. The Man is not just a He, for inside He has his feminine counterpart. Every Woman is not just a She, for inside She has her male counterpart. Male and Female united properly and in harmony, only this defines what is a Man, be it for a male or a female.

Understanding and rationality is Mother to us all. Wisdom is our Father. When Mother and Father unite in holy matrimony, their merger gives rise to knowing. And knowing is the seat of Identity. And Identity is who you are! Identity above defines for each of us our reflections of identity below.

A society that surrenders itself to whims of emotion is rightly compared to a ship in stormy seas. It is most dangerous and life threatening. Many ships have sunk during storms. Great has been the loss of life, and the loss of treasures. As it has been in the past with storms at sea, so too is it today with storms in society.

Emotions are the storm. Emotions thus need to be calmed, and not aroused. Emotions need to be tamed and made subject to Mother and Father. For only understanding and wisdom can guide the stormy emotions into the proper alignment that brings with it calm and peace.

From within the storm, those entrapped therein must gaze above into the place of our Mother, into the understanding that only the Mind can bring.

One crawls up the Supernal Beard like a ladder of salvation. One rises out of emotional turmoil, by gazing upon the understanding of Mother, and seeking within it the intuitive wisdom of Father.

The Supernal Beard is the symbol of the ladder of ascent. It represents how one arises out of the turmoil of unbalanced emotions, and back into a state of inner calm and peace. This is the salvation of the individual, when one is set free from one's tormentors, both those external, and especially from the one's internal, inside of oneself.

From the depths our lost and isolated selves cry out for the salvation that only the greater Identity can bring. The Supernal

Beard is our life-line. It symbolically represents the desire for inner clarity and one's pursuit of understanding and wisdom. It covers one's navel and includes one's sexual energies. It covers one's heart and includes one's passions. The Beard represents the path and the Way from confusion to understanding, and from foolishness to wisdom. So, climb the beard. Calm the storm. Discover salvation.

Salvation does not come to you as a gift from outside. Salvation arises from within you, it is your personal, and natural growth and maturation. Salvation comes to the one who unleashes it from within, and allows it to manifest in one's life, and in the world at large. Only this salvation can calm the stormy seas that today are destroying society.

Let the one who ascends the Beard take heed and know what to do. Let the woman be a man, and let the man be a man, so that together, male and female may unite and become Supernal Man, the great Identity above.

Know the secrets herein, for they emanate from the source of understanding above, and contain within them, the hidden wisdom. Enough for now.

46. What is Right

Feb. 25, 23 motzei shabat

You know what is moral!

You know what is right and proper.

You even know right from wrong.

In spite of social brainwashing,
you are not an idiot!

If you choose to do the wrong things,
your own poor decisions will punish you.

In order to submit to the authority of God,
one must obey the Word of God.

No cutting corners! No rationalizations!

If you wrongly harm another person,
God in Heaven sees, and you will be judged.

Don't try to hide behind repentance.

There is no repentance without reparations!

When you mess up, be prepared to pay the price.

God is indeed merciful,
but only to those who themselves show mercy.

Go ahead! Keep walking your present arrogant path!

Keep bowing down to all the modern false gods.

See how they will save you in your hour of need.

Judgment is very close. Go ahead, keep on denying it.

You won't be denying it for too much longer.

Make peace with your Maker!

Make peace with those whom you have harmed.

In this righteousness (tzedaka) there is salvation from death.

Pay attention now, or pay the price later.

May your hearts, ears, and eyes open to God's Word (Torah).

May you experience the Divine Truth,
and live accordingly, and not die.

Be blessed! Shalom.

47. Schoolhouse Earth

Feb. 26, 23 predawn

Life on this Earth is school, nothing more and nothing less.

Life on this Earth is not supposed to be Heaven, nor is it supposed to be Hell.

In case you have not yet noticed, things happen every day that are not under our control, and are beyond our reach to influence. And yet, these very same things affect us in many ways. One might conclude from this that there is nothing that one can do, but this is not true. While one cannot control what happens to one, one can indeed control how one chooses to respond to everything that happens.

One is responsible for one's own actions, one's own feelings, and one's own thoughts. No one controls these other than oneself. Although there are elements in modern society that want to convince us that some people have no control over their thoughts, feelings, and behavior, this is not true.

It is true, however, that some people have serious difficulty in controlling their thoughts, their feelings, and their behaviors. Such difficulties should, by no means, be accepted as an excuse for one person being harmful to another. Being harmful to another can be abuse. And abuse is always wrong!

Ultimately, life here on Earth is school. We are here to learn how to deal with difficulties and how to overcome adversity, weakness, and our own foolishness.

Life here on Earth is school. For some school is easy, and for some school is hard. Regardless of how difficult life's lessons may be (or not be), they are lessons to be learned nonetheless. And learn our lessons, we will! One way or another, in one lifetime or in many, what each individual isolated, lost soul needs to be taught, it will be taught, and it will remain in school until its lessons are learned thoroughly and absorbed completely.

For some this may indeed be Hell on Earth, but if this is so, then it is a Hell of one's own making. Part of learning is to realize this, and to let go of Hell. The only way out of Hell is to graduate out of it. Yet so many individual isolated souls must love the trials and tribulations of Hell because they always choose to stay there, even when the doorway to exit remains wide open.

Life on Earth is School. School is about learning. Life on Earth, as everyone is forced to eventually realize, is temporary. We are each here for a limited, finite time. We come and we go. Some stay longer, some stay for only a short time. However long our sojourn here is, we are here for a reason. One who fails to search out one's personal reason, and who fails to discover it, and implement it, will be forced to repeat the process all over again, from scratch. Each time that one repeats the process, the lessons do not become easier to learn.

Many people suffer in life here on Earth because of lessons not learned. Life on Earth does not have to be this way. Life on Earth does not have to be difficult. But individual lost souls choose to struggle. They learn from the animals in the wild that life is supposed to be a struggle for survival, and so they choose to fight, and to ravage others to secure what they believe to be their security. But there is no such security, not for animals, and certainly not for lost human souls.

Lesson One to be learned is that we are not animals. While our bodies are the product of this physical Earth, that which makes one a sentient, aware creature is not of this Earth. This is true for animals and humans alike. Understand and know that even animals have souls. And so do plants, and so do those things which we consider to be inanimate (without life). Even planet Earth herself is a sentient being, as are all the other stars and planets. All things natural are alive, for this is the way of Life. All lifeforms are in school. We are each brought here, or brought to any other place, or to any other world, or to any other dimension to experience the realities of that place, and to learn lessons therein.

Human souls have graduated beyond animal consciousness. And eventually human souls will graduate beyond being human. Others who came before us have already graduated from being human. Many of them now serve as our teachers in a higher dimension. Many of us now will eventually graduate schoolhouse Earth and join the teaching staff.

Life on Earth is about focusing on life's lessons. Anything that distracts from this sacred work is called in ancient literature, "strange activity." In religious terms, this strange activity is called Idolatry. Idolatry is a psychological condition that transcends any limited understanding of the concept that is presented by religion. Idolatry has little to do with the worship of this or that so-called god. The false gods that are worshiped are the lies and false beliefs that motivate individual lost souls to act in way that are disharmonious with nature, with the natural Way, and certainly with the lessons that life is here to teach us.

There is nothing wrong with enjoying the temporary things of this Earth while we are here. Yet, to pursue these pleasures with fanatic abandon is harmful to one's soul. Realizing this is one of life's lessons.

One has one's portion in life, as allotted by higher Wisdom. One will not achieve more that one's portion, although many do indeed steal the portions of others. Another one of life's lessons is to learn the age-old commandment, "do not steal." One who steals in one lifetime will find oneself a victim of theft in many lifetimes to come. No matter what it takes, the higher Wisdom will teach the isolated lost soul that stealing does not secure one's place in this world, and that all such activity is wasteful, and is thus "idolatrous."

Let one who is ready pay heed to this lesson. Let the one who is ready embrace these words. Choose life! Seek out its personal meaning for you. Do not be a slave to external interests. Free your soul. Learn your Way. Return to your place. In this one will accomplish one's destiny. One will thus graduate schoolhouse Earth, and take one's rightful place among the stars in Heaven, whose brightness and power is only but a dream here on Earth.

48. The Soldier

Feb. 26, 23 evening

A soldier understands what it means to be obedient to God.

This is why God's people are also called God's army.

To fight for God does not mean to express violence.

To fight for God means to battle one's personal inner demons, and to defeat them totally.

To fight for God means to stand up for, and to practice moral, right, and proper behavior.

To fight for God means to fight evil and immorality in all its forms within oneself and outside of oneself.

To fight for God is a moral and righteous obligation. We call this a mitzvah.

We do not seek to rationalize away the Divine Way, on the contrary, we embrace it first in our hearts, and only then in our minds.

We do what is right simply because it is what is right – no further reason is required.

Religion is great when it serves God. Religion is bad when it serves man.

Our mission and our message is not to promote religion, but rather our mission and our message is to promote the Word of God (Torah), and our necessary obedience to the Divine Way.

Without true sincerity there is no true religion.

God does not ask what our excuses are. Like a Commanding Officer, the Lord of Armies expects His soldiers to follow orders, and to get the job done, no matter the cost.

When Torah speaks, one's response must always be, "Sir, yes Sir!" And then proceed to perform the required acts of service, and of righteousness.

Follow God, follow orders. Don't ask why! Rather know why within yourself, within your very soul.

The good soldier follows orders. God's soldiers receive the blessings of their rewards through the actions that they perform.

Pray to God. Ask to receive your personal marching order. They are present in the Torah. Find your path and serve your Commanding Officer with dignity. In this there is the highest reward, and the greatest peace within.

49. Torah

Feb. 28, 23 morning

Torah was brought to Earth for two reasons. Reason #1 was to transform the inner individual. Reason #2 was for the transformed individual to change the world.

Torah that is external to one is not true Torah. One may be very religious, and very observant, and still not have Torah within.

Assimilation acts like a strong wind upon those who express Torah culture, but who have no internal Torah. The wind blows and all of one's external cultural expressions are exposed to be nothing more than skin deep. Torah that is not internal is no Torah at all. This is why today we see so many who are religious on the outside, but who are far from Torah on the inside.

For the superficially religious, this is all that they want to know, they judge themselves and others by external expressions of religion, and have no idea about the depths of darkness in their souls.

Long ago, from the beginning, we were told to place Torah upon our hearts. Today this commandment is rationalized away and twisted into a statement of philosophy. So few takes the Torah to heart, and all wonder why so few have a direct and personal relationship with the Source of Torah, YHWH.

For many, YHWH remains a reality that is distant, detached, abstract, and purely philosophical. This is the way of those who embrace only the externals of Torah.

YHWH is the internal Torah. One cannot know YHWH all the while that one has not embraced Internal Torah. To experience YHWH within requires of one the internal transformation that only Torah can bring. For YHWH and Torah are one.

Let the academics show off their intelligence. Let the learned show off their learning. How fitting is it that we human beings have already created thinking machines that can memorize and recite back more Torah books, than any human being alive. Book learning is a thing for machines, not for living, breathing, human beings who are bonded with YHWH.

The Sage is called a man of wisdom. The Sage is one who knows enough about what the books say, and then proceeds forward beyond the words in the books towards their inner concealed truths.

True, religion is to be found in books, thus the books have their place. But YHWH is found in life. The only book wherein which YHWH is found is Torah. And Torah is alive, sentient, and aware. YHWH and Torah are to be found everywhere and in everything. The Scroll of Torah contains only the Torah's garments. One must penetrate beneath its surface in order to discover Torah's soul. And the soul of Torah can be seen everywhere where YHWH is. Knowing YHWH begins outside of the books.

Knowing YHWH begins with Fear! Yes, Fear! Not awe, not wonder, and not amazement! Know Fear!

Be afraid, be very afraid. YHWH is the Reality of realities. All this world and everything in it is only a temporary illusion, whose worth is only for the moment, but no more. Everything in this world is nothing in comparison to YHWH. One who does not know YHWH has much to fear, for everything that the shallow and blind soul holds dear is nothing, and will pass like blowing wind.

Reason #1 for Torah to come to Earth was for the transformation of the inner person. We have not accomplished this task, and because of our collective failure, Reason #2 has also not been accomplished.

Yes, fear YHWH, for His mighty wind has only begun to blow, and it will continue to blow stronger and stronger, blowing away all the falsehoods and foolish attachments that blind souls cling to.

Torah will reign supreme, but only within those who embrace it internally. The rest will be gone with the wind. This is the Way of the World. This is the Way of YHWH.

Religion is not one's salvation! Being religious saves no one. Let history bear witness to this. The only salvation is YHWH.

Know YHWH embrace His Torah internally, and the Mark of Salvation will be seen upon your forehead. Judgment will see that you are chosen and pass over you. As for the rest, their judgment is their own fault.

The Light of YHWH will reign supreme. Torah will shine like the Resurrection of Life. The superficial and the shallow religious, who observe without sincerity and without the Fear of YHWH will be gone.

Let the externally religious embrace Internal Torah and know YHWH thereby. For without this return to Truth, they will be blown away when the mighty wind comes and blows away their superficial, external world.

Give thanks to YHWH for He is good, for His (true) mercy endures forever.

50. Submission

March 1, 23

Sometimes when life gets complicated, we forget some of the simplest of things. One lesson for us all to remember is that when something gets broken, it needs to be fixed.

We have many problems in our society. Global war seems to be just around the corner. Almost every country is experiencing unrest. The cost of living just goes up and up, while the quality of living seems to be going down. No matter which way we turn we see a world full of chaos. Is this the way things are supposed to be? Certainly not!

In the beginning when God created the Heavens and the Earth, there was universal chaos. God's first act was to introduce the Divine Light. The Light served to bring order into the chaos. And this set the pattern for all things, for all times.

When a system get broke, it falls into chaos. It seems very evident that this is where we are today. That which fixes chaos is the orderly Divine Light. To put it bluntly, a world without God is chaos, whereas a world with God provides both order and peace.

Yet, let me make one point very clear. I am talking about God, and not about religion! Religions today have become as corrupt as the immoral people who embrace them.

Indeed, one of the greatest things keeping people away from God is the behavior of the religious who proclaim to be close to God. Why would anyone want to embrace a religion whose practitioners embrace all sorts of immoral and unrighteous behavior. Today both one with religion and one without religion act in ways that can only be said to be Godless!

Like I said, the solution to our problems, both in society and within each of ourselves, is a sincere return to a personal relationship and experience of the Divine Light. Only this can change a bad heart into a good one.

God is Alive and Well. And long ago we were warned what happens when one abandons the Divine Way to follows other strange and foreign paths. The greatest Judgment that Heaven places upon us is to let us alone and to suffer the consequences of our own actions, without the Divine Hand intervening in our lives, to help fix things. And here we are today, in the chaos that we ourselves have made.

A return to God is what we each need. This is not a call to become religious. Rather, this is a call to become righteous and moral. This is a call for each of us to retire into whatever area of privacy that we may have left and cry out directly and personally to God. Apologize to God for the darkness of your own making, and beg for Heaven to send you the Divine Light. A change of heart is what leads to change of destiny.

The Divine Light is what fixes all problems. Do not allow the Light to be dimmed by the behavior of those who claim to be carrying its torch.

Submission to the Will of Heaven is primary. Not my (personal) will, but your (Divine) Will be done!

Do not fixate upon the temptations that draw so many astray. Such pursuits are nothing more than modern-day idolatry, and those that pursue them are no different than the idolaters of the past. Do not be one of them!

Place God first, above all things. Pray all the time. You don't need words. God knows your heart. Cry out from within yourself. And if you are honest and sincere, God will hear you and your life will begin to change.

51. Secrets of the Universe & Love

March 3, 23

All the while that one is seeking out the secrets of the universe, one may very well be missing out on the practice and application of those very same secrets in one's daily life doing normal things.

The secrets of the universe are truly great and profound. They surround us no matter where we look. And herein is the secret behind the secrets. One does not have to look very far for them. For the secrets of the universe will reveal themselves right here, right now in one's everyday normal affairs. All one has to do is to look to see them.

The problem, of course, with the reception of secrets is their recognition. The problem is that no one recognizes the profound secrets even when they are right in front of one. The problem is not in the revelation, the problem is in the recognition. If one does not know what one is looking for, then even if what one wants is directly in front of one, one will not recognize that there it is.

There is a part of each of us that is not limited to the confines of our space-time reality. There is a part of us that is right now present in a higher dimension, experiencing life there with the same ease and interaction as we experience life here. And that higher part of us sees and knows everything that we see and know, and yet we do not see our own higher part, nor experience what it experiences. It is clear that the vision, the insight, and the movement is only one way. I know that this reality may be difficult for one to visualize. So let me try to give an example that may help us see the unseen.

Our space-time reality in which we reside at present consists of what we call three dimensions. We can move backwards and forwards (1), right to left (2), and up and down (3). We live this, and thus know it well.

Now, let us imagine a flat sheet of paper that has characters drawn on it. Let us imagine that the characters on the flat sheet of paper are alive, and sentient beings. Their space-time reality is limited to the flat sheet of paper. Thus they have the ability to move backwards and forwards (1), and from right to left (2). What they cannot do is to move up and down (3). There is no up above the paper or down below it. Such movement would be inconceivable for those living on the surface of the flat paper.

Now, along comes one of us, living as we do in 3D. We are above the paper. We can see the whole flat sheet of paper in one glance. Yet, those on the flat sheet of paper have no concept of "up," thus they cannot look up and see us looking down at them.

So, what happens if one of us in 3D takes the edge of one's finger and touches the surface of the 2D flat sheet of paper? Once the finger makes contact with the paper's surface, it appears there, and those living on the paper can see the finger materialize, as if from out of nowhere. It does not look like a 3D finger, for to those living on the 2D paper, there is no such thing as 3D.

Now when one lifts one's finger from off the paper, that which was once present on the flat sheet of paper 2D space is no more. It disappeared as strangely as it appeared. In our 3D reality, all one did was to touch the paper and then remove one's finger. But that act created a stir in the 2D world disturbing their sense of reality.

Just as it is between 2D and 3D reality, so too is it between 3D and 4D reality. The higher part of our self is like the 3D finger that touches 2D space.

When it comes to searching for the secrets of the universe, one does not need to look far away. They are here with us, concealed in our everyday affairs. The secrets do indeed have their source in the 4D space-time around us. And the way to access 4D space is not by building expensive and powerful technological machines, but rather by accessing that hidden part of ourselves that is already present and living in 4D space. So, the way out to the 4D is through our expanding our 3D awareness of the reality of our being.

Expanding 3D awareness is a process of introversion on our parts. We look within in order to reach outside. The greater universe is at our finger tips, for those who can gaze within and recognize what it is that one wants to see.

What are the secret of the universe? For me to answer this question would be the same as if I told 2D beings to "look up." There is no "up" for them. Thus they would see nothing. For me to tell them to "look up" would thus be a waste of time, and would reinforce for the 2D guys that there really is nothing there to be seen.

When however, I tell the 2D guy that he is really a finger touching a flat sheet of paper, I tell him to experience being a finger, and to feel the greater body to which the finger is attached. When it dawns on one that one really is a finger, and not just an image, one's sense of experience will guide one to sense and to feel that which was not sensed or felt before. Thus, the finger becomes aware of the greater body of which it is a part, and we here in 3D space-time equally become aware that we are only a part of a higher dimensional reality.

One who gazes within will discover the true nature of the higher reality. This reality is one of energy. It is an energy of passion, it is an energy of bonding. In human terms, we call this bonding energy, love.

Of all the things that one may spend one's life to acquire, the only thing that one can take with one once one leaves this physical world is love. All the money, all the power, and the possessions stay behind. All of them only have a 3D reality, and thus can no longer exist in higher dimensions.

But love is an energy. Love is the energy of the universe itself. Here on Earth we only experience a small part of it. But the part of love that we do experience here on Earth is intense. One thing we each should know for sure is that of all things, love survives. It is even more real, and more intense in its natural environment of 4D space. This is just one of those universal secrets right here, right now.

One who seeks out true love will discover it, and its power. It comes into our 3D space, just like the finger enters 2D space as described in the example above. Love seems to come from nowhere. But it is always there. All one has to do is to become aware of it, and then to embrace its reality.

Love for (and with) another begins with love for (and with) oneself. The one who recognizes this and lives it vibrates the energetic message of readiness to move forward in life. Internal love leads to external love. This again is one of the hidden secrets of the universe, one that is to be found right here, and right now, for the one who is open to see it.

Love is supposed to be one's normal state. The lack of love is abnormal. The restoration of love into one's life is the true key to happiness. One of the greatest secrets of the universe is simply love. Why make the search and experience for it so complicated? Experience it within, and allow it to naturally manifest. How simple, and yet how profound. One of the greatest secrets of the universe is to be discovered in one of the most normal and natural human things.

52. Mother's Womb

March 6, 23 predawn

Learn a lesson from life itself. Unless a fetus develops first in the womb of its mother, it cannot be properly born to live life here on Earth. There must always be internal development before there can be external development. This is the Way of nature, it reveals the Will, the Mind, and the Hand of the Creator.

Life, and nature itself are our teachers who always guide us in the proper paths of living. Those who extract themselves from the multitude of distractions that human societies have created and return to nature and the natural way will experience firsthand the Way of things as they really are.

All too many people talk and proclaim that life means this or that, and how one is supposed to live accordingly. Yet, do any of the talkers ever silence themselves long enough to listen to the natural Voice that speaks to us from throughout nature itself?

We are inundated by many who each want to tell others how they should live, and what they should do. Each one is so convinced that their way is the right way, regardless of the numerous hardships and struggles that such ones face because of their life choices.

Yes, sometimes life is a struggle. Sometimes we must fight just to stay alive. Indeed, there are good times, and bad times, as well as easy times and hard times. So, what is one to do? Those who allow themselves to be simple, those who remove themselves from the burdens of the ideas, beliefs, and demands of others, simply observe what is the true nature of their surroundings and act in accordance to what is natural and necessary for the moment.

The secret of success in life is learning how to bend and to be flexible in light of life's constant movements and changes. Those who demand to be rigid when flexibility is called for are often broken and shattered.

Yes, there is a right way and a wrong way for almost everything. Yes, there is a constant for righteousness and morality. But even constants are subject to fluctuations. One must be careful to never manipulate this truth and to use it to justify that which is wrong and evil. But at the same time, the one who is wise, the one who learns from nature itself, sees the movement of the Hidden Hand behind all things, and responds accordingly as is necessary.

Those whose thoughts are too rigid will not understand these words. Those whose hearts that have traces of selfishness and greed will seek to manipulate these words. But nature itself conceals within it the Hidden Hand of the Creator. Those who deny nature and the natural Way also deny the Presence of the Hidden Hand concealed within both. The rigid mind will not see. The contaminated heart will not hear. Those who choose to be both blind and deaf by distancing themselves from nature and the natural Way will face the consequences of their choices.

Learning to listen to nature begins within oneself, within one's thoughts and within one's heart. One must heal one's choice to be blind and learn to see with flexibility, and not always with rigidity. One must heal one's choice to be deaf and to cleanse one's heart of any desire, temptation, and distraction that causes one to drift away from the natural Way that conceals within itself the Hidden Hand.

First the fetus must grow before it is born. First one must change oneself internally before one can change oneself externally.

All those who make external changes before internal changes are going about change backwards. External change is only skin deep. It gives the appearance of change, but lacks the depth of change. Some say that such external, superficial change is good enough. But the wise know how false this foolishness is.

First the fetus must grow in the concealment and safety of the mother's womb before it can be born. And as we know, birth itself does not ready one to stand independent in this world. Infancy is a most precious and delicate time. One must be very careful in the nurturing and protection of the newborn. As it is with the birth of the body, so too is it with the birth of consciousness.

Right and wrong, good and evil, truth and falsehood, while these are all objective states, nevertheless, their applications are as many as are situations. Only the flexible will be able to navigate the diverse course of life in peace. Only the pure of heart will hear the natural Voice that guides one along the chosen Way.

Each individual who is contaminated with the multitude of distractions that human societies have created must return to the womb of the Mother. Nature and the natural Way is our Mother, even as the Creator is our Father. None of us are orphans, our supernal Parents are alive and well, and cry out daily for their wayward children to return home.

And so we see in flexibility, we hear in purity of heart, and by these we know the natural Way, and by knowing the natural way, we come to see the Hidden Hand behind it all. It all begins within the womb, the internal development that comes before the external development. The womb of the Mother is open and awaits the return of Her children, for only therein will they be cleansed, nourished, and born anew. Only then will the wise child be born, and begin the long path towards psychic adulthood.

53. Glasses for Psychic Vision

March 7, 23 Purim

Speed is a relative thing, so too is motion. What is fast for one may be slow to another. What is movement for one may be stillness to another. Everyone sees and judges through one's own eyes.

The only concern with all this is when individual perception becomes subject to influence from an outside source. Essentially, along comes some outside source, whether this be a person of influence, or the influence of society itself, and informs the individual that what one sees, one does not see, and that what one believes to be true, is not true.

Instead of naturally accepting one's own perceptions, the outside source comes along and convinces the individual not to believe one's own self, but to rather believe the outsider. When this occurs, and one's turns off one's own natural perceptions of reality, and instead adopts the perception of reality from another, one ends up becoming lost to oneself. Speed and motion are no longer what they naturally are, and how they naturally appear. Instead speed and motion, and everything else, is defined by what you are told to believe. You are coerced into believing the perceptions of the outsider, and torn away from believing that which you know deep inside yourself to be the real truth.

To be certain, one's individual perceptions internally can rightly be compared to one's physical vision (of the external world). Not everyone can physically see clearly. It is well known that many need mechanical vision adjustments. It is a blessing of our times that we understand the science of optics and have made glasses so that through them their many users can see physical things more clearly. Let it not come as a surprise that just as one may need physical glasses to help correct physical vision, so too may one also need psychic glasses to help correct one's psychic vision.

With regards to physical vision one gazes out and can see what is in front of one. One will recognize it and act accordingly based upon what one sees and perceives. This is our normal daily experience. When however we shift from physical vision to psychic vision so many of us are next to blind. Over our psychic eyes are layers upon layers of the beliefs and instructions from outsiders whose sole intent is to make us as blind as can be, with the intent to prevent us from seeing their movements.

What one has over their eyes are psychic blackout glasses whose intent is not to help one see, but rather to block out everything that one does naturally and normally see. And in the blind lack of psychic sight, the speed and motion in the ever-present and real psychic realms go on unseen, and worse, unbelieved.

Rightly have we been taught that before one learns something new, one must first unlearn something old. Our psychic blackout glasses need to be tossed aside, and new helpful psychic glasses must be put on in order for one to learn to again see clearly in the psychic realms. When this occurs, and one sees the influences of the outside sources, one will then easily be able to guard against them, and walk around them, avoiding them as one would avoid a physical obstacle observed with one's physical eyes.

So, what is one to do? How does one remove one's dark psychic glasses, and replace them with ones that will enable one to see clearly in the psychic realms? The answer to this is straightforward. But this answer takes us directly into the realms of the many layers of disbelief that the outsiders have placed upon one.

Let us begin by peeling away one of the layers of darkness to reveal a concealed truth. But remember this, all concealed truths are only truths once one sees them and experiences them for oneself. To accept a truth in any other way only adds another layer of outsider influence over your own inner vision. We wish to avoid this. But the outsiders wish to maintain this, and to reinforce it.

Therefore, when one takes the necessary steps to restore one's own psychic vision, one must take things slowly, and not fast. Indeed, one will move, but one will move at one's own pace, and not at a pace that an outside source tells one is the right or wrong way to be.

Step one in removing darkness from one's inner eyes is to become aware that one is not alone. One is not cut off, not from one's own higher (internal) identity, and not from the universe at large. And yes, we must introduce here that one is a creation of the Creator. No matter what one does, feels, or believes, this truth will never become untrue.

In this world of the many layers of lies, the reality of the Singular Divine Creator (and Law-Giver) is the One Truth that has been layered over the most. After all, the greater the Source of Light, the greater the need and the effort to cover it up for those who wish to conceal this truth.

The truth is that one is never cut off from God. And one must come to experience this truth for oneself. And in doing so, one's internal psychic vision will begin to improve. Yes, the initial outreach for the experience of God (and not just the intellectual belief in a Divine Being) is the first pair of psychic glasses that one "wears" in order to help correct one's psychic vision.

Speed is a relative thing, so too is motion. What is fast for one may be slow to another. What is movement for one may be stillness to another. Everyone sees and judges through one's own eyes. With regards to one's search for the experience of God, these truths will become self-evident.

Discovering the reality of the Divine is not an intellectual process, it is an experiential journey that takes one through one's own heart, one's feelings, and one's thoughts (be they clear and correct, or clouded and confused). One step at a time, one will peel away the layers of lies that outsiders have placed as blinders over one's eyes. One step at a time, the light will begin to come through the openings that one is making within one's psychic vision. For those along this path of discovery, there is always motion. For some, perception will be slow, and for others it may appear to be fast.

With God as one's internal anchor, call upon the Presence and the Force of the Supernal Truth. In time, one's sincerity will bear fruits. In time, the layers of darkness will be peeled away. In time, one will discover the Light. And once this happens, one will be guided by the Light and shown how to better clarify one's own inner psychic vision. Suffice it for now, for one to take this first step.

The many other steps to follow will each become apparent in its time, in its place, and in its right way.

54. The Destruction of Destruction

March 9, 23 predawn

Why is one surprised when the inevitable eventually happens? Does one really believe that one's disbelief actually makes the inevitable go away? This type of thinking is the worst type of arrogance and delusion.

One who is wise can foretell what will inevitably and eventually occur based upon what is happening now. Forecasting the future is not a precise art. No one can foresee all the details of what will (or will not) be. But nevertheless certain general patterns in one's personal life and in society in general, when present, send out clear messages that the present path will lead to a foreseeable future. One may deny the inevitable all that one wishes, but the inevitable will continue to draw closer all the while that one ignores the present, and continues along a path that makes a certain future become inevitable.

We have great power in our hands. We can choose wisdom, or we can choose folly. We can choose the path to peace, or we can choose the path to war. Yes, we choose to build bridges, or we can choose to destroy them. And understand a very clear truth! Building takes a long time. Destruction can happen in an instant.

One with wisdom guards one's tongue. One knows that not all words need to be spoken, and not all truths need to be told. Sometimes, silence and concealment, at the right moment, and in the right way, come to be far superior that speech and revelations.

Building takes time and contains many steps. Each step must be done in its right time, and in its right way in order for the building to become stable and strong. With destruction, all that one needs to do is to destroy. With confusion and chaos, destruction is inevitable. And when the spirit of destruction reigns supreme, the wise silence their speech and conceal their truths, for fear of the destruction of both wisdom and truth.

When a storm arises, one seeks shelter. When destruction reigns supreme, one gets out of the way. One cannot stop a storm with words. Wisdom and truth are no match for the spirit of destruction. When one sets foot along the path of self-destruction, wisdom and truth cry out screaming for one to turn back, but they alone cannot turn one from one's downward spiral.

There is only one power that can confront the force of destruction and that is an equal or even greater force of destruction. Yes, destruction destroys destruction. As bizarre as this may sound to some, the wise understand. For there is destruction whose sole purpose is to destroy everything, and then there is destruction whose sole purpose is to destroy the spirit of destruction, and in its place rebuild anew a strong and solid edifice what will reign in peace!

The secret of victory in war is to fight for peace. Peace must be for all, or there will be peace for no one. When the wise wage war they seek to build, even if they must first destroy. When the fool wages war, they seek to destroy for destruction's sake and have no foresight, nor plan, as to how to rebuild after the destruction.

When the wise wage war and win, they rebuild right way, and there is peace. When the fool wages war and wins, they do not rebuild at all. Darkness reigns supreme, and humanity returns to depravity. We have seen this cycle many times in our recorded history.

Who is wise? The one with foresight. But the prerequisite for proper foresight is understanding. One must be able to both gaze within oneself and to equally gaze out upon society and reads the signs for what they really are!

One must have the courage to accept uncomfortable truths. One must learn discretion when to speak and when to remain silent. One must understand the difference between that which leads to war for the sake of destruction, and that which leads to war for the sake of peace.

And above all, one must understand what it means to be a peace-maker. Peace and peace-makers have their reserved time.

The wise who understand know the difference between the time for war, and the time for peace. The wise who understand proclaim peace when it can be heard, proclaim war when it must be heard, and remain silent when the time is right to remain concealed.

Wisdom and foresight reveal to one what will inevitably come to pass. Therefore the wise who understand take the proper precautions and make the proper preparations. And as for those who deny the inevitable, they take no precautions, and they make no preparations. When the storm comes, they are swept away, and no amount of denial of truth will change the inevitable once it comes to pass. Let the one with ears hear; and the one with eyes see, and with wisdom and understanding, know what to do.

55. Study Talmud

March 9, 23 morning

The reason why Judaism always emphasizes Torah study is to teach its students rational thinking skills.

One must have a free mind in order to live a free life.

Talmud teaches us to question and to inquire.

Talmud learned this this from life itself.

Life is about the expansion of mind and consciousness.

Torah is life; life is Torah. Study life and you study Torah – this is Gemara.

The secret of success is a strong mind.

The secret of freedom is an enlightened mind.

Learn HOW to think – not WHAT to think.

Study Torah and you will understand.

56. Hard Times are our Teacher

March 10, 23 predawn

There is an old saying that "adversity is the mother of invention." This is very true. Another old saying is, "when the going gets tough, the tough get going." Both of these statements point to a single truth.

Good times are easy, but they can make one weak. Bad times are hard, but they can make one strong. Both good times and bad times are the norms for everyone throughout life. Is this the natural way? It does seem to be so. We tend to desire the good and easy times, and we tend to shy away from the bad and hard times. Is this the natural way? It does seem to be so.

But we need to pause here for a moment and contemplate the way of life itself. For nothing is haphazard. Nothing is random, like the blind materialist insists. Everything happens for a purpose. To everything there is a cause, and to everything there is deeper meaning, with some meanings being deeper than others.

When bad and hard times come, their purpose in being is to strengthen the weak. And as we see, the harder the times, the stronger are those who come forth from them. While those who had to suffer those hard times certainly do not reminisce about them, but at the same time, they would never give up the strengths that they have earned due to going through them.

Hard times are a crash course in character building. During hard times, tough choices have to be made. Sometimes one's very survival is at stake. Sometimes one makes extreme decisions that would normally never be made, but at that moment of hardship and crises, the extreme decision is the right one, and maybe even the necessary one.

Each one of us has an internal list of priorities. Each one of us has our values, and our morals. Some things may be easy to compromise, others things may be hard to compromise, and then there are those things which will never be compromised! Oh really?

It is in moments of crises that our values and morals are severely tested. It is easy to do the right thing during good and easy times. Even when times are challenging, most can gather the strength to still do the right thing. But what happens during desperate times? Can one still do that which is right and proper, when one's own survival, and perhaps the survival of loved ones, is at stake?

What we do during good and easy times is a façade of social nicety. Even the worst of people act nice in good and easy times. But when the niceties of everyday life are peeled away due to hard and challenging times, then one's true face is exposed, and we discover who are friends, our neighbors, and our selves really are.

Many times, the face of a sheep turns into the face of a wolf. And also, it happens that many times the face of the weak turns into the face of the strong. How interesting is it that hard and trying times tend to reveal one's true essence. The surface façades of personality and societal position are stripped away. And none of this is haphazard.

To everything, there is a reason and a purpose. Hard times come upon us all, each in their own way. It is during these hard times that one's true character is tested. It is during these hard times that one's true personality is exposed. This is all by Divine design; the universe does indeed operate in ways that are mysterious to us. But let us not concern ourselves with the universe right now, instead let us focus on ourselves.

When hard times come and our character is tested, and our true personalities are exposed, what is revealed may indeed come as a shock to oneself and to others. But there is no such shock to the higher powers, those who know and operate this universe. For them (whomever they may be), they see our true faces all the time. They know who is weak but who appears strong, and they know who is strong, but who appears weak. They also know who is righteous but who appears bad, and they know who is bad but who appears righteous.

It is the way of the universe, to instruct us here in schoolhouse Earth. One of the lessons each of us needs to learn is what is the nature of our true faces? What is the truth about our character? What kind of individual is one really? For during good and easy times, each of us wears a mask of our own making. We always appear to be something that we may indeed not be. And along comes the Way of nature, and imposes hard times and crises upon us, during which our masks are stripped off, and one's true personality is exposed.

Our lesson here in schoolhouse Earth is to learn the truths about ourselves. Hard times come to teach us about ourselves. For everything has a purpose and a meaning. Hard times serve a vital purpose and role in the development of individual consciousness. As hard as these times may be, they are as much our friend as they are our enemy.

The truths about ourselves lie concealed under the layers of masks that we ourselves place over our faces. The universe arranges circumstances to bring us into times when our masks are stripped off so that we can learn the truths about ourselves. Schoolhouse Earth is our teacher. Hard times are our teacher. The Power above already knows the truth of our being. The hard times come to educate ourselves about ourselves. The hard times reveal to each of us our true inner selves. And this is then something that each of us has to deal with, for better or for worse.

So, when the times get tough, the tough get going. They tackle life head-on and do what needs to be done in order to thrive and survive. Will they act with morals and righteous values? Time will tell, for each individual is different.

When the strong discover that they are weak, and the righteous discover that they are evil, each negative revelation provides for one the opportunity to change one's ways, and to return to a higher caliber of morals and values. This is the Way that we are taught here in schoolhouse Earth. Rewards come to the one who changes for the better. And needless to say, so too do punishments come upon those who go from better to worse.

Embrace hard times for the opportunity that they are. Make the best of them, and allow them to bring out the best in you.

57. True Religion

March 11, 23 Motzei Shabat

I mourn what has become of religion in general. Belief in God is supposed to lead one to adopt and to live by a code of righteous behavior and high morals. Yet, with religion today, we see so much emphasis on external appearances and so little focus on what really matters, which is the transformation of the individual personality.

While it is true that God does call individuals into His Divine service, nevertheless such a calling never makes the one who is called any better than anyone else. Being chosen by God is a task and a burden; it is a tough and often thankless job. But those chosen by God seldom have the freedom to walk away from the Divine call.

When God chooses one to act as a vehicle of service, one may be very unaware of the movement of the Divine Hand. One will discover that one's behavior acts like a catalyst of causation. This is the Way God works. He chooses individuals, in either small or large numbers and directs the course of affairs in their lives. Granted, everyone really does have free will, and in an instant, can choose one's path through life. Nevertheless, and needless to say, God knows all this, and chooses one regardless, knowing full well what a person will or will not do.

In Biblical times, God chose political leaders of vast empires to act savagely against others. God aroused the greater power to conquer the weaker, with all the devastation and destruction that comes along with it. God directs human history along these courses so as to implement the hidden and unknowable Divine plan. Nothing has changed since Biblical times. God acts the same way with modern empires as He does with ancient ones.

As individuals, each person can choose how to respond to the events in the world around one. When individuals and collectives act inappropriately the Divine course of correction goes into play. Nature takes its course. Judgement manifests; and we witness the rise and fall of nations. This is the way that it has always been. And this is the way things shall remain.

The Hand of God is upon all. Religions were established with the intent to create the positive transformation of human souls. When this does not happen and religion becomes just an empty shell, then indeed religion becomes like a drug that one takes to feel better. But this is not what religion is supposed to be about.

Real religion has no need to preach doctrines and dogmas. Real religion should be able to be learned directly from nature Herself. Real religion disciplines out-of-control human emotions that lead to bad behavior. Real religion expresses itself through actions, rituals and behaviors that are universal in nature, and which teach the value of the harmonious.

Religions in general proclaim great visions about the greater scheme of things that for the most part cannot become subject to rational analysis. But this does not matter. When a religion relates a story in one of its holy books about events that happened long ago, it does not matter whether or not such events relate actual history or not. Religious books are not written to be history books, they are meant to be expressions of higher morals and values.

Therefore, whether or not the stories that they tell are historical or not does not matter because the stories that they tell are real, valid, and true, regardless of their historicity. A lesson about righteousness and morals does not have to be based upon only historical facts. A lesson about morals and righteousness transcends the limits of its narration. The lessons about morals and righteousness are universal and true because they speak to the inner essence of all humanity, and proclaim a message and a way for all human beings to follow and to strive to fulfill.

These universal messages are called archetypes. They are universally true and apply to us all. Their truth is psychological and psychic. This is what religion is supposed to be, a proclamation and an expression of the universal truths that apply to all humanity. This is how religion is supposed to transform the human soul. This is the Way how God speaks to us all.

When a religion forgets its universal, archetypal purpose, its symbols and metaphors are transformed and become something very small, something very divisive, something very isolating, and something very external. This is how God becomes exiled from the very religion that proclaims to speak for Him.

When religion forgets its universal core value then it degrades into a tribal mentality of one way being the only right way, and thus all other ways come to be seen as wrong and evil. When this occurs, religious boundaries are established, and religious bigotry is born. This leads to religious hate, and to religious prejudice, violence, and war. Certainly, none of this comes from God, and certainly none of this serves the greater purpose for which religion was originally established. But this is what happens when the internal experience of transformational religion is replaced with the external expression of cultural and ethnic religion.

Internal religion unites and transforms souls. External religion creates divisions and the isolations of souls. Internal religion brings souls closer to God. External religion drives souls further away from God.

For one to become religious it must mean that one has discovered the universal, archetypal message and then strives to live it in one's life. However, what we see today when one becomes religious is usually only a superficial adoption of a culture, an ethnic identity, and set of ideas and beliefs that separates one from the rest of humanity, instead one uniting one with the whole of humanity.

Such isolating beliefs may have certain short-term beneficial influence over an individual. But if the individual does not learn how to mature within the context of one's chosen form of religion, then instead of being of service, one's religious expression can become a disservice to one's soul. And this is what we see with so many religious expressions today. This is what happens when one's religion is only superficial. One should never be satisfied with one's external expression of religion. Such an expression rarely has anything to do with God.

Today, humanity needs true religious revival. Humanity needs a revival of the underlying truths and archetypes that define true religion. This is the only way for an individual in particular, and for humanity, as a whole, to rediscover and to reconnect with the Reality of the Living Active Being of existence, which we call God.

One should focus on those religious principles that transform one's soul, turning one into a greater, more moral, righteous, and compassionate human being. When this is achieved then one can rest assured that one has found true religion, regardless of which cultural form of expression one has chosen for oneself. One will discover the underlying Unity of all, and in this one will come to experience the Reality of God. This is the ultimate goal, and purpose of all true religion.

58. Deflect Verbal Attacks

March 12, 2023

Know your own identity– and know the identity of your enemy!

If one does not approve of you – who cares?

Why should the opinion of a stranger have any value in your eyes?

There will always be those who will attack you, so, defend yourself!

Step 1 in Self-Defense is to not allow an attack to succeed.

This is true even if the attack is only verbal.

Deflect verbal attacks by paying them no attention.

Again, who cares about what a stranger says?

Let the words of a stranger be as distant to you as is the stranger himself.

When one reveals oneself to be your enemy – watch them closely, but do not attack them.

The enemy wishes to provoke you to attack him.

In this way you are portrayed as the cause of conflict.

Deflect the words of your enemy – ignore them.

If the enemy chooses to become physically violent, only then should one respond in like kind.

Get ready by getting tough!

Strengthen your weaknesses.

Overcome all obstacles!

59. The Balance of Up & Down

March 13, 23

Which is more important, pursuing awareness of the great sublime secrets of the universe, or fulfilling one's mere, mortal, and mundane responsibilities here in Schoolhouse Earth? How one answer's this question reveals the essence of one's personality.

Regardless of materialistic denials, there really are multiple higher dimensions of reality surrounding us at all times. Regardless of any official denials by certain powers that be, there really are multiple races of higher intelligent beings that come and go back and forth into and out of our galaxy and our dimension at all times.

Yes, we are not alone. And it is "they" who have an agenda with regards to us. And it is "they" who truly control what happens here in Schoolhouse Earth! Due to the profound nature of this reality, it is no wonder then that certain types of individuals crave to experience these other-worldly realities and to interact with them.

Then again, such grandiose speculations may be all well and good, but practically speaking, for the majority of us, we have our daily affairs and concerns that take up all of our time and energy. What is happening "out there" is nice, it might even be entertaining, but needless to say, one is still "right here" and not "out there." Therefore, one pays attention to the here and now, and does not pay too much attention to what's "out there," nor has one any real interest in knowing about it.

True, maybe there really is a "them" who controls the grandiose affairs hidden from the eyes of man. But practically speaking, "they" are not here addressing one's personal problems. "They" are not here paying one's personal bills, nor leading, directing, or even offering advice about one's personal life. So, whether or not "they" really do exist (or not), who cares? Schoolhouse Earth is the only reality that one knows, and therefore, it is the only reality that one cares to know. Who can deny this very practical and realistic outlook?

So, it seems that we have a split. There are those who crave to know what's "out there," and then there are those who crave to deal with the "here and now." These two concerns and interests identify two different types of personalities. One focuses on the beyond, and the second focuses on what is in front of one at the moment.

Those who gaze beyond consider those others who do not share this craving for experience to lack passion and imagination. Those who cling to the here and now consider those whose constant gaze is elsewhere and not on the relevant and practical that is before them to be dreamers, and worse, some consider them to be delusional, and sometimes even dangerous.

It does seem that those who gaze beyond have a flexibility of outlook not often shared by their "here and now" focused counterparts. Like I said, we have here two different personality types. And each type may indeed mutually exclude the other. Each sees life different from the other.

Which type of personality one may possess does not seem to be a matter of choice, but rather it is, as if, one is born into it. Whether or not this is true can be debated. But, needless to say, such debate is pointless and irrelevant. Essentially, what we have are different types of individuals who spend their time here in Schoolhouse Earth in different ways.

And who is to say which way is the better? While it may be very nice, and even entertaining to seek out the secrets of the universe, still, is this really one's true purpose in life? Did one actually come here to Schoolhouse Earth to pay all of one's attention to those things happening outside of school? Would it not be more proper to think that if we come here to Schoolhouse Earth, and are entrenched in the life herein, that maybe we should be focusing on it, and not something else?

While this conclusion should be glaringly obvious to most, still, nevertheless, those of the other personality type are not swayed.

They know that their mission here in Schoolhouse Earth is to look beyond it, discover what is to be discovered, and then to do something with the revelations that they have received. Now, who can say that this endeavor lacks merit? Without revelation and discovery life here on Earth would become stagnant, and boring.

And so, we have those who look up and contemplate, and those who look down and work. We have both dreamers and doers. Both make up the population here in Schoolhouse Earth, and both offer their contributions, which it turns out are both necessary and important.

And now we ask the inevitable question, are the two personality types really so mutually exclusive? Is it not possible for both predilections to exist simultaneously within the same individual? The answer of course is yes! And indeed, most of us are a combination of both! It is only the very rare individual who exclusively expresses one of these predilections to the total exclusion of the other. Such individuals are actually the extremes, of one side or the other.

The vast majority of Individuals here in Schoolhouse Earth are in-between with each, having an element of interest in the beyond (be it great or small), and equal focus on the here and now, paying attention to the job and work at hand. It is the discovery of balance between the two within each individual that is part of one's mission here in Schoolhouse Earth.

So, to answer our initial question, which outlook is more important? The answer is that they are both equal in value. Each one has its time and place. Each individual needs to learn one's own personal internal balance, and to devote proper time to each pursuit, as is right for the person, for the place, and for the time. This is one of the great lessons that one comes to Schoolhouse Earth to learn.

How each individual learns this lesson is unique to the individual. No further instructions can be given one from the outside. Only the exploration and discovery of one's true personality can guide one's way.

60. Clarity of Mind

March 13, 23 morning

Clarity of mind is the greatest acquisition.

Life often moves faster than the speed of thought. Therefore, one must have a trained mind that can respond instantly to whatever materializes.

A clear mind thinks ahead and sees what is coming.

Thus when the moment arises, the clear mind already knows what to do.

It does not need to waste time to think – the clear mind already knows.

Action is taken without any inner conflict or confusion.

One's whole is united and focused to respond.

Therefore, one responds to the world with power and force.

One becomes a victor, and not a victim.

Train your mind – know the difference between emotions and thoughts.

Clear the mind from unwelcome emotional persuasions.

Keep emotions in check – never repressed – but under control.

Free your mind – harden your body – control your heart.

Become the warrior you have the potential to become.

All begins with the training of the mind – so, go get busy!

61. Embracing the Bat Kol, & the Concerns Therewith.

March 19, 23 evening.

I have encountered a fear amongst certain people.

I have been approached on more than one occasion.

I have been asked if maybe I am revealing too many Heavenly secrets.

Maybe, they ask, if it would be best if I conceal the secrets that I so readily reveal. Maybe, they say with concern, the reasons why I suffer from health issues is Heaven's way to warn me that I had better keep quiet!

I have a single word response for all such concerns: Nonsense!

The only thing for one to fear is God. The fear of God is the beginning of wisdom. Knowing God is the beginning of understanding.

But today, because of such rampant religious hypocrisy in all the religions, many times religions themselves serve to be the greatest impediment to people discovering the reality and the experience of God in their personal lives. Instead of religion bringing one closer to God, religion performs the opposite function, and pushes people further and further away.

The non-religious see the immoral and unrighteous behavior that many religious individuals perform, and respond with disgust. The non-religious look how many in the religious camps use their religion as a mask to conceal their lack of morals. One who knows God, knows better!

This is why the fear of God, which instills within one a healthy dose of respect towards all things, is the first step in the service of the Divine. Fear God, and know that the first ones to receive Divine punishment are those who are religious on the outside but immoral and corrupt on the inside. One who fears God has nothing else, or no one else to fear.

Now, let us address the topic of the revelation of secrets. From where does revelation come from? It comes from a place deep inside of one. Some may call this inside place one's imagination, or one's mind. But regardless of the source of revelation, one thing is certain about it, and that is that it seems to come from nowhere.

Nowhere is actually a real place. It is just that it is outside of space and time. It is outside of consciousness. Thus to the individual, nowhere seems to be a non-thing. But this non-thing is actually a some-thing of its own. We are the ones who are limited in understanding. Thus the source and the place from where revelations come into consciousness is not seen; the source is inaccessible to us, and therefore it appears to us that the revelation comes from out of nowhere.

But nowhere is somewhere, and nothing is something, all in the higher dimensions which are the true form of the reality that surrounds us. One who gazes into the nothing will see something that comes forth from the nothing. It comes into the place of thought, from what seems to be no place. But no place is actually a place, a space, and a reality all its own.

Knowing this higher dimensional reality is a great (and necessary) accomplishment for each human soul. Granted, this is the source of the Supernal Secrets. But the reason why they are secret is because no one has penetrated far enough into the unknown to bring forth from there knowledge that is to be known.

Our purpose here in Schoolhouse Earth is to reconnect the part of us here with the part(s) of us there. Our job is to unite ourselves into our original unity. While some consider the lessons about this to be a secret and worthy of concealment, those who have already achieved knowing, understand that the opposite is the truth.

Knowing the higher realities is not meant to be an intellectual statement of beliefs in an unexperienced reality, but rather it is meant to be experienced, and embraced, and thus to transform one's life and one's consciousness.

Therefore, one who experiences the higher reality and who can show others how to experience this for themselves is obligated to do so. To conceal this truth would be considered a crime against worthy and ready souls.

One is, however, meant to, and even obligated to conceal certain truths and to maintain their secrecy when one is dealing with those souls who are not yet ready to embrace the experience of the higher realities. Too much light in an unprepared vessel is never a good thing. Too much information in a mind not properly prepared to handle it can cause the mind to be damaged. We have seen this happen since ancient times, and we most certainly do not wish to ever see it again.

So, for those souls who are not prepared to receive, we conceal from them that which can cause harm to their minds. However, for those souls who are ready and open to receive, it is our obligation and our privilege to serve as conduits of revelation, and to fill up their ready-and-waiting minds.

And now let us address what for some may be an ominous topic, the subject of "Them." I speak of the entities who reside here on Earth but in higher dimensional realities of our Earth. They are supposed to be our school teachers. There is not just one kind of "them," but many.

Speculators, mystics, and philosophers have been trying to describe "them" and their kind for as long as we have recorded written documents. Every culture, every civilization, and every people have always had legends about other entities who either inhabit our Earth, or who come to visit it regularly.

Throughout the ages these Others have been given many names, the most generic and popular are angels (who are the visitors), and demons (who are the other-dimensional Earthly inhabitants). Today due to the decline in beliefs in traditional religions, the Others are now lumped together and called Aliens and Extraterrestrials. And yet, one who will do the research to study will discover that the stories told today about Aliens and Extraterrestrials are pretty much the same stories told throughout the centuries about angels and demons.

The terrible hidden truth that "They" most likely do not want to become too well known is that the Others of today (Aliens and E.T.s) and the Others of the past (angels and demons) are one and the same groups of entities, each doing their tasks, and performing their services, just like they always have throughout history.

Yes, some are supposed to be our teachers here in Schoolhouse Earth, but not all of them. Indeed, some of our teachers are also tasked to serve as teachers to some of the Other indigenous races here in the higher dimensions of our Earth.

Speculations aside, these multiple Others do exist, and it does not take much practice and training for any one of us here on this physical Earth to sense and become aware of their presence. We do not need to read stories in a book about Them and what they do. We can cultivate experiences for ourselves, be these experiences with either good entities or bad ones. And like I addressed above about the source of revelations and insights that come into one's mind, it may very well be the case that it is one of Them (good guy or bad guy) that is doing the whispering within one's psychic ear.

Over many centuries each of our world religions have created many myths about the Others. We have numerous stories and legends about both angels and demons. What these myths and legends do is to distort the reality of these Others, and blur their methods and purposes. Only those individuals who have had personal experiences and encounters with any of Them actually have any idea as to who they really are, what they really do, and what they really want. Those without experience are filled with what they have learned from books, however fantastical, whereas those with experience know better.

Now, here is the dilemma. Those who think that they know don't listen to those who really do know. So, why is this so? Would it not be logical for those with experience to teach those without experience? Yet, those who learn from books readily dismiss and often condemn the experiences of those in the know. Why is there such closed-mindedness? Maybe we should contemplate an uncomfortable possibility.

Maybe some of these higher entities have an agenda of their own to misdirect what it is that human beings believe about them. We do find expressions of this belief in many of the world religions dating back through all of recorded history. Maybe those who learn the books but who have no experience are unconsciously being misled, and are equally being unconsciously influenced to dismiss and to silence those who know the truth. True? False? The answer to this will depend upon whom we ask, those who read the books, or those who have actual experience.

Granted, some levels of knowledge and experience require training and maturity on behalf of the receiver. But this knowledge and the experiences required to receive it are necessary parts of human evolutionary growth. This knowledge must be guarded and dispensed with wisdom, this is true, but in the end, it is nevertheless dispensed. Individuals grow and mature. They learn, they see, and they understand. They learn to see and to interact with the higher dimensions and shake off their mortal human bonds. This is the purpose of Schoolhouse Earth, and the Will of our Creator.

But do all the races of higher dimensional entities, including those placed within Earth's domain to serve as teachers, guides and governors share this view and purpose as outlined, and ordained by the Creator. According to both the books, and those with experience, the answer to this is that no, not everyone works towards this goal. Some have an agenda of their own. Some wish to withhold knowledge, experience, and growth from human beings for their own purposes. Not for naught are we taught that there really is both good and evil in the higher dimensions, just as there is here on Earth. If anyone wants to squelch the dissemination of true knowledge, it would be some of Them.

So, now we can address the question that I raised at first. Are there any Others who might have an agenda to inflict distractions, pain and suffering upon one who would rock their boat by revealing the secrets of the real operations of the reality around us? The answer to this is a resounding yes! There are a number of lower (higher-dimensional) forces who do not always follow the edicts of Heaven, and instead of serving humanity, act against its best interests.

Would these entities take an interest in me (personally)? This, I personally doubt! I cannot bring myself to believe that even everything that I have exposed, taught, and written over the past 30 years would have enough of an interest in it to attract the attention of these higher dimensional beings. But then again, what do I know?

Do other-worldly entities get involved with personal human affairs? Yes, they do, all the time. Some are directed to do so by Powers On-High associated with and working for God. Others act with more of a free hand. Nevertheless when these free operatives act as they will, their actions are noticed, as are the wayward actions of human beings. Both then become subject to judgment and when necessary, retribution.

When negative and harmful higher dimensional beings involve themselves in the personal affairs of a human being they are usually doing so for some personal reason on their own part. They normally do not involve themselves within areas that do not affect them personally.

So these negative and harmful entities are usually not the ones who would be involved in a psychic attack against one who reveals Heavenly secrets. Frankly, such harmful and malevolent entities could care less about such secrets. They would only attack such an individual, or for that matter, any other individual, who acts against their personal interests. Such interests on their part would include their enslaving the minds and the bodies of their chosen victims off of whom they feed as psychic vampires.

Mess with their food, and they might in their own way "bite" someone. Yet, we have numerous ways of psychic self-defense to guard ourselves against such attacks. These entities, however disturbing and dangerous as they may be, are not the ones we concern ourselves with in regards to those who object to the revelation of secrets.

There are other entities who are not negative and harmful, but who are also not the highest authority, nor connected to it. These entities seek to serve in holiness, and they do. However, their understanding of their service is through the narrowness of Divine severity. As such this group (or race of beings) interact with human beings, but in a way that appears to be very human in and of itself.

This group might view the revelation of secrets in a negative light, and might possibly act on their own accord to punish the one who makes such revelations. Again, this group offers the true practitioner no real danger. For the one who truly knows the Heavenly secrets, whether or not one reveals what one knows, is certainly also in direct communion with God's holy Name. In case any of these lower entities were engaged in opposition to the properly trained person, such opposition would be quickly removed with a small and sincere prayer that one offers to God. So this group, like the one mentioned above, is not a cause for alarm.

62. Echo of the Voice

March 20, 23 predawn

Beyond all groups of higher dimensional beings there is the Presence, the Reality of the Divine. For most, the Presence of the Divine is merely an intellectual concept that one acknowledges. One believes in God and believes that God is in charge of all. Yet, most believe that God is so remote and so detached from everyday human affairs that to try to reach out and touch God is an impossible venture.

Those who think along this line believe in God and equally believe that God has no direct contact with us. As such God remains distant, whereas the many other higher-dimensional beings are far more close. So, rather than seek out the Creator, who is believed to be far too distant, the majority of seeking souls endeavor to make contact with the lower higher-dimensional beings, some of whom are very open to communion with physical human beings for reasons of their own agendas.

It is a lot easier for the average person to contact lower higher-dimensional beings than it is for one to energetically align oneself properly in order to commune with the Echo (Voice) of the Divine. The reason why God is sensed to be so distant from humanity is not because of God. In reality, God's Presence is immanent. It is right here, right now. But, because human beings in Schoolhouse Earth tend to be naughty students who do not learn their lessons properly, the Immanent Presence of God is not felt or seen at all.

Layer upon layer of contaminants cover over the psychic eyes of the average layman, convincing them, however wrongly, that God is far removed. The reality is that it is the human soul that removes itself from God, and not that God removes from humanity the Immanent Divine Presence. Our lessons here in Schoolhouse Earth is to direct us to experience this truth.

When, therefore, a good student arises here in Schoolhouse Earth, and learns well the lessons here to be taught, such a student therefore naturally becomes sensitive to the Immanent Presence of the Divine. It is only natural and normal then for such a student to want to share with the world what one has learned. There is nothing wrong and everything right with this.

The Echo of the Divine Voice will then speak within such a student's mind and heart to instruct such a one how to best express and relate one's lessons. When this occurs, lessons are taught, classes are given, and sometimes even books are written. Some may consider this form of communion with, and from the Divine to be prophecy, but it is not prophecy. This form of communion is only with what we will call the Echo of the Divine Voice that permeates all things. In ancient times, this Echo was personified, and called the Daughter of the Voice, in Hebrew, a Bat Kol.

When the Echo of the Voice is perceived, one normally feels compelled to express and relate what one has experienced. Throughout human history here in Schoolhouse Earth we have had a number of such communions. The lower higher-dimensional beings are often very well aware that such communion has been established. They are, needless to say, powerless to prevent it.

So what they do is to try to manipulate its distribution to other human beings. After all, some of these lower higher-dimensional beings have their own agendas with certain human beings whom they use for their own purposes. This relationship between themselves and their corralled humans is not part of the lesson plan here in Schoolhouse Earth. Yet, the higher Powers-That-Be tolerate the situation and use it to teach the corralled human souls to yearn for freedom. And freedom is always found in the hearing the Echo of the Divine Voice.

And so the lower higher-dimensional beings act in their own interests to silence the Echo of the Divine Voice by doing whatever they can to weaken the ones who emanate its Presence here in Schoolhouse Earth. And this is no easy task for these lower higher-dimensional entities! Those who emanate the Echo resonate with an energetic frequency very different from the lower higher-dimensional entities. Essentially, the two operate on completely different band widths and thus the lower one has no influence over the higher, whereas the higher does indeed have influence over the lower.

The lower higher-dimensional beings will thus search out any opening in the energetic bands that interact with one's physicality. When they wish to deter one who emanates the Echo of the Divine Voice, the lower higher-dimensional entities will seek out a weak spot in such a one's physicality, and exploit it. This is why the proverbial righteous appear to suffer. They are doing the right things in the right ways, but certain lower powers-that-be take objection and seek to thwart their efforts. And so life in Schoolhouse Earth continues, as we each learn our lessons about the realities of our situation here, and what it is that each of us is supposed to be doing about it.

Regardless of all the distractions, and wayward students here in Schoolhouse Earth, this planet and the entire reality associated with it (even that which is off-world) is under the sole Authority and responsibility of the Immanent Divine Presence. Nothing goes on here, be it good or evil, that the Immanent Divine Presence does not see and know. And here is where we seemingly all fall short in our Schoolhouse Earth lessons. For the patience and the tolerance of the Immanent Divine Presence is far beyond human comprehension to understand.

Why does Heaven allow and tolerate that which it does? Who has the wisdom to be able to properly and comprehensively answer this question? Why do the righteous suffer and why do the wicked prosper? We can offer all kinds of philosophical answer which may attempt to soothe the troubled mind, but in the end, we do not have any answers that can be subject to analysis and verification. And so we are left without any reasonable answers as to why things are the way that they are.

For those who do not have communion with the Immanent Divine Presence, all one has is the faith to believe that all things will work out alright and well in the end. And that in the meantime, one must still fulfill one's duty here in Schoolhouse Earth and live a righteous, decent, and moral life.

For whatever reasons, known and unknown to humanity, living righteous, decent, and moral lives is the right thing to do. One does not need any type of promise for future rewards. One simply knows what is right and proper and does it simply because it is the right and proper thing to do. This is called righteousness, and this is called faith.

As for those who experience the Immanent Divine Presence and who commune with the Echo of the Voice, they too have a knowing of things that defies words to describe. There are many things that they can indeed share, and they do. And then again, there are other things that the Powers-That-Be, with whom they commune, advise them not to share until the time is right to do so.

And so, those with the Echo of the Voice, aligned as they are with the energetic frequency, which is religiously called Kedusha (holiness) do as they are directed, and live in peace with their mission.

Granted, sometimes they do fall subject to attack from those lower higher-dimensional entities who seek to thwart their efforts, but the Higher Powers-That-Be see all and know all. They intervene when the time is right, and continue to educate their school children, teaching them many lessons about the nature of Divine patience and tolerance. Even for the righteous and the holy, such lessons are difficult to comprehend.

And so, let me conclude as I began. Believing in fiction and fantasy is nonsense! To surrender to fear and superstition is nonsense, and worse, it can even be idolatrous. It is the way of Heaven to shine Light, and the servants of Heaven do just this. They do not hide the Light, nor conceal it from those who will benefit thereby. As for the detractors, distractions, and wayward students here in Schoolhouse Earth, part of our lessons is to learn how to properly deal with all of them, and learn we do!

Now, I have shared with you many things in this revelation. It is now up to you to put them into practice. Listen for the Echo. Once you hear it within you, you will know what to do. This is how you will progress in your lessons here in Schoolhouse Earth.

63. Mother Nature

March 21, 23 predawn

The universe speaks. It has its own Voice. It does not speak our languages, but being that we are part of the universe, there is a place deep within each of us that hears the Echo of the Voice and understands its language and message very clearly. As long as we exist within the universe, the Voice of the universe is a part of us; it is the foundation stone upon which the rest of all the others parts of us are built.

Understand and know that the universe operates in accordance to its own laws. Unlike human-made laws which are often ignored and violated without consequence, the laws of the universe are to be respected. Violation of the natural laws of the universe often lead to swift and extreme consequences, which can lead to instant termination of the violating entity.

We refer to universal law by a symbolic name. We call these laws Mother Nature. Just like a human mother nurtures her young, she will at the same time punish them, often severely, for not minding her word. Consider the universe, Mother Nature to not be any different.

Mother Nature is one symbolic term used to describe universal, natural law. Others refer to this as the hidden Hand of God. Others refer to this hidden Hand as a Divine Presence, which is Immanently Present within everything from the smallest sub-atomic structures to the grand structure of the entire universe itself.

This Presence is the Source of all natural, universal law. As such, this Presence can be understood to be the universal Law-Giver. And thus we have the universal concept of Creator, who we call God.

Thus any reference or use of the term God as applied to anything other than to the Original Creator and Source of universal, natural law is a mistaken application. As is known, certain religions make a big deal about this. But there is no need for religious involvement here. The universe and its universal, natural laws speak with its own Voice. It certainly does not require any human activity to support, or to validate it. Mother Nature is quite capable of disciplining any of her wayward children, be they human beings, or any other force (personal or otherwise) in the universe.

The Echo of the universal Voice is the Force that sustains all things that the original Voice itself has made to be. The original Voice "spoke" and all things came to be in accordance to "what was originally said." Since then the Echo of the original Voice permeates everything in the universe maintaining its forms, and existence.

The Echo of the Voice can be heard within everything, everywhere. Yet, while its nature can be observed through the scientific studies of natural law, actually hearing the Voice within each of its natural applications can only be heard from within that part of each of us set up and prepared to hear the Echo directly within human consciousness.

Those who are properly aligned within themselves with the universal, natural way will naturally sense the Echo within their relationships with everything natural. Those who are not properly aligned with universal, natural law will naturally lose contact with the Echo of the Voice. And when such contact is lost or broken, Mother Nature always intervenes to restore contact! And sometimes, Mother Nature's chosen forms of reconnection may be considered harsh and even cruel by human standards. Mind you, Mother Nature has her own standards, and cares nothing for what her human children think about her ways and nature.

For us human beings to avoid the harsh natural corrections of Mother Nature, we need to be properly aligned with her natural, universal laws. These laws are etched into everything throughout creation. One learns these laws by observing nature itself, but one must do this carefully and not haphazardly. The natural world outside of us has its own set of rules. The natural world inside of us, that defines for us our identities and our humanity, has its own set of rules that is different from the natural laws that govern the outside world.

We human beings must never confuse the differences between the natural laws external to ourselves, and those natural laws which are inside of us and that govern our humanity. For when we mistake the laws of one for the other, and attempt to apply human ways to the external world, or when we try to apply external ways to our internal worlds we create for ourselves imbalance. And we already know how Mother Nature responds to imbalances!

One who gazes within oneself, to understand one's internal natural way, as it properly aligns with the universal natural way, will by nature come into contact with the Echo of the Voice that speaks within, and which dictates, and maintains natural forms. And remember, the Echo of the Voice is Immanently Present. One can actually engage it in internal conversation and receive from it personal direction. Methods and techniques as to how this experiential relationship can be cultivated and supported is a topic that I have elaborated upon in many of my other books.

From the point of contact between psychic consciousness and waking consciousness the Voice cries forth and bewails the state of those human beings who cannot hear its Echo inside of them. Those who gaze within themselves to this point where waking consciousness melds with psychic consciousness will discover there the Echo of the Voice. The Echo will guide one to where one naturally needs to be. And the one who carefully listens to the Echo will be able to hear a remnant of the original Voice that spoke and brought forth the universe. And this is what we call communion with God.

May you learn to hear the Echo of the Voice within you, and come to recognize its universal, natural laws and truths that will guide you to proper universal alignment with Mother Nature. In this will your Mother Nature and your Heavenly Father be pleased.

64. Redemption

March 23, 23 (Rosh Hodesh Nisan) predawn

Redemption! The religious proclaim that this is what they are waiting for. But does anyone pause to consider, what exactly is this long awaited-for redemption?

The origins of this concept of redemption was in the political area. Peoples who were oppressed, repressed, or enslaved, looked for the day when they would be set free of their overlords and thus be free to live life in accordance to the manner of their choosing. This type of yearning for freedom is essentially psychological and thus it transcends any specific political application.

Redemption is a psychological state wherein which an individual is free to express oneself in that manner which the individual recognizes to be the most true expression of one's personal nature. Needless to say, the subjective expressions of individualized redemption are as numerous as are the people themselves.

For the most part, individualized psychological redemption is most often never overtly sought by the masses of people. Instead, the masses of people interpret redemption in the collective and apply its meaning and application en masse to the political arena. And thus we have freedom movements for whatever groups of people there might be.

One of the earliest archetypal freedom movements was the Biblical Children of Israel who sought freedom from their enslaving overlords, the Egyptians. Most are familiar with the famous Bible story how God sent Moses, who through the power of miraculous plagues that struck Egypt, broke Egyptian resolve and in turn they set free the Children of Israel. The commemoration of this event is still celebrated annually as the Jewish holiday of Passover. But the pursuit for freedom certainly did not end there.

The history books of the Bible enumerate the history of Israel and show how on numerous times in their history they fell subject to an invading force then then oppressed them and enslaved them. Israel would call out to God, who in turn would send a savior to again redeem the people. It is important for us to remember the historical context here. For each savior was a normal human being, and each redemption was political. The internalization of the redemption process to transform one's personality was not an Israelite, nor a Biblical concept.

It was not until centuries later with the rise of the Christian religion that the concept of redemption was internalized and removed (partially) out of the political arena. The entire concept of savior and redemption took on a cosmic interpretation in Christianity. This is very far removed from how the concept was originally understood (and still is understood) in Judaism.

To this day, the two religions see the concepts of both savior and redemption in radically different eyes. The question that we should be asking is, does this difference really matter? Is it really worth arguing over? Must it be the cause of so much dissonance, disturbance, hate and even violence? If we want to adapt the concept of redemption for modern times, then what we need is redemption (freedom) from all the religious interpretations of the concept.

The concept of redemption in the Christian model was projected on to the character of their Messiah who became their personal savior. This approach throughout most of Christianity was mostly political and social. The average Christian layman knew nothing about internalizing redemption personally so as to unleash the truths of one's inner (and higher) Self. Only in rare, mystical circles was the internalization process pursued. But this rarity was not (is not) limited to any one religion. All religions have their inner, mystical schools that seek to internalize redemption and to experience it personally at the psychological (and even psychic) levels.

At the mystical level, which is really the psychological level, individual practitioners of the various faiths often find a common ground that transcends the rigid boundaries of their respective religions. As such, individuals who are separated by external walls of cultural (and religious) divisions can transcend those walls, and find a way to get together in the common spirit of individuation.

We have seen this occur on numerous occasions throughout history, often much to the chagrin of the religious authorities who strongly oppose any expression of tolerance towards member of other faiths.

But we seek redemption, do we not? Redemption that is politically based and defined as one group achieving its freedom from another is a never-ending process. There will always be one group that arises which is weaker than another, and thus subject to sway, influence, and control from that other. As the group gains in strength, so does its resolve for independence and self-determination. Needless to say, this is how and why we always have one group (or nation) fighting another. Each seeks dominance so as to express itself fully as it sees fit. As wise King Solomon said, "there is nothing new under the sun."

But there is one thing that is clear about any and all kinds of political (social and economic) redemptions, and that is that as one group achieves its freedom, this often leads to another group losing theirs. Redemption for some often means oppression for others. It doesn't have to be this way. It shouldn't be this way; but unfortunately in this world, in this epoch in human history, things are this way!

So, when we look for redemption in modern times what are we looking for? When we cry out for a savior, what is it that we expect this savior to accomplish? Is the savior of one to become the next oppressor and dictator of another? How can this truly be called redemption for anyone?

I say that any true redemption must be of the psychological kind. True internal individualized redemption must transcend any and all interpretations of it that are placed upon the concept by religions or any other groups.

Redemption that does not set free the individual from repetitive state of continued bondage to one thing or another is no redemption at all! This is why redemption at the group level has failed over and over again.

Redemption is no redemption unless it is redemption for one and all, and all at the same time. Redemption that is not personally internalized and experienced as a personal transformation is no redemption at all!

And now we understand what redemption is supposed to be. Now we can look upon the prophetic declarations about a coming future redemption and understand that its message is not a political one, nor a religious one, but rather it is psychological one, and even a psychic one.

The promised future redemption is not just for this or that nation, nor for this or that religion. The promised coming redemption is for all humanity. All humanity is to be set free from the oppression, repression, and enslavement to ignorance, illusory divisions, and bondage to physical sensations.

The promised redemption to come is to set free all of humanity (and possibly many other races as well) from the shackles that separate and divide us causing us to identity as one group or another, which of course, is what motivates the rise and fall of all external redemption movements.

There is freedom for all, or there will end up being freedom for no one. Freedom begins internally, with the redemption of the mind from its enslavement to external controls. Freedom grows as the independent mind matures by struggling with itself and with the outside world, and eventually discovers its true parameters of individual identity.

All external forms of independent expression are realized to be only subjective in nature, and are not to be generalized. The enlightened mind realizes that one expression of freedom and how it developed in one culture and form is essentially equal to other expressions of freedom that developed in other cultures, and under different circumstances. In other words, the free and enlightened mind understands to look at the essence of a thing, and not just at its external form.

There is One Source for all. It is the One Source that is the Source for the Voice of Freedom that is heard deeply within the psyche of each individual. True redemption comes to one and to all, when the internal Voice of Freedom is heard and followed.

True freedom in the world begins with the true psychological and psychic redemption of the individuals in the world. This was the original message taught over and over again since ancient times.

The concept of redemption itself needs to be redeemed from its imprisonment within the competing different groups in our world.

When the individual is psychically redeemed and set free to experience the One Source directly and personally, this redemption can then become contagious, and as in the past, with Divine help, this Heavenly contagion can affect and infect us all, giving to one and all, true and eternal freedom, and liberty. This is the true global and cosmic redemption for which we all await! We should never take our eyes off of this goal.

65. Controlling Minds, 1

March 23, 23 pre-midnight

Those who can control the thoughts of others control their streams of consciousness, and thus control their perceptions of reality. And reality is only as real as its perceived experience. Therefore, those who control thought, be it their own, or the thoughts of others control their reality. This is a logical and verifiable truth. The question is how far can this go? How far can reality itself be influenced, if not outright changed, merely by the power of focused and directed thought?

The idea that the mind controls perception and that perception controls reality is all well and good. But again, while we can embrace profound statements that identify the truths that underlie our reality, we still do not experience this reality and this power of thought directly. Granted we have numerous techniques and mental tools that assist one in focusing one's attention on any given thing. We teach that along with this focus comes extra ability within the mind to project its influence. But ultimately who can show a direct causation between the focused mind of an individual and actual change in the real world? *To be continued...*

66. Controlling Minds, 2

March 24, 23 pre-dawn

While there are claims that the focused mind can change external reality, any proofs of such will always be subject to debate. What is beyond debate is that the focused mind does indeed change one's inner reality, especially one's inner perceptions of oneself, and of one's reality. And this reality is what is experienced as the world around us. So, mind control does dictate the shape of our world, but that shape is not molded from the outside in, but rather from the inside out.

Even one's perceptions of higher dimensional planes are subject to one's personal interpretations thereof. While each individual may be experiencing the same reality, no two may recognize that they are seeing the same thing, specifically because they each see the same thing in significantly different ways.

Just as this is true of one's experience of the higher dimensions, we see this same truth played out daily here on Earth. Everyday arguments ensue between people because of perceptions. One sees things one way, and another sees the same thing differently. If not for the sake of discussion, sharing and communication, there could never be any kind of greater awareness, agreement, and consensus. We are taught that our purpose in coming here to Schoolhouse Earth is specifically to learn these skills of communication and to bring together that which is wrongly far apart.

Our purpose here in Schoolhouse Earth is for us to learn the reality of unity. Some of the more powerful human beings here on Earth take advantage of our educational purpose, and for their own benefits seek to unite large groups of people. Their technique in doing so is like what I referenced above; these controllers seek to control the streams of consciousness of those whom they can control.

Some human beings manage to control large masses of others, but never is this for the benefit and good of those masses, but rather for their own personal, and most often selfish agendas. And yet, as we have seen throughout history, the Powers-That-Be allow this behavior to continue for a time, double-time, and half-time (whatever this Biblical term really means).

When one small group or individual controls a large group of people, we call this control slavery. As we know, slavery comes in many different forms, the most effective form being the control of the thoughts of others. Direct what people think, control their perceptions of reality, and they will believe whatever it is that you tell them.

The enslavement of their minds is complete because they do not recognize their own mental prison, and in their enslavement, they consider themselves to be free. Thus they neither yearn for, nor seek any other kind of freedom. Such souls can thus remain in a prison of the mind from one lifetime to the next, totally unaware, and in denial, of their true imprisoned condition. The vast majority of souls here in Schoolhouse Earth are in this position. Indeed, the purpose of School is to free the entrapped minds. As we see such emancipation and freedom is an on-going long-term project.

The path to the freedom of the soul has been taught in many different spiritual schools throughout history. There are many different classrooms here on Schoolhouse Earth. We can rest assured that our teachers in the higher dimensions know very well how to perform their missions.

It may seem strange to us, but it is they, our higher dimensional teachers, who allow, and even often set-up, stronger human beings to dominate and control the minds and perceptions of others. They allow these states of human affairs to manifest so as to teach enslaved minds messages about freedom and redemption. Granted these lessons may take many lifetimes to learn, but nevertheless, the lessons are learned, souls do awaken and yearn for freedom.

When the yearnings for freedom begin to take hold amongst the masses sometimes, as a consequence, the lessons taught in spiritual schools spill out into the general population. And when this occurs, the mind and perception of the collective changes. Then we can have social and political revolutions. This happens more often than most realize. And this seems to be one of the teaching methods used by our higher dimensional teachers here in Schoolhouse Earth.

Spiritual schools around the world throughout history have always taught their lessons using similar methods. The specific method used is always the turning inwards of thought and consciousness, and away from the external influences that seek to control and dominate one's perception of reality. Step one in growth is to recognize that there is growth to be achieved. Step two is to look out around one and to recognize the external influences, and to then make every effort to eradicate them from one's mind and consciousness. These two steps lead to the dawn of freedom consciousness.

One who controls the mind controls reality. Thus there is war! Does an external force control your mind, or do you? Unless you gaze within and explore your own mind, you will never know the truth.

Know then that you have much to learn. Seek out your truth within you; recognize the difference between your own Voice and that of others who seek to control you. Once you develop the spirit of freedom, redemption is not far off. And this is how one learns one's lessons here in Schoolhouse Earth.

67. A Comprehensive Review of the Parameters of Alternate Realities & its Relationship with Psychic Health & Mental Illness, 1

March 26, 23 predawn

How foolish and delusional all of us are. We experience what we experience and thus conclude that such is reality. We are each learned enough to recognize that each individual has one's own personal interpretation and perspective of things. We conclude that there are many different perceptions of reality, but still that there is only one reality. This is a very narrow-minded and limited understanding of the way of things.

But let us declare the obvious. If one is limited and locked up inside a specific reality, a reality that defines for one everything that there is, how then can one come to experience something that is beyond the boundaries of experience? Logic will dictate to us the answer, and say, being that one cannot have an experience of another reality, there is no way for one to confirm or deny its existence.

Any discussion of alternate realities is thus nothing more than speculation. One can imagine that there are such alternate realities, and create in one's mind whatever it is that one may wish. Or one may just as easily choose to not imagine any such things and remain focused on what such a one believes to be the here and now of this reality.

Let us imagine for a moment what another reality may actually be like. How similar or how different is it from what one sees and knows right here and right now? The answer to this question will vary from individual to individual. The parameters of difference or similarity will all be defined by the grandiosity or the limitations of one's imagination.

Imagination here is the key. Imagination is a thought process not limited to the shackles of perceived reality. Imagination often takes on a life of its own, and has on many occasions created very elaborate alternate realities, the likes of which often become as real to one as this reality itself.

Mind you, I am not at all describing here any type of mystical experience, but rather I am describing the creative process of many writers of fiction and novelists. Western secular society is inundated with cultural expressions that are built upon fictional characters and their universes. Characters that have been created for Star Wars, Star Trek, Harry Potter, and other fictional worlds are well known and recognized throughout most of the world today.

Today we commonly find almost everyone who, in one way or another, is attached to the social media world, and thus attached to one or more of these fictional realities in a very deep emotional way. How much time, effort and emotional energy does one invest in connection to and relationships with fictional characters from this or that fictional universe? Today it is common to see individuals emotionally attached to, and concerned with, the wellbeing of the fictional characters that they know and love. But has one forgotten the reality that such fictional characters do not exist, and that indeed their entire universes are nothing more than the creation of some author, and brought to life in the production companies that make television programs and movies. In clear terms: none of it is real!

All characters portrayed and seen in novels, television programs, movies and online videos are fictional, are they not? And if they really do not exist outside of the imaginations of those who contemplate them, are they indeed worthy of interest, and all the more so an investment of emotional energy? After all, why should one care about what happens to this or that fictional character? After all, nothing is actually happening to such a character, because such a character doesn't really exist!

And being that such is the case, if one chooses within one's imagination to fantasize about a character having a fate different from that portrayed in a book or film, who is to say that what one imagines is any more or less real than the imagination of the writer of the book, or the producer of the film?

If one does not like the way that a character is portrayed in one form of fiction, one can easily imagine for one's character another fate. What difference does it make if one's imagined storyline for the character is not the same as the one portrayed in the media. After all, fiction is fiction. None of it is reality, and none of it will ever become reality, other than in the subjective imaginative mind of the individual.

But with this statement I have revealed a great secret about the power of mind and thought. It is very possible, and indeed it is often done that one creates an alternate reality all of one's own, within the recesses of one's imaginative thoughts. For most people this ability is good and healthy, and it can enable one to daydream and to become inspired about making this reality, the one in which we live, to be a better one.

For some, however, the alternate realities which are created within themselves can become a dark and fearful place from which one may very well have a hard time escaping. If such an individual is overcome by the dark and fearful imagined world within, and the perceptions of one's inner reality overtakes one's perception of outer reality, then the individual may become trapped in a hell of one's own making. Again, we see this all too often in today's society. We call this state mental illness, and psychosis.

One who suffers from a form of delusional mental illness often cannot be convinced that the reality which such an individual experiences is not real. As such, the afflicted individual interacts with the rest of the world from within one's internal mental prison, acting in ways that the rest of the world does not understand, and cannot experience.

For the afflicted individual, one's reality is the only reality, whereas for everyone else, the reality of the afflicted individual is not real at all! So, let us ask the obvious question. Is the reality experienced by the one whom we define as being delusional and psychotic any less (or more) real than the reality experienced by another? The health care professional treating such an individual will certainly say that the psychotic patient is crazy, and that such a one's reality is not real. Of course, the patient will strongly disagree.

Such is the power of imagination. It seems to have the power to create not only fantasy, but also alternate realities as well. The problem of course is that while the mind of the individual exists in an alternate reality within its psyche, the physical body still resides in this reality, and remains subject to the parameters of reality as defined here. It is the lack of proper interaction with this reality, as defined by the standards established in this reality, that define the parameters of mental health and psychosis in the first place.

After all, numerous individuals create alternate realities for artistic expression (books, television, movies), without confusing their created realities with the one in which we all live. So, there are realities and then there are realities. Some are more real than others. As for which reality is real seems to be a matter of perception.

Maybe the boundaries of experiential reality are grander than one thinks, or that one wishes to speculate. Is it possible that not every crazy person is really crazy? Is it possible that maybe some individuals labeled as psychotic may indeed be in touch with something outside of the boundaries of what the majority considers to be real? To the surprise of many, it has already been ascertained by some mental health practitioners that there is far more to the psychotic mind than simple out-of-control imagination.

To be continued...

68. Psychic Health & Mental Illness, 2

March 27, 23 predawn

Does every thought that one thinks emanate from one's mind? This most likely is true. But even though we say that thought emanates from the mind, we are left with the question, how did the thought get into the mind in the first place? Here is where we transcend the narrow limitations of those who refuse to see beyond this single reality.

It has been shown with numerous examples of psychiatric cases that many times thoughts come into an individual's mind from a source that is not from the external world (or environment). It has been shown that some thoughts come into the mind, not from the outside material world, but from another source, which is both internal and external at the same time.

In order for this to be understood, it is necessary for us to recognize that the individual human mind is not an isolated thing. The individual human mind, at its unconscious source, is not a disconnected isolated entity unto itself. Rather each individual mind is, in a way, plugged in to a greater collective mind, which today is called the collective unconscious. Essentially, all of us share in what we may call a hive-mind, a collective of souls that is actually a singular super-soul of which each of us is only an individual part. For the masses this is not an experienced reality, whereas for mystics from all schools and walks of life, this experience has been universal.

The individual mind is thus two-fold. It contains its unique individual self that is molded by one's environment and external world. But all of this that we recognize as the identity of the individual is not built upon a blank slate. With birth, each child is born with a fully preexistent personality. This is the innate internal true identity of each individual.

As each individual grows up and matures, one's personality is influenced by the external world, but it is not totally created by it. What one is, and always is, remains with one throughout one's life. Indeed, one's purpose and mission in life here in Schoolhouse Earth is to enable one's innate personality, one's true inner self to manifest free and clear of any intervening contrary influences from the outside world. In psychology this process is called individuation, which is the process of one becoming an individual.

It has also been discovered that this process of individuation is guided by a higher hand. Thus, the events that happen to one during one's life are not considered to be happenstance. One's life is guided by an internal (higher) guiding force with the intent to bring about within one the revelation of one's true identity. In psychology this guiding hand and its relationship in assisting one's psychic (psychological) development, is referred as there being a teleological direction to psychological individuation.

The forces that work upon the human mind are again two-fold. First, there are the well-known and understood external forces. We see their influences and understand them relatively well. These influences help develop the external structure through which the internal innate personality manifests itself. This external structure of identity which develops due to one's environment in the Torah/Kabbalah tradition is called one's Nefesh level of soul.

The second force that works upon the mind arises from the internal forces of one's innate unconscious higher self (true identity) which itself is always tapped into the collective unconscious and receives influences and input from there on a regular basis. This internal structure is not so well-known, and is most certainly not understood, at all! This greater part of our minds is far too expansive to be concentrated into the limitations of the conscious mind. That is why the mind becomes split, with the higher truer part of our selves being relegated to that which we call, the unconscious. This interior domain of true identity which one is born with, and which directs one's life to manifest and emanate is called in the Torah/Kabbalah tradition one's Neshama level of soul.

So, in religion, we refer to the Nefesh and Neshama levels of souls, whereas in psychology we refer to the conscious and unconscious parts of the mind. The two models (religion and psychology) are referring to the same realities, with the only difference being the names that are unique to each system. With this duality of mind understood, we can now better understand the topics of psychosis and the perceptions of alternate realities.

As one psychologically develops and matures in this physical world many external influences bombard one with messages, ideas and beliefs that may fundamentally challenge or condemn elements of one's innate (and true) personality. When this occurs, most individuals do not stand up and fight the external influences. Such a concept of rejecting external influences is only an awareness that manifests well along the process of maturation. It is rarely (if ever) there in youth. So as the process of individuation naturally proceeds, it is often met with external influences which contradict its teleological (higher hand) direction. When this occurs, the conscious mind often rejects the internal influence, and represses it outside of consciousness.

Also, as one matures, one is often faced with choices and circumstances in life that are very uncomfortable and unpleasant. The memories of these experiences are repressed out of consciousness. Together the combination of all these repressed feelings and memories combine in a place where all other memory is stored. This collective domain within the mind is called one's personal subconscious.

The personal subconscious resides within one just below consciousness, and just above one's unconscious. It is an in-the-middle layer. In the Torah/Kabbalah tradition, the personal subconscious is called the Klipot, which are the husks or shells that cover over one's inner true self (one's Neshama soul), blocking and perverting its manifestation and influence upon the conscious Nefesh level of soul.

When the subconscious becomes filled with rejected feelings, and blockages from the higher self, this part of the mind becomes the source of negative imagination. In other words, this is the place where nightmares come from. The subconscious stores within it every image and every memory of everything that the conscious mind has ever been exposed to. And thus when one's conscious mind (Nefesh) is not in proper alignment with one's own inner (higher) self (Neshama), deep down within one feels this detachment.

Combine this with how one may be forced to feel or act in contradiction to how one feels and believes to be correct, and the multiple forces within the subconscious can concoct a unique cocktail of emotional upheavals expressed through very unsettling imaginative elements. These subconscious storms erupt into the conscious mind and overwhelm it. When the subconscious content vomits up into the conscious mind, thus preventing the conscious mind from interacting with the external world in its expected way, this is the state that we call mental illness, with one of the worse forms being psychosis.

Let us understand more about the so-called illusionary experiences within psychosis. Again, for the one experiencing such an altered state of reality, their experience of reality is as real to them as our experience of reality is to us. But there is a big difference between the two. The psychotic state is a state of illness. While what they perceive does have a reality of its own, it is still nevertheless a skewered reality of something trying to express itself from within one's personal subconscious.

To be continued...

69. Psychic Health & Mental Illness, 3

March 28, 23 predawn

The makeup of psychotic hallucinations are a unique cocktail of the images stored in one's personal imagination. The teleological influence from within the unconscious acts within the subconscious to create imagery and experience for the conscious mind to perceive and to understand. This is the process of how dreams operate. However, within the context of psychoses, the dream-making function that arises from within the unconscious gets tossed around in the subconscious thus creating imagery and impressions that represent fear, and other negative emotions. Both dreams and psychotic delusions emanate from one's unconscious, the difference between the two is the difference between mental health and mental illness.

Being that modern minds are inundated with imagery from all genre of fiction, those images that can evoke emotions are usually the ones chosen by one's unconscious to represent the psychic/psychological message that it is endeavoring to send to the conscious mind. This is why both dream language and psychotic hallucinations are always very pictorial and rich with intricate imagery.

The unconscious mind does not speak with words, it has no mouth. The way the unconscious communicates is by creating emotional impressions that can be sensed and deeply felt. These impressions are regularly expressed through the multiple forms of imagery that are available in the recesses of one's memory. Thus dreams and psychotic hallucinations speak a language of symbolism that communicate the impressions arising from the unconscious, be it one's personal unconscious, or from the collective unconscious itself.

One can now understand the operational functioning of the human mind, and how there is a single method of communication between the unconscious and conscious. This single operational method gives rise to the wonder and profundity of dreams (be they night dreams or day dreams), and it also gives rise to nightmares, fear, panic, anxiety, and outright hallucinations (within all the senses). The healthy mind receives the dreams. The mentally ill mind receives the nightmares. The method of communication is the same for both. This is why it is imperative for one to not condemn the operations of consciousness simply because there exists the possibility for consciousness to become ill, in the same way as the physical body can become ill.

Communication between one's unconscious mind and one's conscious mind is imperative for life. One cannot learn any real and important life lessons if one's teleological approach to psychological individuation is ignored, rejected, or worse, interpreted to be something negative and harmful.

Modern psychoanalysis follows in the footsteps of the ancient meditative schools that work with individuals to explore one's individual subconscious with the intent of working through all of one's twisted and harmful influences that reside therein. The process of cleansing one's subconscious, to remove all of one's personal Klipot is the joint focus of both psychoanalysis and meditative training. Indeed, both models, the modern and the ancient, serve the same function for healing the human soul.

In light of this insight that the modern model of psychology and the ancient model of meditative training are working towards the same goals, we can see why and how the merging of the two for the sake of psychic healing is a benefit for all.

One's mind becomes filled with the images that one is exposed to throughout one's life. If one is at peace with one's own inner self, then one's subconscious will work with one's unconscious to create and to bring into consciousness images and impressions that are positive, healing, and creative. Whereas if one has not yet resolved one's issues with one's own subconscious, then the images experienced arising from the subconscious will be clouded, confusing, and often frightening. While one may not suffer from complete mental illness and psychosis, one may still indeed suffer from some milder forms of mental or emotional imbalance that requires the services of the psychologist, or a spiritual-health provider.

One of the many forms of emotional imbalance that inflicts so many today is the misguided association of thoughts and attachment of emotions with fictional characters and their relative universes. So many invest so much psychic energy and emotional passion into things which have no reality, and absolutely no importance whatsoever. Social media sucks in people's attention and attaches them to the false and unreal. This disassociation from reality leads to individuals caring more for fictional characters, and less for real other people in the lives. Mind you, this is nothing new in human society. Religions based upon myths, legends and idols have been doing the same thing throughout history.

The reason why the fictitious can become a source of psychological illness is due to the fact that sometimes the human imagination when coupled with human emotions tends to blur the line between what is externally real, and what is internally real. No one can deny that fictional characters do not exist in the external world, whereas due to human imagination and emotion, they most certainly do exist in one's internal world. A problem occurs when the demarcation between these two worlds becomes blurred, and one loses the ability to tell the difference between internal reality and external realty. A level of this lack of psychic clarity may occur within many people, but those who only daydream are usually not affected by an uncontrollable and overwhelming influx of subconscious impressions into one's conscious mind. It is one thing to fantasize about something in fiction, it is quite another thing to somehow believe that one's fantasies are externally materialized.

While most people today do not secretly embrace the belief that their favorite fictional character from television or a movie is actually real in real life, still, there seems to be widespread beliefs in other things that are just as fictional. However, when an individual believes in a fictional reality, one's imagination, coupled with one's emotions, creates such an internal reality, which one comes to believe and embrace as being as real as anything else in the external world. This psychological mechanism is how people believe in their religious icons, and how others embrace all kinds of wildly imaginative beliefs.

Mental illness arises when the imaginary in the subconscious becomes so real that it overwhelms one's conscious mind filling it with confusion. The internal reality is very real, but only internally. Thus psychology and meditative training both place focus about discovering what lurks in the inner recesses of the individual subconscious, with the intent of bringing mental wellness to mental illness.

So, in a way, the delusions of the psychotic mind are real, in their own internal context and subjective meaning. One's own unconscious messages can get twisted within the strata of subconscious content, and turn good into evil, and evil into good.

One who is subject to trauma and who cannot physically escape it will often disengage from their conscious mind, and the trauma of the moment, and seek refuge within an imagined altered state of consciousness within oneself. Needless to say, when this occurs, it often happens that the trauma causes such a schism in the mind that normal consciousness can become split, with the memory and trauma of the terrible experience being repressed, adding layers of negative content to the subconscious.

Being that the modern mind has become inundated with all kinds of fictional beliefs, alongside fictional characters, it is no wonder that when one delves through one's personal subconscious that these fictional characters are seen, and experienced to be real. If taken literally this can tend to reinforce one's sense of delusion.

When, however, fictional characters do pop up in thought, be it normal daydreaming imagination, or in the upheavals of hallucination within mental illness, it is the unconscious that is using these images, because of the emotional association with them, to relate its message. This is why the images experienced in dreams (daydreams or night dreams), and well as those experienced in psychotic hallucinations should never be dismissed as unimportant or irrelevant. These images serve as archetypes emanating from the unconscious. They are messengers. Due to the emotional component attached to them, they seem very real. But what *is* real is their message, and not their person. The mentally healthy mind understands this. The mentally ill mind does not.

Within meditative traditions when one meditates it is not at all uncommon that whatever forces that one may contact in the trance state may materialize in one's mind in the image of one of the set beliefs that one has had exposure to at one point in time. If one's mind is frightened or panicked one may experience visions of demons, ghosts, vampires, and other monsters. This type of imagery can affect the psychotic mind, and it can just as easily affect the normal one that allows such images and beliefs access to one's thoughts and emotions.

To sum up matters, the human mind is a very complex organism. The mind is clearly not limited to the organic human brain, nor is the information stored in the mind exclusively from external sources. Consciousness is clearly not limited to the Nefesh level of soul.

The Neshama level of soul only influences the Nefesh from a psychic distance. The wholeness of the Neshama itself never becomes completely accessible and revealed. Due to the imaginative faculty within the mind, whatever imagery one is ever exposed to is stored in memory, and is activated when the unconscious (or subconscious) calls it up. And memory is not an exact procedure. The imagination can take stored memories and due to the influence of the subconscious twist and turn a memory into something that is clearly unreal.

One who seeks psychic clarity and a true and real experience of higher realities must know and understand the way in which such realities manifest in the mind. One must recognize the subjective nature of the images that package one's experience.

The process of mind that leads one to experience higher states of consciousness is a singular one. One who is in a state of mental health can indeed have a profound and helpful psychic experience. The opposite is also true. One who is in a state of mental illness, can have an equally profound, but negative, and harmful psychic experience.

Prophetic states and psychotic states are very closely related, and at the same time, they are the opposites of one another. The difference between them is the difference between mental health and mental illness. It is vital and important that one does not confuse the two states, thinking one to be the other. For this is how psychic experience becomes condemned, and psychotic behavior becomes praised. In an upside-down society, like ours today, this state of chaos is all too often the norm.

Mental health is the state of redemption from mental illness. This is why the archetype of redemption and freedom is so much a part of the human psyche. The freedom sought by the individual is first a psychic/psychological one. This is where one must focus one's pursuit of freedom and emancipation. Without this vital internal step, all such external steps will be doomed to failure. Redemption begins within oneself.

70. The Way of Reincarnation & Individuation, 1

April 2, 23 predawn

There are many paths, but there is only one way.

But the one way is not for all, it may not even be for two. The one way is the one way for the individual. And each individual is different.

Nature and the universe itself is built upon its laws. Natural law is both flexible and rigid at the same time. One who understands natural law will be able to bend it and work with it. For the one who understands it, natural law is flexible.

One, however, who does not understand natural law approaches it in a spirit of rebellion. Instead of working with the law, to understand its natural parameters, one seeks to break the law in any way possible. One who defies the law and seeks to break it will find natural law very rigid indeed, and most unforgivable.

The laws of nature came first, even before nature itself. We are part of this universe, thus we are part of nature. We are all thus under its authority and limited by its parameters. When we seek to understand the law and respect it, then we can discover ways and means to work with it for our betterment. Natural law will then serve us, as we serve it.

There is only one way. There is only one way for the individual to fit into natural law. The one who knows one's own way will understand how to best navigate life through the parameters of its laws.

There are many ways. There are as many ways as there are individuals to walk the many paths. But the common denominator of all proper paths is that they all conform to natural law, and all of them walk within its parameters.

There are many paths, and not all of them conform to natural law. There does exist the unnatural.

As nature itself is subject to the laws that preexisted it, so too is anything unnatural. That which is unnatural will clash with natural law; it will defy it, and proclaim its independence from it. The unnatural operates in the opposite way of the natural. As such it cannot for long maintain any semblance of strength, balance, or longevity. The unnatural, by definition, will be self-destructive, although it may not recognize this within itself.

The laws of the universe flow and operate in accordance to their preexistent pattern. Within such parameters, there may very well arise the unnatural. Its presence is tolerated for a time. Its existence is not without purpose. For whatever reasons known within the preexisting laws of nature, the unnatural comes into being, serves its purpose, and eventually faces its inevitable fate of annihilation. In a universe of natural law, this is the law for the unnatural.

Another natural law governs the way of life. Life and death is simply a process of ever-changing forms. In this universe, in accordance to its laws, life itself takes on many different forms. Life grows, and learns from one form to the next. Each form is called a lifetime. Each form is thus the body of life, for the moment.

We must understand a reality which we already know, but all too often fail to recognize its significance, and that is that life itself is alive. Life is sentient, conscious, and with purpose. Each expression of life we call a soul. When life takes on a form, we call this form its identity. But as forms change, so do identities. But life itself, like the laws of nature themselves preexisted this universe. Indeed, the universe came into being just so that life could take on its many forms, and to learn the many lessons that being in many forms offers to teach.

The soul, which is life itself in one of its many expressions, comes into this universe, subject to its laws and parameters, specifically to learn how to best manifest itself and bring itself to full self-awareness. Life thus pursues multiple natural forms within the seamless infinite numbers of forms. Life begins its expression in the small and simple, and expands from form to form until it reaches the big and complex. All these lessons identify for the soul how best one can use natural law for one's advantage and self-expression.

One also learns along the way the true nature of the unnatural. One learns the ways and parameters of the unnatural even as one learns the ways and parameters of the natural. One learns, often from experience, not to mix the two. One learns that the unnatural flows opposite to life itself, and thus it defies the universe for as long as it lives. And in its time, the universe itself brings an end to an unnatural force.

Life and death of forms is a natural part of the life cycle itself. This is called good. The unnatural, because of its inherent need to self-destruct only embraces the death of forms, and not its continual renewal. This force of the unnatural is called evil.

Good and evil are ingrained within the laws of the universe. Some call the execution of this law karma.

To be continued...

71. Reincarnation & Individuation, 2

April 3, 23 dawn.

Life on Earth is indeed evolutionary. But the evolution of which I speak is the evolution of consciousness. Long ago when souls first entered Schoolhouse Earth their mission was to learn and understand the parameters of this material universe.

Long ago souls only knew what they knew. They were what they were, with no growth and no change. It was a very stagnant system. Then when other dimensions came into being, offering within them many new experiences about new expressions through which life can manifest, many souls (but not all of them) were attracted to the newness, and craved to experience it. And so, to Schoolhouse Earth (amongst many other places) they came.

Life is directed towards its manifestation. Whatever be the circumstances, life will find a way to thrive in that time and place. We look out at our universe from the limited and narrow perspective of life on Earth as we see it, and we contemplate whether or not life can exist on other planets, in environments that we human beings consider to be hostile to our present form of life. Human beings speak about life as we know it. But anything, as we know it, is so very limited, and narrow. There is so much to life, about life, and about other types of life that we human beings cannot even imagine all the while that we are limited here to our Schoolhouse, learning our lessons about the here and now.

Life exists everywhere and in everything. We may not see it; we may not recognize it, but it is there nevertheless. Even here in Schoolhouse Earth our narrow and limited perspective prevents us from actual experience and interactions with the many other forms of life here.

We all know that animals are alive, but most humans consider them to be dumb beasts unworthy of consideration. But animals also have thoughts and feelings. No, they do not think and feel like we do, but they think and feel nevertheless.

Even plants can think and feel in their own way. Plants can even talk with one another, and with us, but how many human beings are aware of this? How many human beings can communicate with animals and plants? Granted, we can talk with them; many do so all the time. But how many human beings can hear and understand the voice of the animal or of the plant? When they talk back to us, we do not know how to hear. Animals and plants talk with us all the time, but due to our narrow and limited understanding of what is intelligent life, we do not consider the animals and plants intelligent enough to communicate with us, and therefore we do not here them when they do communicate with us. So, who is the dumb one, us or them?

Even that which we consider to be inanimate, or in other words, void of life, is always possessing life. Fire, air, water, and earth are the traditional expressions of the matter-forms of energy, gaseous, liquid, and solid states. Each of these is not a life-form unto itself, but within each form life can manifest in its own unique way. This is how the planet Earth itself is considered to be a living, sentient lifeform all its own.

Yes, the Earth itself is alive. The Earth itself has its own soul, its own identity, and its own will and purpose of being. Our planet Earth is not just an insignificant rock, it is a living, breathing, thinking, and feeling organism, just like we are.

Earth Herself is alive, and it is She who hosts Schoolhouse Earth upon and within Herself. For many this may be a very difficult concept to grasp. But ancient scientists, philosophers, and mystics all knew this to be true. Many knew this truth, not through speculation, but with actual experience and interaction with the soul (spirit) of the Earth.

Not for naught do we call our planet Mother Earth. Not for naught is Mother Earth referred to in the Torah/Kabbalah as Malkhut, the Kingdom of God. God in Heaven is our Heavenly Father. Earth is our Earthly Mother. Together, they give rise to human beings. Mother Earth provides the ingredient for our bodies, and Heavenly Father allocates the souls to inhabit them. And this is the foundation of operations here in Schoolhouse Earth.

Over all these multifaceted operations the laws of nature rule, dominate, and direct. It is natural law that dictates and directs each soul as it chooses a body-form through which to materialize here in Schoolhouse Earth.

Each soul is born on Earth in the form that it needs for the moment, through which it will learn its present lessons. Thus not all souls are born human. Indeed, not all human souls return into human bodies.

Due to their individual level of learning and receptivity, human souls previously born into human bodies, may indeed reincarnate into non-human forms. Human beings can be reborn into animals, plants, and trees, and they can even be placed within inanimate objects such as rocks. Wherever a soul needs to be in order to learn its lessons, that is where natural law will direct it, and enforce its being there. This is how natural law works through the directives executed by our Heavenly Father, and our Earthly Mother. The secrets of this operation is one of the most profound area of contemplation in the mystical schools of the Kabbalah.

All souls incarnate to learn their lessons. Each soul needs to experience, and to personally understand the Way of nature, and the parameters of natural law. In other words, each soul needs to know and embrace that which is natural, and to equally know and to shun that which is unnatural. Each soul is here to learn how to experience, and thus how to know and discern the difference between that which we call good and evil. This lesson is a universal one which has its many applications of expression, with each being unique for the lifeform to which it pertains.

The universe and natural law does not make mistakes. It is very true, and presently realized by more and more human beings, that not all human souls are incarnate into the forms that they identify with as essential to their identity of being.

Schoolhouse Earth is here to teach a soul many different lessons. These lessons teach us how to discern and know the differences between natural and unnatural, and between good and evil. It is for us to learn these things, and to understand them. Therefore, human souls are incarnated in various forms, and in various ways, so as to best bring about the wisdom inherent in these lessons.

We must know and understand that there never is that which we can call a karmic accident. Everything happens for a purpose. Every incarnation has its purpose. It is up to the individual to discover for oneself what one's personal mission and goal is for one's present incarnation and life.

If one finds oneself in an incongruent position in one lifetime, one must seek out why this is so, and what one is supposed to do with this insight. Learning to experience the boundaries between the natural and unnatural come into play here, for how can one learn right from wrong, unless one experiences them personally.

Schoolhouse Earth has within it many different grades, just as do the schools that we humans send our children to. Each of us is in one grade or another. Each of us is in our present grade to learn our lessons therein. Only once the present lessons are learned can one be promoted to the next grade. Failure to accomplish this requires that the soul be left back in the present grade.

It is also possible for a soul to degenerate and to fall backwards in grades. This is when human souls reincarnate in non-human forms. Each of these incarnations is to teach the human soul its lessons, the very same lessons it did not grasp while being incarnate as a human being in the previous lifetime.

To be continued...

72. Reincarnation & Individuation, 3

April 4, 23 dawn.

Why am I here? What is my purpose in life? What am I supposed to be doing; what is it that I am supposed to accomplish? We ask these questions because something deep inside us tells us to. Our own inner (higher) identity that seeks expression acts as the teleological force to bring about our individual individuation. Yet this road is a unique path, with each path being special for the individual who walks it. No two people walk the exact same path. No two people end up in the exact same place. Just as in the physical world one cannot have two people standing in the exact same place, so too is this in the psychic realms.

Each soul can be compared to a part of the body. Some souls are arms, some are legs, some belong to the heart, while others belong to the head. Some souls make up the ears, others make up the eyes, and so on. This metaphor rightly describes how all souls are uniquely different from one another, and yet are still one in that they are all united in the greater, singular supernal body of our collective source. In mystical philosophy (and not just in the Kabbalah), this collective of souls is called Supernal Man.

Supernal Man is a living conscious entity. Each one of us is a part of this greater whole. Each individual part (soul) is therefore directed to learn about and to experience the consciousness that is the reality of the whole. Essentially, Supernal Man desires and thus accomplishes that each and every part of Itself become aware,

357

sentient, and conscious unto itself. In this way, Supernal Man knows each and every part of Itself. It becomes a fully aware entity.

To accomplish this, each part of Supernal Man takes on an identity of its own. Each part (soul) is guided by its own teleological force to explore, to discover, and then to become that which it truly is in the greater scheme of things. Any and all pursuits of identity here in Schoolhouse Earth are only a reflection of one's true identity. No identity accomplished here in Schoolhouse Earth that is associated to one's present lifeform is permanent. As such, all temporary identities are only echoes of the greater whole.

All temporary identities serve to provide one with one's lessons for the here and now. And as one graduates from one grade to the next, one places aside one's previous identity and works to explore, discover, and become the next (temporary) one. This is why previous incarnations are usually wiped from memory. One does not need to focus on the past. One instead needs to focus on the here and now.

There are no karmic accidents. You are here, where you are at. You are meant to be here. You are here to learn your lessons. Anything that distracts you from your learning is therefore harmful to you, and thus bad for you. And our world is full of distractions that serve to harm us in bad ways.

But all this is controlled by the Higher Hand. We are put into turmoil of chaos specifically so that we can learn how to discover and recognize both peace and stability. This is our present lesson plan in our present grade here in Schoolhouse Earth. Each of us has our mission. Each of us has our goal.

My mission and goal is different from yours. Yet, we each go about finding our own in the same way, by seeking out our inner teleological guiding force, and following its lead. As I said, when I began, there are many paths, but there is only one way. One way for the unique individual that you are. So, find your way, and you will find your peace. This is how one learns one's lessons here in Schoolhouse Earth.

73. A Message About the Fall of Modern Egypt/Babylon

April 9, 23

A terrible war has been fought. The opposing forces fought for far more than mere life and death. The final battles continue to this day.

The war today is fought in many ways, with most of these ways being concealed from the minds and the attention of the general public. Nevertheless, it is the general public that has already succumbed to an ancient enemy, and is now being devoured by it.

For the most part, the general public does not even see its own downfall and demise. How sad it is to watch the conquered suffer and die, with them not even being aware of what is happening to them.

The great rule of conquest is this: Control the minds of people, and they will willingly and even desirously surrender to your will, and submit to your authority.

It is easier to conquer the mind through manipulation than to conquer bodies by force of arms.

Lie to the people! Manipulate them! Subtly and slowly twist and turn their thinking process. Transform them little by little. Instead of there being a battle between "us" and "them" redefine ideas, words, and concepts. Turn "them" into "us." And thus, turn evil into good, and turn freedom into slavery. This is how war is fought today. It is fought in the battleground of public opinion manipulation. And the public has already lost!

What we once thought as being right is now vehemently condemned as being wrong. One who was clearly our enemy is now viewed as being not only our friend, but also our savior! The enemy has infiltrated our minds, and has successfully turned "us" into "them."

They have already won the war because that which made "us" to be "us" no longer exists! That which made us to be special, right, proper, and good and has rooted out of us, and ruthlessly destroyed out of our minds and hearts. What remains is a mess; a cesspool of selfishness that seeks only hedonistic pleasures.

The mighty have fallen, and in their place the ancient enemy has ascended. And yet the face of the ancient enemy remains concealed and hidden.

Even when the ancient enemy moves to destroy all that is left of freedom, the clueless public will willfully play along, and like mindless sheep follow their new shepherd. But this new shepherd will not guide his flocks to greener pastures. No! This new shepherd is driving his flocks to the slaughterhouse.

The new shepherd is a carnivore who craves the flesh of his fresh meat. He will devour the general public until next to none remain. And the mindless pool of selfish hedonists care nothing for what happens to the "other guy" as they watch the "other guy" be devoured. Little do they know that their carnivore shepherd will soon come for them, and there will be no "other guy" to raise the alarm, to protest, or even to care. Such is the victory of the ancient enemy as he devours his sheep!

Since ancient times the wise and the prophets spoke, warning the public about the consequences of putting their faith into false gods. And today, there has arisen a widespread global religion that has been fanatically embraced by the general public of sheep. They worship a false god of our own making. The god of the world today is money!

Money and wealth is the false god today worshipped by the general public. One who has money and wealth is looked at as being successful, and desirable. The wealthy have become the new priesthood who show off their wealth encouraging all others to abandon every sense of morals and decency in order to accomplish wealth for themselves. Wealth is the only definition of good. Less wealth is evil. Poverty is the new leprosy.

Yet the minds and hearts of the wealthy are full of darkness, and are bankrupt of all morals, decency, and dignity. And it is these three things that have been rooted out from the general public. It is these three things, morality, decency, and dignity that were once rightful beacons of light, that have now become badges of shame and dishonor. Evil has become good. Wrong has become right. And the rewards of evil are more and more hedonistic pleasures.

The wise have been defeated; their wisdom is silenced. Those who have always had little have what little they have taken away from them, forcing them to become dependent and enslaved to those who have robbed them of everything. Without wisdom and the wise, foolishness and fools abound. It is they who corral the sheep for the carnivore shepherd and his final solution.

And the general public sees not, nor knows not about what is happening, and denies intensely all the signs about what is coming. They are too busy worshipping their false gods of money, and hedonism.

The general public is living a life of lies. They are living in a false reality of their own making. And they have been controlled and manipulated into not caring at all about it. This was the plan of the carnivore shepherd and it has worked out for him very well. And now the carnivore shepherd eats very well, with the general public being his, and offering him from among themselves, a great menu of culinary choices.

In ancient times, the hedonistic societies of Egypt and Babylon arose and contaminated the world. Because of their internal imbalances, each fell in its time, destroying the general public who embraced them. In recent times, hedonist Egypt and Babylon have been reincarnated. Today the hedonist society of the world is nothing more than the revived spirit of the ancient empires of vile idolatrous hedonist filth. As they fell in the past, so too are they falling today. Babylon falls! But who today cares? Egypt is doomed! But who today listens?

The Devourer has worked for a very long time behind the scenes manipulating everything in its hands. It is the Devourer who resurrected Babylon and Egypt, knowing well how the ancient empires enslaved their people. It is the Devourer who will topple the empires that he himself has remade. It is the Devourer who will then take his place as the grand false idol of them all, dispensing wealth, and hedonistic pleasures upon those of his sheep that he readies for the slaughter. And still the sheep follow mindlessly, even to their own slaughter.

Today, the wise are silenced, and those with eyes are told not to look, and not to see. But the wise survive, and those with eyes do look, and they do see. But the wise and those with eyes remain silent. For wisdom today has shown that folly reigns in place of wisdom and blindness rules in place of sight.

So the wise and those who see use their wisdom and their sight, and they flee the crumbling ruins of modern day Egypt/Babylon. They seek shelter outside the domain and outside the reach of the Devourer.

Of course, such a flight comes with a cost. The wise, and those who can see, must leave behind hedonistic ways, and must abandon the pursuit and worship of wealth. This may indeed lead many into poverty. But it is better to be righteous and moral in poverty than to be evil and immoral in hedonistic wealth!

But even these sentiments are condemned by the Devourer and his many minions. And the Devourer seeks out those who still oppose him to root them out and to destroy them once and for all, forever. And so the wise, and those who can see, silence themselves in order to survive. They conceal themselves in order to avoid the detection of the Devourer and his many minions. The wise will remain concealed until after modern day Egypt/ Babylon falls, and even after this until all that is meant to perish perishes.

For wisdom survives all upheavals. The righteous and the moral will remain forever. No matter how bad the battle; no matter how great be the conquering Devourer, no matter how devastating the destruction, righteousness and morals will survive. For the righteous, the moral and the wise place their faith and their fate in the True God who is the Maker of the Heavens and the Earth.

Worse times are coming. The fall must be complete. The Devourer is set free to devour as is his destiny. The general public of sheep will be devoured because they lack the wisdom to avoid this fate, they also lack the will to change their ways. And so, they will face their chosen destiny.

Yes, the great battle has already been fought. The casualties are high, and the dead do not even know that they have long ago died! But all this will soon become apparent, as it must.

There is no message here for the fallen, for the sheep, nor for the hedonist idol worshipper of modern wealth. There can be no message for those who embrace blindness and call it sight, and who embrace deafness and call it hearing. No, there is no message for them, not here, and not anywhere else as well.

This is a message for the wise, for those who can still see, and for those who can still hear. The message is simple: Persevere! Egypt/Babylon must fall. Do not try to save it. Instead get out of the way of its destruction. Save yourselves. Cast away all the idols and false gods that are still embraced today. They are not benign and unimportant. They are reservoirs of evil that will infect your soul. Their evil influence will never top trying to turn you from being one of "us" and transforming you into one of "them." Cast away evil, for only then will you be able to do good.

Let those who still have vision see. Let those who can still hear pay attention.

This message is now delivered. But who is open enough to receive it?

Ma'amar'im – Sayings

1.

To children, I explain.
To adults, I inform.
Adults understand on their own.
They can see the wisdom of a thing
without having it spelled out to them.
We call this maturity.
Head rules over heart.
The clear mind brings harmony
to the storm of unbalanced emotions.
Maturity is as maturity be.
Only the inner adult will understand.

2.

Dreams unfold naturally;
they always bring change.
Fear not, nor hinder,
the natural flow of change,
or else your dreams may never blossom.

3.

Here is a very unpopular truth!
If you want something done your way,
then do it yourself!
No one can do what you want
better than you, yourself.
Do not wait for God to work for you.
God is waiting for you to work for yourself!
And why is this truth so unpopular?
Because it leaves no room for laziness!
Each of us must arise, and work hard
in order to accomplish that which
God has already blessed for us.
Now, get up, and get to work!

4.

Always be honest with yourself!
Know what you want, and don't compromise!
Be willing to embrace
that which is right for you,
and to let go of that
which is wrong for you.
Have the courage and resolve
to do what is best for yourself.

For if you do not place yourself first,
who else will?
This is how we simplify life,
and create peace.

5

You can always close your eyes to the truth,
but that does not make the truth go away,
or make the truth to be true no more.
When you close your eyes to the truth
all it does is makes you blind
and unaware of
what is really going on around you.
Being blind when one does not have to be
is not a wise way to be!

6

When life pushes you,
and tries to hold you back,
push forward with all your might!
Never surrender to circumstances!
Make your own decisions!
Choose your own course!
Right or wrong, good or bad,
your decisions are yours!
This is what makes you
master of your own destiny!
Be the warrior, be the master, not the servant!

7

Life is like riding a bicycle.
Once your learn how to balance
you can ride along smoothly, with ease.
Without balance, life is like a storm.
You can then be tossed and turned
from side to side without mercy.
Learning balance is not hard,
but it does take time.
Once learned, it is a lesson never forgotten!
Take the time, make the effort.
Discover your balance,
and ride through life in peace.

8

It takes courage to see the truth.
It takes resolve to confront
what is wrong in our own midst.
It takes tenacity to keep up the good fight,

to stand out against the crowd,
and to make every effort
to stop the blinded masses
from again going over the proverbial cliff,
bringing pain and suffering upon us all.
Act properly now,
or face the consequences later.

9

You do no one any favors
by allowing the weak to remain weak.
You do more harm than good
when you do not intervene
to make a bad situation better.
You contribute to the problem
all the while that you do not confront
what needs to be challenged,
and force issues that needs to be addressed.
Love is not what you feel, it is what you do!
If you love someone for real
then "kick a**" when the moment requires
a show of true love.

10

Change is inevitable, why seek to avoid it?
Growth is the way of life, why seek to hinder it?
Strength comes from weakness,
and wisdom comes from folly.
This is the natural way of things,
why seek to deny it, why seek to resist it?
We always change from weak to strong,
and from strong to weak,
but we move forever forward
from folly to wisdom never to return to folly again.
This is the way of healthy life.
No denial, no resistance.

11

I am made up of very many parts, yet, I am one.
All my parts operate together
and enable me to be the me that I am.
Our world is made up of many parts,
yet we are one, and we are not one.
We are one in the sense
that we are part of the greater whole.
We are not one in the sense
that we do not act like

we are part of the greater whole.
In this lack of unity we never realize
the greater identity of the united whole.
This is a shame, and loss to us all.

12

Nature requires balance
between all the natural forces.
Challenge them as we may,
we cannot change what is natural balance.
One who lives by one's own rules
in contradiction to natural balance
is living in a state of imbalance.
Nature will not tolerate this for long.
Nature herself will do whatever needs to be done,
in order to restore natural balance.
To oppose the correcting forces of Mother Nature
is the very definition of foolishness.

13

I learn from nature
everything that it is that I need to do.
I learn from heaven
everything that I need to know
about how to be fully human.
Being fully human guides my mind.
Being of the earth guides my actions.
I unite my actions with my mind,
and allow my heart to understand with wisdom.
When my mind and heart are one,
then all my actions are righteous and natural.
Then, there are no conflicts, nor any mistakes.

14

Without emotional stability
one's life is like a ship at sea
during the greatest of storms,
tossed from side to side,
always in danger of being capsized, or sunk.
Ships at sea require a strong captain
to survive the storm.
The human heart needs equally strong direction.
Discipline and control your emotions!
Do not let them control you!
Allow your enlightened mind to heal your broken heart,
and to give birth to wisdom rising up from within you.

15

The greatest danger facing the warrior
is one's own inner instability.
Even when muscles are strong,
and martial skills perfected,
one whose emotions are not under control
will always be defeated,
not by one's enemy, but by one's own self.
Head over body, mind over heart,
the warrior knows this, and understands.
Discipline is The Way, it is only natural.
Thus the natural warrior is invincible.

16

When I gaze at the world around me
I look for opportunities.
When others gaze at the world around them
many see only obstacles.
We are both seeing the same thing,
yet I see an opportunity whereas
another sees only an obstacle.
How is it that the same thing
is seen in two different ways?

17

Never allow words to anger you!
Deflect them, neutralize their power!
Do not give others power over you
to harm you, or control you
through the words that they speak.
Words only have the power that one gives them.
Remain calm, stay balanced.
Your calmness and balance
will cause your opponent
to lose his calm, and his balance.
Thus weakened, your opponent is easily defeated.
Master yourself, guard your tongue.
In this, wisdom unites with action, and creates peace.

18

You think that you are smart?
Good! So be smart!
Prove yourself correct!
You think that you are strong?
Good! So be strong!
Again, prove yourself correct!
On the other hand,

do you think yourself stupid or weak?
This is bad! Prove yourself wrong,
and become smart and strong!
You can choose to be either
good or bad, right or wrong.
The power is in your hands, use it wisely!

19

With my open eyes I see the world around me.
It seems to me to be very real.
With my eyes closed, I dream,
and I see the world inside me.
It too seems equally real to me.
I thus live in two separate worlds.
I am in the one, and then I am in the other.
Who can say that one world
is more real than the next?
I know that my inside world can come outside.
This is why I see it. I make it real.
This is my internal power,
to make my dreams come true.

20

I am my own best friend.
At the same time, I am my own worst enemy.
My greatest struggle is inside myself.
My greatest ally arises from within me,
and gives me incredible strength,
and wise guidance.
My enemy within seeks to weaken me
with confusion of thought,
and uncontrollable outbursts of emotion.
I fight back by maintaining calm, and balance.
I know how to conquer and devastate my true enemy.
I do it by simply allowing myself to be the real me!

21

Learn wisdom and proper living from Nature herself.
For only Nature herself defines the natural.
Nature does not accommodate weakness,
nor should we.
What is weak must become strong.
What cannot get along,
must learn to get along, or it will perish, naturally.
Yes, there are some things that we must tolerate,
then there are those things which must not be tolerated.
Learn from nature!

She may be cruel, but she is always truthful,
and always works for the greater good.
So too, should we!
This is the Natural Way. There is no greater love.

22

Life is a battle! Why does this upset you?
Life always has its ups and downs.
Why do you complain?
There are always good times and bad.
Yet, what differentiates one from the other
is not what they actually are,
but rather what they are perceived to be.
Some see obstacles, others see opportunities.
Some see hard times, and are crushed by them.
Others see hard times, and are challenged by them
to rise to the occasion, and to conquer
even the greatest of foes.
This, after all, is life!

23

Get tough!
Face your adversity!
Overcome it.
It does not really matter
how to overcome it.
Do what works.
Be creative! Be imaginative!
God is the author of creation and origination.
So, be like God, and be creative and originate!

24

Get the job done! That's it!
It doesn't matter how you feel!
It doesn't matter what you think!
All that matters is what you do,
and how well you do it!
The universe does not care about your complaints.
The universe will not slow down,
or become less complex,
in order to make your time here any easier.
Do what needs to be done, and do it right!
Stop complaining! Stop wasting time!
Act! Be bold! Build! Create! Make! Do!
You're here on Earth to accomplish, so accomplish!

25

Like many others I too pray to God,
and ask for Divine blessings.
Yet, unlike many others I do not sit back
and wait for God to answer my prayers,
to shower me with the gifts of Heaven.
Instead, as best as I am able,
I take matters into my own hands,
and work hard to create, form, and make
the best that I am able to create, form, and make.
In this I discover that I am already blessed,
and that I already possess the gifts of Heaven.
All I have to do is to use them.
Why is this not more well-known?

26

Many people often carry
heavy burdens from their past.
These burdens hinder their present lives,
and make day-to-day affairs
more difficult than these affairs need to be.
Why does one choose to carry
such an unnecessary burden?
It is because no one has told them that it is okay
to put the burden down, and to leave it behind.
Leave the past in the past, do not let it haunt you.
Do not let it burden you anymore.
Bury the dead, and move on in peace!
Let go, and let live!
Only you can free yourself!

27

When I do what is natural,
everything seems to move smoothly.
This is the meaning of blessing.
And when I act with the best of intentions,
and yet still experience unexpected resistance,
I recognize that I must broaden the scope of my vision,
to encompass greater information, and knowledge.
This is also a blessing, and it is the act of enlightenment.
Every day I learn something new
about the Natural Way, and I embrace it.
This is the proper Way to channel Heaven,
and to manifest the Higher Way here on Earth.

28

The future is not yet written.
Either we ourselves will decide
how the future is to unfold,
or others will decide it for us.
We already have all the internal power
that we will ever need.
All we need to do is unleash it.
Yesterday is our teacher.
Today is our opportunity.
Tomorrow is the fulfillment of our dreams,
or the dashing of our hopes.
We get to decide which one it is.
And if we do not choose what is right,
how can we complain when others choose what is wrong.

29

We are all warriors.
Every day we battle the darkness
of our own surroundings.
Every day brings us stillness, and movement.
Silence and noise, good things, and bad.
This is the natural order.
It is the way it is.
The only thing that changes is us.
The warrior contemplates the Way of Life,
and seeks to walk the path of life,
by struggling against the path of death.
Nature only changes when we bring about the change.
We are thus warriors,
struggling to bring the best out of nature, itself.

30

There are secrets in nature that we cannot know.
And why can we not know such things?
The fault is not in nature, the fault is in us.
For nature has no need to hide her secrets.
It is we who cannot be entrusted certain knowledge,
at least not until we are mature and responsible enough
to use this knowledge with wisdom and discretion.
The more that we act in accordance to nature,
both the nature surrounding us, and the nature inside us,
the more aligned we become with the Natural Way.
The more that we are one with the Natural Way,
the more of nature's secrets will become known to us, naturally.
Secrets are entrusted to adults, not to children.
Which then, are we?

31

I gaze upon others, and see all their faults.
I wonder about how it is that I see all this.
As I contemplate further, I have a revelation.
The faults that I see in others
are the same faults that I can now see in myself.
Again I contemplate, and question:
Do I really see the faults of others,
or perhaps I only am seeing my own faults,
that I am projecting on to them.
Yes, I have my faults, but do others share my faults?
I contemplate yet again, and I realize that
sometimes our faults are not the same, but sometimes they are!
So what I see on the surface is rarely ever the whole truth.
I need to look deeper in order to ascertain more certain truths

32

For some, nature can appear to be cruel,
and daily living can appear to be harsh!
There is no escaping this perceived reality.
The enlightened one, however, looks upon
the perceived cruel and harsh,
and seeks to turn everything negative
into something positive.
This is the power of the human mind,
and the purpose of human consciousness.
We are never slaves to destiny!
While we cannot control everything that happens,
we most certainly can control how we choose to respond!
Destiny is ours to create, nature cannot hinder this!
This is the power and the fulfillment of the enlightened soul!

33

Mastery and dominance
is the domain of the disciplined soul.
The master of oneself
bows to no other master,
be it outside of oneself, or inside of oneself.
The master of Self
controls one's own destiny,
and decides one's own course.
Whatever happens will happen,
but the Master of Self
chooses how to act, and acts accordingly.
The Master of Self controls nature internally,
and is therefore a Master of far more than just mere self.
Contemplate this, and discover my secret meaning.

34
Heed now my advice,
and your life will be happy, and at peace.
Never, ever slow your pace
to enable another to catch up to you,
or to keep up with you.
If they can't keep up,
then it is a crime for them to slow you down!
Pass them by, and leave them in the dust.
This is both your destiny, and theirs!
Also, never ever speed yourself up
to try to keep pace with another!
If you wish to move along slowly to enjoy the Way,
then by all means, do exactly that!
You move at your pace, and let others move at theirs!
This is the natural Way of things, and it must be obeyed.
Each person must march to the beat of one's own drum.
Each person must dance to the tune of one's own music.
Never march to another's beat,
never dance to music that is not your own!
Be who you are, and let others be who they are!
When everyone walks the path unique to oneself,
we have internal harmony, and peace.
The inner harmony will lead to a content world.
This is the key that unlocks both happiness, and peace.
Open these doors inside yourself,
and discover this truth personally, inside yourself.

35
The inside world and the outside world
are two parts of the same whole.
If you don't fix the one,
the other one will remain broken until you do!
Stop trying to redefine nature!
Stop trying to fight that which cannot be fought!
Learn the Ways of nature, and the Ways of Wisdom.
Combine your understanding of both,
and with this knowledge,
you will be able to change the course of the universe.
This is, after all, only natural,
for it is our purpose and our destiny.
Embrace it! Make peace!
Restore the ancient to its rightful place, and complete the circle.

36
Be careful about turning against another!
Be careful not to give into hate!

For once you walk down this dark road
allowing insult, hate, and harm towards another,
you have unleashed an uncontrollable terror!
Today, it is you who turns against the other.
Tomorrow, it will be the others
who will turn against you!
When you turn against the other,
you start a chain reaction
that, in the end, will take you down
alongside the other that you want to take down.
There is no escape!
What goes around, comes around!

37

The most important, pivotal moments of life
are never recognized as they happen.
So treat every moment, and every decision
with caution, and care.
What you consider in the moment
to be small, may indeed be big.
Often, what is done, cannot be undone.
Gaze forward from the present moment
into the, as yet, unwritten future.
Ask yourself, is this the path that I truly wish to walk?
If so, then embrace it. If not, turn aside, now, before it's too late.
You are the master of your own destiny, captain of your own ship.
Choose your course with wisdom and insight.
Be guided by a settled mind, and not by an unsettled heart.

38

Dispel evil with good!
Dispel lies with truth!
Never attack straight on,
announcing your next move!
Strike from the side.
Never let your foe see you coming or going.
In this world, our foes are many.
They are strong, and we are weak.
They are many and we are few.
BUT! While they may be wise, we can be wiser!
In your wisdom is your victory.
Know your wisdom first, before you strike.
In this way, your brilliance will blind your foe.

39

In tough times we always choose,
to either stand firm and fight,

or to cut loose, and take flight.
In some battles to flee is wise.
In other battles to flee ensures defeat.
Internal battles must always be fought.
One can never take flight from the inner enemy.
One's own inner demons will never give one rest.
One's inner demons must be totally defeated
in order for one to have true, inner peace.
Thus we fight the good fight
in order to win the greatest victory!
Conquer yourself, and you become
master of your own destiny.

40

The height of arrogance is for one to think
that one can control the world.
One who does not respect nature
will not be respected by nature.
The height of foolishness is for one to act
without consideration of the consequences.
While our proper actions are our best assets,
our shortsighted decisions are what lead us
to the unpleasant circumstances in life
that we must tolerate, and suffer.
One who knows one's place,
and embraces it without complaint
will find oneself exactly where one needs to be.
Move if you have to, but reside in your natural place.

41

Fight or flight, which path do you choose?
Flight will take you
into the realms of fantasy,
wherein you can dream whatever it is
that you wish to dream.
Fight will take you
in the world of reality
wherein which you will have to struggle
in order to make your dreams come true.
Which do you choose,
the easy path of fantasy,
or the difficult road to reality.
The choice is always yours!

42

FAITH can make the unreal to become real.
Lack of faith can make the real

to become unreal.
There are always distractions.
There are always doubts.
There will always be those
that will seek to destroy faith
out of fear for what faith can make real.
Stand firm in your faith.
Believe until the waters part,
and your freedom from slavery is accomplished.
No matter how difficult the obstacles,
overcome them with FAITH.

43
It is clear!
We are all created in the Image of God!
We are thus all equal in the Eyes of God!
Yes! We are all different, we're supposed to be!
When united, our differences come together
and make us strong in unity!
When divided, our differences weaken us,
and make us easy to dominate, and control.
The Word of God is in all things, and is for everyone!
The Path of Torah offers a profound wisdom
that benefits all who will respect it, in truth.
Torah, like God, like nature itself, is for everyone!
Enough divisions! Unite!
Let the Path show you the Way of Respect & Unity!

44
To stay stubbornly entrenched
against the natural flow of change
is a sure way to pass on,
even as the past itself passes on.
This is a most unwise course of action.
Everything changes its form,
even when essence remains constant.
Those who mistake form for essence
believe that staying true to form
is the same as staying true to essence.
This too is a most unwise course of action.
Those who know the Way of creation and its Creator
know that to all things there is its proper time.
Knowing the right time enables one to do the right thing,
in the right time, in the right place, in the right way.

New Sihot

The Klipot of the Subconscious

May 1, 23

In all practices of psychic/spiritual ascent such movements cannot and do not occur without difficulties. The existence of these difficulties is recorded in a code-like fashion with the meditative experiences of the prophets Elijah (Kings), and Ezekiel (Chapter 1). Generally, these difficulties are described as a storm (1), a cloud (2), and a fire (3). These three perceptions are symbolic expressions of states of mind that the individual aspiring ascendant will always experience. These three states of mind are the layers of congestion, confusion, and terror that an individual experiences every time that one seeks to disengage from the physical body and the normal level of waking consciousness associated with it.

When we speak of psychic/spiritual ascent, it needs to be made clear that this experience is a psychological one. No one is physically ascending anywhere. What is happening during this process is that one's conscious waking mind expands conscious awareness to include experiences from other, higher states of reality. Essentially, the psychic ascent is a reintegration between an individual's lower and higher identities. But becoming aware of one's true, higher identity (Self) is hindered by a layer of thought that has been pushed out of memory. This intervening layer consists of the above mentioned, storm, cloud, and fire. In psychology this layer of thoughts is called one's personal subconscious.

This is why authentic Ma'aseh Merkava teachings are essentially a very in-depth psychoanalysis. Each individual who aspires to successfully tap into one's personal unconscious, which in turn connects one to the collective unconscious, must first pass through one's own subconscious and all the repressed content that resides there. Mind you, this is no easy task, as any modern psychologist can testify.

Since ancient times, aside from techniques of connection, each aspiring student also had to cleanse oneself of all inner intervening psychic content. We see clear evidence to this in the words of the Biblical prophets and other writings when they call for one to repent and to cleanse one's heart before God. Since Talmudic times, the law has been enacted that Ma'aseh Merkava had to only be taught one-on-one between master and student. This is because the relationship between them was actually one of psychoanalyst to patient.

It is imperative today that modern practitioners of the Merkava system realize the underlying psychological reality of that which is sought. Otherwise, modern practitioners may be pursuing a fantasy idea of what Ma'aseh Merkava is believed to be in their minds, but which has no basis in reality. It is because many modern practitioners do not know how to get to where they want to go (spiritually/psychically) that they never end up getting there. Thus the first Klipah of the mind storm, which are the cacophony of confused ideas and thoughts must be peeled away and discarded. The road to Truth cannot be traversed by one who carries lies. One must unlearn what one has learned, and re-experience for oneself the truth of things.

Creator & Creation

May 2, 23

Look around! What do you see? Do you see the Way of creation, or do you see the way of human beings acting in and against creation?

In the past, I have always spoken about nature and the natural way. This is the common language understood by most. Nature simply means that the universe operates in accordance to its natural laws. Science pursues an understanding of these laws and builds upon this understanding their theories of the universe. There is nothing wrong with this pursuit, however it is very narrow and limited in scope.

There are those in science, who in their rebellion against the Creator, create for themselves a theory of the universe which is so far-fetched that it goes beyond science fiction, and even beyond the tolerances of imagination. In order to deny that the Creator created nature, thus rightly to be called creation, the rebellious scientists seek to proclaim that the universe created itself, that the laws of nature created themselves. Indeed, the rebel scientists take one step further and instead of saying that these things created themselves, they say that the universe was always there, that it is eternal, without beginning, and without end. One who gazes out and looks upon every reality that we know sees the glaring contradiction of such a false proclamation.

Creation had a beginning, and creation will have an end. The length of its life may not be able to be determined by the minds of modern human beings. But we know that all life has its end, and thus all life has its beginnings. This is true for all life, no matter how small, or how large.

A question is often proposed that asks, if the universe was created at a specific point in time, what then existed before that point in time? This is a valid question, however limited it is in perspective.

We have always known that there have been many other universes. Some came before us, some exist side-by-side with us, and yet others will come after us. Each of them is equally a creation of the Creator. As for what came before us, there was another universe of sorts. It still exists, but it is different from our universe in the same way as a child is different from its parent.

While modern science will speak of the beginning of the universe as a big bang, it might be more accurate to describe the beginning of our universe as the big birth. Our universe was birthed by the one before it. And that universe was birthed by the one before it. How many times this process has been repeated is not known to us human beings. Each universe is a child of its parents. The Ultimate Source, which started the whole procedure, this is the one whom we call God.

As distant as this might make God sound to be, such a perception is an illusion. The Creator of all universes rules over them all and through them all by the Laws that the Divine has instilled within each one. Indeed, the Presence of the Divine and the Divine Consciousness exists within each of its creations, acting through its creations, and experiencing life in its many multiple forms through each creation. This again is true of all creations be they small or large.

For those who cannot directly experience the reality of the Divine Presence, belief of its Presence will have to suffice. Belief is what the mind accepts to be true, even though there is a lack of experience thereof, and thus no confirmation of its truth. Be this as it may, the believer accepts the truth, even without being able to see it and to experience it first-hand.

Long ago, the Presence of the Creator spoke with humanity and taught us a Code of living standards that are designed to stabilize our position within the created order of balance. We were taught how to live with one another, how to behave, what to do, and what not to do. These standards were embraced by those who could experience, and were received as commandments by those who could not experience, but who believed nevertheless.

But this happened a long time ago. Since that time, many believers have ceased believing. As such they care not for the created way of creation, nor for its commandments that mold and strengthen righteous and moral human behavior. And because they rebel against the ways of creations, they seek to rebel against the Creator. And so, they try to remove any awareness of the Presence of the Divine Mind.

Instead of referring to creation, the very word of which implies that there be a Creator, they instead simply refer to a nebulous nature, that is simply there, without beginning, without end, and certainly without a Creator. For this reason alone, we must always remind everyone that nature itself is merely a creation, and thus we should refer to it properly.

There are created laws that operate here in creation. These laws are rigid and strict. One violates the laws of creation at one's own peril. Within each of these laws resides the Consciousness and the Presence of the Creator. Long ago when the Code was bestowed upon us the laws therein were designed to reflect and to mirror the universal laws of creation itself. Thus one who adheres to the Code is one who is balanced with all creation. And the opposite is also true, the one who rejects the Code and does not discipline oneself to behave properly as ordained by the Creator is out-of-sync with creation, and in opposition to it. Such individuals then serve as agents of destruction as opposed to agents of creation. Even one with a simple mind can look out upon one's fellow human beings, and see the vast number of destroyers among us.

The creation declares the Presence of the Creator. It is clear for all to see. But there are those who do not want to see, and more so, they also do not want others to see either. Therefore those who do not want to see seek to blind the eyes of others so that they too will not see. They concoct all kinds of fables and stories such as the universe created itself, or that it is eternal, and thus there definitely is no Creator. One can thus act any way that one chooses, without regard for righteousness and morality. They have created a new law of their own that states, do whatever it is that you want, this is the new law. And being blind to the Presence of God, and equally being blind to the consequences of their actions, many are deceived by these false arguments, and fall out-of-sync with creation and its laws. But like we already know, the laws of creation are rigid and firm. Those who violate them will indeed suffer the consequences of their actions.

What human beings need to understand is that the concept of time is very subjective. Time is perceived by us here on Earth in one way, and time is perceived very differently in the Eyes of the Creator. The details of these differences may not be known to us. But we must never think that because the Divine Presence does not intervene immediately in accordance to our time-frame that there is no intervention at all. This is very much untrue. The Divine Presence sees all and knows all, and acts to realign its universe and all the parts therein, be they great or small, all in good time, as is ordained by a Higher Wisdom.

Those who continue to deny this, and who continue to act in their out-of-sync ways will eventually be realigned. They will be taught their lessons. They will learn and be reformed. As for how this will happen, and when, this is known to the Creator. And those who seek to experience the Divine Presence will be granted insight into the operations of creation. And for all others, each is in the Hands of Higher Wisdom. Each will be dealt with in good time.

Ma'aseh Merkava & Psychology

May 3, 23

The most difficult language on Earth to understand is the language of one's own unconscious as it attempts to communicate with the conscious mind.

On a regular basis our conscious mind is inundated with feelings, and impressions, as well as pieces of memories from dreams. We often have no idea from where such feelings and impressions come from, and we all the more so often haven't a clue as to what our dream symbols mean to us. Our conscious minds are aware of these things, and yet we have no idea as to how they got into consciousness, and why.

From the point of view of normal, waking consciousness, the unconscious and all of its impressions and images are for the most part unwelcome visitors who serve no functional purpose. Our very prejudiced society tends to focus on external reality to the point of denying internal reality, and to look upon its involvement with consciousness as an intrusion. The more the mind becomes material and rational, the less it becomes open to and aware of its own inner content, drive, and purpose.

This separation and repression of unconscious content that seeks to bubble up into consciousness helps create the middle level of the mind that separates the consciousness from the unconscious; this is the subconscious.

Now I feel that I must digress for a moment to discuss the mannerism in which I write and my personal purpose for doing so.

For those who are well aware of my writings and my person, I am an Orthodox (Jewish) Rabbi, blessed to be trained in the teachings and practices of the Torah's mystical traditions known popularly as the Kabbalah. Now, the word Kabbalah as it is used today, means Jewish mysticism in general, and has within it many different schools of philosophy and practice that are significantly different from one another. Those familiar with me and my writings know that I practice and teach the lessons of the Prophetic Kabbalah, which is a modern term to describe the oldest of Torah mystical traditions called the Ma'aseh Merkava, which is the pursuit of the chariot vision as described in the Bible by the prophet Ezekiel.

Unbeknown to most is the fact that Ezekiel's description of his chariot vision uses symbolic terms in the same way as terms of a different variety are used in later Kabbalah, specifically the schools of the Zohar and the Ari'zal.

All visionary experiences speak in the language of the unconscious because visions do not arise from the external world, but from the internal world. One's individual unconscious is one's higher Self. It is this unconscious higher Self that exists in its own dimensional reality, which is far different from the material, physical reality that the conscious mind acknowledges.

When elements from that other dimensional reality commune with one's higher Self, one receives the impressions of such contact. One's unconscious then passes along these impressions in the form of images into the conscious mind. The images that one's conscious mind receives are unique and subjective to the individual's collective memory and intellect. In other words, the conscious mind can only relate to those things that it understands.

Thus when the unconscious has a message to give to the conscious mind, it sifts through every memory, thought and feeling that the mind has stored, and chooses those images, feelings, and impressions that best fit the message. Essentially, the unconscious message uses the thought patterns, and imagery understood by the conscious mind as its vessels, or as its body in order to manifest. The unconscious is thus like the soul, whereas the conscious mind is like the body. And this association is far more than metaphor. For that which we call our soul, is actually our unconscious higher Self, and it does reside within the physical body, which is dominated by the conscious, waking mind.

As each human life is unique, so too is the collection of thoughts stored in each individual's experience. Thus each experience of higher reality, including prophecy, will be cloaked within the symbols and expressions of the individual. It thus becomes imperative for the individual to recognize the subjective nature of one's revelations of symbols, and to seek their interpretation and meaning. More often than not, a recipient of impressions arising from the unconscious does not understand oneself well enough to grasp the proper and true meanings of one's own revelations. When this happens, the underlying truth of the message received is often overlooked, and thus gets ignored.

Throughout my writings I have endeavored to speak about the truth of things, about the relationship between various levels of consciousness, without having to resort to the traditional usage of popular Kabbalistic metaphors. Why use terms like Sefirot, Olamot, and Partzufim if the reader does not have a clear and precise understanding as to what these words, and the realities underlying them, actually mean.

I find it far better to use modern terminologies familiar to most from such well-known and popular fields of knowledge and study such as psychology. If I talk about various levels of souls, and their ascents or descents, most will not understand the underlying reality of such a discussion. Many take the symbolic words to be literal and thus draw all the wrong conclusions about the lessons to be learned. When, however, instead of taking about souls, I talk about levels of consciousness, and how one expands consciousness (or how consciousness contracts), this description is more widely understood. The message can therefore be successfully communicated.

Essentially, modern day Ma'aseh Merkava is in-depth self-psychoanalysis. One who understands this properly at least has the chance to succeed in receiving a modern-day version of the chariot vision, which will manifest in the symbol forms familiar to modern minds. This is why understanding one's own personal symbols that arise from one's own personal unconscious are of paramount importance. And equally why one must do the psychological work to clear out and heal all the subconscious content within one's mind in order to receive a clear and correct communication.

This psychological explanation of the Ma'aseh Merkava explains what the Biblical prophets did in their day but in our language. This is why I pursue this style of writing and teaching. I live today, so therefore I speak the language of today. Those who learn this lesson, and apply it stand the chance of becoming a part of the living tradition that dates back to the earliest of times.

SECTION FOUR

THE SEVEN ESSAYS

Chapter 1

Neshama & Nefesh:
The Story of You, Before & After Life

You have heard it said, "If at first you don't succeed, try and try again."

This about sums up Heaven's attitude towards the education and evolution of the human race.

Only spiritually immature souls, no more developed than the youngest toddler, would ever associate one's human identity with one's temporary physical body, and with the equally temporary subjective identity that is born along with it, and dies along with it.

Let me give an example. Once upon a time, there was a life-force entity, who was just One from a greater Whole. The One exists. Period! If we choose, we may call the One a soul, consciousness, or whatever. Names are not really important. One gazes out upon the universe and realizes that One either wants to, or needs to learn a lesson about something or another. So, One then enrolls in school.

This school in which One will learn One's lesson requires that One fully emerges into the school, so as to receive "hands on" training. One then enters the school, which for the sake of our example is the planet Earth. One chooses an indigenous lifeform in which to become incarnate, and through which the lessons of planet Earth will be learned.

As One incarnates here on Earth, the new lifeform (body) is given a name. This name now becomes associated with the identity that One will embrace all the while that One remains on Earth at this time, learning the lessons for which One came to Earth in the first place.

So, One has One's natural and normal identity. Let's call this identity Neshama (remember what I said about names). Neshama comes to Earth, incarnates in a body which is then given its own name and identity. Let's call the body name Nefesh.

So, Neshama (One) goes through life on Earth during this lifetime known as Nefesh. However, as is the way of all finite matter, forms are always in a constant state of change, flux, and impermanence. In time, the body that Neshama inhabits is returned to its elemental forms. (The body dies). When the body dies, Neshama leaves the body and moves on. But what happens to Nefesh?

Nefesh is only the temporary identity that Neshama uses while inhabiting that specific body. When the body dies the Nefesh association dies along with it. Now, while the Nefesh association dies, this does not mean that Nefesh dies. For Nefesh is only the temporary identity of Neshama. So, when the body of Nefesh dies, the identity of Nefesh, and everything about it, including every memory, feeling, and what have you, is absorbed into Neshama.

So, while Nefesh the body dies, the reality of Nefesh lives on as part of Neshama. Nefesh becomes the lesson learned by Neshama while here on Earth.

Now let us take this one step further.

Neshama, the consciousness, soul (whatever) has a best friend, whom we shall name Nishmat. Nishmat wishes to join Neshama on a journey to Earth. So Nishmat also incarnates on Earth as did Neshama. Nishmat takes on a body and is given the name Nafsha.

On Earth, Nefesh and Nafsha hangs out together. Nefesh was born a male, while Nafsha was born a female. As is the way on Earth, Nefesh and Nafsha marry and live out life on Earth as husband and wife. When it is time to depart Earth, Nishmat leaves behind the body (and identity) of Nafsha. Nishmat absorbs all that was Nafsha, and her lessons learned on Earth.

So, now back in their indigenous forms, Neshama and Nishmat are friends again, only now they have a deeper relationship because of the lessons they learned while being Nefesh and Nafsha on Earth.

So, Nefesh and Nafsha never really die. Although their bodies go the way of all finite forms, the essence of their nature, (their souls), which are Neshama and Nishmat remain forever, enriched by their previous experiences.

Essentially, the temporary identities of Nefesh and Nafsha are reabsorbed back into the greater identities of Neshama and Nishmat. This can be repeated numerous times, with Neshama and Nishmat embracing within themselves multiple temporary identities alongside their original One.

And so it is with us.

Each time our Oneness incarnates here on Earth, it creates for itself yet another temporary identity. Over the many experiences (lifetimes), while the temporary identities of past lives may be forgotten, the lessons learned from them serve as active and vibrant influences on the present temporary identity.

This is why it is often the case that one may receive an impression, a knowing, and an awareness of some truth or reality that transcends the boundaries of the experience or memories of the temporary identity. Such a knowing is described as being internal, meaning that it arises up from within the mind, from a realm of mind that we know is there, but we lack access to. This part of the concealed mind is called the unconscious.

It is the unconscious that connects the temporary identity with One's true reality of being. (Or in the case of our example, what connects the temporary Nefesh with the immortal Neshama). Being that the unconscious serves as the conduit between the temporary and the permanent, it is what we call the pathway to higher consciousness, or the doorway into a higher dimensional state of being.

It is through the unconscious that Neshama interacts with its Nefesh identity. Neshama (in the unconscious) knows everything that is going on. Nefesh, on the other hand, has no such knowing, and essentially is left with only the smallest amount of inner awareness.

When Nefesh pays attention to the subtle prodding of Neshama from within the unconscious, all goes well for Nefesh. When Nefesh does not listen to the Inner Voice, then Nefesh feels alone, and lost. Only with the death of the body can Nefesh be reabsorbed into Neshama.

Nefesh is born to learn the lessons offered in Schoolhouse Earth. Nefesh is born here while Neshama sits back, and like a parent (or Higher Self), watches Nefesh grow and learn.

Neshama prods and directs Nefesh all the time, this usually occurs in that time-period when Neshama and Nefesh chat; this is time of sleep. This is the normal order of operations. When all things go well, life on Earth serves as the rewarding, enlightening experience that it was designed to be. However, things do not always follow the normal order. Sometimes things get messed up. Sometimes the dreams of Schoolhouse Earth are turned into a nightmare. When this happens other procedures need to be implemented.

Sometimes the lessons to be learned here in Schoolhouse Earth may not be the most pleasant or enjoyable. Neshama oversees the birth, growth, education and return of Nefesh. Neshama knows in advance which lessons may or may not be easy to learn, but accepts the experiences of such. Neshama recognizes that all that Nefesh feels or possibly suffers is only for a very short moment, and is necessary for the learning process.

Nefesh, on the other hand, has no such insights as to the purpose of its present sufferings. Nefesh feels what it feels and responds as it will respond. Sometimes Nefesh acts in one way which serves for its betterment. Sometimes Nefesh acts in an opposite way that further leads to its own harm.

It is rare, but sometimes it does happen that the life of Nefesh goes wrong, and takes on paths not meant for it by Neshama. If all of Neshama's corrective interventions fail to correct Nefesh's course, it is known that sometimes Neshama quits school and withdraws Nefesh prematurely. When this happens Nefesh is often quite damaged, and it may take a while before Nefesh can be reoriented safely back into Neshama.

What I have described here are only a very few of the instances and interactions that occur in the ongoing educational process of Neshama.

In one way, we are all Neshama, and in another way, we are also all Nefesh. The Neshama/Nefesh story is thus our own. Each of us while here on Earth live a separate Nefesh identity. We often fail to recognize that we are all part of the greater whole of the One Neshama. And so, our Nefesh lives, temporary as they are, continue here on Earth, learning what we were sent here to learn.

This is our story, before, during and after our current cycle of Nefesh identity here in our present temporary experience, here in Schoolhouse Earth.

Chapter 2

Real Angels & the Nature
of their Dual Dimensionality

"And he lifted his eyes and saw, and behold, three men were standing beside him."
(Gen. 18:2)

"God brought the angels to him in the likeness of men."
(Rashi comm. to Gen. 18:1)

"Angels do not possess bodies or corporeal being."
(Maimonides, M.T. Y.T. 2:3)

"But such words contradict Scripture.
It is forbidden to listen to them, all the more to believe in them!"
(Nachmanides, Torah comm. to Gen. 18:1)

The Torah is full of stories that describe angelic encounters. In most instances, the angels are described are appearing like relatively normal human beings. But looks can be deceiving.

Were these encounters physical and tangible, or were they prophetic visions experienced only within the mind of the individual? This is the age-old debate amongst Rabbinic scholars, be they of either the philosophical or mystical schools. But is this debate really a debate? For one thing is certain: there is a lot more to angels than is currently understood.

Angels are not what we think that they are. There is a side to their reality that is not covered, nor discussed in any book of either the philosophical or mystical schools.

Throughout most Rabbinic literature, especially in recent centuries, there seems to be an incredible lack of any direct, personal experiences with known angelic beings. Therefore, most of what the Torah Sages and Kabbalists understand about angels is learned from books, and we do have a good number of books that discuss the subject.

However, for the most part, all this information is academic in nature. It is based upon philosophical speculations often originating in either Aristotelian or Platonic thought. Almost never are there recorded any actual and authentic direct personal experiences and interactions.

Most discussion about angels in Torah literature that is meant for public consumption is watered-down in order to present angelic beings as mild-mannered helpers from God that act to intervene in the lives of the everyday person. This portrayal makes angels look like magical creatures from some imaginary make-believe world who perform wondrous miracles, the likes of which we would wish would happen to us.

Such portrayals, however moralistic and inspiring, are still nothing more than child-like stories fed to the masses to entertain and to edify. Such stories, and the metaphysical speculations of Sages, either Kabbalistic or philosophical, have created for us what is, for the most part, a completely fantastical portrayal of beings, not indigenous to our Earth, who are very much real, and who are, in reality, very different than what we have been led to believe.

As is clear from the religious literature that discusses angels, one correct point is that there are many different types of angelic beings. Angels are not all the same, and we have no idea as to what they really are, and what function and purpose they perform in the universe, with regards to humanity, or outside of such a narrow context.

Let us remember, there are full species or races of angels. Most students of the Bible have heard some of their names at least once. And being that they are called by different names, the understanding is that they are different from one another. Therefore, a Seraph is not a Hayah, who is not a Cherub, who is not an Eril, who is not a Benei Elohim. What each of these races are we cannot accurately describe. All that we can say about them is what is recorded for us in our literature. And our literature only speaks of individual entities, and does not, and cannot address the function of an entire angelic race.

For example, in Ezekiel's visions, he sees both Hayot and Cherubim. But how many of each does he see? Is the number seen by the prophets all that there is of that species? Are there only four Hayot, or perhaps are there billions (or more). We cannot say. And if there are such a large number, what function are they performing elsewhere in the universe? Granted, four of them serve in the Merkava chariot (as described in Ezekiel's vision in Ez. 1), but what about the other four billion? What are they doing?

We also make the mistake to refer to all these other-worldly entities as angels. Remember, angel in Hebrew is Malakh, which means a messenger. So of the four billion or so Hayot, how many of them are in the Divine service functioning as messengers? All of them, some of them, or a very few number of them? We simply do not know.

Those who are not interacting with us human beings are the ones not sent by God to interact with us. As such, they are not messengers, as such they are not, technically speaking, angels! They are nevertheless other-worldly beings, and by nature they are thus extraterrestrial. (And to this day, there are still many students of angelology who object to my usage of this clearly applicable term).

Regardless of whatever these other-worldly beings actually are, they each have their individual identities, and thus their individual lives. Granted those lives might be very radically different from our own. Then again, maybe not. Maybe there are some angelic races who are not too dissimilar from us humans, and then again, there may be one or more angelic races out there who are radically different from us, and thus have no desire to be in contact with us.

Since the earliest written records we have always associated angels as existing in some nebulous place called Heaven. Throughout most of recorded history if one were asked, where is

Heaven, one would simply point up to the sky, and usually have no further details to describe where Heaven actually is.

In ancient prophetic literature, descriptions of Heaven were expanded to include multiple Heavens. Some of the descriptions actually elaborated, even if just a little bit, what goes on in each of the Heavens. While many of these descriptions are imaginative with the intent to be moralistic and inspirational, some of the information might have come from those prophetic practitioners who actually did travel outside their physical bodies to actual other worlds. Again, the difference between those with experience of other realms and the beings who dwell there, and those that just speculate about these things, is staggering.

Descriptions of encounters with angelic beings should never begin with a story-like fairy-tale mentality that often begins with a "once upon a time" attitude. We create for ourselves layer upon layer of myth, fantasy, and outright delusions every time that we engage the topic of angels from such a detached point of view that lacks all sense of any kind of personal encounter.

One of the many fantasies that is popularly portrayed is that angels only appear to certain holy and righteous individuals. We are wrongly taught that angels do not appear to everyday people, because everyday people are not worthy of such a sublime experience. Contradicting this we have numerous examples from the Bible itself, as well as throughout later Torah literature. Angels can and do appear to whomever it is that they wish, regardless of our beliefs as to whom they should and should not appear to.

As I have mentioned above, there are entire races of what we call angelic entities. We are taught (but we cannot confirm or deny) that the vast majority of them serve Heaven in one fashion or another. And we are taught, and there are those of us who know from personal experiences, that the angels with whom we interact with here on Earth are but the smallest percentage of angelic entities who are out there. We are only aware of those with whom we interact (in the past or present). As for the rest of all these other races, and their populations in the billions (or more), we cannot even begin to speculate.

There is so much that we do not know. It is therefore worthless to speculate about that which one does not know, and cannot know. What we can talk about, even beyond speculation, and into the realm of actual experience, is the nature of those angelic entities with whom we do have contact.

We can talk about what we know! And what we really know is very different from what the masses think that they know. What we really know from experience can be quite frightening for those who still embrace their fantasies, and who are reluctant to budge from their belief in them.

For the most part angels are proclaimed to be "spiritual" beings. But what exactly is the definition and nature of something spiritual is nebulous at best. Spiritual is simply defined as something not physical. Spiritual lacks all material form and substance. Little do most know that this definition of spiritual has its source in Grecian philosophy and not in Torah. But be this as it may, let us explore the actual reality of what is, what we call, "spiritual."

Today, with modern scientific discoveries, we have become much more aware of the realities surrounding us than what we knew centuries ago. Today, we can acknowledge that there are real, non-physical, completely non-material realities out there. But we do not call these realities "spiritual," today we call them energy.

We know that physical form (be it solid, liquid, or gaseous) is made of matter. Matter is made of atoms and molecules that vibrate and spin at certain speeds. The one thing that all material forms share is that all speeds of their internal movements are under a speed limit that we today call the speed of light. Science has demonstrated to us that if matter is sped up to the speed of light it no longer remains material but is converted into energy. So, energy is faster-than-light existence.

To return to angels. There are those who insist that angels are non-corporeal; that they are non-material intelligent entities. They are often portrayed as non-corporeal beings of light. If this is indeed the case, then we must conclude that real "angels" are entities whose existence vibrates in a higher energy frequency that do we human beings.

Angels are thus beings of light. This makes them to be beings of energy. As energy beings they are a form of life that is non-biological and non-organic. This is not life as we know it. But if these entities are real, then modern science needs to expand their definition of what is a lifeform.

We also understand that we live in three-dimensional space with a fourth dimension of time. Yet, we have come to understand that there are other dimensions above these. There are dimensions of being, which by our definition are filled with energy (and not matter). Are these dimensions our fabled "Heaven?" Are these higher dimensions the natural home of these hyper-light beings (or at least of some of them)?

What are dimensions that move faster-than-light really like? Are they made up of their own forms of atoms, molecules and the like? Modern science as best as we presently understand might indeed say yes. Thus, there may be entire races of beings, living on distant planets, each doing what is does, all existing in higher dimensions, the likes of which is even hard for us to imagine.

The human soul is also an energetic entity that only temporarily inhabits the physical body. The soul is experienced as the individual mind, housed as it may be, within the organic, physical brain. And this is what human beings and higher entities share in common. We are both energy-based lifeforms who have the ability to materialize in the three-dimensional world of solid forms.

Human souls enter this physical dimension by inhabiting and enlivening the chemical combinations that merge together to form a human fetus. The length of sojourn in this physical dimension is thus directly coordinated with the health and life of the physical body that a soul inhabits and enlivens.

Human souls enter this dimensional plane in a rather rigid way. Souls are intensely attached to their physical bodies, never leaving them to go too far, or for too long. Because the soul sojourn in the body is so extreme, any and all memories of pre-body existence is blocked out of the mind consciousness that associates itself with the temporary identity established with the body. This situation of temporary amnesia is not total. Souls are programmed to leave the body and body consciousness on a regular basis in order to commune with the higher dimensions. It is during these periods (the sleep of the body) wherein which the soul receives education, information, and knowledge about a good number of pertinent and relevant things.

We need to understand that the reality of soul communion with other souls, be they incarnate in human flesh or not, is a constant human experience. Just because a portion of soul becomes entrapped within the temporary consciousness associated with the life of the body, does not mean that the portion of soul has lost all contact with greater reality. No contact is ever lost or broken. However, the temporary identity associated with the body does many times block out of conscious awareness any other realities or communications with them.

Normally higher entities should be able to commune with souls openly and regularly all the while that these souls are encased in physical bodies and the temporary identity established along with it. In other words, the body and its temporary identity should not be serving as hindrances or blocks to communication. Yet, this normal state of openness is exactly what gets lost. And as it does, the entities of the higher dimensions need to resort to other means of communication in order to get through to the entrapped soul. These other means are what we have come to know as angelic visitations.

Angelic visitations come in many different forms. Only some of them are recognized for what they are as they are happening. The case in point is that of the three visitors who appeared to Abraham (re. Ge. 18). The Rabbinic commentators reflected opposite opinions as to whether this encounter of Abraham's was either physical or "spiritual." Yet, what if it were both? What if this encounter occurred in parallel dimensions simultaneously? But in order for us to understand how these types of parallel realities transpire, I must elaborate some further points.

The Torah narrative makes it very clear that three very physical visitors came to see Abraham. Maimonides, true to his Aristotelian outlook, understood that this episode must be visionary, and not physical, simply because angels cannot become physical. Nachmanides made his opinion of Maimonides's view very clear when he stated, "*But such words contradict Scripture. It is forbidden to listen to them, all the more to believe in them!*" And this brings us back to where we began this essay.

As higher-dimensional beings whose apparent natural habitat seems to be in a hyper-light state, we may very well indeed be surprised to think that such beings can materialize into physical forms in this lower-dimension of physical space time. But why should we go so far as Aristotle and Maimonides to conclude that such a thing cannot happen? Maybe these two great minds of their times could not have conceived of the possibilities that today we can consider because of our expanded understanding of science and technology. We can consider that which they did not!

Higher-dimensional beings, however different that they be from us, are still not God. We do not consider higher-dimensional beings to be all-knowing, and ever-present. These attributes we ascribe only to God and not to any of His messengers. Granted, this may or may not be true, but in the presence of the lack of any evidence, we should never consider ascribing to created entities any force or power that we presently believe is exclusively the dominion of the Divine. What this means is that angels and other higher-dimensional beings still exist bound by whatever laws of physics that rule over the dimensional plane of their being.

As we have already mentioned, higher-dimensional human souls leave their hyper-light existence to become cloaked in physical bodies. This is the natural process of birth. However, human souls can also come to inhabit a physical body (usually of another) for a brief period of time. This is called an Ibbur wherein a human soul temporality inhabits a human body side-by-side with the body's host soul. This Ibbur soul comes and goes into and out of human bodies as needed and as directed by a higher-technology that we do not understand.

Thus hyper-light beings can and do enter and exit human forms on a regular basis. This same rule also applies to those entities whom we call angels. If we can enter and exit into physical forms, then so can they. But this conclusion only provides us with a possibility. There are also other possibilities that we must address.

Maimonides is convinced that higher-dimensional beings can only be met while one himself is in a state of higher consciousness. In such a state one acquires the ability to experience beyond the physical, and thus one can meet and greet there indigenous beings of that dimension. Thus for Maimonides, the visitation with Abraham must have been a vision, and could not have been anything else.

We have already learned that hyper-light beings have the technology which enables them to temporarily enter into our lower physical space-time dimension. Now here is an interesting idea to consider. All throughout our discussions, we have been describing angels as hyper-light beings who are indigenous to higher dimensions. We also need to consider whether or not this is entirely true.

As we saw from the Biblical narrative of the Sons of God coming to Earth and marrying human women (ref. Gen. 6) some angels must be totally physical. So, if the Sons of God referenced in Genesis 6 can be physical, then so too can the angels referenced in Genesis 18.

The only question that we can ask is about their natural, indigenous state prior to their presence on Earth. Is it possible that these angels (and thus all their species) are not non-corporeal beings at all? Is it possible that like many other extraterrestrial races out there, some angels are just as corporeal as we are?

What we know about angels only comes through our individual encounters with them. Those who commune with angels usually do so here on Earth (or near-by) in one sort or another of astral out-of-body form. In other words, we shift consciousness into our energetic bodies and then meet other energetic entities in a higher-dimensional energetic reality. But just like we human beings exist in physical forms, and these forms are our present indigenous forms, what can we say about those others whom we meet? Do they also have some indigenous form which they inhabit and put aside in order to meet with us in Vision?

Abraham met three men, who were angels. They sure looked like men, and acted like men. And yet we say that they were angels. We then say that after they finished their mission here on Earth that they returned to "Heaven" (wherever and whatever that may be). So, once they arrived back in Heaven, what forms do these angels exist in there?

In Heaven, are these angels non-corporeal hyper-light beings similar to human souls? Or is there a Heaven wherein which some angels are actually corporeal (in one form or another) similar to our present human forms? Being that there are many different species of angels and higher-dimensional beings, it is very possible that they can exist in a number of different parallel dimensional forms, on worlds that are (or are not) corporeal within any definition of the word.

We are left to reconsider the disagreement between Maimonides and Nachmanides. Maybe these extraterrestrial beings that we call angels are from a non-corporeal indigenous state which they temporarily leave in order to come here, or maybe it is we who leave our terrestrial abode to meet with these hyper-light beings in a higher dimensional plane. Or, maybe, just maybe, these beings (or some of them) may very well indeed by physical, just like us, and inhabit some form of physical body, just like us?

If this is the case, then maybe, if and when they may wish to interact with human beings from time to time, they too, just like us, may shift into an altered state consciousness inhabit an astral body, travel through hyper-space, and meet with other similar out-of-body entities equally engaging in astral travel. This last consideration would certainly fit the conceptions of both Maimonides and Nachmanides. These entities, which we call angels, could thus be corporeal and non-corporeal both at the same time, in a fashion not to dissimilar from ourselves.

These are all lovely speculations that we can add to our Aristotelian and Platonic considerations. Or, maybe better yet, we can practice the out-of-body techniques for achieving higher consciousness, project our minds out of body and go meet these entities in the higher planes, and ask them directly more about themselves, and their lifestyles.

We do believe that these entities are real and thus they are really there. Maybe we should not discuss these things anymore, but rather go find out for ourselves. Maybe they are waiting for us to do just this?

We will never know until we take that next step and reach out. Once they reach back to us, we will then have experience, and not just speculation. Then we will know with a knowledge that is knowing, and we will have taken a great leap forward in our human evolution. Maybe, this is not such a bad thing at all.

Chapter 3

Dybukkim, Shedim, & the Fallen Angels Among Us Today

"Demons are among us. They are possessing our souls! Be afraid! Be very afraid!"

Well, maybe not! Maybe these scary old ghoul-type demons conjured up by Hollywood are only as real as the silly movies in which they appear.

But I am sure that there are many out there who live their daily lives in fear of these other-dimensional beings, be they real or imagined.

So, let us address the issues of the reality of demons, and what is their real way of interaction with the human race.

First of all, according to almost every religious and spiritual tradition that I know of, demons are a very real race of beings with whom we share our planet Earth. Now, this statement alone, I know, will unnerve many of you, but it shouldn't. For once we understand a little more about demons, we will come to view them more as a race of intelligent, yet potentially dangerous beings who mind their own business in their own place, rather than as evil minions of the Devil out to cast our souls into Hell.

Each religious culture and tradition has its own understanding about malevolent spirits that inhabit our Earth. But these spirits are not necessarily demons. The understanding of demons embraced in the modern secular world has its origins in the teachings of the Catholic Church (think of the movie, The Exorcist). The view of the Church has been around for a long time and their views and ideas reach far beyond their own borders.

But the Torah understanding of demons is not so black-and-white simple as it is for the Church. Indeed, our brethren in Islam know of the demons (whom they call the Jinn) in a way very similar to our Torah.

The Talmud and peripheral Rabbinic literature is full of revelations and information about demons (Shedim). So, let no one say that belief in demons is relegated only to the Kabbalists, for this is not so. Torah-based rationalists since the days of Maimonides have wanted to dismiss the actual tangible reality of demons, but such an outright denial would put one into outright denial of our Talmud and our Rabbinic tradition. No true student of Torah would ever do such a thing. There are real Shedim, but for the most part, they are not what most people think them to be.

When we think of Shedim (and Jinn) we conjure up thoughts of evil ugly beings, who are the minions of the Satan, whose sole intent is to harm and torture naïve human souls. We think of Shedim as the ones who possess human beings (as portrayed in countless movies). But this is not accurate. Those entities that possess human beings are not Shedim at all. The spirits that possess human beings are called Dybukkim (from the root word, dybbuk, which means "to cling"). In reality, they are the disincarnate human souls of the dead that seek to enter into, and take control of the body of another living person in an attempt to take control of those bodies so as to coerce and manipulate their behaviors.

Dybukkim are the souls of the dead who are fleeing the afterlife and who are terrified to face their Heavenly judgement. They thus run away from the Angels of Judgement sent to retrieve them and seek to hide within the bodies of living human beings and to experience life all over again through them. Needless to say, such activity is considered a very serious spiritual crime. There is an entire group of Angels assigned to the task of hunting down these wayward souls and upon discovery to drag them into the afterlife, to face their just sentences.

For the most part Dybukkim go to great lengths so as to not appear as evil ugly monsters. They are most often malevolent, lost human souls whose intent it is to live again through their hosts. They do not seek to destroy their hosts, nor torment them. However, most Dybukkim are thrill seekers and unrepentant hedonists. They often compel their hosts to performs acts of wanton lust so as to experience those pleasures through them. We have often heard someone say that they don't know what led them to act in the certain way that they did. Sometimes wanton, reckless dangerous and immoral actions are not ones of personal choice but rather ones of compulsion from a hidden soul that possesses one.

Dybukkim almost always focus on hedonistic pleasures. They usually do not concern themselves with philosophical issues. In other words, a Dybbuk rarely engages its host in inner dialogue trying to get the host to adopt a different philosophy of life, or to convert to another religion. If any such inner dialogue was to occur it would be for the purpose of expanding opportunities of hedonist pleasures.

Almost all exorcisms are geared towards the removal of the disincarnate human soul who is fleeing judgment and hiding out in a naïve human host. Exorcisms of this kind can often be a frightening experience. To this day, these unfortunate events still occur. However, most authentic Kabbalist exorcists will never divulge personal experiences other than in the most general of ways. There are still a great number of secrets with regards to souls and the afterlife which most "in the know" agree should be kept secret.

About a hundred years ago, however, one Rabbi did lift the veil and wrote about his exorcism encounters. This Rabbi was R. Yehuda Fatiyah. His book, Minhat Yehuda, HaRuhot Mesaperot (the Spirits Speak), is available in English translation. I, myself, translated large selections of the text in 1993. Since my efforts, others have come forth and translated the entire book. It should be readily available for those interested in this topic. But be warned, such reading is not for the easily frightened.

Now that we have discussed Dybukkim and distinguished them from the Shedim, let us return to discuss the Shedim and discuss what it is that some of them actually do.

First and foremost we must declare that Shedim are not the Fallen Angels spoken of in Genesis 6. These Fallen Angels are another group that we will discuss shortly.

Shedim are a race of beings, created by God, who are indigenous to our Earth. They are an elder race to humanity and we share our Earth with them. Like human beings some of them are righteous and good, while others of them are wicked and evil. The righteous and good ones usually stay far away from human beings and rarely interact. The bad ones, however, are the ones with whom we need to contend.

Now, with this being said, we need to reveal that this Earth upon which we live is far grander and greater in scope than what meets our physical eye. Anyone with meditative or astral travel experience may have visited other realms right here on Earth that do not seem to exist anywhere here on Earth. This is no contradiction, neither is it a delusion. The fact is that there is more than one dimension of life right here on our Earth. Many different races share our Earth with us, but each inhabits its own relative dimension of time and space. And this may or may not include Inner Earth and the realms existing down there (be they in this dimension or parallel one).

In classical literature (Avot d'Rebbe Natan, and elsewhere), it is said that Shedim are like human beings in three ways, and like angels in three ways (as to which angels, reference is not made, nor is it important). Like angels, Shedim can (apparently) fly, be invisible, and know the future (for as much as 30 days to come). Like human beings, Shedim eat and drink, sexually procreate, and die. This description helps us draw some interesting conclusions about the actual nature of these created beings. It also arouses some concerns with regards to some modern-day issues associated with aliens and alien abductions.

Shedim give the appearance that they fly and that they can be invisible. Rather than subject these powers to myths and legend, let us understand them more scientifically. In order for real Shedim to act in this way, it will mean that they exist side-by-side with us in a higher, parallel dimension of space and time. They act in the ways that are normal and natural for that dimensional plane. Although they exist in their dimensional plane, they also have access to ours. They seem to have this access in an easy and natural way.

Human beings can also access the higher dimensional plane inhabited by the Shedim (and others), but this requires of the human advanced training in meditative practices that enables one to travel astrally outside the physical body, limited as it is to 3-dimensional space.

What is interesting to note is that Shedim procreate sexually. And we have a long history of documentation detailing numerous episodes of Shedim breeding with, and procreating with human beings. As strange as this may sound to some, it seems to happen so often that one may question just how irregular it really is.

For hundreds of years, Rabbinic Sages have written works documenting how Shedim sexually breed with human beings, and do so with great desire. Indeed we have documentation of human/Shed marriages, and in one such instance (recorded in the book, Kav HaYashar, 68-69) the hybrid offspring of such a union actually appears in a human court of law (Beit Din) to plead their case over a right of inheritance.

Human/Shed hybrids are said to be highly sought-after in the Shedim realm and are considered to be something like a noble class. When one reads in modern UFO literature about so-called alien-abductions, these patterns sound identical to those attributed in the past to Shedim. Maybe this association will help those who believe in aliens, but not in Shedim to finally become aware that the two are most likely one and the same.

For centuries Shedim have ran a breeding program to infiltrate themselves among human beings. While the ancient literature on this subject is there, it often goes untranslated, and thus unnoticed.

But there are authors today who have noticed the hybrid program, and the many hybrids amongst us. Authors like David M. Jacobs, and John E. Mack have covered this subject and have published some very interesting observations and conclusions, the likes of which most certainly do not contradict anything in Torah literature.

Whatever it is, and whoever is behind it, there does seem to be a hidden agenda by some higher dimensional beings to solidify their forms here in our 3-dimensional space-time. As to what this agenda may be, we will discuss shortly. However, there is more to this story. We have yet our third group of entities who are not Shedim, and who are not disincarnate human souls. These are the Fallen Angels (the Sons of God referenced in Genesis 6) who have become entrapped here on Earth. Let us now discuss them.

Genesis 6 speaks of a group of Angels who descended to Earth in the attempt to make this world a better place (at least from their own point of view). Unfortunately they themselves fell victim to the same crushing energy forces of physicality that compromises even the most spiritual of souls. Rather than remain fluid, balancing themselves between the higher and lower dimensional planes (as do the Shedim), these Angels, like Adam before them, became completely immersed in this physical dimension. They ended up succumbing to physical lusts and began to mate with human women. Their hybrid children (the Nephilim) thwarted and corrupted the natural order, turning the world into a sexually perverted and violent hell. The Bible relates to us what happened soon thereafter with the Flood of Noah.

So what happened to these Fallen Angels after the Flood? What happened to their children, the Nephilim? Where are they today? While the written Torah does not discuss the details of this, the Oral Torah does reveal the secrets.

The Fallen Angels were not human beings. Although they could take on human form, they were not bound to it. They existed in the same dimensional plane as do the Shedim. This is why many times (for many different reasons) one group is mistaken to be the other. But the Fallen Angels came down to Earth with good intent, despite being rebellious. The punishment of Heaven towards them was most fitting. Being that they came to help humanity, their punishment was that they would be forced to complete the job. They were sentenced to remain earth-bound until the ultimate repair (Tikun) of the Adamic race is complete.

Heaven established a special body of angelic governors who serve as the "Angelic Princes" over the nations (the lower Heavenly Sanhedrin). These Fallen Angels, who have not yet been able to re-ascend to Heaven serve as the spiritual Sanhedrin (court) that directs the course of nations. They receive their instructions from the Watcher Angels who in turn receive their instructions up through the chain of command directly from God.

And so the Princes of the nations, the original Fallen Angels reign over the affairs of humanity, all the while that God pursues His plan for the ultimate redemption of humanity.

Now, these Princes have not yet been able to realign themselves with Heaven's purified energy field. Therefore, they still suffer from some of the effects experienced by being subject to contact with the Earth's energy field. In other words, these Fallen Angels still do not act angelic.

It is well known (even from the Bible) that angels fight with one another. For example, in the Book of Daniel, we see that the angel Gabriel who was on a mission from God to bring Daniel an answer to his prayer, was stopped at the border of Persia (where Daniel lived) by Persia's angelic prince.

The Prince of Persia has jurisdiction over his domain, even to the point of being able to prevent entry to a visiting angel, even one with the stature of Gabriel. Gabriel had to return to Heaven and bring Michael along with him in order to contend with the angel of Persia. Michael, who some believe is actually a Metatron, overrode the Prince of Persia, something that Gabriel was not capable of doing.

So, to this day we have the Angelic Princes of the nations, who live side-by-side with the Shedim. Most likely these Fallen Angel Princes dominate the Shedim (for better or for worse) and use them however it is that they see fit. But just how far this

411

relationship goes we cannot say. What we can say is that both races share the same dimensional plane, and according to many sources, both inhabit Inner Earth.

It is interesting to consider the relationship of the Shedim breeding program, the hybrids born from it, and the alleged infiltration of large numbers of these hybrids in the present human population (just as it was in the generation of Noah). Ancient lore and modern UFO lore seem to overlap and merge into one. But are we talking about mere stories and legends or is there something more to all this? Are there really hybrid human/shedim living among us? How would we ever know? What would we look for? How would they be recognized? While modern UFO lore has no answer to these questions, ancient Kabbalistic teachings do have answers.

Unlike modern scientific models, ancient religious and spiritual traditions from around the world speak about the existence of the Soul. A Soul is simply the true energetic entity that lives within the shell of whatever body it inhabits. We human beings have a Soul. We have an Adamic Soul. The Adamic Soul resonates its own unique energy frequency and vibration. Other lifeforms each have their own level of soul, each with its own unique energy frequency and vibration.

Most of us today have lost all sensitivity to read or to feel the energy vibrational signatures of another. Nevertheless a remnant of this still exists in many. How many times have we met someone, or have gone somewhere and suddenly get a really bad feeling about the person or place? Some call this a "gut-instinct," but regardless of what it is called, the sensation received is quite real. Anyone experiencing such a sensation knows very well how true this is, regardless of the voices of others who may wish to be rational (in their own minds) and to dismiss such feelings as fantasy.

In ancient spiritual teachings taught throughout history around the world, students have been trained to become sensitive to these energetic signatures and to distinguish between one type and another. In Biblical times, we called this type of sight, "Ruah

HaKodesh" (Divine inspiration); today many call this clairvoyance. Descriptive names are not important, what is important is the cultivation of this refined insight that enables one to read energy signatures.

Angels, demons, normal people, people with a dybbuk, animals, extraterrestrials, each has their own unique energy signature. Regardless of the form of body they inhabit, one sensitive to energy signatures can see from a distance who is who within the physical body. Many today call energy signatures, Auras. Thus the clairvoyant read the Auras of people and can see within them almost a full "technical readout" of their soul, and the condition of the soul. Those who correctly and successfully perform "energy-healing" make use of this technique.

One frightening thing is clear. Not all human beings today have human souls. This is very clear to those with the clairvoyant eye. But even the rest of us can recognize non-human souls simply by looking at the behaviors, feelings, and thought-processes of a person.

Those who act cruelly towards animals (and most certainly towards other human beings) may very well be doing so because they lack a human soul. Also, we see a rising number of individuals who are not only non-religious, but actually anti-religious. We see a growing animosity towards anything related to God, Scripture, and traditional religion and moral values.

We see a growing hatred towards God and an equally growing adoration of the Satan, and the hedonistic negative world-outlook that it entails. Individuals of these orientations tend to have very shallow moral values, and are often a danger to others, and many times, even to themselves. They defy anything and everything sacred and holy and do so with joy and zeal. Individuals of these orientations emanate a "spirit" from them that few people fail to recognize.

When, however we seek to identify the soul origins of certain individuals, needless to say, we must be very cautious. There is no shortage of evil and wicked individuals out there who act with total disdain and disregard towards others, and towards life itself.

Such behaviors do indicate that one's energy signature may indeed be something other than human, but it is not proof positive. Great discretion is required to read human souls. Be it clairvoyance or Ruah HaKodesh, only the one with the psychic eye can truly recognize psychic things.

Human souls are created in the Image of God. As such, there is an inherent sense of morality and goodness within the soul. Now, granted, not everyone created in the Divine Image lives up to the lofty potential that lies within them. But there is still a big difference between those who do wrong due to weakness or confusion and those who chose to do wrong willingly and knowingly, in seeming defiance to all things right and good. These different types of individuals clearly emanate different types of auric energy signatures. While most cannot see them, many can sense or feel them.

Now, let us ask the unasked question. Why would Shedim, and alongside them Fallen Angels desire or want to merge with flesh and blood human beings? What advantage does being human offer to any of these other entities? What is their agenda? The answer to this is rather simple, although at the same time, it is rather diabolical.

Fallen Angels, who are now the Princes of the Nations, and Shedim each have their own individual agendas, which just so happen to overlap. Remember, each group live here on Earth, but in a slightly altered parallel dimensional state. Angelic Princes and Shedim both can and do take on physical human appearances and interact with humans all the time. But, for whatever reasons guided by the laws of physics that their original forms are subject to, they cannot maintain human forms for any long-term period. Apparently, their human manifestations are only temporary. Maybe it requires of them too much energy to maintain those forms for any length of time. So, in order to adjust this natural state of theirs, they seek human DNA. Thus the more human DNA that they have (through interbreeding) the more they are able to maintain a presence in this dimensional plane. And now, let us address why it is that they want to do this.

Our physical human forms enable us to experience a wide variety of sensations. We are all aware of the levels of intense pleasure that can be received through numerous forms of physical activities. These include the usage of narcotics and alcohol, sexual promiscuity, and all other forms of behaviors that cause chemical secretions in the human brain that create pleasure.

The physical human body has been designed to experience these things. But apparently, the original form of the bodies of the Fallen Angels, alongside the original form of the bodies of the Shedim did not have such chemical receptors in their brains. Thus they could observe the pleasure responses in human beings but they were not able to experience them for themselves. Even when they took upon themselves a temporary human form, this only enabled them to have a temporary and limited experience of human pleasures.

Essentially, these races were jealous of the human ability to experience sensations. As we know our experience of sensations occur due to chemical reactions in the human brain. Is it then a surprise to us when we hear of alien abduction stories that speak about sexual experimentation and the specific removal of certain chemicals from either the human brain or body. Whoever is performing these "abductions" is clearly looking for something specific. And as wise King Solomon said, "there is nothing new under the sun."

The Fallen Angels and those Shedim who have joined their cause have been pursuing this research for thousands of years. It is only in modern times that we human beings are beginning to understand that there really is a rhyme and reason to all the ancient stories about demonic abductions, human sacrifice to "demons" and all other similar accounts. Throughout the centuries (and even in recent modern times with the operation of the Nazi death camps), willing human beings have been participating with these other races to "feed them" human lives.

Human souls and human bodies are joined together by the universal energy field. This field goes by many different names, such as Nefesh, Hiyuli, Qi, Orgone, Prana, Kundalini, Shekhina, and now (I believe) Zero-Point energy. This is the Life Force of the universe. It is also the universal commodity of value. Consider it to be the money of the universe. In order for a human soul to inhabit a human body a certain amount of Life Force energy must be drawn in by the two in order to merge them into one. This merger them becomes a living and vibrant human being.

The original bodies of Fallen Angels and Shedim could not absorb this Life Force energy in such a pure and unadulterated state. They therefore needed to water it down in order to be able to use it. By influencing human behaviors to be more in alignment with the direction and compulsions that the Fallen Angels and certain Shedim can place within human minds, human life force energy becomes diluted and thus consumable to these other races.

The weakened life force is then conserved and used to construct more permanent human bodies, within which these other races can inhabit. This is what has been behind the hybrid breeding program since its inception. According to the Torah, the breeding program began long before the coming to Earth of the Fallen Angels in Genesis 6. Some Shedim began this program when they first influenced Kain to kill his brother Abel. The original realignment began with Kain's soul. This is what led to the almost total loss of his genetic progeny. Of course, some did survive the flood and prospered afterwards, but not on the face of this Earth, (but this is a topic for another time).

To become human so as to experience human sensations in full, this has been the obsession of these other races for a very long time. But we should not conclude that this is their only agenda.

Remember, the Fallen Angels are the Princes of the Nations. They are here under Divine command to guide the course of humanity to the good goal of righteous and moral behavior. They cannot fulfill their mission if and when humanity (or those appearing to be human) are all acting wantonly with violence and out of control hedonism.

No, those who are out of control must be brought under control. And this is where the hybrid breeding program takes its last step. These Princes of the Nations and those Shedim serving under them have sought to manipulate human beings, both genetically through their breeding program, and socially through their infiltration of human society. The end purpose of this program is to remove independent free will from the hearts and minds of human beings. Their goal is to create a race of docile human beings, who will do what they are told. In this way the Princes of the Nations can turn to God and proclaim, "behold, we have brought peace to Earth, and unity to humanity."

Of course, the cost of all this is the perennial imprisonment of the very human (Adamic) soul sent here in the first place to accomplish all these things. But the Fallen Angels want it this way to prove to Heaven that the only good and docile human beings are the ones who are not fully human by Divine standards. Of course, this is not the Divine plan. And so the Fallen Angel plan and the Divine plan are at odds with one another.

Righteous and moral human beings, who stand by their faith and belief in God and their respective religions, try to maintain a lifestyle of independence and morality outside of the influence of our Earthly Overlords. And so there is ever growing conflict between those who serve the plan of the Fallen Angel Overlords and those who still stubbornly cling to God. And so, we have the setup for the final battle of Good versus Evil, the likes of which has been written about and prophesied for many thousands of years.

So, here we are, living in a multidimensional reality. We human beings are normally only aware of a single dimensional reality. Other races of this Earth, living side by side with us exist in the higher dimensions alongside this one. As such these higher dimensional entities can enter and exit our dimension at will. Their entrance or exit appears to us as if they instantly appear out of nowhere and then dematerialize back into nothingness. This is only our perception because we do not have the consciousness nor the sensory apparatus built into us to see the higher dimensions.

These higher dimensional beings recognize that human souls have a great life force energy source packed into them. They also know present human limitations. Therefore, for the most part, these higher dimensional entities look at human beings as a lower life form, and as a food source, corralled and ready to be harvested.

The Fallen Angels and their Shedim cohorts have an agenda. They are seeking the maintenance of their own races, while at the same time, keeping humanity under control for their own personal benefits and usages.

Above the Fallen Angels in the chain of command are the Watchers. As Watchers their job is to observe, not to engage. They see what the Princes of the Nations do, but they do not judge; that is not their job. Yet, at the appointed times the Watchers give their reports to the authorities above them, and Judgement is ordained only by God Himself.

God watches humanity and equally God watches the activities of the Shedim, the Fallen Angels, and anyone else who gets involved with "Experiment Earth." God observes how individual human beings respond to the numerous choices and decisions that are placed daily before them. We are judged by our actions and our choices.

Throughout human history there have always been infiltrators, non-human souls who inhabit human bodies, who then rise to positions of power, and in turn wreak havoc upon humanity in all too many ways. We can recognize them as the perpetrators of wanton violence, depravity, hatred, and cruelty. These behaviors alongside rampant hedonism, which is an uncontrollable obsession with physical sensations, thrills, and pleasures, are good markers to identify foreign souls concealed within human bodies.

So, what is one supposed to do with the information revealed herein? For the most part, this information is academic in nature. It is meant to be informative and that's all. But for some others the insights revealed herein might inspire one to make every effort to live a moral and righteous life.

In the days of Noah, God sent a flood over the Earth to remove the contamination of the hybridization common in those days. Prophecy states that in the days before the coming of Mashiah, there will be many great battles. Yet, the greatest of battles is the internal individual struggle wherein each human being must decide to which influence he will succumb.

Each human being must decide if one desires to identify and associate with one's spiritual origins, or with the new image and identity that the forces of the Other Side (Sitra Ahra) have in store for the human race.

God allows this scenario to play out. God sees all the non-humans in human bodies who blaspheme Him daily. God doesn't care about the petty behaviors of wayward non-human souls. Those incarnate into human beings who do not belong here will be returned to their places of origin, just as it was done in the aftermath of the Great Flood in the days of Noah.

In the meantime, we each see the culture war raging around us. We are falsely led to believe that it is a war between two social factions with different political visions. But the present war is far more than this. It is a war between the Heavenly forces themselves. It is a war between good and evil, between human souls, and non-human souls.

This insight should not come as a shock to anyone. It should be clear and evident. Those who hate God, His Word, and His Way rebel against these things with great joy and pleasure. They revel in their new human forms hoping to subdue all humanity to their whims and ways. And God watches to see who will succumb, and who will stand strong.

A new flood of cleansing will soon come to cleanse the Earth again. Life on Earth must spiritually evolve and progress onto its next stage of existence. We call this the Messianic Age. This present period of testing here in Schoolhouse Earth will determine who gets promoted into the Messianic Age, and who will be left back, to start life from scratch all over again on some distant foreign world.

Chapter 4

Identifying the Fallen Primordial Kings & their Agenda in Modern Times
(The Queens of SAG d'SAG)

To understand the present, one must understand the past. The turmoil and trouble that our society faces today had its origins long ago in the prehistoric past. We must return to the beginning to understand the present. Only in this way will we be able to foresee the future and take the necessary steps to safeguard ourselves.

Long before the Fallen Angels, and long before the Nephilim, there were the fallen Primordial "Kings" who "reigned in the Land of Edom prior to there being a King in Israel." Our history begins here.

These fallen "Kings" were the ones responsible for the original Shattering of the primordial Vessels, elaborated upon in depth in the Kabbalah of the Ari'zal. The existence of these "Kings" is not just as a literary metaphor. The ancient primordial "Kings" were/are real. Indeed, to this day, they clandestinely move their concealed hand, and bring havoc and destruction to our world, even as they brought to their own.

The true meaning (and identity) of just who are these fallen "Kings" needs to be clarified and understood.

First and foremost it must be stated and clearly understood that the fallen "Kings" as is made clear in the writings of the Ari'zal were actually the fallen "Queens."

The Shattering of the Vessels which gave rise to the Klipot (domains of evil) happened in the realm of the Supernal Female (the Sag d'Sag d'AK). Thus, the primordial worlds and the pre-Adamic civilizations that arose under the influence of these "Kings" were all Female dominant. They were all Matriarchal societies.

Although R. Vital, the redactor of the Torah of the Ari'zal, did not believe in the physicality of these primordial worlds, almost all the other Kabbalists, including R. Vital's own students, did believe them to be physical. And in light of modern archeological evidence from around the world, it appears that the majority of the Kabbalists were correct.

Therefore the spiritual Kabbalah of the Ari'zal needs to be understood in alignment with the Kabbalah that reveals to us the reality of the physical pre-Adamic civilizations (Malkhut d'Malkhut, or BEN d'BEN).

It should thus be clear to us that Atlantis, Lemuria, and the other very physical pre-Adamic civilizations (here on Earth) from the previous Shemitah (cosmic time period) were all Matriarchal societies. They were all reflections of the fallen feminine SAG of AK. (I discuss many of the details of the Kabbalah of the Ari'zal in my book, The Evolution of God. Interested readers should consult there for further, deeper information).

Ancient history aside, what makes this information relevant today is that the source of the chaos and confusion in modern society is due to nothing other than the resurrection of the ancient imbalance that has returned and which dwells among us with its own nefarious plans.

The ancient Darkness has revived right before our eyes. The fallen "Kings" (Queens) have returned and have executed their plan to return to dominance. And the majority of people remain blind to all this because they do not know what it is that they are looking at.

The true psychic psychological cause of human suffering is well discussed in the Torah of the Ari'zal. However, the language of the Ari'zal's Kabbalah is most cryptic. All too many students study the words of the texts without ever grasping their full meaning, or seeing the ramifications of their practical applications. Those who study abstracts never seem to grasp the concrete. But due to present threats, we can no longer remain so disconnected and in the dark.

Darkness comes before the Light. This is a clear Biblical teaching from the opening verses in Genesis. The Ari'zal's Kabbalah teaches the same thing.

The Primordial Light that would shine forth from the Eyes of Adam Kadmon was the Light of the expression of the Nikudot (of the TaNT'A) of SAG (of AK). The Nikudot represent the second of the four worlds, Beriah, which itself is a female expression. The Name SAG (63) also represents the second world Beriah. Thus the Light that came forth from the Eyes of Adam Kadmon was a feminine Light; it was the feminine of the feminine. It is the Source of the first Hey in the holy Name YHWH.

It is this Source above that gave birth to each of the Seven Kings. Emanating originally as SAG, and from SAG, each of the seven "Kings" should rightfully be referred to in the Feminine, and thus as "Queens" instead of "Kings."

The primordial Shattering of the Vessels occurred because the seven lower vessels (HaGaT NaHiY'M) of (the female) SAG were not properly aligned with their Source, which is the Upper Lights (SAG, MAH, BEN of the Ta'amim of SAG), which are the A'HaF of AK. These are the Lights of the Ears, Nose and Mouth of Adam Kadmon. (Remember, all references to the Supernal Man, AK, and to the body parts thereof are all symbolic representations of psychic psychological realities).

The Ears (Ozen), Nose (Hotem) and Mouth (Peh) of AK (Adam Kadmon) originally manifested the primordial Light of the Ten Sefirot, prior to their being differentiated into individual and unique Sefirotic identities and personalities.

The Ears of Adam Kadmon was the Source of the initial revelation of the concealed Primordial Light within AK. The Light then proceeded to manifest through the Nose, and finally from the Mouth. But the Ears was the original Source of the manifest Light.

As the Lights of the Eyes came forth, the Keter, Hokhma and Binah of the SAG knew and understood their place. Male and Female emanated in proper polarity and were thus correctly aligned. The Supernal Mind emanated intact.

When however it came time to manifest the lower Seven Sefirot of the SAG, it is said that they (the lower Seven) could not connect to the original Source of the Light emanating from the Ear. Essentially, the Seven could not, or would not listen to the Voice of the Ear. They could not see it, nor hear it. As such the pattern of the emanated triad of Keter, Hokhma, and Binah of the Eyes was not seen, nor heard.

The lower Seven Sefirot of the SAG embraced the fullness of emotion and at the same time blocked out all contact with the balance and harmony of the balanced Supernal Mind. This embrace of emotion disconnected from a proper, clear, and lucid mind caused the misalignment of the lower Seven, which then led to their shattering and fall.

And so as each of the Seven lower Sefirot of SAG came forth from the Eyes of AK, the cryptic language reveals that the pattern of their emanation was flawed from the outset.

The Seven lower Sefirot rule the domain of heart and emotions. In order for emotions to be maintained in balance they must manifest in proper harmony and alignment with the forces that we know as male and female. In Kabbalah, male and female are referred to as MAH and BEN, but most people today are aware of this primordial reality under the name given to it from the Orient, this being Yin and Yang.

These lower Seven Sefirot of SAG that shattered and fell, were all female. They did not manifest their male counterpart. They had no MAH component to balance them (no Yang to complete Yin). As such instead of emanating aligned in columns (right and left), the Seven emanated one on top of one another in a straight line.

This rigid form of dominant female expression denied and repressed their male counterpart. As such when the Supernal Light of the Absolute Creator (Ayn Sof) entered into these vessels of the Seven lower Sefirot, the vessels, being imbalanced and out of alignment, were incapable of receiving the Divine Light (which Itself is always Male dominant). The Light was too powerful, too strong for the female vessels to embrace. Because they were not in balance with a male counterpart all Seven lower Sefirot were forced to express dominant female (SAG) characteristics. And this is why the vessels shattered and why the "Kings" (Queens) died.

Know now and understand the great mystery! What the Kabbalah reveals to us is not a lesson in history. These events are not something that happened long ago in time. The imbalance and the shattering of the vessels, and the fall of the Primordial Kings (Queens) is a psychic, psychological event that repeats itself continuously in the minds and souls of every human being. The Shattering of the Vessels and the Fall of the Primordial Kings is happening right now, in the lives of so many people around the world who fail to align with the Supernal Mind.

Fallen souls fall specifically because they allow their emotions to dominate and lead their lives blocking out the natural balance of the Supernal Mind which itself is the Source of every human mind (soul).

The primordial Kings (Queens) is a state of psychic psychological imbalance that was embraced and personified by the souls of the political, spiritual, and social leadership in pre-Adamic times. Their souls are not Adamic! Although these souls mingle with human souls to create hybrids amongst us, they are nevertheless not Adamic. This is why they seek to restore the form and values of the fallen society in which they lived.

But the ancient society was not destroyed by accident or due to natural causes. The pre-Adamic civilization was destroyed because of the behaviors and the consequences thereof of the people who lived then. The ancient Matriarchal society was notoriously anti-male. The ancient Matriarchal society was almost totally emotionally based, viewing rationality as a male-form of thinking which was to be shunned. Because they were so out-of-sync with the primordial Supernal Male, this is what led to their collapse.

To correct the primordial Shattering of the Vessels of the Matriarchal society of the pre-Adamics, God brought in a Rectifier from the outside. This was Adam (the MAH). Adam is both male and female, but in proper alignment and balance with one another.

Adam was then brought to Earth with the intent of gathering up the sparks of Light that became entrapped within the shards of the Shattered Vessels. Adam was to be dominant, and the remnant of the Matriarchy would be subservient to his lead. As such Adam was to be the male, to the pre-Adamics being the female. The Kabbalah of the Ari'zal called this the Yihud of MAH (Adam) and BEN. The BEN, spoken of here, is Malkhut. But Malkhut was not always Malkhut. She was at first Binah, the upper Hey of YHWH. Only with the Shattering of the Vessels, and the fall was she toppled and became the lower Hey of YHWH under (and subservient to) the Vav (MAH-Adam).

Originally, Adam was from a foreign (higher) dimension, which itself is an expression of YHWH Himself for the lower worlds. Adam was to rectify the broken world outside of Eden. Eden was his training ground. But the pre-Adamics resented having a new order imposed upon them. They were resentful and resisted this new male oriented world, and they were determined to do something about it.

One of the wisest and strongest of the pre-Adamics, one who knew how to lie, and to manipulate, was sent to infiltrate Eden. This enchanter, this Nahash (serpent), naturally approached Eve the female and performed his (her?) bewitchery upon her. Eve then toppled Adam, and then the two, equally and side-by-side, were cast out of Eden and onto the face of the Earth to work long and hard so as to accomplish their mission here on Earth. Thus we have the Kabbalistic history of our world.

The story recorded in Genesis happened a long time ago. But the struggle between the pre-Adamics and the Adamics continues to this day. The struggle will soon reach its peak and then the final Tikkun (rectification) will manifest, bringing harmony, alignment, and peace to our world and to the universe. MAH and BEN will be rebalanced. And BEN will return to Her rightful place as SAG, only now fully rectified. This is the secret of the verse in Zechariah (14:9), *"on that day will (Yihyeh) YHWH be One, and His Name One."*

But until the ultimate End comes, we have a struggle on our hands, with the souls of the pre-Adamics who are now comfortably fully cloaked within Adamic bodies. For millennia the pre-Adamics ran their breeding program to create better and better human hybrids. Only in this last century have they finally succeeded in creating the perfect hybrid.

Now these hybrids are everywhere in positions of power and influence. And the only way to recognize them is through their energy signatures. And this is why the hybrids, disguised in human form, have for many centuries now, been the ones leading the charge to root out of civilized society any acceptance of, or tolerance towards the development of latent human psychic abilities. The less who can see them, the more that they can go unnoticed, and be free to pursue their nefarious plans.

Today, so many precious few know how to see or read energy signatures, thus the hybrids walk unnoticed amongst us. They are the ones who taught us to repeatedly tell the big lie until everyone comes to accept it as truth. Their plans, to date, have worked out, all in accordance to the Divine plan. Today, we hear of all sorts of stories about aliens and alien abductions. Little does anyone suspect just who these real "aliens" actually are. They are not from Outer Space, they are from a place much closer to home.

Hybrids, those with the souls of the fallen "Kings" (Queens) can still be identified by their behaviors. This is clearly documented in the Zohar (1, 25a), only there they are called the Erev Rav (the mixed multitude). In brief here are some tell-tale behavioral signs that we can watch for, to help us identify them.

All of them have a "knee-jerk" vindictive hatred towards anything Biblical, and especially anything Patriarchal. They despise Biblical morality, especially anything to do with business honesty, and sexual modesty. This is why they are the foremost outspoken proponents for atheism, paganism, and any sort of new world order that completely and totally replaces a world order with anything Biblical in it. They essentially want to remove the Adamic presence and influence from Earth, and to restore things to the way they were 14000+ years ago before the disaster that destroyed their civilization.

Their method of operation today is the same as it was in the past. They totally deny God as an authoritative Dominant, who is to be feared (as declared in the Bible). They equally seek to block any real contact with the collective higher rational Self (their Source in Binah), this is why they make every effort to block all types of real psychic growth.

They manipulate and persuade people and things emotionally. They compel people to act without thinking. They forcefully seek the restoration of the ancient Matriarchy and the suppression and repression of anything male-dominant. They are the ones who coined the phrase "toxic-masculinity." They are the ones who seek to corrupt men by confusing their sexual identities, all in an attempt to destroy "manhood" (the MAH of YHWH).

They convince people that the only true god to worship is self-indulgence and pleasure. They teach others to crave and pursue intensely pleasurable physical sensations, thus creating an addiction for more and more stimuli (this leads to the growth of perversions). They are very big hedonists, who because they deny the supernal world seek every extra pleasure that this physical world can provide. Needless to say these pursuits after pleasure lead to all sorts of perverted abusive behaviors.

These are the behavioral results of the Shattering of the Vessels. Without proper alignment with the proper Supernal Pattern of creation, these hybrid souls run amuck on Earth creating havoc and destruction.

God has His plan. God tolerates the imbalance for a while, for out of it will come balance. We know what prophecies say. We know that once all the Sparks of Holiness have been sifted out of the Fallen Kings (Queens), they will no longer have anything upon which to feed. At that time, they will fade away for good.

We are not yet at the End, but it is coming closer. We see this with everything happening all around us. And just as the one side speeds up its agenda of domination and destruction, so does the Light increase so as to offer an alternate for those who seek it and who are willing to embrace it.

And so now you can identify the resurrected Fallen Primordial Kings & their agenda in our times. And if you are paying attention, you already know what you can do about it.

Chapter 5

About Demons

1

Remember!

Shedim always come disguised as angels of light.
They deceive one with words of love and life
and in the end deliver only hatred and death!
They come to steal your souls!
Torah warns us to stay faithful to the Word of God,
and to shun everything
that tries to persuade against it.
Beware!
Many are the deceived who do not know that they are deceived!

2

How can one tell the difference between an authentic angel of light,
and a demon disguised as one?
Know these things:

An angel of light does not lie to you.
An angel of light will refuse to appear to you all the while that you
are not holy enough to receive it.
The angel fills your mind with the awe and fear of God.
The angel encourages you to repent and to serve God and to obey
His commandments.

On the other hand:

A demon always lies to you.

A demon disguised as an angel comes to anyone, and fills one with messages of acceptance and love.

The demon lies to you, and tells you that you are okay, when you are far from okay in the eyes of God.

The demon fills your mind with feelings of love and acceptance. The demon tells you to be spiritual and that there is no need for organized religion.

The demon convinces you that rebellion against the Word of God is being true to God.

But the god of the demon is the Satan; Satan is its master, and the demon seeks to make you subservient to his master.

To the demon, all human souls are food! They seek to control your thoughts and feelings so as to control your actions. In this way they can feed off of you as they desire. And all the while you believe that you are growing spiritual, when in truth you are sinking deeper and deeper into the depths of uncleanliness.

What I tell you now are uncomfortable truths!

Many today are servants of demons and slaves to the Satan, and they do not have a clue about the subservience of their own souls to the forces of evil.

Only obedience to the Law of God gives one strength to resist demonic deceptions.

Only subservience to God offers any protection against the evil of soul snatchers!

Fear God! Follow His Torah! Stay clear of spirituality that disconnects one from the revealed Word of God from Sinai!

There are many demons around, they disguise themselves in all shapes and sizes; they proliferate especially on social media.

Guard your souls by following these rules. Keep yourselves safe.

And remember! Greater ones than you have been deceived and have fallen!

Guard your souls for true! May the protection of God and His Torah be with you.

3

*"Does the LORD delight in burnt offerings and sacrifices
as much as in obedience to the LORD's command?
Surely, obedience is better than sacrifice,
compliance than the fat of rams."*

1 Samuel 15:22 (JPS, 1985)

Obedience and compliance!
Get it?
This is the Way of HaShem and His Torah.
Do not accept any imitations!
One who does not uphold the codes of righteousness & morality,
as outlined by HaShem in His Torah,
simply has no portion in either HaShem or His Torah.
This should not be controversial!
It should be common sense!

4

In the beginning God created the Heavens and the Earth.
Everything was created by God, and all Laws are ordained by Him.
God has ordained what is moral and immoral,
and what is right and wrong.
God alone decides what is right and good,
and what is wrong and evil.
God's Laws and God's Word are one; this is the Torah.
Torah declares God's Word and God's Will.
Torah declares what is right, good, and Godly,
and what is wrong, evil, and demonic.
The wise submit to God and obey the Divine Will.
The fool rejects the authority of God
and obeys one's own misguided thoughts and desires.
The wise are blessed by God.
The fool is cursed by God.
There is no shortage of fools; there is no shortage
of evil declaring itself to be good.
The righteous live by God's Law.
One cannot be righteous in the Eyes of God,

all the while that one rejects the Divine Law.
Repentance – returning to God in humble submission
to the Divine Will and Divine Law
is the only way to avoid the Divine curse
and the suffering and judgment that is to come.
The cursed fool mocks and blasphemes,
continuing in one's evil ways.
Do not mistake Divine patience
for a lack of the Divine Presence.
Every day we pray for the judgment
of those who violate the Law of God.
We show no remorse when Divine Judgment is executed.
Instead we say, Barukh Dayan HaEmet,
Blessed is the True Judge.
Let those who rebel take heed and repent, while there still is time.

For your salvation, dear God, we await, amen!

Chapter 6

The Teachings of
Rabbi Yehuda Fatiyah of Yerushalayim:
Demonic Activity in Modern Times

Introduction

Every now and then a person non-observant in the ways of our Torah asks me: "How come we do not see miracles today, as there were in Biblical times?" My answer is always the same; I tell them that they are not looking in the right place to see the modern day miracles. They ask me where they should be looking; I point them to Rabbi Yehuda Fatiyah.

Born in Baghdad in 1859, Rabbi Fatiyah rose up to be the foremost student of the Ben Ish Hai. He had said regarding himself that he was the reincarnation of Rabbi Yehuda Landau, a great Ashkenazic halakhist, author of the responsa Nodah B'Yehuda.

Rabbi Fatiyah said that he had to come back to Earth, for although in his previous lifetime he was a great sage and pious man, he did not fulfill his Torah obligation to study Kabbalah. So in this life, the study of Kabbalah was his main focus and tikkun (rectification).

Amongst his many works, which include multiple commentaries to the holy Zohar and the Etz Haim, Rabbi Yehuda authored Minhat Yehuda. In it, in Parashat Yehezkel, Rabbi Yehuda writes of his experiences with earthbound souls, and the exorcisms he performed.

Even among Kabbalists this was not the norm; Rabbi Yehuda was a step above the rest. My own teacher, HaRav Meir Levi zt'l told me that when he was a child he had met Rabbi Yehuda, and when Rabbi Yehuda cast his eyes upon him he ran out of the room. I asked Rabbi Meir why he had run; he responded that he was afraid, because Rabbi Yehuda's eyes were so intense.

The most important and famous episode regarding Rabbi Yehuda was his involvement with the infamous Circle of Blood.

According to the August 14, 1987 issue of the Jerusalem Post Magazine, Rabbi Yehuda persuaded the British Command in the Land of Israel to give him and two others the use of a plane and a pilot. He instructed the pilot to fly a large circle completely around Israel (including parts of Egypt) while Rabbi Yehuda performed "kapparot" – the traditional slaughtering of a chicken performed prior to Yom Kippur, the blood of the chickens being thrown out of the plane. Rabbi Yehuda thus made a Circle of Blood surrounding Israel.

While some might think this the act of a desperate man, it seemed to have served its purpose. The author of the article quotes the pilot of the plane as saying: *"Shortly afterwards, Rommel attacked and the lads in the mess used to kid us. 'Fat lot of good those chickens of yours have done', they said...but they were wrong. It was Rommel's last fling. Three weeks later came Monty's advance from El Alamein. The rest is history...Mind you, I wouldn't have believed it had I not flown the mission myself."*

Do not underestimate the power of a Kabbalist, especially one of the caliber of Rabbi Yehuda Fatiyah. His students and his students' students teach in Jerusalem to this day. Rabbi Yehuda Fatiyah ascended above on the 27th of Av, 5702.

Here is a selection from the works of Rabbi Yehuda Fatiyah.

The Difference Between Dreams
that Come from Angels & that Come from Demons.
A True Story of Demonic Deception & Influence.

Sefer Minhat Yehuda (Parashat Miqetz 47)

"And in the morning, his soul was agitated." (Ber.41:8). This infers that his soul was not agitated in his dream as he slept, but only in the morning when he awoke and contemplated the meaning of his dream. Then was he deeply troubled from within.

We find a similar case with regards to Nebuchadnezzar and his dream, where it says (Dan.2:1), "His soul was troubled and his sleep left him." For he was awakened from his sleep by his dream, and his soul was troubled within him. He could not return to sleep.

This then is the way of a true dream that comes through an angel. One's soul is not troubled while one sleeps when seeing the dream, only after one has awoken. The reason for this is that it is not God's desire to frighten a person or cause one trouble while that one sleeps. [A dream comes] specifically to make one aware of what [Heavenly] edicts have been made concerning oneself or others. This is so that one may make efforts to rectify their sins. If so, why then should one be bothered while one sleeps?

This is similar to the prophecy that Isaiah spoke to Hezekiah, King of Yehuda, that he would die, and not live (2 Kings 20:1). Our sages have said [regarding this episode] that [Hezekiah] would die in this world, and not live in the world to come. He asked [Isaiah] why. [Isaiah] answers because you did not marry and beget children. [Hezekiah] responds, if so, let me marry your daughter. Isaiah says that it is too late for that, the edict has already been issued. Hezekiah says Isaiah, Son of Amotz, silence your prophecy and leave. For I have received from the House of my father's father [King David], that even if a sword is dangling over a man's throat, he should never stop awaiting [God's] mercy. For if the edict has already been issued, and there is no more hope, why then did God send you to me? You do have good news to tell me.

Thus, it is with a bad dream that is shown to a man through an angel. For were it not possible to nullify the edict by one's prayers, fasting, and charity, as well as one's repentance for what one has done, why then would the person be shown the dream at all? This is what our sages have taught [Ber. 55A] regarding the verse, "God has done this, so that you will be in awe of Him" [Koh. 3:14]. This refers to [showing one] a bad dream, so that one will be in awe of God. This being so, why should the dreamer be disturbed while he sleeps?

This then is the rule: The dream that comes through an angel will be neatly arranged. It will not be a mixture of conflicting matters. It also will not be fearful and terrorizing at the time of the dream. More than this [while within the dream] one will see oneself as if one were completely awake. If all these conditions have been met regarding a dream, know for sure that the dream is true, and that it has come from an angel, and that this is a 1/60 portion of prophecy [Ber. 57B.]

However, the dream that comes through a demon has another way to it. The demon stands next to the person while he sleeps a light sleep, and whispers in his ear frightening things, and fragments of things from various subjects. These things trouble the person's mind and make him afraid. His heart beats faster, and he awakens because of the heightened fear.

These demons remain standing there [at the person's side], and rejoice and laugh at him in that they were able to frighten him. When the person returns to sleep, they in turn bother [the person] all over again. They continually repeat this. No man will escape this until he repeats the bedtime Shema prayers.

There is also another way. When the person is awakened, he should say, **"Tameh Tameh Barah Lakh M'kan"** [unclean one, unclean one, be banished from here]. Say this three times. Then the demon will leave, and the person will rest securely. If one has an enemy then he should say, **"Tameh Tameh Barah Lakh M'kan V'lekh Etzel Ploni Ben Ploni V'hav'hi'lehu"** [unclean one, unclean one, be banished from here, and go to the home of so and so, and bother him]. The demon will then do whatever he is commanded.

If you wish to experiment with this, whisper in the ear of a young child while he is sleeping a light sleep, and say to him I have bought you all kinds of sweet candies, and I have placed them in this box nearby. When the child awakens from his sleep, he will ask about the candies, and where they are. This is what is written in Sefer Hasidim 135 and 441.

Therefore most dreams that are frightening and disturbing usually occur when a person is in a light state of sleep, such as at the beginning of one's sleep, or at its end when one is about to awaken, for only then is the brain able to receive those [demonic] images, and not when the person is deep asleep.

Know, that even if one recites the bedtime Shema Israel prayers prior to sleep, if one is awakened from one's sleep by a crying baby, or for whatever reason and then returns to sleep, the demons can then have sway over him, to frighten and disturb his sleep with frightening images. One must recite again the Shema Yisrael prayer a second time. One must at least recite the first verse and Baruch Shem, as it is written in Sha'ar HaPesukim, Shir HaShirim on the verse, "I sleep" [SOS 5:2].

Also know, if a person has a demon bonded to them through sexual immorality, they [the demons] then have the power to breach the fence of the reading the Shema so as to fulfill their desires [through the person]. The regular reading of the bedtime Shema will therefore not be affective. One will have to read it with great devotion, word by word.

I will also reveal to you now new things. The demons have learned about the things that mankind cares about, and show them to people in their dreams. For example, one who sees [in a dream] that his tooth has fallen out, or that a cow is slaughtered before him, or that one is fasting, or wearing black garments, or going barefoot etc..., a person [should no longer] be concerned about these [types] of dreams, with the exception if one is called up to the Torah by name. Even so, the one who is not concerned will receive a blessing.

Sometimes the demons show people bad things. If that person is a fool and believes these dreams, then the demons [themselves] bring the evil of the dream into physical reality, in order to fulfill the dream. [In this way the dreamer] learns to believe in his dreams. Sometimes when a Voice is heard proclaiming [a proclamation] in Heaven about some evil that is to come, [the demons] reveal this to a person in his dreams in order that the person will come to believe in his dreams.

Now this person needs to know that if he fasts over these dreams, or makes atonement or offers charity, and doesn't ask a Rabbi who knows how to differentiate between dreams that come through angels and those that come through demons, know for sure that this person will be destined to see horrible and evil dreams. For the demons rejoice that they did not work for naught over this person. These demons are called, "Shedim Nukhrain" (Gentile demons), who teach evil.

There are other demons who are called, "Shedim Yehudain" (Jewish demons) (Zohar, Bamidbar 253A). These have a different way about them. They make themselves appear as the ancient [Biblical] prophets, or as the Talmudic sages. There are those who make themselves appear as the judges of Israel and as great famous rabbis who have passed on to the other side. They all appear with great beards and crowns upon their heads, like the righteous and the pious. Sometimes they say that they are Abraham, Isaac, or Jacob, or Elijah the prophet or the like. One must be careful to ask them directly if they are the Biblical patriarchs [themselves] or if they just have the same names. Thus, you must also ask of Elijah. You must be very analytical regarding any answer [these demons] give you. For many a time they give an answer that is not exactly clear. If their answers are not clear, know that they are demons.

[These demons] can do even greater things than this. They can show to a person the image of the heavens, the image of the throne of glory, and the angels of heaven. [These demons] are careful not to frighten a person. On the contrary, they command the person to study Zohar and Psalms every single day. At night they arouse him to awaken to pray [the midnight service] Tikun Hatzot. Sometimes they command the person to immerse a number of times in the mikvah each day, and to constantly change his clothes. [He is told] to abstain [from relations] with his wife. After all this [these demons] make the person accept upon himself all kinds of afflictions and fasts. If this person does all these things, [these demons] then strike him and command him never ever to reveal the vision of them or what they show him to anyone else (for fear that they will be *exposed a demons). In the end, the person's mind is completely caught up with [these demons], to the point that he goes insane. Eventually [these demons] cause the person to suffer seizures. May God protect us.*

These demons come at the beginning of a dream. Afterwards they appear even while the person is awake. Sometimes they come just as a person is awakening. Many times people, men and women, have come to me, who have seen things while they are awake. I cannot get into all the details, but I will relate one story as an example.

In Tammuz 5671 (July, 1911), after the afternoon Shabat prayer, a young boy age 11 was brought before me. He said that he could speak with Elijah the prophet face to face, and not just in a vision or with puzzles. Any time that he would want [to speak with Elijah] all he had to do was call him, and he would immediately come. The only condition being that he [the boy] had to be alone, with no one else there [to see].

I said to him, enter this room, and ask him [Elijah] if he is truly Elijah the prophet. This the boy did. And he answered me; "I am truly Elijah, why does Yehuda doubt me?" (I am the Yehuda being spoken of). I said to the boy, this is none other than a Jewish demon whose name happens to be Elijah. This is not Elijah the prophet. You are being plagued by Jewish demons. Come and I will recite the prayer against demons over you, then will this Elijah flee from you. The child said to me, that this is certainly Elijah the prophet, and that you can do whatever you wish, and we will see who will be the victor.

After I prayed over the boy a number of times, he went into a private room to see whether Elijah would come. Elijah immediately came as he had done in the past. I was truly surprised by this. So, I took the child and went to see Rabbi Shimon Agasi zt"l, who was then alive, for him to examine the child. After he had examined him, [Rabbi Agasi] said that this was truly Elijah the prophet, and not a demon. I disagreed, and told him that it is a demon.

We both agreed that together we would all go after the Saturday evening prayers to see Rabbi Ya'aqob, the son of Rabbi Yosef Haim (the Ben Ish Hai) so that he may examine him. After he examined [the boy] in a number of ways, he too said that for certain this was Elijah the prophet of blessed memory. I disagreed with them both and nullified their proofs.

I requested of them to let me test [the boy] one more time. I said to the child that he should tell Elijah to translate to him the verse in Jeremiah, *"Ki'd'na Tem'run L'hom Ela'haya Di'Sh'maya V'ar'ka La Avadu Ye'vadu Me'ar'ah U'min T'hoht Sh'maya Eleh"* (Then shall you say to them, the gods that have not made the heavens and the earth, they shall perish from the earth, and from under these heavens. Jer. 10:11).

If [Elijah] translates this verse into Arabic (the spoken vernacular then), then it is possible to consider that maybe he is Elijah the prophet and not a demon. For the demons know the language of Aramaic (the language of this verse), for they [the demons] speak Aramaic and show evil dreams, and whisper into the ears of those who speak Aramaic. However, this verse speaks about their inevitable destruction. They do not wish to hear it, all the more so to translate it into any vernacular language.

Thus when the boy asked Elijah to translate the verse, Elijah said, that he had no time to waste there, for he had to leave [the boy] and go write down the merits of the Jewish people [for the heavenly court]. Elijah said that he was in a rush. When the boy told me of this response, I said to him, go back and tell [Elijah] to translate the verse of which I ask, for it is very important [that he do so], so that we may know for sure that he truly is Elijah. Elijah again told the boy that he was in a rush. I said to the boy, say to Elijah, that he has been conversing with us for a good while [why all of a sudden is he in a rush?], when it should be easy for him to translate this verse, instead of wasting time trying to get out of doing it. Only in this way, by translating this verse, will the Sages be convinced.

When the boy said these things to Elijah, he got angry and proclaimed "Hai HaShem" (As HaShem lives), I will never appear to you again for you do not believe that I am Elijah the prophet. Immediately [Elijah] disappeared and never reappeared to the boy.

After Elijah departed, Rabbi Agasi and Rabbi Ya'aqob said to me, that in their opinion, this was truly Elijah the prophet, for it is his way to swear by saying "Hai HaShem" (As HaShem lives). And our Sages have said (Meg. 3A) that even demons do not say the Name of God in vain.

I said to them that [this Elijah] was a demon, and that he did not say the Name [of God] in vain. Firstly, he fulfilled his word, he promised that he would leave and not return, and that is what he did, therefore, what he said was not in vain. And more than this, in essence [Elijah] never said the Name of God at all! He did not say Hai – Yod Key Vav Key [the true Name of God], nor did he use the Name Adonai. He said, Hai HaShem, using the word "HaShem" i.e., the letters Hey Shin Mem [this is a reference to the Name of God, and not the Name itself, at all). This is nothing other than pure deception [on the part of this Elijah]. The Sages finally agreed that I was correct.

Now, to get back to our subject. Up until now, I have been explaining the difference between dreams that come through angels, and those that come through gentile or Jewish demons. Now, I will explain more about the essence of dreams and how they are to be interpreted. This I do with the help of my Rock and Redeemer.

One must know that all dreams come in very concealed images. This is for a number of reasons. The first is that [the fulfillment] of the dream will not be for a number of years. The second [reason] is [that the dream] comes to admonish a person for the sins that they have committed. The third has to do with matters between a husband and wife. I will give you an example of all of these. The first reason is a known thing, such as the dreams of Joseph who dreamed about his brothers, or the great image envisioned by Nebuchadnezzar, or the dreams of Daniel. All of these came in the form of very concealed images because their fulfillment was still very far off. In accordance to the level of the concealment within the dream vision, so is the distance [in time] of its fulfillment.

Earthbound Spirits & Possession

Sefer Minhat Yehuda (Parashat Yekezkel)
"Then He said to me: 'Prophesy to the spirit; prophesy, son of man, and say to the spirit, 'Thus says my HaShem: Spirit, come forth from all the four winds; breathe upon these slain, so that they may live'." (Yehezkel 37:9)

This pasuk speaks of the dead of Israel who have been murdered. They were all dumped together into one (specific) valley, and left for their bones to dry out. Now Yehezkel was standing by them and prophesying to them in the Name of HaShem. The bones then started to come back together in their rightful positions. Then muscle and flesh were formed over them, finally to be covered with skin; yet there was no spirit (of life) within them. Then did Yehezkel start to prophesy, to tell the spirits to return to their bodies, in order that they may live. All this is explained in Perek (Chapter) 37.

Now, when he prophesied to the spirit, he called the spirit to come from "all the four winds". According to Rashi, these "four winds" are the places that the souls have wandered over the face of the earth; from there they shall be gathered and brought. If this is so, in accordance with Rashi, we then must say that until now (meaning the time of Yehezkel), these souls had not yet entered into the Garden of Eden but were instead hovering upon the four winds of the earth. This was due the fact that they were evil individuals, as it is taught in Sanhedrin 92B...Therefore all these years, these souls did not even merit to enter into Gehinnom (Hell); they were earthbound...

These souls are referred to in the Zohar (Saba d'Mishpatim 99B) by the name "Neshamot Artila'in", meaning they are naked souls, without having bodies. Now, I know very well that everyone greatly desires in their soul to know what becomes of one's body and soul after they depart from this world, until they reach their final rest in the Garden of Eden with the souls of the righteous and pious. Therefore have I decided to write this book, based on what I have found written in the Zohar and the writings of the Ari z"l, as well as what I have asked of these earthbound spirits, that have entered into (other) people, and who have come to me in order for me to heal them.

I would ask of the spirits all types of questions, such as what happened to them after their deaths, being that they did not go to hell, nor have any knowledge regarding it, since they did not yet merit to enter the (rectifying) fires of hell. Yet, there was one (spirit) who, after I had prayed (and received permission from the Holy One, blessed be He), did return to me, after he was rectified and had gone to Gehinnom. The spirit explained to me the uppermost level of Gehinnom wherein he was punished, and what happens to the others who are punished there. He also explained to me what is to happen to him after he is released from Gehinnom and allowed to proceed to the Garden of Eden.

Know that all the sins and transgressions that a person does by themselves, with the exception of the (residue of the) sin of Adam, certainly causes them to be encased in a klipah, and the contamination of the serpent; each in accordance with their own individual sin. However, everything is, of course, dependent upon an individual's repentance; for by the repentance that one performs, one has the ability to cast off from one's self the contamination that comes forth from sin, even if the sins be great ones. Yet, the contamination and klipah that cling to us due to the sin of Adam – these are not affected by repentance, simply because it was not the individual who sinned. Yet, (because of the sin of Adam) we are all destined to die. Then is this blemish rectified by death; for the person is then buried and the flesh returns to the dust. Thus is the klipah, which clings to us from the sin of Adam and Hava, removed.

With this can we understand the punishments inflicted upon the soul while still in the grave (Hibut HaKever). After a person is dead and buried, immediately there come four angels, who (spiritually) open up the grave and expand it to be the exact size and depth of the person buried therein. The soul and body are rejoined...the reason being that the klipah is still attached to the soul. Each of the angels then grabs the soul from every angle, and beat him until the klipah has been broken and removed from the soul. Therefore is this called Hibut HaKever (literally, the beating within the grave).

After the Hibut HaKever, the four angels depart and leave the soul standing by the grave. Immediately thereafter comes another angel, powerful and cruel and very frightening. He grabs the soul and takes it through the Kaf HaKelah (literally, the hollow of a sling – this is the name given to that transformation period between the physical and the spiritual). The soul is hurled up to the outer gates of the Heavenly Tribunal (Beit Din). Two angelic messengers of the Court come forth and escort the *naked soul within. If it be a female soul, she is given a garment large enough to cover her private parts. The soul then enters before the Court, in order to stand trial.*

Now pay close attention, and hear what the spirits have told me about their being in front of the Heavenly Tribunal. I will write this all down case by case; from this shall a person learn what should be his path, and what to do therein. In order not to omit relating about the spirits who had come to me for healing, I will start off writing about them. They were very much in distress due to their punishments; therefore, all my efforts were to release them from their torments as early as possible.

In the year 1900 (5660), a woman came to me by the name of Hannah Bat Akiba. She was possessed by the spirit of a woman whose name was Jahlah Bat Amam, who was an adulteress who had relations with an Arab man who very much wanted to despoil her. She also acted like a Muslim (and not like a Jew). After a few tries, with the full congregation involved, and the use of seven Torah scrolls and seven shofar blasts, (the spirit) finally left Hannah and she was completely healed.

Another time, on Thursday the 20th day of Adar I, 1902, a woman by the name of Haviva Bat Rahmah came to me. She was the wife of Ya'aqob Yosef Dayida. She was possessed by the spirit of Aharon Nisim Kohen, who died without children and was an ignorant man. With only a little effort I was able to make him leave.

A third time, on Sunday the 14th of Kislev, a woman by the name of Noam Bat Leah came to me. A spirit by the name of Ya'aqob Ben Gazalah had entered into her. He was a rich and powerful man in the city of Bozra; he had pity on his own name and the name of his (still living) family. He left her within thirty days; however, on the 17th of the same month he returned and reentered her. By the power of Yihudim (spiritual meditations), I was able to extract him on Friday the 19th of Kislev.

A fourth time, on Monday the 22nd day of Kislev, 1902, a man by the name of Reuben Ben Moshe Mani Ben Rahmah came to me. He was possessed by a spirit by the name of David Johanan who was a shoe repairman. His mother's name was Aziza. I was working with him until Friday the 16th of Shevat. On that day while I was performing Yihudim upon him, all of Reuben's bones began to shake. Suddenly his leg shot forth, straight and hard. He felt as though all the bones in his leg had been broken; his toes separated, and the spirit left his body through his big toe. Yet, it did not hurt him, even as I had commanded the spirit to do. Now all of these experiences regarding the spirits and what I have spoken with them, I have all these things written in depth; yet, I have not written this all here, because it is not relevant to our present discussions.

The topic of earthbound souls and possessions was a specialty of Rabbi Yehuda's. This excerpt is only the introduction to the section of Minhat Yehuda entitled "Ruhot HaMesaperot" (The Spirits Speak). The following selection can be interpreted to be rather frightening. It is pretty intense to gain a glimpse as to what is waiting over on the other side for the unprepared.

The Evil Soul of the False Messiah Shabtai Tzvi Strikes from Beyond the Grave

On Monday, 22 Kislev 5663, a man named Reuben Ben Moshe Mani Ben Rahama came to me. He was possessed by a spirit named David Yohanan...

While I was yet working with him, another man, Yehezkel Ezra Ben Yisrael came to me. His family name is Bakhur. He said to me that for a number of years evil thoughts would pop into his head as though from nowhere. During the silent Amidah prayer, or during Kaddish or Kedusha, he would hear a voice within him saying, "Give up your religion, convert and become a Christian" (God forbid).

These thoughts were so powerful that they would disturb his concentration, preventing him from answering the Kaddish or Kedusha. It had not been twenty years since he had gone to Rabbi Yosef Haim (the Ben Ish Hai) who sent a letter to HaRav Eliyahu Mani in Hebron. The response was that (Bakhur) had a great klipah within his heart, and that he (Rav Mani) couldn't help him.

The Ben Ish Hai consulted with me at that time and told me to write a mezuzah, and prescribed that Bakhur should wear it over his heart. This however had no effect. Therefore he had returned to me to inquire whether he had a spirit within him.

Being that Bakhur was an honest God fearing man, I consented to his request. I started to perform Yihudim by his ear, the Yihudim used against spirits. Thus the breath of the Yihud enters into his ear, and then into his organs, for the breath of the Yihud disturbs the breath of the spirit.

While I was reciting the Yihudim into his ear, Bakhur started to laugh. I asked him what he was laughing about; he answered and said that he can almost hear another person inside himself, and he is very viciously cursing you, saying this one's Rabbi, Yosef Haim (the Ben Ish Hai) advised you to wear a mezuzah, he should take the mezuzah and place it up his Beit HaBoshet (the embarrassing place) (God forbid). Now his student has become the Rabbi. He is only half of his Rabbi, Yosef Haim. In this way did the spirit curse me and mock me.

Upon hearing all this, I returned to recite Yihudim by his ear numerous times, without interruption, until such a time that the spirit was cursing, twisting and turning within Bakhur's heart. But I would not pay the spirit any mind. In the end Bakhur inquired of the spirit within him, he said, "Ask Yehuda what does he want from me?" I said to him, "I want to know from what city you come and what is your name. I want you to tell me the absolute truth. If you lie to me, I will show you what I can do by placing severe punishments and sufferings upon you".

The spirit answered Bakhur saying that there have been a number of people like Yehuda who tried to get me to reveal my name, but they weren't able to get anything from me. I am stronger than stone. I do not open up to just anyone. I said to the spirit, "If so, I will continue to try, and we will see who will be successful in the end.

If you are truly a strong spirit and are accustomed to sufferings, then prepare yourself to suffer the travails of the the Yihudim, for they are like an unquenchable flame, and they are more painful then hell itself; for I will not leave you alone until you truthfully tell me your name and whence you came.

You will suffer all this pain for nothing, because you do not submit to me. You are causing all this suffering to fall upon you, and not me." I started again to recite Yihudim by Bakhur's ear as I did previously; I also blew the Shofar close to his ear with the meditations that are appropriate for this.

Bakhur started to scream. "Enough, enough!! I surrender." The spirit now wanted to tell me his name and place of origin. Yet I wasn't ready to listen. For I know it is the way of the spirits to be like Pharaoh, they only surrender for a moment then they go back to being stiff necked. Therefore I decided to show the spirit the power of the Holy Names. Only when I was finished with the Yihudim was the spirit tired and worn down, and asked me to give it time to relax from its travails.

Afterwards, the spirit asked me, "Why do you seek to know my name and place of origin? Why do you need to know this?" I said to the spirit, "So that I can rectify your soul and allow you to ascend to the Garden of Eden, so that you won't suffer from being earthbound anymore."

The spirit said, "This is not possible, not for you or for your rectifications. I do not wish to go to the Garden of Eden."

I said to the spirit, "Again you challenge me?" I brought my mouth close to Bakhur's ear so as to again recite the Yihudim. The spirit then screamed within Bakhur's mind, and said it would reveal its name.

It said its name was David Ben Savti Ben Rivka from the city of Izmir (Turkey). He said that he was an apostate and that he had slept with gentile women, and that he left no children, and that he had possessed Bakhur some seventeen years earlier.

The spirit then asked why I had flipped the world over on him. He said, "I have never hurt (Bakhur) or caused him any harm, and if you are so concerned about these insignificant thoughts, I will be careful from now on not to cause him evil thoughts. Just leave me here in my place, for if I were to leave, where would I go? Where would I find rest?"

Bakhur said to the spirit, "Go to Gehinnom". The spirit answered, "I am not yet worthy to enter into Gehinnom, for I am guilty of sleeping with a menstrual woman, a gentile woman, and a prostitute. Please don't go again to Yehuda, for I can't stand it. Let me stay here in my place, and I will not bother you further".

All these things did the spirit speak within Bakhur's mind, and he (Bakhur) would speak them to me. Being that I really didn't want to deal with spirits, I made a condition with the spirit. If it would return and place evil thoughts in Bakhur's mind, I would set my hand against it.

Only a few short days had passed when the spirit returned to its evil ways and brought evil thoughts into Bakhur's mind. Bakhur came to me and related what was happening.

I started to recite Yihudim by his ear. I commanded the spirit that this time to truthfully tell me his name, for the angel who oversees the Yihudim already had revealed to me the spirit's name and place of origin. (This frightened the spirit). I told the spirit that I would continue to recite a number of Yihudim by Bakhur's ear until he revealed to me his name, even as the angel had told it to me.

The spirit was very disturbed by this, and he said he name was Tzvi, and that his mother's name was Rivka, and that he was from Izmir. I commanded him to tell me the truth; for initially the spirit said his name was David Ben Savti, and now he says his name is Tzvi.

I asked him outright, "Aren't you none other than the notorious Shabtai Tzvi from Izmir, who made himself to be a messiah?" The spirit answered that this was the truth.

I asked him, "If so, you died in the year 1666; it has not been 237 years from your death. Tell me where you have reincarnated until now? How were you judged?" The spirit answered me mockingly, "Even if you get for yourself enough paper to write a book and enough pens (I will not tell you), for these things are none of your business. Now, you are late for your class in the Yeshiva. Your students are awaiting you, they are looking for you. How much time will you waste, delaying here with me?" I saw that what he said was true. I arose and left for the Yeshiva. I decided I would finish this work tomorrow.

While in the Yeshiva I met Rabbi Shimon Aharon Agasi; I related to him this matter of Shabtai Tzvi, and how he had possessed the soul of Bakhur. Rav Shimon went and told these things to Rabbi Yosef Haim (the Ben Ish Hai). Together they warned me not to continue with Shabtai Tzvi, fearing he would hurt me, God forbid.

The next day, Bakhur came to me, and I started Yihudim for Shabtai Tzvi. From within Bakhur, Shabtai Tzvi began again to curse me with awful curses. Bakhur would tell me all.

I stopped the Yihudim, and started to speak gently to the spirit, words that would touch his heart. I spoke with him saying, "Let me ask you some questions: What is my strife with you? Do you think that I wish to take revenge for what you did when you were alive?"

The spirit answered that he did not think this. I asked him, "Do you really think my intent with these Yihudim is to cause you harm so that I will receive a Heavenly reward for my endeavors with Bakhur?"

The spirit said, "It's not that." I said, "For Bakhur is a poor man, he cannot pay me for my services. Why then do you think I am troubling myself taking time away from my learning, if not for the sake of your soul? For is it still not a spark from God above? Can it not shine like the most brilliant pearl? It is only due to sin that you have fallen. The Holy One, blessed be He is above all, and the Source of all. It is by His design that you entered into Bakhur's body, so that by such, your soul would have a limit and end to its sufferings by the work I am doing with you. I am making the endeavors to rectify you. What then is my sin, my blemish that you curse me with all these horrible curses?"

The spirit said to me, "I can't stand the sufferings of the Yihudim."

I said to him, "It is the way of the world that if a person is sick from an illness deep inside the body, the doctor has to open up the body in order to remove the cause of the illness. Even if this causes much pain, the person suffers it so that he can get well. He doesn't curse the doctor. As for me, it is not my way to discuss things in such depth with the spirits, for the vast majority of them are quite ignorant, and can't tell the difference between what is good for them and what is bad. However, I know what I know. I know that you are a very learned individual. You know how to judge for yourself what is for your own good and what is not. Therefore, I am correct in what I am doing with you, and your curses can have no effect upon me; for I know that your soul does not truly wish to curse me. It is the klipah that surrounds you that is forcing you to act thus. Therefore, I forgive your soul." These were my words with Shabtai Tzvi that I spoke with kindness and respect (towards him). Rabbi Yosef Haim and Rabbi Shimon Agasi had both told me to be aggressive with him.

When I finished my words, the spirit answered me in the words of a wise man. "I will not conceal from you a thing. For even though I suffer from the Yihudim, like a man who has wounds in the flesh, and along comes the doctor who covers the wounds with vinegar and salt, until it can hurt no more; yet, when the Yihud is finished, I do feel that my flesh has softened, and that the wounds are healing. I feel at ease. And now, I agree with your path. I want you to perform Yihudim upon me. And even if I jump or scream, pay no attention to my pain, for I scream due to the tremendous pain."

I told him that this was still not enough. When a person becomes drunk, and stumbles around, falling into a pit of mud, he cries out to those passing by to help him up. It goes without saying that the one in the mud helps those helping him to pull him out of the mud. He doesn't depend on them to do all the work. In relation to this I ask you not to place your full burden upon me. I will work to remove the klipah from surrounding you on the outside, but you must make the efforts to remove your klipah from within yourself. HaShem will help us both. The spirit answered, "Yes. Yes, let's do it and prosper."

I started performing a number of Yihudim, and the spirit would scream horrible screams. Yet I would not pay attention to his screams until I was exhausted from performing the Yihudim. The spirit also was tired and exhausted from all its travails. It was not able to speak anything for a good amount of time.

After this I asked the spirit if the Yihudim had helped rectify him. The spirit said, "Yes, yes, your honor, I feel that the weight of the klipah is lighter upon me." I then asked him, "How thick is the klipah that is left upon you?" The spirit answered, "Without exaggeration, it is at least two feet thick."

I asked him, "I have one question to ask you: tell me, does the ball of the sun revolve around the earth, or is it stationary in the heavens, or it is suspended in the air of this world?" The spirit answered me, "Do you wish for me to enter my head between the great mountains (meaning the souls of the Talmudic Sages, dwelling above) so that they will crush my head? What you find written in the books, learn. I have no business in these matters." I asked the spirit a number of other questions, yet here I will only write the answers that were given to me, and from the answers I'm sure that you will understand what the questions were.

I am he, Shabtai Tzvi. My death was by hanging. I did not repent of my sins. I was buried in a gentile cemetery. While I was yet alive the klipah would materialize before my eyes. They are what caused me to become evil. I did not keep myself in holiness.

[The spirit told me that] he has reincarnated numerous times that cannot be counted. He merited to achieve the levels of nefesh and ruah. When the neshama started to manifest within him is when it happened what happened. Now he acknowledges that Moshe, our teacher, upon him be peace, is true, and that his prophecy is true, and that his Torah is true. Yet all this will bear him (the spirit) no fruits; for being that he is dead, he is not obligated to observe the mitzvot (Shab. 30A). The merits he had earned from any mitzvot that he did perform are already gone.

At this point, Rabbi Yehuda inserts this side note: (Evil spirits can only speak in the heart, but not in the mouth. I give witness to this. In 1914, a virgin woman came to me who was then 35 years old. She was blind in both her eyes. She had reincarnated within her the soul of a Rabbi that was of my generation, who I had known very well. With all this, he would only speak within her heart and not within her mouth, even though she was blind. She did not study Torah, and this Rabbi was attracted to her while he was still alive. Even now he was trying to get her commit a sexual sin with another Rabbi, saying that from their union would the Messiah be born. Yet, she did not listen at all to his voice. After performing Yihudim and making efforts, the identity of this Rabbi was made known to me, as well as the fact that he had desired her...

This then is the reason why the spirits speak only in the heart, and not in the mouth. They do not want to be recognized. This way they can be mocking and maligning. In Sha'ar HaGilgulim 22, 22A, it is written, "When one reincarnates in a person, it is done in one of two ways. The first deals with the souls of the wicked, who after their deaths are not even worthy to enter into Gehinnom (hell) -- they enter into the bodies of living persons here in this world. The second manner is when a soul impregnates a person by what is called an "Ibbur". This soul bonds (with the living person) in great secrecy.

Thus, if that person then commits a sin, the incarnated soul within can then overpower the soul of that person whom they are inhabiting, and cause that person to sin further and to deceive it into going in an evil direction. Until here are the words of the Sha'ar HaGilgulim. It is possible that what the Rav (the Ari z"l) meant here when he referred to the souls who "bond (with the living person) in great secrecy" is that they do this for the reason mentioned above, so that they will not be recognized, and thus they will be free to mock and otherwise trouble the public. Let us return to our subject.)

With regards to Bakhur, he was the reincarnation of the ruah (aspect of the soul of Shabtai Tzvi). The nefesh aspect was still living in an animal in the forest. It did not want to be in this place, nor did it want to ever reincarnate in the body of a Jew. It wanted to stay in the forest.

(Regarding Shabtai Tzvi), he was 35 years old when he died. I asked him a number of other questions that he did not want to answer me, for he was still encased in a klipah two feet thick.

After five days I again spoke with the spirit in a softer tone, and I saw that he had relented tremendously. He was actually remorseful over the sins that he had done. He was now very anxious for me to try to complete his rectification. He now abundantly blessed me and the members of my family. He said he wasn't saying all this (talk about repentance) for my sake, but rather because it was true.

(He told me) that his first sin was that he had fallen victim to committing adultery. And that it is true what they say about him, that he had had a homosexual affair while he was wrapped in his talit and tefillin. He even once sent a young man to have an illicit adulterous affair with his own wife Sarah, telling the boy what was written in the Torah, "All that Sarah says to you, listen to her."

After his death he was punished with demonic beatings for twelve years. Until now he had always reincarnated into wild animals. Being in Bakhur was his first time possessing a human.

He then explained to me why he was able to enter into Bakhur to possess him, the reason being that once Bakhur, when a young man, gave a young girl a (forbidden) kiss. This Bakhur did 30 years ago. Prior to this, the spirit said, he would hang around Bakhur's proximity, because Bakhur was from the same source soul as he, the spirit, was. (The teachings referencing this are in Sefer HaLikutim, Yirmiyahu 8:14)...

For the sake of one forbidden kiss was an opening created for the spirit to come in and possess Bakhur. Yet the spirit is judged (and punished) every Friday, from the second hour of the day through the fourth hour and a half. The spirit told me that he is punished alongside the spirit of Yeshu HaNotzri in boiling feces.

Regarding myself, the spirit told me, that I am here reincarnated for the second time, and that fifteen years ago I merited to receive the ruah level of soul. The spirit said that it was HaShem who brought him to me, in order for me to rectify him.

Regarding Bakhur, he must learn Zohar every day, in the early hours of the predawn morning, as well as after his meal, for the sake of the elevation of the soul of Shabtai Tzvi Ben Rivka. He must go to the mikvah every day. He must not be concerned with the evil thoughts that pop up in his mind. And when they do pop up, he should recite the verse: **Rahash Libi Davar Tov** "My heart is astir with a good thing." (Psalm 45:2) and meditate upon the holy Name **"Resh Het Shin."** Also meditate upon the holy Name **"Kibel Rinat Ameykha"** (KRA STN) and the evil thoughts will be nullified.

From that day onward, the spirit of Shabtai Tzvi would request of Bakhur that he study more and more Zohar every day, more than the day before, even if this meant taking time out from making a living.

When it came to going into the mikvah, the spirit would cause Bakhur to hurry so fast that he would almost fall down the stairs into the water. The spirit would also awaken him every morning early, in time for prayer.

The spirit also requested of me that I should recite Yihudim for him every day into Bakhur's ear, including the blowing of the Shofar. The spirit thought that by doing all this maybe he would merit to enter Gehinnom.

I asked the spirit when he would leave Bakhur. He told me not to ask. When he was ready to enter into Gehinnom he would leave Bakhur, without having to be asked.

And in truth, this is the way it was. For after a few days, Bakhur was no longer being disturbed in his sleep, I examined him and found no traces of the spirit of Shabtai Tzvi.

Thus ends a true story of demonic possession, what caused it and what efforts need be made to rectify such a terrible situation. Let us all learn from this a lesson, to safeguard and protect ourselves. Evil surrounds us. It can only be neutralized by the good within us. And there is no good but Torah, the Word of the living God.

Chapter 7

Opening the Third Eye

There is a veil over your eyes. You cannot see it, and you cannot see beyond it. Because of this, you do not believe that there is more to see. But there most definitely is a whole reality out there beyond what the eye can see and what the mind can conceive.

Long ago we have been taught that in actuality we have three eyes. With two we gaze upon the physical world around us. With one we gaze upon the rest of the world that is invisible to the other two eyes. This third eye is indeed only a metaphor, but it represents an innate human ability to experienced, understand and to interact with the higher dimensional planes in which we exist simultaneously with this physical one.

But we are told over and over again that there is no third eye, and that there are also no higher dimensions to be experienced. Law #1 of brainwashing is to tell the big lie over and over again until the majority comes to accept it as true. And this is exactly what has happened.

Even though that you yourself see, you are told that you do not see, and that there is nothing to be seen. You can directly experience the reality of another dimension, and you will be told that you are crazy and in need of hospitalization, or that you are possessed by a demon and in need of religious ritual intervention. Either way, the one who can actually see is taught from youth to lie about what one sees, and to never talk about it to anyone. This is a terrible act of abuse against the human soul.

The horrible state of affairs is nothing new. The veil that has been pulled over our eyes is referred to in the Bible as the forbidden fruit of the Tree of Knowledge, Good and Evil. What the Biblical metaphor is referring to, and what real event underlies the Biblical narrative actually means is not relevant here to our considerations.

What we must understand is that we are all, as a race, handicapped. We have been blinded in our metaphorical third eye. And we are lied to when we are told that psychic development is a function of the mind, when it most certainly is not limited in any such a way.

The third eye does not see through the power of mind. Intellect plays no role here whatsoever. The third eye sees through our individual bio-energetic bodies. These are the constructs of energy which maintain a higher level of consciousness, and exist simultaneously in this physical world and in higher dimensions. These constructs of energy we have come to call a soul. And as we know there are five levels of soul, each of which experiences its own higher dimensional plane.

We are forever present in higher dimensions at the very same time that we are present in this one. Death of the body simply means that the vessel that enslaves us to perception of a singular reality is removed. This enables one to return to where one was before one became entrapped in singular dimensional perception.

One does not need to permanently leave the body in order to temporarily leave the confinement to the perception of the singular reality. One can learn to shift one's awareness from one level of soul to the next. Some call this out of body travel. Some call this telepathic or clairvoyant experience. Some call this seeing with the Third Eye. Regardless of the name that it is called, embracing a parallel alternate consciousness of a higher dimension is a real thing that is normal, proper, and accessible to anyone who practices the exercises in order to accomplish it.

SECTION FIVE

KAVANOT OF THE MERKAVA

YHWH (Hawaya) Meditations

The Practice of the YHWH Merkava: Using the Name YHWH as a Tool for Psychic Diagnosis & Spiritual Healing

"I place YHWH before me, always."

Psalm 16:8

The foundation of prophetic Torah meditation is the contemplation and visualization of the holy Name of God, YHWH.

As is well known, the Name YHWH has no well-known pronunciation. YHWH is erroneously pronounced either as Yahweh or Jehovah. Both forms are historically inaccurate and wrong. So, if we know what is wrong, the question is, do we know what is right?

The answer to this takes us into the heart of Torah's prophetic meditation. For in order to meditate upon YHWH, we must first define our terms. What is meditation? And what is YHWH?

To define meditation and to outline its practices is easy. This has already been done countless times in all too many spiritual traditions from around the world. Yet, when it comes to the Name YHWH, we encounter something different from anywhere else.

YHWH has no well-known pronunciation for a reason. The reason is that YHWH is not what we think It is. We know YHWH as the Creator, and Master of the Universe. But our understanding of these concepts is so primitive that it borders on the idolatrous.

YHWH is not a person, or a being. There is no knowing YHWH in the normal rational sense of knowing. Yet, YHWH is our God and King. And our God and King is not a person or a being! We can say that YHWH is spirit, but what does that mean? What is spirit, and for that matter, what is spiritual?

We have all too many questions, and all too few answers. Intellectual contemplations of this nature can only lead to very limited revelations. The source of true insight and knowing will therefore not come from intellectual contemplation. Prophetic Meditation looks to experience YHWH personally and based upon such experiences only then to draw conclusions as to the reality of YHWH.

The Kabbalists look at the Name YHWH as a code. They have broken down the Name YHWH and apply to each of the four letters of the Name, Yod, Hey, Wav, and Hey multiple concepts, terms, and associations. We will shortly address these things. But before we do, we need to understand that YHWH, who is not a person, or a being, is nevertheless a coded representation for something literally "out of this world."

In Biblical times, understanding of what YHWH is progressed through the centuries. The Patriarchs understood little about YHWH. They knew that He was the Creator of the universe and the only true God. But that is about it. Later, Moses had actual close encounters with YHWH, in a way that no human being has had either before, or since. Scripture enumerates some rather strange encounters of Moses with God. These include God placing His Hand over Moses' face, and Moses seeing YHWH's backside. All this language recorded in Torah makes it sound as if God has some sort of form and body.

Later Judaism emphatically denies that this is the case and proclaims these descriptions are symbolic metaphors, with deep mystical significance. Most likely, this is very true. Yet, the real nature of YHWH still remains to us as an unknown.

The later prophets speak of YHWH's grandiosity. YHWH is Master over all, and Director over the affairs of humanity. YHWH is not limited to being the God of the single nation, Israel. YHWH is the Lord of all humanity. YHWH is the God of gods, and Lord of lords. YHWH is essentially not only The Boss, but YHWH is Boss of bosses. But what exactly is YHWH? To say that He is God defines a function of YHWH, but what is YHWH in essence, beyond His ethnic association with Israel.

Like we said above, the answer to the question, what YHWH is will never be answered by philosophical, or other academic contemplations. The only way to know what is YHWH is to experience YHWH. We know for sure that YHWH far transcends any association with any one people or faith. We know for sure that YHWH far transcends any idea or concept that we embrace about God, about a Heavenly Father, or a Divine King. The Kabbalists recognize YHWH to represent the archetypal pattern of existence itself. YHWH thus is more than a Name, and title, or reference to any being or identity. YHWH is! And that about says it all!

King David wrote, "I place YHWH before me, always." In order for us to do likewise, we must understand the associated patterns, concepts, and ideas that the Kabbalists have associated with each letter of YHWH: Yod, Hey Wav, and Hey. As we form the patterns of association, we will come to embrace the pattern that is YHWH. Thus, when we turn to YHWH in meditation, we will soon experience that we are not interacting with an individual, Divine, or otherwise, but rather we are interacting with the Consciousness, and the Sentience of Life and the universe Itself.

The Name YHWH, instead of just being the Name of the "tribal-God" of Israel has been transformed, or maybe better to say, has been realized to be a representation of the parts of the universe.

Let us begin by enumerating the concepts of the Kabbalah and how they correlate to the letters of YHWH.

To begin with, we know that YHWH is not actually a Name. We should maybe better refer to it as representing a concept. YHWH is formed from the Hebrew root verb, HWH (howeh), "to be." When the letter Yod (Y) is added to the root verb form, it changes the verb from the passive tense to the active tense. Thus HWH "to be" becomes YHWH (being). YHWH is thus "Active Being." YHWH is the activity of Being in the general sense. YHWH is thus the "being," the "awareness," and the "consciousness" of everything. YHWH is thus the consciousness and sentience of existence.

This is the reason why the Sages prohibited the verbal recitation of the Name. YHWH is not a Name like all other Names. YHWH is a concept that conceals within it the secrets of Life itself. Who can comprehend this? Who can embrace this? Who can take this all within? No one! YHWH is far greater than anyone, or anything. As such, the Name is set aside and subjected to a unique rule of sanctity so as to proclaim its grandiosity.

According to the Kabbalists, the four letters of Y-H-W-H represent the four basic levels or dimensions through which we human beings experience reality. The four dimensional levels are: the psychic (also known as the spiritual), the intellect (also known as the rational thinking mind), the heart (the realm of emotions), and the body (the realm of form, be it physical or otherwise).

There are four dimensional realms, each is represented by a letter of YHWH. The first letter Y (Yod) represents the psychic (spiritual). The second letter H (Hey) represents the intellect (conscious mind). The third letter W (Wav) represents the heart (emotions). The fourth letter H (Hey) represents the body (form). Thus, together we have: Yod (psyche); Hey (mind); Wav (heart); and Hey (body).

YHWH represents the whole of the pattern, and at the same time, each of the four within the pattern are complete and whole, in and of themselves. Thus, we have a whole and complete YHWH for each of the four dimensional realms. In order to represent this reality in visual form, the Kabbalists have devised a system wherein which the letters of the Name YHWH are each spelled out in different ways, in order to derive unique numerical values for each spelling. Each of these unique spellings thus comes to represent the wholeness of YHWH in each subjective realm of the four dimensions.

The Hebrew letters Yod, Hey and Wav can each be spelled in unique ways. Yod is always spelled with three letters: Yod (itself), Wav, and Dalet. Hey can be spelled in three different ways. Hey can be spelled Hey Yod, or Hey Alef, or Hey Hey. Wav also can be spelled in three different ways. Wav can be spelled Wav Yod Wav, or Wav Alef, Wav, or Wav, Wav.

The Hebrew alphabet has no separate system of numerical symbols. The letters themselves are the numbers. For our purposes here, we need to know that Alef is 1, Hey is 5, Wav is 6, and Yod is 10.

When we wish to refer to the Presence of YHWH in one of the four dimensional planes, the Kabbalists have devised four different spellings of the letters that spell YHWH. Before we enumerate them, we must first learn the names that the Kabbalists have ascribed to the four dimensional planes.

When it comes to the study, practice and experience of true Kabbalah, knowledge, and awareness of the names of the dimensional planes, and how YHWH is manifest in each is essential. The names ascribed to the four dimensional planes are as follows: Atzilut is the name ascribed to the realm of the psychic intuitive. Beriah is the name ascribed to the realm of the rational intellect. Yetzirah is the name ascribed to the realm of the emotional heart. Asiyah is the name ascribed to the realm of forms and bodies.

For each dimensional plane the Presence of YHWH is expressed by unique spellings of the letters of the Name. Each unique spelling has its unique numerical value. Thus, the Presence of YHWH as manifest in each dimensional plane will be expressed as the Name YHWH of a specific numerical value. The four spellings of the Name, and their numerical values are as follows:

For Atzilut. Yod (Yod, Wav, Dalet) = 20, Hey (Hey, Yod) = 15, Wav (Wav, Yod, Wav) = 22, and again, Hey (Hey, Yod) = 15. Together 20+15+22+15 = 72. Seventy-two in Hebrew is represented by the two letters Ayin (70) and Bet (2). Ayin, Bet is pronounced like a word, AB. This spelling of the Name is thus the YHWH of 72. This is the Name as it is associated with the dimensional plane of Atzilut, the domain of the psychic intuitive.

For Beriah. Yod (Yod, Wav, Dalet) = 20, Hey (Hey, Yod) = 15, Wav (Wav, Alef, Wav) = 13, and again, Hey (Hey, Yod) = 15. Together 20+15+13+15 = 63. Sixty-three in Hebrew is represented by the two letters Samekh (60) and Gimel (3). Samekh, Gimel is pronounced like a word, SAG. This spelling of the Name is thus the YHWH of 63. This is the Name as it is associated with the dimensional plane of Beriah, the domain of the rational intellect.

For Yetzirah. Yod (Yod, Wav, Dalet) = 20, Hey (Hey, Alef) = 6, Wav (Wav, Alef, Wav) = 13, and again, Hey (Hey, Alef) = 6. Together 20+6+13+6 = 45. Forty-five in Hebrew is represented by the two letters Mem (40) and Hey (5). Mem, Hey is pronounced like a word, MAH. This spelling of the Name is thus the YHWH of 45. This is the Name as it is associated with the dimensional plane of Yetzirah, the domain of the emotional heart.

For Asiyah. Yod (Yod, Wav, Dalet) = 20, Hey (Hey, Hey) = 10, Wav (Wav, Wav) = 12, and again, Hey (Hey, Hey) = 10. Together 20+10+12+10 = 52. Fifty-two in Hebrew is represented by the two letters Nun (50) and Bet (2). Nun, Bet is pronounced like a word, BEN (which is the opposite spelling of Nun, Bet. It is considered easier to remember BEN, Bet Nun, because it is also the Hebrew word for son). This spelling of the Name is thus the YHWH of 52. This is the Name as it is associated with the dimensional plane of Asiyah, the domain of forms and bodies.

So, in review, when we wish to use the Name YHWH and experience it within, our experiences will arise from one of the four internal domains of our human experience. In order to be able to distinguish, and to differentiate which experience of YHWH one is experiencing, we have the four different YHWHs, which again are known by their numerical values 72 (AB), 63 (SAG), 45 (MAH), and 52 (BEN).

Another thing, when the Kabbalists make reference to the Name YHWH, they refer to it by rearranging the letters to spell the Name in a manner which can be pronounced. Instead of saying, YHWH, or just HaShem, the Kabbalists say HWYH, pronounced Hawaya.

Thus, when referring to the manifestations of Hawaya (YHWH) in the four dimensional planes, the Kabbalists will refer to the Hawaya d'AB to reference the psychic intuitive; Hawaya d'SAG to reference the

AB, 72 [ע"ב]   יוד הי ויו הי

SAG, 63 [ס"ג]   יוד הי ואו הי

MAH, 45 [מ"ה]   יוד הא ואו הא

BEN, 52 [ב"ן]   יוד הה וו הה

rational intellectual; Hawaya d'MAH to reference the emotional heart, and Hawaya d'BEN to reference to the forms and bodies. The prefix "d" is Aramaic and means "of." Being that Zoharic literature is mostly Aramaic, the later Kabbalists have incorporated some Aramaic into the Hebrew vernacular.

Now that we have differentiated the Name YHWH into its four forms of manifestation in the four dimensional realms, we can continue to elaborate on the Name and its correlations with the Ten Sefirot.

In brief, the Ten Sefirot, while considered to be the descending grades of Divine radiance in the outside world, really needs to be viewed as being the internal pattern for all things in existence.

A full exposition of the Ten Sefirot is beyond the scope of this present chapter. However, we do need to review the basics in order to apply them within the context of our meditative practices.

Again in brief, the Ten Sefirot correspond to different elements within the human experience, as well as to correlative body parts within the human anatomy. Each of these Ten differentiated elements, needless to say, manifests its own unique expression of YHWH (Hawaya). To differentiate these, the standard four-letter

Name YHWH is used (ten times), but with each reference being differentiate from one another by the association of different Hebrew vowels written into the YHWH Name. Now, each Name of YHWH (Hawaya) with a set of vowels is not meant to be recited with those vowels. The vowels are not placed there to promote pronunciation, but rather to visually identify a Sefirotic association.

It is best to diagram the Ten Sefirot, their internal applications, their bodily associations, and their corresponding spellings in this chart. I will repeat the chart further on and there discuss its usage.

The Ten Sefirot and their Correlations				
Keter (Crown)	Collective Unconscious	Skull	YHWH with Kamatz	יְהֹוָה
Hokhma (Wisdom)	Personal Unconscious	Right Brain	YHWH with Patah	יְהֹוַה
Binah (Understanding)	Conscious Mind	Left Brain	YHWH with Tzere	יְהֹוֵה
Hesed (Mercy)	Expansion Influence	Right Arm	YHWH with Segol	יְהֹוֶה
Gevurah (Severity)	Contraction Influence	Left Arm	YHWH with Shva	יְהֹוְה
Tiferet (Glory)	Balance Influence	Heart	YHWH with Holam	יְהֹוֹה
Netzah (Victory)	Desire to Impose	Right Thigh	YHWH with Hirik	יְהֹוִה
Hod (Majesty)	Desire to Receive Benefit	Left Thigh	YHWH with Shuruk	יְהֹוֻה
Yesod (Foundation)	Creative, Sexual Energy	Genetalia	YHWH with Kubutz	יְהֹוּוּוּה
Malkhut (Kingdom)	Body Consciousness	Feet	YHWH with no vowels	יהוה

In the general meditation called the Merkava, all ten of these correlations are contemplated, along with numerous others (as will be seen) that correspond to other body parts and functions.

In review, we have explained how the Name YHWH is far more than just a Name; it is rather a symbol that represents the entire pattern of known existence. The Name YHWH can be spelled out in four different ways, referred to by the numerical values of the spellings AB (72), SAG (63), MAH (45) and BEN (52). These correspond to the four dimensional planes of Atzilut (the intuitive), Beriah (the rational), Yetzirah (the emotional), and Asiyah (the physical) elements of our human experience. We also apply ten different sets of vowels to the Name to associate it with the Ten Sefirot, which themselves refer to specific elements in the human psyche and physical body.

With these fundamental correlations understood, we can now proceed and return to the beginning, and put into practice Psalm

16:8, which states "I place YHWH before me, always." Now that we know what YHWH is, and how we can apply it, we can proceed to these applications.

When we begin to visualize the Name YHWH, we recognize it for what it is, the greater pattern of our existence. We look at each letter of the Name and understand that each one has its unique correlations.

Yod corresponds to the dimensional plane of the psychic intuitive, Atzilut, and thus the Name AB.

Hey corresponds to the dimensional plane of the rational intellect, Beriah, and thus the Name SAG.

Wav corresponds to the dimensional plane of the emotional heart, Yetzirah, and thus the Name MAH.

Hey corresponds to the dimensional plane of forms and bodies, Asiyah, and thus the Name BEN.

Yod is AB. Hey in SAG. Wav is MAH. Hey is BEN. These correlations become very important once we begin the process of visualizing the Name.

The prophetic tradition in Torah makes use of both inner vision and outer sounds. Reciting combinations of holy Names that are configured towards a specific purpose is a common prophetic practice. I have discussed these methods in great detail in my books, Yehi Deah, Parts 1 & 2. Our present technique of using the Name YHWH is different from these others. Meditating upon YHWH is exclusively an internal visualization exercise.

Our visualizations of the Name YHWH are far more than a mere mental exercise of inner vision. The Name YHWH represents Reality itself. As such, the Name has a "life of its own." When one visualizes and interacts with the Name, autonomous things begin to occur within one's mind. We learn about the meaning of the Name, and its many correlations because these things will begin to arise out of one's unconscious all by themselves, without any prodding on part of our conscious thoughts, will or desire.

Warning! YHWH is alive! Bringing YHWH into your consciousness opens a door to higher realities, that once open, can never be truly shut ever again. Proceed only if you are willing to move forward, because once started, there is no turning back!

One begins this meditative practice by first understanding well the meaning of YHWH and its integral parts. With this information stored away in one's mind, the autonomous nature of YHWH can begin to operate within one's unconscious. YHWH operates to bring to consciousness greater awareness, insight, and sensitivity to the reality of the greater world in which we all live.

One memorizes the Name YHWH in its original Hebrew form. Once this is done, one can visualize the Name within one's mind at any time, in meditation, or at any other time of the day. The form of the Hebrew letters is well known, and their shapes are simple enough for one to memorize without too much difficulty. And with this being said, I will emphasize that the form of the Name YHWH that we memorize and use, is not the original historical form used by the Biblical prophets.

The Gemara (BT, Sanhedrin 21b) records a discussion among the Sages as to what was the original script of the Ten Commandments. Historically the Paleo-Hebrew script was in use during the centuries following the Exodus through the exile into Babylon. This means that every Biblical prophet who called upon the Name of YHWH visualized it in the Paleo-Hebrew.

During the Babylonian exile, this script was changed for the one that we use today. Rabbinic Sages and Kabbalists alike seek to defy history and declare that the modern script of Hebrew, called Assyrian, was the original script of revelation from Mt. Sinai. The Kabbalists especially are emphatic about the sacredness of this script and base many Kabbalistic teachings upon the shapes of the letters in modern script.

Therefore, almost everyone today who meditates upon and visualizes the Name YHWH does so in the modern Assyrian script. However, there are the private few who remain historically faithful to the Biblical prophets and (in secret) use the Paleo-Hebrew script to visualize the Name YHWH.

As for which of these scripts one should use, unlike many of my peers, I will leave the choice up to the individual to choose for oneself. The two scripts each generates its own power and energy signature. If one wishes, try to visualize both, one at a time. See what they feel like and make your decision accordingly as to which one to use.

Now we come to the practice. First, memorize the Name YHWH in the script of your choice. At all times during the day, keep the Name YHWH in mind. Focus on making its presence more and more real in your thoughts at all times. Realize that the Name YHWH is alive! It is Life itself! It is Being itself.

YHWH includes within it all of our psychic, intellectual, emotional, and physical experiences, and is the source of all these things. YHWH is all! Cultivate a sense and an awareness of this this, always! As YHWH lives, YHWH will take root in your unconscious. As you merge and bond with YHWH; YHWH merges and bonds with you.

There is a meditative technique taught originally by R. Abraham Abulafia and quoted by R. Hayim Vital wherein which as one visualizes the Name YHWH, one should visualize it as a living Being in abstract human form standing in front of you, waiting to engage you in conversation. And then one should start a meditative verbal dialogue with a personified version of the Name.

The nature of this inner verbal dialogue and our interaction with the Name YHWH is where the real depths of personal revelations are to be experienced. While the Abulafian method relies mostly on open expression in the inner dialogue to manifest revelations from the unconscious, R. Vital places emphasis on the appearance of the letters themselves.

When one gazes upon the letters YHWH, regardless of the script, how do they appear within one's inner vision? Are the letters big or small? Are the letters sharp and rigid, or fuzzy and fluid? What color are the letters? Can one visualize all four letters of the Name simultaneously, or do some letters appear and not others? And most importantly, how does one feel when performing this visualization? Does one feel emotionally drawn to bond with YHWH, or maybe one feels awe and fear, and instead feels like keeping a distance? These, and many other questions arise.

When working with a master Kabbalist who is personally guiding one's training, the teacher will ask the student what is seen. The student, needless to say, must focus one's inner attention and endeavor to not only see the letters of the Name, but also to feel them. The nature of this interaction reveals the status of the student with regard to the Name. Sharing these insights with one's teacher enables the teacher to properly guide the student into better, and deeper insights into oneself, and about the reality of YHWH.

What one sees is a reflection of one's inner self. The nature of this inner vision, which is subject to constant change, needs to be understood in great depth. In order to acquire this understanding, one then takes the next step after the visualization of the Name, and actually engages the Name in inner dialogue and conversation, Abulafian style, letter by letter.

For example, one can visualize the Name, and following the Abulafian method, imagine that the Name is personified. One can then interact with the Name in the form of inner dialogue. One can approach the first letter of the Name, Yod, and gaze at it carefully. One can them engage the Yod in direct inner conversation.

One greets the letter, and in one's imagination allow a dialogue to develop not limited by one's conscious mind. When visualizing the Name or any letter thereof, it will appear in a way that is unique to the individual. One may see it in one color or another, big or small, or however. One should pay attention to one's inner vision, and ask the letter (or the whole Name), why does it appear in one's mind in this specific fashion?

It might very well be that the letter (or Name) may not be aware of how it appears to you, and in turn, might ask you why you see it as you do, and not as it sees itself. Needless to say, this type of response is very purposeful to expand the discourse between you and it. The nature of such an inner dialogue can prove to be most revealing, about oneself, and about the nature of the reality around us.

One who engages in this style of dialogue may or may not imagine an inner voice actually speaking to one. One may instead just feel impressions within one's mind that such and such is what is. These impressions may indeed be truthful, or they may indeed be false. Yet, one pays attention to these impressions and continues to inquire as to the truth or falsehood within them.

Over time, and contemplation, with YHWH as your guide, your inner sense of discretion will grow considerably. As one cultivates a sense of trust in the Name (or individual letter), one will be able to sense and discern many different things. This is how the Name YHWH is used to develop psychic clarity and prophetic abilities. This was the method used since Biblical times. This is the meaning of the word, "always," as in the verse, "I place YHWH before me, always" (Psalm 16:8). In Biblical times, this sense of inner knowing was called Ruah HaKodesh (Divine inspiration).

One must remember that each letter of YHWH reflects its own unique expression of the dimensional realities in which we live. Each letter, therefore, reflects the realities and insights of its respective dimension.

Yod will reflect to one insights and realities with regards to one's personal interactions in the psychic, intuitive arena. The Yod will manifest one's personal blockages, limitations, and areas in need of growth, refinement, or repair. Such insights are revelations into one's personal access to the domain of Atzilut. In more advanced meditations, for greater insights into this specific domain, one meditates and visualizes the expanded Name AB (72), interacting with it, as one would with the simple Name.

Hey will reflect to one insights and realities with regards to one's personal interactions in the realm of intellect, rational thought, and analytical abilities. The Hey will manifest one's personal blockages, limitations, and areas in need of growth, refinement, or repair. Such insights are revelations into one's personal access to the domain of Beriah. In more advanced meditations, for greater insights into this specific domain, one meditates and visualizes the expanded Name SAG (63), interacting with it, as one would with the simple Name.

Wav will reflect to one insights and realities with regards to one's personal interactions in the realm of emotions, feelings, and the heart. The Wav will manifest one's personal blockages, limitations, and areas in need of growth, refinement, or repair. Such insights are revelations into one's personal access to the domain of Yetzirah. In more advanced meditations, for greater insights into this specific domain, one meditates and visualizes the expanded Name MAH (45), interacting with it, as one would with the simple Name.

Hey will reflect to one insights and realities with regards to one's personal interactions in the realm of the physical, be it with regards to one's physical health, or possibly other matters relating to the outside world. The Hey will manifest one's personal blockages, limitations, and areas in need of growth, refinement, or repair. Such insights are revelations into one's personal access to the domain of Asiyah. In more advanced meditations, for greater insights into this specific domain, one meditates and visualizes the expanded Name BEN (52), interacting with it, as one would with the simple Name.

The same rule of visualization applies to the specific Names of AB, SAG, MAH, and BEN as would to the basic Name YHWH. Appearances and interactions need to be encouraged, embraced, and understood in order for psychic development and personal growth to manifest.

Now that we have discussed the Name YHWH within the context of the four dimensional realms and the letters that manifest them, we will now proceed to elaborate upon the Name YHWH as it is experienced within the Ten Sefirot, and within the parts of the human body that correspond to them.

472

First, remember what the Sefirot are believed to be. The Sefirot are believed to be cosmic forces that define the pattern of known reality. Most Kabbalists believe the Sefirot to be only abstract externals, but this is not so!

The Sefirot exist and defines for us human beings our pattern, and our perception of reality. The Sefirot are the blueprint for our human souls; they describe and define us. As such when we contemplate the Sefirot we do not look upon them as abstract externals that are subject to philosophical analysis and examination. Rather the Sefirot are us! They are within us, and we are within them!

The Ten Sefirot correspond to the patterns within our psyches, and within our physical bodies. This has already been shown in the above chart. Contemplate this chart and learn it well. For when one wants to, or needs to connect with the Sefirot, one needs to embrace the proper form of the Name YHWH and use it to gaze within. When the Torah states that humanity was created in the image of God, it is referring to the internal pattern of the Sefirot.

When we wish to contemplate our internal Divine Image, we turn to the Sefirot, and Sefirah by Sefirah, body part by body part, we gaze within ourselves seeing the Name YHWH in each. As in the general exercise, we visualize the Name YHWH in each specific body part, with its unique vowels. And as we gaze upon the Name, we again note what color is the letters, whether they are big or small, clear or fuzzy and whatever else.

On the following page is again the chart of the Ten Sefirot and its body correlations. We will elaborate on them now.

The Ten Sefirot and their Correlations				
Keter (Crown)	Collective Unconscious	Skull	YHWH with Kamatz	יָהָוָהָ
Hokhma (Wisdom)	Personal Unconscious	Right Brain	YHWH with Patah	יַהַוַהַ
Binah (Understanding)	Conscious Mind	Left Brain	YHWH with Tzere	יֵהֵוֵהֵ
Hesed (Mercy)	Expansion Influence	Right Arm	YHWH with Segol	יֶהֶוֶהֶ
Gevurah (Severity)	Contraction Influence	Left Arm	YHWH with Shva	יְהְוְהְ
Tiferet (Glory)	Balance Influence	Heart	YHWH with Holam	יֹהֹוֹהֹ
Netzah (Victory)	Desire to Impose	Right Thigh	YHWH with Hirik	יִהִוִהִ
Hod (Majesty)	Desire to Receive Benefit	Left Thigh	YHWH with Shuruk	יֻהֻוֻהֻ
Yesod (Foundation)	Creative, Sexual Energy	Genetalia	YHWH with Kubutz	יוּהוּווּהוּ
Malkhut (Kingdom)	Body Consciousness	Feet	YHWH with no vowels	יהוה

When contemplating a specific Sefirah, one does so by contemplating the correlating Name of YHWH demarcated as it is by its specific set of vowels. One then visualizes the Name of YHWH with that set of vowels either hovering over or penetrating within the specific body part.

Remember, the Name with the vowels is not meant to be read or recited aloud. The addition of the vowels is only for the purpose of identification, and not pronunciation. Reciting the Name with the vowels adds nothings to the meditation and may indeed be a violation of the sacred law not to pronounce the sacred Name inappropriately. If, however, one wishes to mentally contemplate how the Name would sound with the vowels, without verbally expressing it, one may do so within one's mind and imagination.

We will use the Sefirah Keter as our example. Keter is represented by the Name YHWH with the Kamatz vowel written under all four letters (see chart). One visualizes YHWH with Kamatz around one's skull. One can visualize YHWH as one wishes hovering over one's skull, like a crown over one's head. Mentally, one can chant within Yah Hah Wah Hah ("Ah" being the sound of the vowel Kamatz). This would be the internal chant (mantra) for the crown/skull.

One focuses one's imagination upon this place and contemplates how YHWH with the Kamatz represents the Divine radiance that is the source of the Collective Unconscious, and how this permeates all existence. One attempts to feel sensations within one's thoughts, or one tries to internally visualize a form of this reality. One must then pay careful attention to what one senses, or to what one is imagining, for this is how message and meaning will come to one about one's personal Keter.

If one wishes, one may use the Abulafian technique here and visualize YHWH with Kamatz as some form of individual or being standing opposite one (or in any other similar fashion). This imagined form specifically represents the Sefirah Keter and your personal relationship with it.

This imagined entity within your mind may indeed represent something autonomous, something much more real than just your thoughts. This imagined entity may serve as your personal Magid (spirit guide) to the revelations about the Sefirah Keter. But because this imagined entity is YHWH with Kamatz, its arena of revelation is limited to Keter. But pay attention! The imagined entity might act of its own and give you an impression or actual visualization of the Name changing its vowels from Kamatz (in Keter) to whatever. If this were to happen (and in advanced practice, it often does), this means that one is being guided from within and is being shown a path from Sefirah to Sefirah (be this consecutively, or not). One requires wisdom, understanding and insight in order to grasp what it is that one is being shown.

The method of contemplating the other Sefirot in other parts of the body follows this same pattern. It would be counterproductive for me to elaborate how this is to be done with each Sefirah. One must learn how to practice this technique autonomously, as directed from within, and not just from words written in a book.

This meditation is meant to be practiced, and not just learned as an academic exercise. The general pattern of how to proceed is clearly outlined for the Sefirah Keter. One should be able to figure out for oneself how to do this for the other Sefirot. Trust YHWH to guide your imagination.

At this point, let me share with you the words of R. Hayim Vital from his Sha'ar Ruah HaKodesh (4a-b), that I referenced above. R. Vital here merges the visualization of the Name with the parts of the body and adds in visions of color and their correlative meanings. He uses this example to provide the practitioner with a psychological tool, similar to a Rorschach ink-blot test used in psychological testing.

"One way for a man to know his sins is to meditate in his mind on the four letters of the Name YHWH, written in block (Assyrian) Hebrew. This is the meaning of the verse "I have placed YHWH before me always" (Ps.16:8).

When one meditates on the Name, if he has sinned and thus blemished any one of the four letters, then that letter he will not be able to meditate upon clearly. He can thus know the source of his weakness.

When meditating upon the Name, if the letters appear as if written in black ink, know that this one's soul emanates from Asiyah.

If the letters appear red, then the one who sees such emanates from Yetzirah.

If the letters appear white, that soul emanated from Beriah.

If the letters appear not only white, but glowing and sparkling, this soul emanates from Atzilut.

By this can a man know to which level his soul clings. In this way also, a man should meditate on the name YHWH as if placed in every organ or member of his body, be it his face, hand and so on, if there be something lacking (of the letters in a specific area) the man can then identify his sin.

The true and highest way of perceiving YHWH in meditation is to see the Name as a burning fire. If one perceives the Name as such, then that one is without blemish and is complete."

In this selection from R. Vital's Sha'ar Ruah HaKodesh, he raises a topic that needs to be elaborated. This is the realistic matter of each person's individual blemishes. I already briefly addressed this topic within the context of the four dimensional planes. Let us also apply it within the context of the Ten Sefirot.

As human beings, nobody is perfect. Every one of us suffers from some form of blemish in one area of our being. Every one of us emanates an energy signature which manifests our Sefirotic identity with regards to our balance or imbalance with the universal forces. Every individual has one's strengths and one's weaknesses. Many of these will manifest as blemishes in one's energy signature.

When one meditates upon the Name YHWH in general, and in particular, the nature of one's unique and particular experiences, impressions and visualizations reflect what is happening within one's psyche and body at that time. Essentially, we can use the Name YHWH as an examination tool. By paying attention to how we autonomously experience YHWH, we can come to recognize our individual blemishes, weaknesses, and limitations.

These are not shown to us in order to put us down, or to hold us back. On the contrary, we seek to experience these, as we would seek a diagnosis from a doctor, so that we may proceed towards healing, and a cure for our ailment. So, our interactive experience with the Name YHWH, in general, and in particular is far more than a mere meditation, it is also a technique for psychic and medical diagnosis. Once one realizes what one needs to address, one can go about it in the best, and most practical way.

The Kabbalists take the Name of YHWH into all the different parts of the body, whether or not these parts correspond to a Sefirah. By visualizing a unique expression of YHWH in the eyes, ears, nose, and mouth, one visualizes surrendering these orifices and their functions to Divine service. Essentially, by visualizing YHWH in them, one is offering oneself to serve as a vehicle through which the Light of YHWH can express itself here on Earth. The vehicle referenced here is called a chariot, in Hebrew, a Merkava. Thus, the name of this meditation of placing the Name of YHWH in all parts of one's body with the intent of sanctifying oneself to Divine service is the Kavanot of the Merkava. And so, we refer to our practices as the Practice of the YHWH Merkava.

Now let us address how the Name YHWH is to be expressed through the eyes, ears, nose, and mouth. The order that we shall follow will be that of the order of emanation of the Lights that came forth from Adam Kadmon giving rise to the primordial worlds of the Akudim and Nikudim. Essays that explain these

Kabbalistic teachings can be found in my book, The Evolution of God. We do not need to digress to discuss these details here. Suffice it for us to know that the order to follow for these visualization meditations is the ears, nose, mouth, and eyes.

[5] הַ [58] אֹזֶן

[ס"ג, 63] יוֹד הֵי וָאו הֵי

יוֹד הֵי וָאו הֵהַ ג' אֹזֶן

We begin with the Ears. The Hebrew word for ear is Ozen, spelled Alef (1), Zayin (7) Nun (50), the numerical value of this is 58 (1+7+50). From the supernal Ozen (ear) of Adam Kadmon (Primordial Man) comes forth the initial manifestation of the five-level soul NaRaNHaY. This is the realm of the dimensional plane of Beriah that is within Adam Kadmon. Thus, the Ozen (ear) manifests the letter Hey (the first Hey of YHWH). Numerically the Hey is 5. We add the 5 representing the Light of the Ear of Adam Kadmon with the value of Ozen (58) and we arrive at 63 (5+58). 63 we recognize as the YHWH of SAG, the Name that represents the rational, logical mind. And thus, the rational mind is associated with the sense of sound, emanating into the ear, bringing to the mind comprehension, and understanding.

There is yet one more kavanah to the ear, which is expressed in a special way of writing the expanded form of YHWH. We arrange the spelling of the expanded form of YHWH to be numerically equal to the value of the word Ozen (ear). This is as follows Yod (Yod, Wav, Dalet = 20) as in AB. Hey (Hey, Yod = 15) as in SAG. Wav (Wav Alef, Wav = 13) as in MAH, and Hey (Hey, Hey = 10) as in BEN. This form of YHWH is the unique form for the ears and is visualized any time when hearing and understanding is involved in one's meditation. We perform this visualization for both the right and left ears.

The Nose. The Hebrew word for Nose is Hotem (spelled, Het (8), Wav (6), Tet (9), Mem (40). Together this is again 63, SAG (8+6+9+40). In the deeper Kabbalah, the visualization of YHWH in the Nose is divided between the internal, concealed portion, and the revealed external portion. This division represents our

478

breathing process, where the inhale is concealed, and the exhale is revealed. And so, for each there is its own unique visualization.

For each nostril, one visualizes inhaling the Name SAG. Often in the Merkava diagram found in Hebrew books, these Names of SAG are here written vertically, as opposed to normal horizontal script. This is to indicate the action of inhalation.

ף ﬩ ף
ﬡ ﬡ
ﬡ ﬡ
ﬡ ﬡ

אהיה אהיה אהיה חילוניות
אהיה יהוה אהיה ג' חיים

As one exhales one visualizes the Name AHYH (Ehyeh) three times. AHYH (Ehyeh) is numerically equal to 21. Three times this gives us 63, SAG. In addition to this there is one additional visualization added here in the exhalation from the nose. We visualize the Names AHYH (Ehyeh) 21, YHWH (26), and again AHYH (Ehyeh) 21. Together, the numerical value of these three Names is 68 (21+26+21). This is the numerical value of Hayim (life). For breath is the spirit of life. One visualizes both of these groups of Names upon exhalation.

The Mouth. The Hebrew word for mouth is Peh, its numerical value is 85. What comes forth from the mouth? Speech. In the Hebrew language speech is formed with combinations of the 22 letters of the alef-bet. Speech is the verbal expression of thought. Thought comes from the mind.

יוד הי ואו הי
אחהע' גיכק' דטלנת' זסשריץ' בומף
כ"ב אותיות דכ' מולאות הפה
יוד הי ואו הי אהיה פנימיות הפה
יוד, יוד הא, יוד הא ואו א ג' פה חילוניות
קול יהוה ג' יופיאל ע"כ דבור אדני
קול ודבור יאהדונהי

The mind is the dimensional plane Beriah, corresponding to YHWH of 63 SAG. So, SAG (thought) wraps itself in words made up of 22 letters. Thus, we have 63+22 = 85, the numerical value of Peh, mouth. This then is the first visualization of the Merkava of the mouth. We visualize the unity of thought (represented by SAG), and speech (represented by the 22 letters of the alef-bet).

Thought is manifest in the Sefirat Binah, the dimensional realm of Beriah represented by YHWH (Hawaya) of SAG. But thought has its origins in even deeper realms of the unconscious. The Name AHYH (Ehyeh) is often associated with both Binah and the Sefirah Keter, which here represents pre-cognized thought. Thus, the union of YHWH of SAG and the Name AHYH (Ehyeh) represents the inner mouth. The concept of "inner" here is referring to the source of both thought and speech, the "inner" recesses of the mind.

The numerical value of SAG (63) and AHYH (21) is 84. For the Kabbalists, this is close enough to the numerical value of Peh, 85. They simply add the value of 1 to represent the word itself. This addition of 1 is called a Kollel. Adding a Kollel to a numerical value is a very common practice amongst Kabbalists. Personally, however, I chose not to use these additions. I find that if we seek to force numerical equalities by adding extra values from here or there then we miss the significance of equivalences that are precise.

The outside of the mouth is represented by expanding the form of the Name YHWH of MAH, as follows: Yod (Yod Wav Dalet) 20, Yod Hey (Yod Wav Dalet – Hey Alef) 26, Yod Hey Wav (Yod Wav Dalet – Hey Alef – Wav Alef Wav) 39. Together, 20+26+39 = 85, Peh. This Name is chosen to represent the external aspect of the mouth. For as the mouth reveals the concealed thoughts of Binah (the Supernal Mother, Imma). The speech that comes forth is what builds the body of Zeir Anpin (the Supernal Son). Mother gives birth to son; the mouth "gives birth" to speech.

The speech that comes forth from the mouth is two-fold. First there is the Voice, the undifferentiated sound emanating from within, without being formatted and structured into words. The unstructured Voice is the "sound" of the inner or upper worlds, the essence, the soul, and the life that takes form and structure and becomes speech. Voice is therefore represented by the Name YHWH, for YHWH reality is never structured in accordance to the rules of our physical dimension of space-time. We thus unite the Kol (voice) with YHWH. This is the "Voice of the Lord." The numerical value of Kol (Kuf, Wav, Lamed) is 136. The angelic Name

Yofiel (beauty of God), one of the Names of Metatron, has the numerical value of 137. According to the Kabbalists, that is close enough to reference it to a word with the value of 136 (Kol). I have already expressed my opinion about this above.

As we have the Voice, so too do we have Speech (Dibur). Speech (Dibur) is the form and structure of the Voice as it manifests here in these dimensions of physical space. The Name associated with Speech is ADNY (Adonai). Thus, the unity of Voice and Speech (Kol and Dibur) is represented as the union of the two Names, YHWH and ADNY (Adonai). This represents the general union of Heaven and Earth, and/or the spiritual with the physical. The letters of these two Names are knitted together to form one single Name of eight letters. This eight letter Name is found throughout Kabbalistic liturgy, especially whenever the Name of God is mentioned in traditional Jewish prayers. This, in and of itself, is a separate meditation that will be covered at another time.

The Eyes. The Hebrew word for eye is Ayin, spelled Ayin (70), Yod (10), Nun (50). The numerical value of Ayin is thus 130. The Name YHWH is numerically 26, thus five times (x) YHWH is 130, the value of Ayin (eye).

יהוה יהוה

יהוה

יהוה יהוה

ג' עין

The Supernal Eye sees all. Thus, we visualize that which the eyes see, and this, of course, is the Name YHWH. YHWH is visualized five times to correspond to the five general Partzufim (Sefirotic Faces), which are Arikh Anpin (Keter), Abba (Hokhma), Imma (Binah), Zeir Anpin (ZA-Tiferet), and Nok (Malkhut). Five also corresponds to the five-part NaRaNHaY soul. Five also corresponds to the letter Hey.

The five Hawayot (YHWHs) are the standard visualization for any meditative practices using the eyes. For example, when one recites the Friday night Shabat prayer, the Kiddush over a cup of wine, one is to priorly visualize the image of the five Hawayot (YHWHs) within the reflection of the wine in the glass that one is holding. One performs this visualization for each eye separately.

דעת עליון

יוד הי ואו הי   יוד הי ואו הי

יוד הי ואו הי   יוד הי ואו הי

יוד הי ואו הי   יוד הי ואו הי

יוד הי ואו הי

דעת תחתון

יְהֹוָה   יֱהֹוֶה

Da'at. Da'at is Knowledge, but this is not like any Earthly knowledge that we are normally familiar with. The Supernal Da'at is the external expression of in internal Keter. Da'at is the inner knowing that is received when the intuition of Hokhma is properly received within the understanding of Binah.

When Hokhma (AB) and Binah (SAG) combine (symbolized as the Zivug, sexual union of Abba and Imma), they give birth to a "son." This is Zeir Anpin, the six Sefirot of the heart. And Da'at, the external expression of the concealed Keter serves as the inner soul, or source of ZA. What all these metaphors mean is that once intuition is understood within the mind/soul, this gives rise to an inner conviction that defines a path for action. The pattern of the path is ZA (also Torah), the soul of the path is Da'at.

Da'at itself, being that it is the external expression of Keter, has its own subjective inner and outer (concealed and revealed) forms of expression. The Supernal Da'at is expressed by seven times (7x) the Name SAG (63). 63 x 7 = 441. 441 is the numerical value of the word Emet, Truth! The Supernal Da'at is the ultimate Truth! External Da'at is represented simply by the Name YHWH. Yet, in order to distinguish YHWH in Da'at, like with all the Sefirot, a set of vowels is ascribed to the Name. Being that the other Sefirot have already used all the other vowels, the vowels ascribed to YHWH in Da'at are the base vowels of the letters. Yod is with a Holam vowel, Yo. Hey is with a Tzere vowel, Hey, and Wav is with a Kamatz vowel, Wah. The final Hey is like the first.

Being that Da'at is the byproduct of Hokhma and Binah, the YHWH of Da'at is thus written twice to visualize to the meditator its dual source.

The Feet. At the bottom of the Merkava chart there is listed a special holy Name. This Name is formed by knitting together YHWH of 72 (AB) and AHYH (Ehyeh) of 161 (KASA). The numerical value of this name is 233, the value of the Hebrew word for foot, Regel. This concludes the internal Merkava. What is interesting to note about this knitted Name is that it represents the highest forms of the manifestations of both YHWH and AHYH (Ehyeh). AB and KASA represent Atzilutic elements, and yet they are found here in Asiyah. This is to indicate, as the Sefer Yetzirah says, the end is in the beginning, and the beginning is in the end.

We begin at the highest level and work to the lowest, only to discover that the lowest only bring us back to the higher, in a spiral-like movement.

161 *72*

אלף הי יוד הי   יוד הי ויו הי

יוד אלף הי הי ויו יוד הי הי

161 + 72 =233

ג' רגל

In the traditional Merkava kavanah, there is one more visualization that focuses on the external form represented by the Name Elohim. Up until now, all our visualizations were based on the Name YHWH, emphasizing their internal nature. This final step visualized the "Image of Elohim." The five letters of the Name Elohim (Alef, Lamed, Hey, Yod, Mem) are correlated with the Ten Sefirot in this manner. The Alef of Elohim correlates to the Keter, the Gulgalta (skull). The Lamed of Elohim correlates to three Sefirot Mohin (brains), HaBaD (Hokhma, Binh, Da'at). The Hey of Elohim correlates to the next five Sefirot, Hesed, Gevurah, Tiferet, Netzah and Hod. The Yod correlates to Yesod. The Mem correlates to Malkhut.

א כתר גולגלתא

ל חב"ד ג' מוחין

ה חגת"נס

י יסוד

ם מלכות

These then are the individual sections of the Merkava practice. Now that we have reviewed them all, we can put them together into a concentric whole, applying the meditation prophetically, instead of academically.

The YHWH Merkava is designed to focus consciousness on transforming one's physical and psychic self into a conduit for higher dimensional energies, manifesting them here on Earth. The word Merkava means chariot. A chariot is a vehicle of movement, it carries a rider from point A to point B. The YHWH Merkava essentially is the practitioner. One surrenders oneself to become a vessel and vehicle through which the higher dimensional energetic Force that we call YHWH manifests Itself within every part of one's psychic and physical being. But this is only point A. Point B is the destination to which one must now channel the YHWH energetic Force, to where it is needed most.

In modern pseudo-kabbalistic prayerbooks designed for public, popular use, the Merkava meditation has been reduced to a prayer which one can recite like any other prayer. While this does make the concepts of the YHWH Merkava accessible, it nevertheless robs the meditation of its depths. In my book, Walking in the Fire, I published a full translation of the prayer form, along with commentary. For those wanting a condensed form of this material, I recommend you there. And now, for the deeper version.

The YHWH Merkava is a visualization exercise. This is how it was developed, and it is most effective when practiced in this form.

The procedure should be simple enough. One merely visualizes the Name YHWH in all its different symbolic forms, in each and every specific aspect of one's being or body. In order to accomplish this, one needs to learn to give one's imagination free reign to wander within one's thoughts.

The practice of Hitbodedut (mental isolation) here becomes essential. One must withdraw one's thoughts and daydreaming from external distractions, and instead focus them on one's inward spiritual adventure. Step by step one allows one's imagination to take on a life of its own within one's mind. One begins by visualizing the Name YHWH generically, without expansion, without vowel, without anything! Just focus on the Name!

Make believe that you can see the Name standing before you, not as blocks of inanimate letters, but rather as a living being (or beings). Engage in an internal dialogue with whatever first pops into your thoughts. Do not try to control or direct this. Let it happen naturally. So, for example, although you might want to begin at the beginning of the Name, with the first letter Yod, your personal imagination might redirect you towards another letter first. If this happens, it is not by mistake. There is a reason for everything! Begin then by engaging that which you experience first.

Begin the internal conversation by asking, "OK, why are you here? What am I supposed to understand from you popping up first in my mind?" Allow your mind to isolate itself from all outside distractions and focus on the moment. This is daydreaming at its best. Keep up the inner dialogue.

Instead of trying to rationalize and intellectualize this experience, pay attention to how you are feeling, as opposed to merely just what you are thinking. Do not ignore the thoughts that are popping up into your head. Rather, engage them emotionally. Ask why they are there. Pause and reflect how those thoughts make you feel. Indeed, those very thoughts and feelings that pop up initially are guides and signposts to direct you along your way into deeper contemplation, exploration, and revelation. Do not fear this. Embrace it!

The natural order of the YHWH Merkava follows the order of the Sefirot. One begins with Keter, and works one's way down the Sefirot, with the addition of the other body parts in their order. This natural order way is very rigid, and many times, the deeper one gets, one realizes that one's imagination may not be directing one down this structured form. Let this be!

Follow your imagination. Give your thoughts and feelings free reign. You will be shown that which you need to see. It is this fluidity that separates the Merkava meditation from being an intellectual contemplation of the theoretical Kabbalah and transforms it into a living experience of the Prophetic Kabbalah.

So, like I said above, when you visualize the Name YHWH is each body part, don't focus on the vowels; they are just there are guideposts, nothing more. Focus on the letter as they appear in that body part as related to that Sefirah.

When contemplating one's psychic, mental, emotional, or physical health and status, use the four versions of the Name AB, SAG, MAH, and BEN. Instead of focusing on the form of the letters, trying sensing how they feel to you. Such feelings, arising from deep within you will be a reflection of where you stand with regards to YHWH in that specific place.

Unless one feels otherwise guided, one should follow the proper order of the meditations. Within the framework of the body this is the proper order to follow.

Keter, Hokhma, Binah, Right Ear, Left Ear, Right Nostril, Left Nostril, Mouth, Eyes, Upper Da'at, Lower Da'at, Hesed, Gevurah, Tiferet, Netzah, Hod, Yesod, Malkhut. This is the general order. In prayerbooks, this order is called the Tikun Nefesh, Rectification of the Soul.

The Merkava diagram is also found in many different prayerbooks, especially those following the Kavanot of R. Sharabi (the Rashash). One finds the Merkava diagram strategically placed in four specific locations throughout the Shaharit morning prayers. These four locations demarcate the psychic ascent through the worlds that one is supposed to be focused upon while reciting the prayers. A more detailed description of this is covered in my book, Walking In The Fire, wherein which I translated and explained in brief the Kabbalistic ascent through the worlds weaved into the morning prayers. I will digress to briefly review this.

As we know there are four kabbalistic worlds We refer to them as dimensional planes. The four are Asiyah (the physical), Yetzirah (the emotional/astral plane), Beriah (the realm of mind and thought), and Atzilut (the realm of the psychic, the Source of the Sefirot). All prayers are supposed to be psychic, and not just a mere recitation of mindless words. Therefore, all prayer is said to be in the world of Atzilut. Therefore, the four worlds in the Shaharit morning prayers are the four subjective worlds of the world of Atzilut. In others words, the Asiyah of Atzilut, the Yetzirah of Atzilut, the Beriah of Atzilut and the Atzilut of Atzilut.

The division of the worlds follows the order of the prayer service. The morning prayers begin with the recitation of the portion called the Korbanot (the Sacrifices), which needless to say does include other related prayers. This section is the Asiyah of Atzilut. Each ascent between worlds is performed by the recitation of the Kaddish prayer. The Kavanot of which is far beyond the parameters of this present lesson. Once the Korbanot are recited, followed by Kaddish, one enters into the psyche of the Zemirot (the Psalms), these are the Yetzirah of Atzilut. When these are finished, Kaddish is again recited and one begins the reading of the Kriyat Shema (the Shema Yisrael and its blessings), this is the Beriah of Atzilut. And finally, one recites the Amidah (the Standing Prayer), the Atzilut of Atzilut.

The reason for my digression is to discuss the Merkava diagram which is found with each ascent into each of the four worlds. Essentially, the diagram is the same in each of the four places, with one specific exception. In the meditation (Kavanot) of the eyes, which as shown above is five times the Name YHWH, each order of the worlds expands the five Hawayot (YHWHs) to express AB, SAG, MAH and BEN, in ascending order.

עין דאצילות	עין דבריאה	עין דיצירה	עין דעשיה
יוד הי ויו הי [ע"ב]	יוד הי ואו הי [ס"ג]	יוד הא ואו הא [מ"ה]	יוד הה וו הה [ב"ן]
יוד הי ויו הי [ע"ב]	יוד הי ואו הי [ס"ג]	יוד הא ואו הא [מ"ה]	יוד הה וו הה [ב"ן]
יוד הי ויו הי [ע"ב]	יוד הי ואו הי [ס"ג]	יוד הא ואו הא [מ"ה]	יוד הה וו הה [ב"ן]
יוד הי ויו הי [ע"ב]	יוד הי ואו הי [ס"ג]	יוד הא ואו הא [מ"ה]	יוד הה וו הה [ב"ן]
יוד הי ויו הי [ע"ב]	יוד הי ואו הי [ס"ג]	יוד הא ואו הא [מ"ה]	יוד הה וו הה [ב"ן]

From the prophetic perspective, rather than just look at the diagram and acknowledge the concept that it represents, we extract the visualization of the Eye, and use it independently to gaze within ourselves within each of the four dimensional realities in which parts of us reside. So, one seeking insight into something physical or bodily can gaze upon YHWH of BEN, using the Name repeated five times (as shown above). One uses the other Names in similar fashion for gazing into the emotional, mental, and psychic realms.

We can now draw this meditational ritual to a close. Let us put all the pieces together to create a concentric whole, for those who will want to use the whole. Remember, even if you start out to use the entire Merkava, you can stop at any place along the way, and stay there for as long as one feels necessary.

In the prayer version of the Merkava, a proclamation begins the procedure. It simply says, behold I am dedicating myself to become a Merkava for the sake of the unity of the Holy One, blessed be He and His Shekhina. The majority of those who say these words really have no idea as to what they mean. So, in brief let's explain them.

Every meditative state begins with preparation, so if you plan to use the entire Merkava in a single meditative session, then make the necessary preparation that I have discussed in so many of my other writings. Just remember this: you don't have to go into a meditative state if you are just generally contemplating the reality and Presence of YHWH. This, one is supposed to be doing always (Psalm 16:8), no meditation state required.

The Merkava system begins with the Keter, the source of one's personal unconscious, the Source of the Active Intelligence, the point of contact between the individual Self and the Collective Whole. Visualize YHWH (with or without the vowel Kamatz) as one will feel inclined. Get a sense of how this feels to you. Pay attention to the thoughts that pop up into your consciousness. If you can (or cannot) see the letters of the Name, ask yourself why what you see, sense, feel, or experience, is what it is. Contemplate, or better to say, feel YHWH in your Keter, granting you awareness and expanding consciousness into the Keter domain.

יכ״ין לעשות עלמו מרכבה וכסא לאורס דחלילות דקדוסה.

גלגלתא

מוח שמאל בינה	כתר	מוח ימין חכמה
יְהֹוָה	יְהֹוָה	יְהֹוָה
אזן שמאל	דעת עליון	אזן ימין
יוד הי ואו הה	יוד הי ואו הי יוד הי ואו הי	יוד הי ואו הה
כמס׳ אל יהוה ס״ג	יוד הי ואו הי יוד הי ואו הי	כמס׳ אל יהוה ס״ג
	יוד הי ואו הי יוד הי ואו הי	
פין שמאל דחלילות	דעת תחתון יְהֹוָה יְהֹוָה	פין ימין דחלילות

חוטם

נקב ימין ☐ ☐ נקב שמאל

יוד הי ויו הי	יוד הי ויו הי
יוד הי ויו הי	יוד הי ויו הי
יוד הי ויו הי	יוד הי ויו הי
יוד הי ויו הי	יוד הי ויו הי
יוד הי ויו הי	יוד הי ויו הי

אהיה אהיה אהיה חילו׳

אהיה יהוה ארוה חוטם עס ד׳ אותיות וסכו׳ ג׳ חיים.

פה

ג״י׳ ס״ג וכ״ב אותיות דס׳ מולאות הפס יוד הי ואו הי
אחה״יע ניכ״ק דטלנ״ת זסשר״ץ בומ״ף

יוד הי ואו הי אהיה פנימיות הפה

	יוד יוד הא יוד הא יוד הא ואו נ׳ פ״ס חילוניות
כתר גולגלתא א	קול יהוה, ג״י׳ יופיא״ל ע״ה דבור אדני
חב״ד ג׳ מוחין ל	קול ודבור יאהדונהי
חג״תנה ת״ק ה	דבור ג״י׳ כ״ו מ״ה ק״ל ועשר אותיות והכולל.
יסוד י	יהוה יוד הא ואו הא מספר ואותיות. ס״ס פ״א
מלכות ☐	יוד יוד הא יוד הא ואו יוד הא ואו הא ק״ל

זרוע שמאל גבורה	גופא ת״ת	זרוע ימין חסד
יְהֹוָה	יְהֹוָה	יְהֹוָה
שוק שמאל הוד	בריק יסוד	שוק ימין נצח
יְהֹוָה	יגהוווהו	יְהֹוָה
רגל שמאל נ׳	עטרת היסוד	רגל ימין נ׳
	סלי יְהֹוָה	

יוד אלף הי הי ויו יוד הי הי ☐ יוד אלף הי הי ויו יוד הי הי
כרוך

489

Statement of 42 Principles
of the KosherTorah School
for Biblical, Judaic & Spiritual Studies

Let it be known by the following statements the principles, beliefs and truths that I hold sacred and upon which I have built the KosherTorah School.

1. I believe in God.

2. It is because that I believe in God that I am also able to believe in my fellow human beings.

3. I believe that God created us all, and in spite of our differences, be they those made by God, or those made by us, we are all children of God, created in the Divine Image.

4. I believe that being created in the Divine Image gives each of us a responsibility and obligation to respect one another and to care for one another, that this, above all else, is our human calling and what defines for us our humanity.

5. I believe that God is the origin and originator of all things.

6. I believe that all things came forth from God with intelligent design.

7. I believe that God is a Sentient Consciousness, not to be confused with a person.

8. I believe that God is the information and intelligence within everything in existence.

9. I believe that God is the Universal Mind.

10. I believe that God is not a He or a She, but that God is something far greater than anything we humans can presently possible imagine.

11. I believe that God communicates with that which It has made.

12. I believe that God has a plan, for all things, for our universe, for our planet, and for us.

13. I believe that God communicated with our ancestors.

14. I believe that God directed the giving of the Torah to the nation of Israel at Sinai.

15. I believe that the Torah is an extraterrestrial code that when properly understood can unlock many of the secrets of the universe.

16. I believe that the Torah contains God's Will for the nation of Israel.

17. I believe that the commandments of the Torah are to be observed by the children of Israel, and that the lessons of Torah can be understood universally, and embraced by all.

18. I believe that religions in general, for the most part, divide and separate, rather than bridge and unite.

19. I believe that all religions, including my own, have been infiltrated and compromised with teachings and beliefs that promote prejudice, hatred, division, and other teachings that contradict God's Torah, God Will, and God's Purpose.

20. I believe that it is the moral imperative of all sincere religious individuals, of all religions, to condemn any and all religious teachings, including their own, that promote prejudice and hatred, that these contradict God, and thus must never be taught in the name of God.

21. I believe that we all must make every effort to root out prejudice, hatred, and violence.

22. I believe that it is the Will of God for all humanity to live in harmony with one another.

23. I believe that it is the Will of God for us to all be different, and that our differences be respected.

24. I believe that our differences are merely superficial, and that when we take a deeper look within ourselves, we will find that we are ultimately one, united as we are by the inner Divine Image.

25. I believe that it is God's Will for each of us to individually take this deeper look within ourselves, and to expand our personal perspectives.

26. I believe that all our different faiths, beliefs, and practices may not all be right, and may not be all wrong.

27. I believe that I can be different from you, and you from me, and that this is acceptable as long as no other is harmed, or otherwise deprived of what may be reasonably considered to be rightfully theirs.

28. I believe that we all have equal right, and equal access to God, Its Will and Way.

29. I believe that we can learn much about the Way of God by observing the natural world that God has made, and learn from it how to be natural.

30. I believe that living naturally is God's Will and Way for humanity. We are part of this planet, and therefore, should act as part of it, and not in contradiction to it.

31. I believe that technology and science are God's gifts to humanity.

32. I believe that the purpose of technology, and science, is to enable us to properly understand the natural world around us, and by understanding it better, to live in harmony with it.

33. I believe that it is God's Will for us to explore the boundaries of human imagination and thought, and to make our world and universe a better place.

34. I believe that every human being has the right and the responsibility to earn a living, and should pursue all moral and appropriate avenues to secure one's place in this world.

35. I believe that each human being has the moral obligation and responsibility to do one's individual best to become self-reliant, independent, and to assist our fellow human beings to accomplish the same. I believe this to be the Will and Way of God.

36. I believe that no one should be compelled to accept the views and beliefs of others. No one should be compelled to do anything that the individual finds morally objectionable, unless such behaviors are deemed necessary for the greater good, and agreed to by all parties so affected.

37. I believe that human governments and politics will forever be corrupt as along as corruption rules within the human heart.

38. I believe that there is no one true system of government, other than one directed by moral human beings, with the sincere intent to promote the blessings of prosperity and good for all.

39. I believe that people have the right to live as they will and as they wish, as long as they do not harm any other in any reasonable way.

40. I believe that it is the Will of God for man to prosper and evolve, and that it is the Will of God for each of us to assist one another towards these most sacred of goals.

41. I believe that although many who may come to the KosherTorah School come from walks of life that I personally cannot and do not endorse, I nevertheless welcome all and invite them, if they so wish, to embrace our teaching here at the KosherTorah School, as they may see fit.

42. To express these beliefs and to establish these goals, I have created the KosherTorah School, and invite all human beings, created in the Image of God, to partake in whatever materials of value that I may produce for public benefit.

May God continue to bless you and keep you.

Sincerely,
Ariel B Tzadok

KosherTorah School

About Ariel Bar Tzadok
& the KosherTorah School

Rabbi Ariel proudly welcomes to the KosherTorah School all peoples, of all backgrounds, who wish to learn about the authentic and original Biblical world outlook.

KosherTorah is not just about the Bible.

KosherTorah is not just about Judaism.

KosherTorah is not just about religion.

KosherTorah is not just about God.

KosherTorah is about us!

KosherTorah is about building bridges!

KosherTorah is about becoming a more decent human being!

KosherTorah is about common sense, simple living, righteous behavior, and liberty and respect for all.

For over thirty years, Rabbi Ariel has been a world renowned expert of the authentic, Biblical "Secrets of the Torah" teachings, that many today simply call "Kabbalah."

Rabbi Ariel teaches the sulam aliyah (ladder of ascent) school of Kabbalah, which consists of the Biblical teachings of the works of Ezekiel's chariot (Ma'aseh Merkava), and the prophetic meditative techniques passed down through the centuries.

The purpose of these teachings is to cultivate actual, authentic, and personal spiritual experiences, the likes of which are psychological, and transformational. The purpose of spirituality is to explore one's inner self, and to discover, and unleash one's inner, latent potentials. To this task is the KosherTorah School dedicated.

While knowledgeable of the theoretical/philosophical schools taught by others, Rabbi Ariel places special emphasis on teaching the "other schools" which most today are unaware of, or not qualified to teach. These specifically are the prophetic/meditative and so-called "magical" schools. Rabbi Ariel teaches others HOW-TO practice these ancient methods for each individual to acquire their own unique spiritual experiences.

The KosherTorah School focuses on teaching Biblical, and later mystical literature in a rational way to enable the student to extract their universal teachings from their numerous layers of myth and metaphor.

The school proudly serves the educational needs of a global audience, and welcomes students from all walks of life.

Born and raised on Long Island, New York, Ariel Bar Tzadok studied abroad in Israel for a number of years. He studied in Jerusalem at the premier Sephardic institute, Yeshivat Porat Yosef (Old City), and later in Kollel Hekhal Pinhas. While studying for his rabbinic ordination, he was blessed to become the private student of the renowned Kabbalist, Rabbi Meir Levi, *obm*, the foremost student of the leading Kabbalist of Jerusalem, Rabbi Mordechai Sharabi *obm*.

In June 1983, Rabbi Ariel received his rabbinic ordination (Haredi/Orthodox) from Rabbi Ya'akov Peretz, Rosh Yeshiva (Dean) of Kollel Hekhal Pinhas, and Beit Midrash Sephardi in the Old City of Jerusalem.

Rabbi Ariel augmented his religious education with studies in the other religions of the world, esoteric studies and practices, philosophies and psychological systems, particularly studying Jungian psychology at the Jungian Center in New York.

In 1992, after teaching privately for many years, Rabbi Ariel officially established his school (with the original Hebrew name Yeshivat Benei N'vi'im) to address the growing concerns of spiritual misguidance, and misinformation that is pervasive in the Jewish community at large. Since then, while staying faithful to his Orthodox Torah origins, Rabbi Ariel has expanded the KosherTorah School to meet the needs of an ever widening audience.

Rabbi Ariel is a regular featured guest on the popular TV program Ancient Aliens. He also appears in other TV programs, speaks on radio talk shows, and is published in scholarly journals and newspaper articles. His YouTube page hosts hundreds of his videos and he regularly teaches live public classes on Facebook. He has spoken before religious congregations, university groups and lectures around the country.

Made in United States
Orlando, FL
22 January 2024

42797571R00271